NTC's
Dictionary
of
SPANISH
FALSE
COGNATES

Marcial Prado

NTC Publishing Group
NTC/Contemporary Publishing Company

Library of Congress Cataloging-in-Publication Data
is available from the United States Library of Congress.

Published by NTC Publishing Group
An imprint of NTC/Contemporary Publishing Company
4255 West Touhy Avenue, Lincolnwood (Chicago), Illinois 60646-1975 U.S.A.
Copyright © 1993 by NTC/Contemporary Publishing Company
Printed in the United States of America
International Standard Book Number: 0-8442-7977-3

21   20   19   18   17   16   15   14   13   12   11   10   9   8   7

Foreword

The study of false cognates or, as I call them, *falsos amigos*, is not as simple as pointing out that *asistir* is not exactly the equivalent of "to assist." Although English and Spanish derive a considerable part of their vocabulary from common Latin or Indo-European roots, the two languages have followed such divergent paths of semantic development that meanings of seemingly identical words are often completely different.

Students' problems with false cognates in both English and Spanish have largely been ignored in textbooks and even dictionaries. Too often editors have such an inadequate knowledge of both Spanish and English that the reader is given only one meaning of a word, which may not be the most common or even the most characteristic one. Students who rely on the accuracy of textbook or dictionary vocabulary often produce unacceptable translations such as the case of the student who said he had recently had *pecho de pollo* (chicken breast) for lunch.

"But how are you supposed to know?" students ask in dismay, clutching their Appleton, Velázquez, and VOX dictionaries. "I look up 'sane' and the first offering is *sano*. But you say it should be *cuerdo*." I explain that learning the right word for the right context is part of understanding a second language and comes with experience and patience. Now, students need no longer be discouraged. For anyone seeking a guide to false cognates and a shield against the insidious pitfalls of dictionaries, this is it!

Here you will find an answer to the problem. I have compiled 2500 false cognates that can be invaluable to intermediate or advanced students of both English and Spanish, as well as translators and anyone who wants to learn Spanish or English. The problem of false cognates goes much further than traditional stories of embarrassment, such as that of the American lady who declared "*Juan me embarazó*" (John got me pregnant) when she meant to say that John embarrassed her, or the Spanish gentleman who tried to explain why his wife wasn't pregnant: "She is impregnable, or maybe she is inconceivable."

There are three kinds of false cognates. The truly deceptive cognates are English words whose cognates in Spanish have a significantly different meaning, such as "library" (*biblioteca*) and "*librería*" (bookstore) or "bigot" (*fanático*) and "*bigote*" (mustache). Usually this kind of false cognate is not very treacherous because a bilingual dictionary should clearly define its meanings.

Another type might be called semideceptive cognates, words that may be translated by their cognates in the other language but also have one or more other meanings. For example, *consentir* means "to consent" but also "to spoil" or "pamper" people. Practically all the bilingual dictionaries on the market translate *consentir* only as "to consent." This is simply not the only meaning. Another example is "vicious," which not only means *vicioso* but also *cruel, depravado*. No dictionary explains that *vicioso* applies only to people, whereas "vicious" is used for people, animals, concepts, and ideas. Such vital information is never included in bilingual dictionaries, and for this reason we find mistakes like *una organización difunta*, which sounds as comical and incorrect as *"a defunct child."

Some semideceptive cognates share a common meaning in both languages, but in addition, each term has acquired different meanings. For example, *falso* and "false" share the idea of "untrue," but *falso* also means "counterfeit, fake" whereas "false" also means *postizo* (hair, teeth, breast).

There is a third group of false cognates that we might call "unclear" cognates because they have acquired divergent meanings in the two languages, but they are closely and delicately related. *Conveniente* in *"No me es conveniente ir mañana"* is not the same as "convenient" in "It isn't convenient for me to go tomorrow." The shades of difference between "convenient" and "suitable," "advisable" or "appropriate" are difficult to convey as *cómodo, útil, práctico*. Other treacherous pairs are *sugestión* and "suggestion," *rudo* and "rude." The ability to make such distinctions is a valuable part of understanding a foreign language.

The words in this dictionary occur in a specific context. For this reason, there are plenty of examples to illustrate the denotations of each term. Furthermore, each term occurs within a specific cultural setting. In certain cases, I have added a cultural hint that may be the key to understanding why the two cognates are not interchangeable, such as "corpulent" and *corpulento*, "assault" and *asalto*, "ambition" and *ambición*.

Although a dictionary is not a grammar, I have included the gender of all nouns except those ending in *-o, -a, -ión*, which are easily predictable. The plural of certain nouns has been included, for example *álbum / álbumes*, *suéter / suéteres*, and the contrast between countable and uncountable nouns such as *consejo* and "advice". Furthermore, stem-changing verbs have been marked in parentheses—for example, *consentir* (ie, i)—to account for irregular forms such as *consiento* and *consintió*.

It is impossible to provide all the different dialect variations in the Spanish-speaking world. However, I frequently mention whether a term is used in Spain or Latin America, and I tend to give a little more emphasis to the Spanish of the New World, just as I tend to use American English rather than British English. I have incorporated new spellings such as *bufé*, *bisté*, *cuplé*, *champán*, as well as the new entries in the latest dictionary of the Real Academia Española—which, incidentally, contains over twenty thousand more words than in the previous edition, such as *tiquete* (ticket), *chequear* (to check), *ancestral*, *control*, *reciclar*, *líder*, *opcional*, *controversial*, *implemento*, *champú*. This shows us that languages are alive and that one may expect to find new false cognates, while some others may disappear.

It is virtually impossible to make a complete selection of false cognates, and this book does not claim to do so. But I hope that the false cognates you seek have been included. The translations from English to Spanish and vice versa do not necessarily preclude other possibilities. I have generally included several different terms, especially when entries have a wide variety of meanings.

Acknowledgments

I want to thank my wife Rita for her frequent help, as well as for her moral support in the long years it took to complete this dictionary. I also sincerely appreciate the ideas and hints from all students who directly or indirectly collaborated with me. I must thank Dr. Ronald Harmon and Donald Wadley for correcting the manuscript and for "trying" to help me improve my English. I also acknowledge the financial support that California State University at Fullerton gave me through a sabbatical leave and several grants to carry out the project.

A

abandonado / abandoned *Abandonado* passively means "abandoned, neglected" to refer to things (and to people and animals treated as things); actively, it means "negligent" or "untidy" to refer to people who are careless with clothing, hygiene, etc. Es muy **abandonado** en su ropa. *He is very **negligent** with his clothes.*

abandonar / abandon *Abandonar* can be as negative as "to abandon, desert," or it can be the simple act of leaving, giving up something such as a place or a career. *Abandonarse en* conveys the idea of "to give away, to give in, to neglect." **Abandonamos** la ciudad el lunes. *We **left** the city on Monday.* Desde la muerte de su padre **se abandonó en** su persona, en la casa, en todo. *After his father's death he **neglected** himself, his house, everything.*

abismal / abysmal *Abismal* is not used much and only figuratively to mean "abysmal" ("deep, huge").   diferencia **abismal** entre ricos y pobres */ **huge (profound)** difference between rich and poor*   *Abysmal* is used in the real sense of *profundo,* and in a figurative sense it has the negative connotation of *pésimo, terrible.*   Viven en una pobreza **terrible.** *They live in **abysmal** poverty.*

abnegación / abnegation *Abnegación* does not mean "abnegation"; rather, it conveys the positive virtue of "care, dedication, self-denial." *Abnegation* has a negative denotation of *denegación, negativa, renuncia.*   **renuncia** de su responsabilidad   */   **abnegation** of his responsibilities   Abnegado* is "dedicated, unselfish" and *abnegarse* (ie) means "to care, sacrifice oneself, be dedicated." Es una enfermera muy **abnegada.** *She is a very **dedicated** nurse.* Se **abnegó** por cuidar a sus hijos. *She was **dedicated** to her children. / She **made sacrifices** to take care of her children.* To abnegate is *negarse* (ie) or *rehusar* Se **negó** a donar sangre a la Cruz Roja. *He **refused (abnegated)** to give blood to the Red Cross.*

abortar / abort *Abortar* means "to abort" in the sense of "the miscarriage of a baby" (in women or in animals).
hacerse abortar = *to have an abortion*
To abort is also used in the figurative sense of *fracasar* ("to fail"). Different things and events can "abort," such as flights, plans, projects, as indicated in the headline "Bird Forces Flight to Abort" (*Los Angeles Times,* 12/27/90). La rebelión **fracasó** por falta de apoyo. *The rebellion was **aborted** for lack of support. Abortion* means *aborto* (in females) and also *fracaso* in events and things. [In modern English, miscarriage is used to indicate natural (involuntary) death of a fetus; whereas abortion is used to indicate induced death of a fetus. There is no Spanish word for miscarriage; instead, **aborto** accidental and pérdida del bebé are used.] Tuvo un **aborto accidental** a los tres meses. *She had a **miscarriage** in the third month.* ¿Debe hacerse legal el **aborto**? *Should **abortion** be made legal?*

abreviar / abbreviate *Abreviar* means "to abbreviate, to shorten" a word (e.g., *abreviar una palabra* = "to shorten a word"). In Spanish, it is commonly used to mean "to cut short, take a shortcut, hurry." *En taquigrafía se **abrevian** las palabras. Words are **shortened** in stenography. **Abrevia**, que no tenemos mucho tiempo. **Make it short**, we don't have much time. Vamos a **abreviar** el camino. Let's take a **shortcut**. To abbreviate (a fraction)* is *simplificar (quebrados)* in mathematics. *Abreviación* is "abbreviation." *Abbreviation* translates as *abreviación* and also as *abreviatura* (to indicate a shortened form of a word, such as *Ud.* for *usted*). *La **abreviatura** de id est es i.e. The **abbreviation** of id est is i.e.*

absolución / absolution *Absolución* is not only "absolution, pardon" with regard to religious confession but also "acquittal" in a court of law.
absolución de la demanda = *finding for the defendant*
Absolver (ue) is "to absolve" and also "to acquit." The participle and adjective of *absolver* is *absuelto*, which means both "absolved" and "acquitted." [In Spanish, *el sacerdote y el juez absuelven*; in English, the priest "absolves" and the judge "acquits."] *El criminal fue **absuelto** por el sacerdote, pero no por el juez. The criminal was **absolved** by the priest but was not **acquitted** by the judge. El acusado fue **absuelto** por el jurado. The defendant was **acquitted** by the jury.*

absorbente / absorbent *Absorbente* means "absorbent" (regarding liquids), but it has other meanings, such as "demanding, possessive, absorbing." *un trabajo **absorbente** / a demanding job una persona **absorbente** / a possessive person Absorber* means "to absorb, to soak up" and also "to demand, to be possessive, to suction or suck in" (a vacuum cleaner), and "to catch" (dust). *Esta aspiradora **absorbe** bien. This vacuum cleaner **has good suction**. Esta alfombra **absorbe** mucho polvo. This rug **catches** a lot of dust.*

abstracto / abstract *Abstracto* means "abstract," the opposite of *concreto* ("concrete"). *Abstract* is also a noun, which translates as *extracto, resumen* (m.; "summary"). *Mandé un **resumen** del artículo de 100 palabras. I sent a 100-word **abstract** of the article.*

abusar / abuse *Abusar de* means "to use too much" and translates as "to go too far, to take advantage of, to misuse." [Note that the preposition *de* is required after *abusar: abusar de* + a person or thing.] *No **abuses** de mi paciencia. Don't take advantage of my patience.* **abusar** del tabaco / *to smoke too much To abuse* means "to use immorally" and translates as *maltratar, injuriar, insultar, denigrar. Algunos padres **maltratan** a sus hijos. Some parents **abuse** their children. Abuso* means "excessive use" and translates as "immoderate use, misuse (of authority), imposition on, betrayal (of trust)." *Abuse* means "immoral use" and translates as *maltrato, insulto, injuria. El **maltrato** de los niños debe castigarse. Child **abuse** should be punished. Abusivo* means "excessive, exorbitant, misused, improper." *precios **abusivos** / excessive prices; exorbitant prices Abusive* means *ofensivo, injurioso, insultante. palabras **ofensivas** / abusive (offensive) language*

académico / academic   *Académico* means "academic" in the sense of "scholarly" to refer to university studies, research, etc. (It is more common to use *universitario* and *escolar* to refer to courses, location, syllabi, programs, dress, etc.) [The members of an academy, such as the *Real Academia de la Lengua Española*, are called *académicos* in Spanish and "academicians" in English.] Los **académicos** se reúnen en Madrid. *The **academicians** meet in Madrid.* año (curso) **escolar** / **academic year;** *school* year   En los Estados Unidos sólo se lleva el traje **universitario** durante la graduación. *In the United States, the **academic** gown is worn only during the graduation ceremony.*

acceder / acceed   *Acceder a* means "to acceed to" with the denotation of "to consent, agree"; however, the Spanish term is used much more frequently than the English term. Por fin **accedió** a ayudarme. *Finally he **agreed** to help me.* To acceed to also means *tomar posesión* (of an office or post). El senador **tomó posesión** de su cargo. *The senator **acceeded to** his office.*

accesorio / accessory   *Accesorio* means "accessory" to refer to things, equipment, and parts of machinery, such as a car. It also translates as "additional, incidental, secondary." Los gastos **accesorios** son pocos. *The **incidental** expenses are minor. Accessory* also applies to people who assist or are involved in a crime, which is *cómplice* (m., f.) in Spanish. Ella es **cómplice** del delito. *She is an **accessory** to the crime.*

accidente / accident   *Accidente* (m.) can be as serious as a fatal "accident," but it can also refer to an "incident" or "mishap." It also means "roughness, irregularity, unevenness (of terrain)."
por or **de casualidad** = *by accident*
Fue un **accidente** embarazoso el derramar el café en la alfombra nueva. *Spilling coffee on the new rug was an embarrassing **incident**. Accidentado* means "injured, damaged" (person or thing, such as a car); "uneven" (terrain); and in a figurative sense, "troubled, agitated." Lleva una vida **accidentada**. *She leads a **troubled** life.* La finca está en terreno **accidentado**. *The ranch is on **uneven** terrain.*

acción / action   *Acción* means "action, deed, act" and also "stock" or "share" in the stock market (*bolsa*).
Acción de gracias = *Thanksgiving*
radio de **acción** de la compañía / *the company's **operating** range*   Las **acciones** de la bolsa tienen altibajos muy a menudo. *Stocks very often show ups and downs in the market. Action*, in addition to *acción*, means *acto, medida, disposición, argumento* ("plot" as in *una obra de teatro*).
tomar medidas = *to take action*
Tomó **medidas** fuertes contra los narcotraficantes. *He took strong **action** against drug dealers.*

acento / accent   *Acento* means "accent" to refer to a written accent mark and "stress" to refer to a phonetic accent. It also translates as "accent" to describe a regional style of speaking, for example, *acento cubano, acento de Madrid.* [This usage of *acento* has been criticized, but the term is used in many countries instead of the old terms *tono* and *dejo*. The *Real Academia* has admitted this usage in the most recent edition of its dictionary.] "Mesa" tiene el **acento** en la primera sílaba. *Mesa has the **stress** (is **stressed**) on the first syllable.* Habla con un **acento** (dejo) extraño. *She speaks with a strange **accent**.*

acomodación / accommodation *Acomodación* means "accommodation" to refer to an arrangement or adjustment. *Accommodation* also means *alojamiento, habitación* in a hotel or an inn. alojamiento en un hotel de primera /*accommodation in a first-class hotel*

acomodar / accommodate *Acomodar* means "to accommodate" in the sense of "to adjust, arrange, suit, or offer work to." It is a synonym of *arreglar, hacer sitio, caber, dar trabajo.* The reflexive form *acomodarse* means *sentarse cómodamente* ("to sit comfortably"). **Se acomodó** en el sofá. *She **sat comfortably** on the sofa.* To *accommodate* also means *complacer, hacer un favor.* Podemos **complacer** tus deseos. *We can **accommodate** your wishes.* **Acomodado** means "accommodated, arranged, fixed, suitable," but the most common meaning is "wealthy, well off." Tiene una familia **acomodada**. *He belongs to a **wealthy** family.* **Acomodador** (m.) means "usher" in a theater, church, etc.

acordar / accord *Acordar* (ue) means "to agree on, resolve, remind, tune (in music)." The reflexive form *acordarse de* means "to remember, to recall." ¡Te **acordarás** de mí! = *You'll be hearing from me!* La Directiva **acordó** cerrar la tienda. *The Board **resolved** to close the store.* No te **acordaste** de mi cumpleaños. *You didn't **remember** my birthday.* To *accord* translates as *conceder, dar, otorgar.* Me **concedieron** una beca. *They **accorded** (awarded) me a scholarship.* Accord as a noun means *acuerdo* ("agreement"), *armonía.*
de común acuerdo = *with one accord, unanimously*
Trabajemos de común **acuerdo**. *Let's work with one **accord**.*

acostar / accost *Acostar* (ue) does not mean "to accost"; rather, it means "to put to bed, lay down." The reflexive form *acostarse* is translated as "to go to bed, to lean over or on, to bend over." No te **acuestes** (recuestes) en la mesa. *Don't **lean over (lean on)** the table.* To *accost* means *acercarse a (a hablar), dirigirse a, abordar (una persona).* Los periodistas **abordaron** al Presidente. *The reporters **accosted** the President.*

acreditar / accredit *Acreditar* means "to accredit" as in "to accredit a diplomat or a teacher" (*acreditar* or *reconocer a un diplomático o a un maestro*). But *acreditar* also means "to prove, to credit, to back." No puedo **acreditar** esa historia. *I cannot **back up** that story.* **Acreditado** means "accredited" (teacher or diplomat) and also "well-known, reputable" to refer to persons, organizations, and commercial firms. una agencia **acreditada** / *a **reputable** agency*

acto, acta / act *Acto* means "act, deed, action, ceremony."
acto seguido; en el acto = *at once; on the spot*
acto carnal = *sexual intercourse*
Act can also be translated as *decreto, ley, número* (routine of a performer).
Decreto del Congreso = *Act of Congress*

en fragante = *in the act*
El comediante hizo reír con su **número**. *The comedian got a lot of laughs with his* **act**. *Acta* is "certificate" (of birth, marriage, etc.). The plural *actas* means "minutes" of a meeting. La secretaria leyó las **actas**. *The secretary read the* **minutes**.

actual / actual   *Actual* does not mean "actual" but "present, present-day, current, modern." In a commercial (business) letter, *el actual* means "this month." La situación **actual** es peligrosa. *The* **present** *situation is dangerous*. *Actual* in English translates as *real, verdadero, efectivo, mismo*. El **verdadero** ladrón está suelto. *The* **actual** *thief is on the loose*. *Actualmente* stands for "presently, now, nowadays." **Actualmente** vivimos en paz. *At* **present** *we are living in peace*. *Actually* means *realmente, de hecho, en efecto, en realidad*. En realidad es más barato de lo que parece. *Actually it is less expensive than it looks*. *Actualidad* (f.) means "the present time, current importance, topicality." *Actualidades* means "current events."
en la actualidad = *at the moment; nowadays; today*
Es un tema de gran **actualidad**. *It is a very* **topical** *subject*. Leo la sección de **actualidades**. *I read the* **current events** *section*. *Actuality* means *realidad* (f.).

acuerdo / accord   *Acuerdo* means "accord"; however, *accord* is no longer commonly used in English and has been replaced by *agreement, understanding*. *Acuerdo* also translates as "resolution (in the Congress), sense, wisdom."
estar de acuerdo = *to agree*
de acuerdo con = *according to*
Los embajadores firmaron un **acuerdo**. *The ambassadors signed an* **agreement**. El **acuerdo** sube los impuestos. *The* **resolution** *raises taxes*.

acusado / accused   *Acusado* means "accused" (i.e., defendant in court) if the term is applied to people, but *acusado* also means "marked, strong, outstanding" if it is used with things or habits.
Tiene un acento español muy **acusado**. *He has a very* **strong** *Spanish accent*. Su **acusada** nariz lo traiciona. *His* **prominent** *nose betrays him*.

acusar / accuse   *Acusar* means "to accuse, charge with a crime" and also "to point to, indicate, blame, reprimand." The reflexive form *acusarse de* means "to confess to."
acusar recibo = *to acknowledge receipt*
Los síntomas **acusan** pulmonía. *The symptoms* **indicate** *pneumonia*. **Acuso** recibo de tu carta. *I* **acknowledge** *receipt of your letter*. Lo **acuso** de nuestras desdichas. *I* **blame** *him for our misfortunes*. Se **acusó del** crimen. *He* **confessed** *to the crime*.

adecuado / adequate   *Adecuado* means "adequate, sufficient," as well as "suitable, right, appropriate." Su sueldo es **adecuado** para vivir. *His salary is* **adequate** *to live on*. Es el hombre **adecuado** para ese cargo. *He is the* **right** *man for that job*.

adepto / adept   *Adepto* means "supporting" as an adjective and "supporter, follower, member" as a noun. Mahoma tiene muchos **adeptos**. *Mohammed has many* *followers.* **adepto** del gobierno / *government* **supporter** *Adept* translates as *experto en, hábil, mañoso, diestro.* Ese señor es muy **experto** en la cocina internacional. *That man is very **adept** in (at) international cuisine.*

adherencia / adherence *Adherencia* is not "adherence" but "adhesion, sticking" *(acción de pegar)* and also "ability to hold the road" or "roadholding" (of a car). tener buena **adherencia** / *to **hold the road** well; (to have good **roadholding**) Adherence* (support) means *adhesión, fidelidad* (f.), *apoyo.* **adhesión** a sus creencias / *adherence to one's beliefs*

administración / administration *Administración* is not only "administration" in terms of government *(gobierno)* but also "management, running, headquarters" (office). Una buena **administración** es vital para un negocio. *Good **management** is vital for a business.* Consejo de **administración** / *Board of **Directors*** **administración** de empresas *business **management***

administrar / administer, administrate *Administrar* is "to administer, to dispense" and "to administrate, to rule," as well as "to manage, to run" (a business). **administrar una paliza** = *to give a beating* *Administrador* (m.) stands for "manager, agent," as well as "administrator." **administrador** de aduanas / *customs **officer*** **administrador** de correos / *post-master*

admirable / admirable *Admirable* translates the literary and rather archaic English term *admirable.* Modern meanings of **admirable** are "surprising, astonishing, amazing." una victoria **admirable** / *a **surprising** victory* *Admiración* is "surprise, wonder, amazement," rather than "admiration," which is not used much in this sense. signo de **admiración** (¡!) / *exclamation mark (!)*

admirar / admire *Admirar* suggests a great surprise, and for this reason translates better as "to surprise, amaze, astonish" than "to admire." The reflexive form *admirarse de* means "to be amazed at, to marvel at." Tanta generosidad me **admira.** *Such generosity **amazes** me. To admire* connotes a sense of approval, and a good translation is *elogiar, alabar.* Ella **elogia** mucho a su marido. *She **admires** her husband a lot.*

admisión / admission *Admisión* means "admission" in the sense of "acceptance." Hay un examen de **admisión.** *There is an **entrance** examination. Admission* also means *entrada, billete* (m.; for the theater, movies, sporting events, etc.). Ya no se ven **entradas** gratuitas. *Free **admission** is a thing of the past.*

admitir / admit *Admitir* is "to admit" (admit mistakes, admit to school, etc.) and also "to allow, permit; to acknowledge, recognize; to suppose; to hold (spectators)." **Admitamos** que tenga razón. *Let us **suppose** he is right.* El estadio **admite** 50.000 personas. *The stadium **holds** 50,000 people.* No puedo **admitir** esto. *I can't allow this.* No se **admiten** propinas. *No tipping **allowed.***

adobe / adobe *Adobe* (m.) was loaned to English. *Adobe* refers to a "sun-dried brick." Las casas antiguas son de **adobe.** *The old houses are made with (of) **adobe.** Adobe* in English has been extended to refer to *arcilla* ("clay," the type of dirt used to make *adobes*). En Castilla hay mucha **arcilla.** *In Castile there is plenty of **adobe** soil.*

advertencia / advertisement *Advertencia* means "warning, piece of advice," or "foreword" (of a book). Le hizo repetidas **advertencias.** *She gave him repeated **warnings**. Advertisement* translates as *anuncio.* **anuncios** por palabras (clasificados) / *classified ads (advertisements) Advertir* (ie, i) means "to warn, notice, realize, recommend." Te **advierto** que no vayas. *I **recommend** that you not go.* He **advertido** mis errores. *I have **realized** my mistakes. To advert* means *referirse* (ie, i) *a, hacer alusión a. To advertise* is *anunciar, hacer propaganda.*

aéreo / aerial, air *Aéreo* is "aerial" or "air" (as an adjective).

correo aéreo = *air mail*

fotografía **aérea** / *aerial* photography *Aerial* is also a noun, meaning *antena* ("antenna"). Las **antenas** están en los tejados. *The **aerials** (antennas) are on the roofs.*

afectar / affect *Afectar* is "to affect" in almost every denotation: "to put on, to pretend, to have an effect on, to concern." In some cases, *afectar* carries a negative connotation, such as "to hurt, to damage, to move (with emotion)." **afectar** estar enfermo / *to **affect** being (pretend to be) sick* La escena la **afectó** mucho. *The scene **moved** her a lot.*

afrontar / affront *Afrontar* is not "to affront" but "to confront, to face, to face up to." Hay que **afrontar** al enemigo. *It's necessary to **face** the enemy. To affront* translates as *afrentar, insultar, ultrajar.* However, *afrentarse de* means "to be ashamed of, to be embarrassed." **Ultrajó** a la inocente muchacha. *He **affronted** the innocent girl.*

agenda / agenda *Agenda (el orden del día)* translates in English as "agenda," but in Spanish, *agenda* is also *cuaderno pequeño, libreta,* which is "notebook, diary" in English. Escribo en la **agenda** las palabras que no conozco. *I write the words I don't know in my **notebook**.*

agradable / agreeable *Agradable* is "agreeable, pleasant, pleasing, nice" with the meaning of *placentero. Agreeable,* which comes from *to agree,* also means *conforme, dispuesto, de acuerdo.* Estoy **conforme** con ese plan. *I am **agreeable** (amenable) to that plan. That plan is **agreeable** to me.* ¿Está **de acuerdo** con eso? *Is that **agreeable** to you? / Do you **agree** with that?*

agregado / aggregate *Agregado* means "aggregate, a mass of different things," but the word also applies to people to indicate "assistant" (professor) and "attaché" (commercial, cultural, press, etc.). Ella es la **agregada** cultural en Roma. *She is the cultural **attaché** in Rome.* Es profesor **agregado** de historia. *He is an **assistant** professor in history.*

agresivo / aggressive *Agresivo* in Spanish keeps the original meaning of "attacking, militant." *Aggressive* has upgraded its negative denotation in modern English and turned it into a positive concept. In the business world it has come to mean *activo, dinámico, atrevido, llamativo.* un gerente muy **dinámico** / *a very* **aggressive** *manager* un anuncio **llamativo** (atrevido) / *an* **aggressive** *advertisement* **Agresión** translates in English as "aggression" in the sense of "an unprovoked attack." *Agresor* (m.) means exactly "aggressor, attacker."

agrícola, agrario / agricultural *Agrícola* and *agrario* are adjectives standing for the English word *agricultural.* (There is no such Spanish word as *"agricultural."*)
productos agrícolas = *agricultural products*
La industria **agrícola** es más importante cada día. *The* **agricultural** *industry is more important every day.*

aire / air *Aire* (m.) is "air" (to breathe), "air" (a musical tune), and "air" (conceit). However, *aire* has a broader meaning of "wind" or "draft" *(corriente,* f.*)* and figurative meanings of "elegance, gracefulness, likeness *(parecido),* appearance."
al aire libre = *outdoors, in the open air*
levantar castillos en el aire = *to build castles in the air* (Spain)
echar una cana al aire = *to have a great time*
darse un aire a = *to resemble*
darse **aires** de intelectual / *to put on intellectual* **airs** Se dice que la gente rica tiene **aire** de esnobismo. *It is said that rich people put on snobbish* **airs.** Ayer hizo mucho **aire.** *Yesterday it was very* **windy.**

ajustar / adjust *Ajustar* is "to adjust" in the sense of "to fix, arrange." It also means "to fit, to make fit, to resolve (a difference), to settle (pay accounts), to employ." *Ajustarse a* is "to conform to, to adjust oneself, to agree, to cling." El sastre me **ajustó** el traje. *The tailor* **made** *my suit* **fit.** ajustar las cuentas a uno / *to settle accounts with someone* *Ajustado* is "adjusted, fixed, arranged, settled," and also "tight, close-fitting, close, employed."
resultados ajustados = *close result*
Esas muchachas llevan ropa muy **ajustada.** *Those girls are wearing very* **tight** *clothes.*

álbum / album *Álbum* (m.) is exactly "album" (notice the written accent in Spanish). The plural form is *álbumes* in Spanish and *albums* in English. Nos sentamos por horas y horas, mirando los **álbumes** de su niñez. *We sat for hours looking at his childhood* **albums.**

alcoba / alcove *Alcoba* means "bedroom."
secretos de alcoba = *intimacies* (of married life)
La casa tiene tres **alcobas.** *The house has three* **bedrooms.** *Alcove* means *nicho, rincón (*m.*), hueco.*

alegar, allegar / allege *Alegar* means "to allege" in the sense of "to plead, to claim," a meaning in English that is hardly used anymore. *Alegar* also means "to say, argue, dispute." Los jóvenes estaban **alegando** mucho. *The young men were* **arguing** *a lot. Allegar* (notice the spelling with *ll*) means "to collect, to raise (money), to bring closer." *To allege* is *suponer, pretender, pretextar.*

Allegado is a noun meaning "relative" *(pariente,* m.*),* "close friend." *Alleged,* as an adjective, is *supuesto, pretendido, presunto.* El **supuesto** ladrón se escapó. *The alleged thief escaped.*

alias / alias *Alias,* meaning *es decir,* is an adverb in Spanish signifying "that is, rather, alias, otherwise known as." Francisco, **alias** Pancho Villa / *Francisco, or rather Pancho Villa* Alias in English is an adverb and also a noun whose plural is *aliases.* As a noun it means *nombre alterno* (generally, "false name"). El criminal usa dos **nombres falsos.** *The criminal uses two aliases.*

alienación / alienation *Alienación* means "alienation," in the technical sense of the word, which in everyday English is "insanity." The *alienista,* a psychiatrist, looks after mental patients, but the modern word for it is *psiquiatra.* El **psiquiatra** (alienista) nos aseguró que la **alienación** del paciente tiene cura. *The psychiatrist assured us that the patient's insanity is curable.*

alteración / alteration *Alteración* is "alteration, change," and also "argument, upset *(altercado),* disturbance, irregularity (of pulse), deterioration (spoiling)." **alteración** de la salud / *deterioration of health* Alteration also means *arreglo (de ropa), reforma (de edificios).* El sastre hace **arreglos** de ropa. *The tailor makes alterations.*

alterar / alter *Alterar* is "to alter, change" and also "to upset, disturb, spoil (food, things), distort (the truth), falter (voice)." ¡No **te alteres!** *Don't get upset!* El calor **altera** los alimentos. *Heat makes food go bad (spoil). Alterado* is not only "altered, changed" but also "upset, disturbed, angry, deteriorated (spoiled)." *Altered* also means *arreglado, retocado* (clothes). *Alterable* is "alterable, changeable," and also "spoilable, likely to get upset."

alternar / alternate *Alternar* means "to alternate, change, rotate, take turns." It also means "to mix" (socially) or "to associate" (with people). Le gusta **alternar** con todos en las fiestas. *He likes to mix with everybody at parties.* Los empleados **alternan** cada hora. *The employees take turns (rotate) every hour.*

altitud / altitude *Altitud* (f.) means "altitude" in the sense of "elevation above sea level." *Altitud* is also "height" or "elevation" (above ground, in the air). El avión vuela a 35.000 pies de **altitud** (altura). *The plane flies at an altitude (height) of 35,000 feet.*

alumno / alumnus *Alumno* is not "alumnus" but "student, pupil." Likewise, *alumna* is not "alumna" but "student, pupil." Los **alumnos** parecen no estudiar mucho. *Pupils don't seem to study much. Alumnus* translates as *ex alumno* (note the spelling with two words) or *antiguo alumno. Alumna* translates as *ex alumna* (also with two words) or *antigua alumna.* El director invitó a las **ex alumnas** a la ceremonia de etiqueta. *The principal invited the alumnae to the formal ceremony.*

amasar / amass *Amasar* means "to amass" in the figurative sense of "to accumulate, pile up." In the literal sense, *amasar* (from the word *masa*) means "to knead (dough), to mix (mortar), to massage." **amasar** (acumular) una fortuna / *to amass a fortune* Me gusta comer tortillas, pero **amasar** la harina es otra cosa. *I like eating tortillas, but kneading the dough is something else.*

ambición / ambition *Ambición* keeps the original meaning of the word *ambition* as an "immoral desire to obtain something." *Ambition* in English has upgraded its meaning, so that now it has a positive denotation: "legitimate and noble desire to succeed." Possible renditions are *empeño, dinamismo, atrevimiento, iniciativa.* *Ambicionar* parallels *to have ambitions,* which is better rendered by *empeñarse, atreverse, esforzarse (ue), procurar.* **Ambiciona** convertirse en gobernador, aunque sea comprando los votos. *He **has ambitions** of becoming governor, even if that means buying votes.* **Ambicioso** means "with immoral desire." El actor de este programa es tan **ambicioso** que maltrata a las mujeres. *The actor on this program is so **immoral** that he mistreats women. Ambitious,* in modern English, means *emprendedor, luchador, dinámico.* El joven **emprendedor** se hizo millonario con su esfuerzo. *The **ambitious** young man became a millionaire through his efforts.*

amenidad / amenity *Amenidad* (f.) is an abstract noun and has no plural. *Amenidad* means "pleasantness, charm, grace," in everyday English. Me gusta la **amenidad** de ella. *I like her **pleasantness** (charm). Amenity* is not a common word in English; however, *amenities* is a concrete noun and translates as *servicios, atracciones, prestaciones.* El Club Med ofrece muchas **atracciones.** *Club Med offers many **amenities.***

América / America *América* means "all America," from Canada to Patagonia, and it is divided into North, Central, and South America. *America,* in everyday English, is short for the "United States of America." *Americano* is a person born in any of the American continents. *American* refers to a citizen or product of the United States. Latin Americans use terms such as *estadounidense* (m., f.) or *norteamericano.* In colloquial Spanish *yanqui* (m., f.) and *gringo* are used without necessarily having negative connotations. Algunos **americanos** son pesimistas hacia los **norteamericanos (estadounidenses).** *Some **Latin Americans** are pessimistic about **North Americans** (U.S. citizens).*

amoroso / amorous *Amoroso (cariñoso)* has the sense of "loving, tender, gentle, affectionate."
cartas amorosas = *love letters*
Se porta muy **amoroso** con su hija. *He is very **loving** with his daughter. Amorous* refers directly to sexual excitement to express love, and must be translated as *sensual.* Con su esposa Juan es muy **sensual.** *John is very **amorous** with his wife. Amorosamente* means "tenderly, gently, lovingly." *Amorously* means *sensualmente.*

amplio / ample *Amplio* means "ample, big, sufficient," but *amplio* has more denotations than its English cognate. It also translates as "spacious, roomy, wide, vast, extensive." un salón muy **amplio** / *a very **spacious** hall* una finca muy **amplia** / *a **vast** estate* Vendimos ese coche para comprar éste que es **más amplio.** *We sold that car to buy this one, which is **roomier.***

analista / analyst *Analista* (m., f.) is "analyst" (in science, mathematics, etc.) and also "annalist" (a writer of annals). *Analyst* also means *comentador* (m.; of the news) in Latin America and *comentarista* (m., f.) in Spain. Es **comentador** del periódico *Times. He is an analyst for the* Times *newspaper*. La **comentarista** empezó a las cinco. *The news analyst started at five.*

ancestral / ancestral   *Ancestral* translates as "ancestral," according to the most recent dictionary of the *Real Academia*, but *ancestros* was not included for "ancestors." *Ancestors* translates as *antepasados, mayores, ascendientes* (m.). The *Real Academia* also suggests *solariego, secular* to mean "ancestral." casa **solariega** (ancestral) / **ancestral** home herencia de **los antepasados** / ances tral heritage

anciano / ancient   *Anciano* is used with people to refer to "old" and "elderly," and it is considered more polite than *viejo.* Los **ancianos** merecen respeto. *Elderly people deserve respect. Ancient means antiguo, vestusto, anticuado.* Me gusta leer sobre la Grecia **antigua.** *I like to read about ancient Greece.*

angina / angina   *Angina (de pecho)* is the same as *angina* in English, which in everyday language suggests "heart trouble" (medically, *angina pectoris*). In Spanish, *angina(s)* is used in the sense of "tonsillitis" or some other "throat trouble." El muchacho se queja de las **anginas.** *The boy complains about throat trouble.* Murió de **angina de pecho.** *He died of angina (angina pectoris).*

ángulo / angle   *Ángulo* is "angle" (in geometry) and also "corner" or "bend" (in a pipe or river). En el **ángulo** derecho está el piano. *The piano is in the right-hand corner. Angle is also used in the figurative sense of punto de vista, aspecto.* Hay otro **aspecto** del problema. *There is another angle to the problem.*

animación / animation   *Animación* means "animation" (with life, with cartoons) and also means "excitement, liveliness, activity, bustle." Hay **animación** en la fiesta. *There is excitement at the party. Animado stands for "animated" (as in life or cartoons) and also "lively, inspired, encouraged, busy, bustling."* Está **animado** por sus éxitos. *He is encouraged by his success. Animar means "to animate" (with life), as well as "to cheer up, motivate, enliven, encourage."*

anónimo / anonymous   *Anónimo* means "anonymous" (with no name, lack of individual character), but in the business world *anónimo* translates as "incorporated." **Sociedad Anónima (S. A.)** = *Incorporated (company) (Inc.)* Las sociedades **anónimas** son la base del mundo capitalista. *The incorporated company is the base of the capitalist world.*

ansiedad / anxiety   *Ansiedad* (f.) is not so much "anxiety, worry" as it is "longing, yearning, desire." *Anxiety stands for preocupación, inquietud (f.).*

ansioso / anxious   *Ansioso* is not "anxious" in the sense of "worried" or "uneasy" but rather "greedy, eager." Es muy **ansioso** y lo quiere todo para él. *He's very greedy and wants everything for himself. Anxious means preocupado, inquieto.* **preocupado** por el futuro / **anxious** about the future

antecedentes / antecedents   *Antecedentes* (m.) is "antecedents" meaning "background," but the Spanish term is more common than its English cognate. *Antecedentes* means "background, record, history." [*Antecedente* is only used in

the singular as an adjective referring to grammar and means "antecedent."]
antecedentes penales / *criminal record* ¿Cuáles son sus **antecedentes**? *What is his background?*

anticipación / anticipation *Anticipación (anticipo)* stands for "anticipation, expectation, prediction," and also for "advance" (payment).
con anticipación = *in advance, early, in good time*
Llegamos con cinco minutos **de anticipación.** *We arrived five minutes early.* *Anticipar* is not only "to anticipate, bring forward, expect, predict" but also "to advance" or "lend" (money), "to be early." **anticipar** el alquiler / *to pay the rent in advance*

antigüedad / antiquity *Antigüedad* (f.) is "antiquity" ("ancient times") as an abstract noun and also "seniority." In addition, *antigüedad* is a concrete, countable noun with the meaning of "antique." Le dieron ascenso por **antigüedad.** *They gave him the promotion because of seniority.* tienda de **antigüedades** / *antique shop*

antiguo / antique *Antiguo* translates as "ancient, old, former." *Antique* as an adjective means *anticuado* and as a count noun means *antigüedad* (f.).

antipatía / antipathy *Antipatía* does not mean "antipathy"; rather, it means "dislike, unpleasantness." Le tengo **antipatía** a tu primo. / *dislike your cousin. Antipathy* has been downgraded to refer to *hostilidad* (f.), *repugnancia*. *Antipático* is "unpleasant, unfriendly, uncongenial, disagreeable." Su tía me cae muy **antipática.** *I find his aunt very unpleasant. Antipathetic*, which is not commonly used, means *hostil, contrario, opuesto*.

anunciar / announce *Anunciar* means "to announce," as well as "to advertise" and "to be a sign of." Las golondrinas **anuncian** la primavera. *Swallows are a sign of spring. Anuncio* is "announcement" and also "ad (advertisement), notice, poster." In some countries *comercial* (m.) is used for a television or radio "commercial," although the *Real Academia* does not recognize this meaning.
anunciante = *advertiser, sponsor*
tablilla de **anuncios** / *notice (bulletin) board*

aparato / apparatus *Aparato* is "apparatus" to refer to any machine or equipment, but the Spanish term is one of those cover words used virtually for everything, including when the speaker does not remember the name of something. In some countries *aparato* is the colloquial term for *teléfono*. *Aparato* also translates as "pomp, show, fuss, set (for radio or television)," and "system" (of the body).
sin aparato = *simply, unostentatiously*
Se celebró la boda con mucho **aparato.** *The wedding was celebrated with a lot of pomp.* **aparato** digestivo / *digestive system*

aparente / apparent *Aparente* does not exactly mean "apparent," ("seeming, possible"); it is better rendered as "convenient, suitable." Ese banco es **aparente** para ti. *That bank is convenient for you. Apparent* emphasizes the visual sense and must be translated as *evidente, claro, patente, manifiesto, notorio*. Su tristeza era **evidente**. *His sadness was **apparent**. **Aparentemente** sometimes means "apparently, seemingly," but this term very often means *evidentemente, claramente*.

aparición / apparition *Aparición* means "apparition" ("ghost; appearing by surprise"), as well as "appearance (on the scene or in real life), publication, issue." Hizo su **aparición** a las tres. *He made his **appearance** at three o'clock.* libro de próxima **aparición** / **forthcoming** book

apartamento / apartment *Apartamento* is "apartment" in most Spanish-speaking countries, but in some countries *departamento* is preferred. In Spain *apartamento* is used when the apartment is rented and *piso* (*condominio*, nowadays) is used when it is for sale. En la Costa del Sol hay muchos **condominios** (pisos) en venta. *There are many **condominiums** (apartments) for sale on the Costa del Sol.*

apelar / appeal *Apelar* shares two meanings of *to appeal:* (1) *recurrir en la corte sobre una sentencia*, and (2) *suplicar a alguien*. *Apelar* also has its own denotations of "to resort to, to have recourse to." Señor juez, **apelo** a su buena voluntad. *Your honor, I **appeal** to your goodwill.* **apelar** a la violencia / **to resort to** violence *To appeal*, though, has the basic denotation of *gustar, interesar, atraer.*
derecho de **apelación** = *right of appeal*
La idea de fumar no me **gusta**. *The idea of smoking doesn't **appeal** to me.* encanto sensual (sexual) / *sex **appeal***

apetito / appetite *Apetito* exactly means "appetite." Notice the use of the article *an* in English in the following expression:
tener mucho **apetito** = *to have an appetite*
abrir el **apetito** = *to whet one's appetite*
¡**Buen provecho**! = *Good appetite! (Eat hearty!)*
No sólo quiero abrir el **apetito**, sino también comer medio pollo. *I don't want to simply whet my **appetite**, but to eat half a chicken.*

aplicación / application *Aplicación* means "application" ("to use, put, attach, put in effect") with the meaning of *usar, fijar, poner en práctica (una ley, teoría)*, *etc.* But *aplicación* also applies to people, meaning "industry, diligence, assiduity, hard work." Admiro su **aplicación** en el trabajo. *I am surprised by his **diligence** at work. Application* also means *solicitud* (f.), *petición*. Favor de llenar este formulario de **solicitud**. *Please fill out this **application** form.*

aplicar / apply *Aplicar* is "to apply" (the law, paint, etc.) and *aplicarse a* is "to work, try hard, apply oneself diligently." Se **aplicó** para sacar buena nota. *He tried hard (applied himself) to get good grades. To apply* is also used for *solicitar, dirigirse a, acudir a. Aplicado* means "diligent, studious, hard-working," as well as "applied, put, used." Ella es muy **aplicada**. *She is very **studious**.*

apología / apology *Apología* is not "apology" but "eulogy, justification, vindication." Hizo la **apología** del difunto. *He gave a **eulogy** for the deceased. Apology* translates as *excusa, disculpa.*
presentar excusas = *to make an apology*
Le presento mis **disculpas**. *Please accept my **apology**.*

apreciable / appreciable *Apreciable* emphasizes quality and must be rendered as "worthy, valuable, estimable, audible, sensible (noise)." *El director es una persona* **apreciable**. *The principal is a* **worthy** *person.* *Appreciable* is not exactly a cognate of *apreciable* because the English term emphasizes amount and size and is better translated as *considerable, notable, grande.* Hay un déficit **considerable**. *There is an* **appreciable** *deficit.*

apreciación / appreciation *Apreciación* refers to material value and must be rendered by "appraisal, estimate." [Don't confuse *apreciación* with *aprecio,* which means "esteem."] *Appreciation,* "understanding," refers to moral values: *aprecio, gratitud* (f.), *reconocimiento.* In the business world, *appreciation* is the opposite of *depreciation,* and as such, it means *plusvalía, aumento de valor.* Mostró su **gratitud** con una sonrisa. *He showed his* **appreciation** *with a smile.*

apreciar / appreciate *Apreciar* refers to material value: "to appraise, estimate, evaluate, price." It also means "to notice, observe, make out." Puedo **apreciar** la figura de Diego. *I can* **make out** *Diego's figure (shape).* To appreciate refers to moral values: *agradecer, comprender, estimar.* In the business world, it means *aumentar (subir) el valor.* Le **agradezco** mucho su ayuda. *I really* **appreciate** *your help.* ¿Cuánto ha **subido el valor** del oro? *How much has gold* **appreciated?**

aprehender, aprender / apprehend *Aprehender* and *aprender* are both cognates of *to apprehend,* with its double meaning. *Aprehender (apresar, prender)* means "to apprehend, arrest, seize." *Aprender (percibir, comprender)* means "to apprehend, learn, understand."
aprender de memoria = *to learn by heart*
Los ladrones fueron **aprehendidos** por la policía. *The thieves were* **apprehended** *by the police.* aprehender contrabando / *to apprehend (seize) contraband*

aprehensión, aprensión / apprehension *Aprehensión* is "apprehension" ("capture, arrest") as *detención, arresto.* La **aprehensión** (detención) del ladrón demoró mucho tiempo. *The* **apprehension** *(arrest) of the thief took a long time.* *Aprensión* shares with *apprehension* the idea of "fear, worry": *temor* (m.), *recelo, preocupación.* Tiene la **aprensión** de que va a morir. *He has an* **apprehension** *that he's going to die.* *Aprehensivo (perspicaz)* translates as "perceptive." *Aprensivo (miedoso, inquieto)* means "apprehensive, fearful, anxious, worried." Es tan **aprensivo** que no va a ver a su amigo enfermo. *He is so* **apprehensive** *that he doesn't go to see his sick friend.* *Apprehensive* also means *inteligente, de comprensión.*

apto / apt *Apto* does not mean "apt" exactly. In Spanish, *apto* stresses manual skills, whereas in English, *apt* emphasizes mental skills or capacity. Possible renditions of *apto* are "good at (or for), suitable, fitted, fit for, skillful." Es muy **apta** para los negocios. *She is very* **good at** *business.* Apt means *apropiado, adecuado, capaz, atinado.* Esa cita es muy **atinada**. *That is a very* **apt** *quotation.*

apuntar / appoint *Apuntar* does not mean "to appoint"; it means "to note, write down, aim at, point, score (in sports), dawn, sprout, prompt (in theater)." *Apuntarse* is "to enroll oneself, to enlist," for example, in the army or in an organization. **Apuntó** al corazón y lo mató. *He aimed at its heart and killed it.* El ministro **apuntó** la necesidad de una reforma. *The minister pointed out the need for reform.* **Me apunté** de voluntario. *I enrolled myself as a volunteer. To appoint* means *nombrar, designar, fijar* (time). Ella **fue nombrada** embajadora. *She was appointed ambassador.*

arca / ark *Arca* means "ark," but it also means "chest, coffer, safe, strongbox." **arcas públicas** – *public coffers, treasury* **arca de Noé** = *Noah's Ark* Vimos un programa sobre la búsqueda del **arca** de Noé. *We saw a show about the search for Noah's Ark.*

Arcada / arcade *Arcada* means "arcade" as a "row of arches." In Spain, the term *soportales* (m.) is used more than *arcada,* for example, around plazas. The plural form *arcadas* means "retching, nausea" *(náuseas)* in Spain. La plaza tiene cuatro **arcadas.** *The square has four arcades (rows of arches).* puente de una sola **arcada** / **single-span** bridge *Arcade* or *shopping arcade* translate as *galería comercial.*

arco / arc, arch *Arco* has two cognates in English: *arc* (in geometry) and *arch* (in architecture). But *arco* also means "bow" (for violins, arrows). **arcoíris** = *rainbow* Los árabes usaron el **arco** de herradura. *The Arabs used the horseshoe arch.* **arco** de medio punto / *semicircular* **arch** *Arch* is also an adjective with the meaning of *grande, malicioso.* **gran rival** = *arch rival* **una mirada maliciosa** = *an arch look*

ardor / ardor *Ardor* (m.) is "ardor" in the figurative sense of "passion, eagerness, fervor, enthusiasm" *(pasión, deseo, entusiasmo).* But in Spanish, *ardor* has the concrete meaning of "heat, burning sensation, burn." **ardor de estómago (ardores, agruras)** = *heartburn* El **ardor** del sol puede causar cáncer. *The heat of the sun can cause cancer.* **ardor** (entusiasmo) en el trabajo / *ardor (enthusiasm) for one's work* **Ardiente** is "ardent" in the sense of "passionate, keen, enthusiastic," and it is also used with concrete things to mean "burning, hot." Siente un amor **ardiente** por los bosques. *He feels an ardent love for the forests.* Siento la arena **ardiente** en los pies. *I can feel the hot sand under my feet.*

arduo / arduous *Arduo* means "arduous, difficult, strenuous" in its denotation of *difícil.* Es una tarea **ardua.** *It is an arduous task.* El doctorado parece demasiado **arduo,** pero ésa es una de mis metas. *The doctorate seems too arduous (difficult), but that's one of my goals. Arduous* also has the concrete meaning of *escarpado, abrupto* (terrain). Subimos una loma **escarpada.** *We climbed an arduous slope.*

arena / arena *Arena (ruedo)* is the same as *arena* (of a bullring or circus), but the primary meaning of *arena* in Spanish is "sand." The word also means "dust" as in *arenas de oro* ("gold dust"). **reloj de arena** = *sandglass, hourglass*

arena movediza = *quicksand*
Algunas playas tienen **arena** negra. *Some beaches have black* **sand.** Pelean en la **arena** (el ruedo). *They are fighting in the* **arena.** *Arenoso* means "sandy."

argüir / argue *Argüir* means "to argue" as "to reason, prove, show, conclude" *(alegar, razonar, demostrar* [ue]*).* To argue also has a different denotation: *discutir, pelear* (not with fists but with words). ¡No **discutas** más! *Don't* **argue** *any more!*

argumento / argument *Argumento* is "argument" in the sense of "reasoning" *(razonamiento),* but it is also used in literature to mean "plot, story line." Ese **argumento** (razonamiento) no convence a nadie. *That* **argument** *(reasoning) is not convincing anyone. Argument,* on the other hand, basically means *disputa, debate* (m.), *alegato* (in court), *discusión.* Esa razón es **indiscutible.** *That reasoning is beyond* **argument.**

armada / army *Armada (marina)* is not "army" but "navy, naval forces, fleet." [In modern Spanish *marina* is used more frequently than *armada.*] Mi abuelo fue almirante en la **armada** (marina). *My grandfather was an admiral in the* **navy.** *Army* translates as *ejército,* and in a figurative sense, *multitud* (f.), *mucha gente.* El juego de fútbol del **ejército** contra la **armada** (marina) es famoso. *The football game between the* **army** *and the* **navy** *is famous.*

armar / arm *Armar* is "to arm" only in reference to "weapons" *(armas)* in a real or figurative sense. *Armar* has further meanings: "to assemble, put together (a machine), make (a lot of noise), set (a trap), load (a weapon)."
armar jaleo = *to make a racket (noise)*
Tengo que **armar** la bicicleta. *I have to* **assemble** *(put together) the bicycle.* ¡Buena se va a **armar**! *There is* **trouble coming**!

arresto / arrest *Arresto* is "arrest" with the meaning of "detention."
estar detenido = *to be under arrest*
El ladrón está **detenido.** *The thief is under* **arrest.** *Arrest* in the medical sense of cardiac arrest translates as paro (cardíaco). Murió de un **paro** (cardíaco). *He died from cardiac* **arrest.** *Arrestar* means "to arrest, detain."

arribar / arrive *Arribar* means "to arrive," but it is not used much outside literature.
arribismo = *arrivism (unscrupulous ambition)*
To arrive most commonly means *llegar.*

arsenal / arsenal *Arsenal* (m.) is "arsenal" as "weapons storage," but in Spanish, *arsenal* also means "shipyard" *(astillero)* or "dockyard." Figuratively, *arsenal* and *arsenal* are used to mean "a large amount of anything." Tiene un **arsenal** de libros. *He has an* **arsenal** *of books.* En un **arsenal** fabrican barcos. *They build ships in a* **shipyard.**

arte / art *Arte* (m., f.) is "art" in the sense of "an artistic production." However, *arte* also means "device, skill, workmanship," and sometimes it is used with the downgraded meaning of "trick" or "cunning." *Arte* also translates as "art-

istry" or "artistic ability." [*Arte* is masculine in the singular and feminine in the plural. For example, *este arte* and *estas artes* or *buen arte* and *buenas artes.*]
tener buen arte = *to have a good appearance*
Ciencias y Letras = *Arts and Sciences*
Bellas Artes = *Fine Arts*
Tiene **arte** para convencer a todos. *He has the **skill** to convince everybody.* por amor **al arte** / *for the love of it*

artífice / artifice *Artífice* (m.) applies to people to mean "artificer" (i.e., "craftsman, artisan"). *Artífice* is used figuratively to mean "author, maker." Es el **artífice** de su fortuna. *He is a self-made man (the **maker** of his fortune). Artifice* has downgraded its original denotation to mean *recurso, ingeniosidad* (f.), *truco, artificio.* [Notice the contrast in English between *craft* ("skill, art") and its derived adjective *crafty* ("tricky").] Usa varios **trucos** para vender. *He uses various **artifices** to sell.*

artista / artist *Artista* (m., f.) translates both as "artist" (in the world of art) and as "actor" or "actress" (in the movies or theater).
artista de cine = *film actor*
Pablo Picasso fue un gran **artista.** *Pablo Picasso was a great **artist.*** ¿Conoces a algún **artista** de cine? *Do you know any movie **actors?***

asaltar / assault *Asaltar* is "to assault" with its basic meaning of "attack with violence." *Asaltar* can encompass different terms such as "to break in, storm, raid, hold up, assail." [In recent decades *to assault* has been used with the very negative meaning of "to rape," the worst type of assault. Perhaps this is due to the fact that the number of assaults has been growing very fast. This type of crime is reflected in legal terminology. The Spanish term for *to rape* is *violar* and for the noun *rape* is *violación.*] Una idea me **asaltó.** *An idea **crossed** my mind. Asalto* is "assault" as *ataque violento. Asalto* also refers to a "round" in boxing. *Assault*, for many people, has come to mean "rape," as in "sexual assault."
intento de violación = *criminal assault*
atentado contra el pudor = *indecent assault*
Los culpables de **violación** no reciben castigo suficiente. *Those guilty of **assault** (rape) don't receive sufficient punishment.*

asamblea / assembly *Asamblea* is "assembly" in the sense of "meeting, gathering, congress" *(reunión). Assembly* also means *montaje* (m.), "putting together" (a machine). salón de **actos** (reunión) / *assembly hall* Trabaja en un taller de **montaje.** *He works in an **assembly** plant.*

asbesto / asbestos *Asbesto* is exactly the mineral "asbestos." [Notice that the English *s* is not written in the Spanish equivalent.] In some countries *amianto* is used as a synonym of *asbesto.* El **asbesto** (amianto) es peligroso para la salud. *Asbestos is dangerous to your health.*

ascendencia / ascendancy, ascendency *Ascendencia* means "ancestry, origin, descent." Es de **ascendencia** mexicana. *She is of Mexican **descent.** Ascendancy,* or *ascendency,* translates as *predominio, influencia, ascendiente* (m.). Es una familia de mucha **influencia.** *It's a family of great **ascendancy.***

17

ascender / ascend   *Ascender* (ie) is "to ascend" with the meaning of "to go up" *(subir)*, but **ascender** also has the meanings of "to be promoted (a person), to add up to (an amount)," and "to climb (mountains)." La cuenta **asciende** a 25,00 dólares. *The bill* **adds up to** *$25.00.* La **ascendieron** a gerente. *She was* **promoted** *to manager.*

asesino / assassin   *Asesino* is not only "assassin" (someone who kills a prominent or important person) but also any "killer" or "murderer."
asesino = *murderous   (adj.)*
asesinato = *assassination*
Era un **asesino** pagado. *He was a hired* **assassin.** *Asesinar* is "to assassinate" (i.e., "to kill an important person") and also "to murder, to kill" (any person). La criada fue **asesinada** cruelmente. *The maid was brutally* **murdered.**

asesor / assessor   *Asesor* (m.) does not mean "assessor"; rather, it means "adviser, consultant" *(consejero)*. El Dr. Arana es mi **asesor** (consejero). *Dr. Arana is my* **adviser.** *Assessor* means *tasador* (m.), *evaluador* (m.).

asesorar / assess   *Asesorar* means "to advise, to counsel." *To assess* means *tasar, evaluar, valorar en* and sometimes, *juzgar, considerar.* Me **tasaron** la casa en *$200.000. My house was* **assessed** *at $200,000.*

asiduo / assiduous   *Asiduo* means "assiduous" as "regular, frequent." *Assiduous* is also *diligente, trabajador, porfiado.* Es una secretaria **diligente.** *She is an* **assiduous** *secretary. Asiduamente* means "assiduously" in the sense of "regularly" *(frecuentemente).* Nos visita **asiduamente.** *He visits us* **regularly.** *(assiduously). Assiduously* also means *diligentemente, porfiadamente.*

asignatura / signature, assignment   *Asignatura* means "subject, course." Me matriculé en las **asignaturas** más desafiantes. *I enrolled in the most challenging* **courses.** *Signature* translates as *firma, rúbrica* (the written name of a person). Es una **firma** ilegible. *It's an unreadable* **signature.** *Assignment* translates as *asignación, atribución, trabajo, tarea.* Ya terminé la *tarea* para hoy. *I already finished today's* **assignment.**

asilo / asylum   *Asilo* means "asylum" as a "home" *(refugio)* for orphans and elderly people. *Asilo* is not used to mean "a home for insane people" as is the English term *asylum.* However, *asilo* is also used as *asilo político* ("political asylum"). Ofrezco mi tiempo libre para trabajar en un **asilo** de huérfanos. *I volunteer my free time to work in an* **orphanage.** *Asylum* is traditionally translated as *manicomio* to mean *casa de los locos;* but in modern times, *hospital* (m.) *mental* is a better term.

asistencia / assistance   *Asistencia* is "assistance" with the meaning of "help" *(ayuda)*, but the primary denotation of *asistencia* is "attendance" as an audience (at a concert), a congregation (in a church), or gate (at a game).
asistencia social = *social welfare*
La **asistencia** a clase es obligatoria. *Class* **attendance** *is mandatory.* Siempre aumenta la **asistencia** a la iglesia en la Navidad. *Church* **attendance** *always goes up at Christmastime.* Necesita **asistencia** médica. *He needs medical* **help** *(assistance).*

Asistir means "to assist, help" but also "to attend, be present, come to, witness," as well as "to follow suit" (in cards). *Asistente* means "one who is present, bystander." Sometimes *asistente* is used to mean "servant" and *asistenta*, "maid." The plural *asistentes* translates as "audience, public." *Assistant* means *ayudante* (m.), *auxiliar* (m., f.; professor), *dependiente* (m., f.; clerk in a store). subsecretario = assistant secretary

aspecto / aspect *Aspecto* may refer to "look, appearance" in things or people, and it also refers to "aspect," meaning "point of view" *(opinión).* [Notice that in English *aspect* is not used to refer to *apariencia material.*] Juan tiene **aspecto** elegante. *John has a smart* **appearance.** El problema tiene varios **aspectos.** *There are various* **aspects** *to the problem.*

asumir / assume *Asumir* means "to assume" as "to take on, take upon" (a position, responsibility, control). Debes **asumir** la responsabilidad. *You must* **assume** *the responsibility.* *To assume,* in addition to *asumir,* is most commonly used to mean *suponer, presuponer.* At times, *to assume* takes on the negative connotation of *afectar, fingir* (virtue). **Supongo** que mientes. *I* **assume** *you are lying.* *Asunción* (of the Blessed Virgin) is "assumption" in English.

atacar / attack *Atacar* almost exactly means "to attack" in its general sense. *To attack* and *to assault* are used currently to mean "to rape, try to rape," when the victims of the attack are women. The Spanish term for *to attack* (rape) is *violar.* Si no se hubiera escapado del **ataque,** probablemente la habría **violado.** *If she hadn't escaped the* **attack,** *he probably would have* **raped** *her.*

atención / attention *Atención* is "attention," meaning "mental concentration, care, interest." *Atención* also means "kindness, courtesy, politeness, consideration." The plural *atenciones* means "respect, consideration." Presta (pone) mucha **atención** a las noticias. *He pays a lot of* **attention** *to the news.* ¡Cuidado! *Attention!*

atender / attend *Atender* (ie) is "to attend" as in "to take care of" (affairs, duties), as well as "to listen to, pay attention, wait on, serve." La camarera (mesera) nos **atendió.** *The waitress* **waited on** *us.* *To attend* ("to be present at") basically means *asistir a, estar presente a.* [Notice the required preposition *a* in Spanish.] **Asistimos** al funeral. *We* **attended** *the funeral.* *Atento* means "attentive," as in "paying attention," but the most common usage of *atento* is "polite, considerate, kind, thoughtful." ¡Para ser un niño es muy **atento**! Mira cómo no interrumpe a los demás cuando hablan. *He's* **polite** *for a child! Notice how he doesn't interrupt when others are talking.*

atestar / attest *Atestar* is "to attest" (in court), although *atestiguar* is more commonly used to express the same concept. The most common usage of *atestar* is "to cram, stuff, fill up, crowd, pack." un autobús **atestado** de gente / *a bus* **crowded** *with people* El gordito **atestó** la boca de dulces, como si fuera una ardilla con bellotas. *The chubby boy* **filled up** *his mouth with candies, as though he were a squirrel with acorns.* *To attest* in everyday Spanish is *dar fe de, dar testimonio de* (not necessarily in court), *confirmar, legalizar* (documents). **Doy fe de** que ella es mexicana. *I* **attest** *that she is Mexican.*

atractivo / attractive *Atractivo (atrayente)* means "attractive, charming, appealing." *Atractivo* is also a noun meaning "attractiveness, charm, appeal, allure." En esa compañía tienen salarios **atractivos**. *That company has **attractive** salaries.* Kari tiene muchos **atractivos**. *Kari has many **charms.***

audiencia / audience *Audiencia* is "audience," referring to an event: "interview, hearing." In some countries, *Audiencia* ("court of justice") is used to refer to *Tribunal* (m.) *de justicia*. In other countries, *Corte* (f.) *de justicia* is used. El presidente concedió dos **audiencias** hoy. *The president granted two **audiences** (interviews) today.* *Audience* also refers to people (in a group, as spectators): *auditorio, concurrencia, público.* La **concurrencia** no cesó de aplaudir. *The **audience** didn't stop applauding.*

"auditar" / audit *"Auditar"* is not a Spanish term, although it sounds feasible. *To audit* translates as *verificar, revisar, inspeccionar* (taxes, accounts). *To audit* a class is *ser oyente*. Hacienda **revisa** la declaración de impuestos. *The IRS **audits** income tax returns.* **Es oyente** en la clase de francés. *He **audits** the French class.* *Auditoría* means "audit" ("the act of auditing"), and also means the office of the *auditor* (m.): "judge advocate's office." *Auditor* is "judge advocate." In some countries, the term *interventor* (m.) is used.

auditorio / auditorium *Auditorio* is used to mean "auditorium" in some countries. The *Real Academia* has included this meaning in the latest edition of its dictionary. In everyday Spanish *auditorio* means "audience, public, spectators." El **auditorio** se puso de pie y aplaudió. *The **audience** stood up and applauded.* *Auditorium* can also be translated as *salón* (m.) *de actos, anfiteatro, aula magna, paraninfo*. La conferencia está en el **paraninfo**. *The lecture is in the **auditorium.***

automático / automatic *Automático* is "automatic" only in the sense of "mechanical gear." *Automatic* in English is used in a figurative sense and cannot be translated literally: *inmediato, correspondiente, a la par.* Me dieron un ascenso **inmediato** al recibir mi diploma. *They gave me an **automatic** promotion on getting my diploma.* *Automáticamente* is "automatic" only in a mechanical sense. *Automatically* is used in a real and a figurative sense: *en el acto, ipso facto, paralelamente, a la vez.* El ascenso trae un aumento de salario **en el acto** (a la vez). *The promotion **automatically** comes with a salary increase.*

autorizar / authorize *Autorizar* means "to authorize," in the sense of "giving official permission." However, *autorizar* is used for everyday situations to mean "to permit, allow, accept, approve of." Mi padre me **autorizó** ir al cine. *My father **allowed** me to go to the movies.* **autorizar** una manifestación / **to give permission** for a demonstration palabra **autorizada** / **accepted** (official) word *Autorización*, similarly, is not only "authorization" but also "permission, approval, acceptance." Tengo **autorización** de mi jefe. *I have my boss's **permission.***

avalar / avail *Avalar* is used in the business world for "to guarantee, be the guarantor of," and in the common world, it means "to vouch for, answer for, endorse." **Avalamos** al candidato demócrata. *We **endorse** the democratic candidate.* *To avail* means *valer, servir* (i), *valerse de. Aval* (m.) is "guarantee" as a noun.

Di mi **aval** a mi hermano. *I acted as **guarantor** to my brother. Avail* means *ventaja, utilidad* (f.).

en vano = *to no avail*

avisar / advise *Avisar* is not "to advise" but "to warn, inform, let know," and sometimes "to send for." *To advise* means *aconsejar, asesorar* (paid advice). Le **aconsejo** que viaje. *I **advise** you to travel. Aviso* means "warning, announcement" and in some countries "advertisement."

estar sobre aviso = *to be on the alert*

El ataque del país es un **aviso.** *The attack on the country is a **warning.*** dar un **aviso** al público / *to make a public **announcement*** *Advice* translates as *consejo, asesoramiento.* [*Consejo* is a countable noun, whereas *advice* in noncountable: in Spanish, *dos, tres consejos* is possible; in English, *a piece of advice, some advice.*] Le di dos **consejos.** *I gave him two **pieces of advice.***

axis / axis, axle *Axis* (m.) means "axis" with the denotation of "the second vertebra in the spine." *Axis* in English also means *eje* (m.) as in a sphere or of the planets. La tierra tiene un **eje** del Polo Norte al Polo Sur. *The earth has an **axis** from the North Pole to the South Pole. Axle,* on the other hand, translates as *eje* in vehicles.

azul / azure *Azul* is not exactly "azure" but means "blue" in general.

príncipe azul = *prince charming*

Me gusta la blusa azul **celeste** más que la **azul marino.** *I like the **sky blue** blouse better than the **navy blue** one. Azure* translates only a a shade of blue: *azul celeste* ("sky blue"). *Azure* is generally used only in literature and art. In everyday English, *azure* is replaced by *sky blue.*

B

bachiller, bachillera / bachelor *Bachiller, bachillera* mean "high-school graduate." Ya terminé la secundaria. Soy **bachiller**. *I completed high school. I am a high-school graduate.* *Bachelor* has two meanings: *soltero* ("unmarried") and *licenciado* (roughly a "B.A. degree").
solterón = *old bachelor*
solterona = *spinster*
¿Conoces algún club de **solteros**? *Do you know of a club for **bachelors**?*

bachillerato / baccalaureate *Bachillerato* is not "baccalaureate" but "high school studies." Different countries use different terms for *bachillerato: escuela secundaria, escuela superior, liceo, segunda enseñanza, instituto*. [Note: The building itself is the *instituto* for public schools and *colegio* for private schools.] *Baccalaureate* is the degree received after four years of college or university. It is close to the *licenciatura* in Hispanic countries, although this degree involves five years of study and therefore is the equivalent of a Master's Degree in the United States. Soy **licenciado** en Lingüística. *I have a **Master's** in Linguistics.*

bagaje / baggage *Bagaje* (m.) is "baggage," but only in the sense of "military equipment." In Spanish, *bagaje* is used in the figurative sense of "stock of knowledge" or "academic wisdom." mucho **bagaje** literario / *good **stock** of literary ideas* *Baggage* (luggage), however, refers to all kinds of *equipaje* (m.; "bags, suitcases, trunks"). Llevaron su **equipaje** al hotel. *They took his **baggage** to the hotel.*

bala / bale *Bala (fardo)* means "bale" as "a bundle of goods" such as hay or cotton. The everyday meaning of *bala* is "bullet, shot" and, figuratively, "hooligan." Compré una **bala** de hierba para el caballo. *I bought a **bale** of hay for my horse.* un carro a prueba de **balas** / *a **bullet**-proof car*

balance, balanza / balance *Balance* (m.) is "balance" in the sense of "difference between credits and debits." In Spanish *balance* also means "rocking, roll, rocking chair," and in a figurative sense *balance* means "result."
hacer el balance de = *to make an inventory of*
El **balance** del accidente aéreo es de 280 muertos. *The **result** of the airplane accident is 280 casualties. Balance* also translates as *equilibrio, volante* (m.; *de reloj*).
balanza comercial = *balance of trade*
equilibrio de poderes = *balance of power*
Balanza means "scale" as "a machine for weighing" and also "balance" in the expression "trade, accounts, payments." Uso la **balanza** para pesar los ingredientes cuando cocino. *I use the **scale** to weigh ingredients when I cook. Balancear* means "to balance" as in "to rock or swing; to settle accounts." The reflexive *balancearse* is "to rock, swing." El viejito **se balancea** por horas en la mecedora

(el **balance**). *The old man* **rocks himself** *for hours in his* **rocking chair.** *To balance* translates as *equilibrar, mantener (ie) equilibrio, comparar, cuadrar, compensar.*

balcón / balcony *Balcón* (m.) is "balcony" in a house or building. Las casas antiguas de España tenían **balcones.** *Old houses in Spain used to have* **balconies.** *Balcony* also translates as *entresuelo* in a theater or auditorium. En el teatro prefiero la platea al **entresuelo.** *I prefer the orchestra section to the* **balcony** *in the theater.*

balón / balloon *Balón* (m.) means "football, ball," not "balloon." El **balón** de balompié (fútbol) es redondo. *The* **ball** *for soccer is round.* El **balón** de fútbol americano es oval. *A* **football** *is elongated.* Su posesión más preciosa es el **balón** firmado por Joe Namath. *His most prized possession is the* **football** *autographed by Joe Namath.* *Balloon* translates as *globo.*

banca, banco / bank *Banca* is "banking" ("the business of operating banks") and it also means "bank" in gambling, as well as "footstool." La **banca** ha tenido problemas serios en los últimos años. *The* **banking** *industry has had serious problems lately.* hacer saltar la **banca** / *to break the* **bank** *Banco* is "bank" (of money, of sand) and also "school of fish, bench, pew."
banquillo (de los acusados) = *stand (for the defendant)*
banco de sangre = *blood bank*
banco de coral = *coral reef*
Un **banco** es un supermercado de dinero. *A* **bank** *is a supermarket of money. Bank* has further meanings: *orilla, ribera* (of a river), *loma, terraplén* (m.; "embankment"), *bajío* (underwater).

banda, bando / band *Banda* is "band," meaning "sash, a musical group, a flock of birds," and also "track" (sound), "wing" (of a political party), "line" (in a football field or any other sport). Una **banda** de ladrones robó el tren. *A* **band** *(pack) of thieves robbed the train.* La **banda** derecha es fuerte. *The right* **wing** *is strong. Bando* means "faction" or "party" (in politics), "flock" (of birds), "decree, edict, proclamation." Es muy raro ese **bando** de faisanes. *That* **flock** *of pheasants is very rare.* **bando** de la alcaldía / *mayor's* **decree**

bar / bar *Bar* (m.) means "bar" (for drinks), "saloon, tavern." Un **bar** es más lujoso que una taberna. *A* **bar** *is more luxurious than a tavern. Bar* also translates as *compás* (m.; in music), *foro* (judicial), *pastilla* or *barra* (of chocolate, of soap, of chalk), *barra* (rod, piece of wood, metal, etc.), *tranca* (in a door), *galón* (m.; chevron, military decoration), *barrera, abogacía.*
Colegio de abogados = *Bar Association*
¡Me comí tres **barras** de chocolate blanco! *I ate three* **bars** *of white chocolate!* Debe estar entre **barrotes.** *He should be behind* **bars.** El coronel luce sus **galones.** *The colonel shows off his* **bars.**

baranda / veranda *Baranda* means "railing, banister, handrail." La escalera tiene **baranda** a los dos lados. *The staircase has* **railings** *on both sides.* Cuídate en la escalera. Si no llevas el bastón necesitas agarrar la **baranda.** *Be careful on the stairs. If you don't use your cane, you must grasp the* **railing.** *Veranda* (or *verandah*) translates as *pórtico, galería, mirador* (m.). Las casas del sur tienen **pórticos.** *Houses in the south have verandas.*

barba / barb *Barba* means "barb" (the hair of a feather), but the basic meaning of *barba* is "beard, chin" *(barbilla).* The plural *barbas* is used instead of the singular *barba* to mean "a thick, bushy beard." Juan se rió en mis propias **barbas.** *John laughed in my face.* *Barb* also means *lengüeta* (of an arrow or fishhook), and in a figurative sense, *agudeza* (wit, sharpness), *mordacidad* (f.) or *veneno* (malicious remark). La **agudeza** de su ingenio nos hizo poner mala cara. *The barb of his wit made us wince.*

barbaridad / barbarity *Barbaridad* (f.) is "barbarity" in the sense of "atrocity, cruelty." But the colloquial usage of *barbaridad* focuses on two meanings: (1) "nonsense" (foolish words) and (2) "an 'awful' lot." No digas **barbaridades.** *Don't talk nonsense.* Esa casa cuesta una **barbaridad.** *That house costs a fortune (an "awful" lot).* *Bárbaro* translates as "barbarous, barbarian, barbaric," but in colloquial Spanish the term means "fantastic, fabulous." ¡Qué **bárbaro!** = *Fantastic! Great!* Lo he pasado **bárbaro.** *I had a fantastic time.* Esos soldados son **bárbaros.** *Those soldiers are barbaric.* *Barbarismo* is "barbarism" ("the misuse of words in grammar"). *Barbarism* (from *barbaric*) also translates as *barbarie* (f.).

barco / bark *Barco* means "ship, boat, vessel." [*Barca* is a small *barco,* for example, for fishing.]
barco de recreo = *pleasure boat*
barco de vela (velero) = *sailboat*
barco mercante = *merchant (cargo) ship*
Bark is used for *corteza* (of a tree) and also *ladrido* (of a dog, coyote, etc.). En la montaña se oyen los **ladridos** de los perros por la noche. *On the mountain one can hear the barking (barks) of the dogs at night.* El corcho se hace de la **corteza** del alcornoque. *Cork is made from the bark of the cork tree.*

barraca / barracks *Barraca* is not "barracks"; it means "cabin, hut, stand, booth" (at outdoor fairs, carnivals), a "peasant's home" (in Valencia, Spain). El pastor tiene una **barraca** en la loma. *The shepherd has a cabin on the hill.* La anciana vivió en una **barraca** comodita, situada en medio del bosque. *The old woman lived in a comfy cabin in the middle of the woods.* La feria está llena de **barracas.** *The fair has many stands.* *Barracks* is the term for *cuartel* (m.; military).
mochila = *barracks bag*

barril / barrel *Barril* (m.) (also *tonel* [m.], *cuba*) is "barrel, cask, keg." [Note that one *barrel (barril)* contains 42 American (not British) gallons of oil.]
cerveza de barril = *draught (draft) beer*
El vino fermenta en el **barril.** *Wine ferments in the cask (barrel).* *Barrel* also means *cañón* (m.; of a gun, of a feather), *tambor* (m.; of a watch).
organillo = *barrel organ*
caja del tímpano = *barrel of the ear*
La escopeta tiene **cañón** corto. *The shotgun has a short barrel.*

basamento / basement *Basamento* is used in architecture for "base, plinth" (of a column). *Basement* (of a house or building) translates as *sótano*. Las casas de California no tienen **sótano**. *Houses in California don't have basements.* El **sótano** es frío y oscuro. *The basement is cold and dark.*

base / base *Base* (f.) means "base" as a noun, (from baseball to a statue to chemistry). In Spanish *base* also means "basis" (plural, *bases*) as "the fundamental principle or theory of a system."
sueldo base = *minimum wage*
a base de = *thanks to, by*
¡Qué va! El no tocó la **base**. *No way! He didn't touch the base.* Esa es una buena **base** filosófica. *That's a good philosophical basis. Base* in English is also an adjective with very negative connotations such as *bajo, despreciable, vil, degradante.* Su conducta es tan **despreciable**, tan vil, que ni el mismo diablo la justifica. *His behavior is so base, so degrading, that not even the devil himself would justify it.*

bastardo / bastard *Bastardo* means "bastard, illegitimate child"; however, the term is used much more in English than in Spanish and is one of the most common insults. In Spanish, the term usually is not used as an insult. *Cabrón* (m.) *(hijo de puta, hijo de la chingada)* are used instead.

batería / battery *Batería* means "battery" (electric or military, a set of things). Some countries use *pila* instead of *batería* for radios, watches, etc. *Acumulador* (m.), as well as *batería*, is used to refer to a "car battery." *Batería* also means "percussion, drums" (in music), including the person who plays that instrument. Me regaló un reloj sin **batería** para Navidad. *She gave me a watch without a battery for Christmas.* **batería** de luces [en el teatro] / **footlights** *(battery) [in a theater]* Ringo Starr tocó la **batería**. *Ringo Starr played the drums. Battery* is also used in legal terminology for *agresión menor*. Se confesó culpable de **agresión menor**. *He pleaded guilty to battery.*

bazar / bazaar *Bazar* (m.) is "bazaar" as a "general store with inexpensive merchandise." Me enamoré en un **bazar**. *I fell in love in a bazaar. Bazaar* is also used to refer to *tómbola* or *verbena* (a fair or carnival with rides, games, food, etc.). In some countries *quermese* (f.) is used instead of *tómbola*. Me gustan las **tómbolas** benéficas. *I like charity bazaars.*

benéfico / beneficent *Benéfico* is "beneficent" (i.e., "nonprofit, charitable") and also "beneficial, advantageous." *Beneficioso* is another term for "beneficial."
lluvia benéfica = *beneficial rain*
Es una función **benéfica**. *It's a charity function (performance).* Los empleados de organizaciones **benéficas** también **se benefician**. *Employees of nonprofit organizations usually derive profit themselves. Beneficencia* translates as "charity, public welfare." *Beneficiar* means "to benefit" *(ayudar),* to profit, to exploit (land, mines)." **beneficiar** al género humano / **to benefit** humanity

benevolente / benevolent *Benevolente* (or *benévolo*) translates as "benevolent, kind, charitable," and in legal terminology, "lenient" (for example, a judge's findings in court). El juez fue **benévolo** con el culpable. *The judge was **lenient** with the guilty person.* El cura es **benévolo** con todos. *The priest is **kind** to everyone.*

bigote / bigot *Bigote* (m.) does not mean "bigot," but "mustache" (on people). *Bigotes* are "whiskers" (on cats). [The plural *bigotes* instead of *bigote* suggests that the hair is thick or bushy.] Dalí tenía un **bigote** con guías. *Dalí had a handlebar mustache. Bigot* translates as *fanático, beato, localista* (m., f.; "narrow-minded"). No me gusta la gente **fanática.** *I don't like bigots (bigoted people).*

billete / billet *Billete* (m.) is "ticket" (for a plane, movie, etc.) and also "bill" (banknote, paper money). [The most recent dictionary of the *Academia Real* includes *tique* (m.) and *tiquete* (m.) as loan words from the English *ticket* because these terms are used in some countries.] Pagué el **billete** de avión con varios **billetes** de cien dólares. *I paid for the plane **ticket** with several one-hundred-dollar **bills.*** Cómprame un **billete** de avión a España y te amaré para siempre. *Buy me an airplane **ticket** to Spain and I'll love you forever. Billet* means *alojamiento* (military), *leño* ("firewood"), *moldura* (architecture). *Billetera* translates as "wallet."

billón / billion *Billón* (m.) is a "trillion" in the United States and France. El cielo parece tener un **billón** de estrellas. *It seems like the sky has a **trillion** stars. Billion* in the United States is not called "billion" in England but "one thousand million." To translate *one billion* from the United States to the Hispanic world, the figure *mil millones* is used. [In numerals (mathematical figures), *un billón* needs twelve zeros, whereas *one billion* needs only nine zeros.] La ganancia es dos **mil millones** de dólares. *The profits are two **billion** dollars.*

bistec, bisté / beefsteak *Bistec* (m.) or *bisté* (m.) (both spellings appear in the dictionary of the *Real Academia*) is a loan word from *beefsteak* and the meaning is the same in both languages. In English the term has been cut to *steak*. [The plural of *bistec* is *bisteques* and the plural of *bisté* is *bistés*.] Un platillo popular de Cuba es **bisté** (frito) con papas fritas. *A popular dish in Cuba is (fried) **steak** with French fries.*

bizarro / bizarre *Bizarro* was used frequently from the Golden Age to the last century, but today it is hardly used. The term had the meaning of "brave, gallant, dashing." *Bizarre* has the pejorative meaning of *grotesco, extravagante, excéntrico.* Esa muchacha tiene ideas **extravagantes.** *That girl has **bizarre** ideas.* Es un programa muy **grotesco.** *It's a very **bizarre** program.*

blanco / blank *Blanco*, as a noun, does not mean "blank"; it means "target, mark, goal, aim."   quedarse en **blanco**   /   *to fail to grasp the **point***   dar en el **blanco**   /   *to hit the **bull's-eye** (target) Blank* means *espacio en blanco* (in documents), *laguna* or *vacío* (in history, memory, etc.). As an adjective, *blank* means *en blanco*, as in *un cheque en blanco* ("a blank check"). Llenen los **espacios en blanco** en el formulario. *Fill in the **blanks** on the form.* Los libros antiguos tienen muchas **lagunas.** *Old books show many **blanks** (lacunae). Blanquear* is used for "to whiten, to whitewash," and in banking terms, the illegal action *blanquear el dinero* is "to launder money."   Los bancos que **blanquean** dinero pueden ser multados seriamente. *The banks that **launder** money are liable for serious fines.*

blando / bland   *Blando* is not "bland" because *blando* refers to the sense of touch (*tacto*), and its denotations are "soft, tender, gentle." In a figurative sense *blando* translates as "weak, easy": *una vida blanda* ("an easy life").   un profesor **blando** con los alumnos   /   *a soft (easy) teacher with the students*   Me gusta el bisté bien **blando.**   *I like my steak very **tender.***   *Bland* refers to a person's disposition, as in *amable, suave, afable,* or the climate, as in *templado, suave. Bland* also refers to the sense of taste (*gusto*) in food and drinks, as in *insípido, insulso.* Estos frijoles están **insípidos.**   *These beans have a **bland** taste.*   Cancún tiene un clima **suave.**   *Cancún has a **bland** climate.*

blindar / blind   *Blindar* is not "to blind"; it means "to armor, armor-plate, shield." *To blind* means *cegar (ie), dejar ciego, deslumbrar* ("dazzle"). Se quedó **ciego** durante la guerra.   *He was **blinded** in the war.*   El sol poniente me **cegó.**   *The setting sun **blinded** me.*   *Blindado* is not "blinded" but "armored, shielded." Los tanques de guerra están **blindados.**   *The war tanks are **armor-plated.***   Al Capone usó un carro **blindado.**   *Al Capone used an **armored** car.*   *Blinded* means *cegado, deslumbrado. Blindaje* (m.) translates exactly as "blindage."

bloque / block, bloc   *Bloque* (m.) means "block," as in "a large piece of stone, wood, marble." In politics, *bloque* translates as "bloc": *bloque atlántico* ("Atlantic bloc"). [In modern Spain and Colombia, *bloque* is used for a high-rise apartment building.]
de un solo bloque = *in one piece (block)*
Block also means *cuadra de ciudad (manzana).*
letras de molde = *block letters, print*
Bloquear means "to block, to stop the passage, to blockade (militarily), to freeze (money)." *Bloquear* and *to block* are both used in a figurative sense, for example *bloquear un proyecto,* "to block a project." Estuvimos **bloqueados** por la nieve. *We were **blocked** (cut off) by the snow.* El gobierno ha **bloqueado** (congelado) los salarios para resolver la crisis. *The government has **frozen** salaries to resolve the crisis. Bloqueo* is "blockade" in a military and commercial sense. Cuba tuvo un **bloqueo** militar. *Cuba had a military **blockade.***

boletín / bulletin   *Boletín* (m.) means "bulletin" (publication of a society, a brief official statement) and also "report" (school, weather) or "forecast" (weather). El muchacho temeroso escondió el **boletín** de notas. *The fearful boy hid his **report** card (school **report**).* ¿Ya dieron el **boletín** meteorológico (del tiempo)? *Did they give the weather **forecast** already?* ¡**Boletín** de noticias de última hora! *Last-minute (up-to-the-minute) news **bulletin!***

bomba, bombo / bomb   *Bomba* is "bomb," meaning "an explosive," and it also is "pump" (for liquids) and "bombshell" with its concrete meaning of "an explosive" and its abstract meaning of "sensation" (*sensación*) or "surprise" (*sorpresa*). Nos dio una noticia **bomba.** *He dropped a **bombshell** on us. Bombo* means "bass drum" (*tambor,* m.) and "lottery drum" in a concrete sense, and "song and dance" or "ballyhoo" (*publicidad ruidosa*) in a figurative sense.
darse bombo = *to boast*

Dalí siempre **se daba bombo**. *Dalí always used to **boast** about **himself**. **Bombear*** (or *bombardear*) is "to bomb" and also "to pump (liquids), to bend, to warp *(arquear)*, to lob (a ball)."

bombero / bomber *Bombero* means "fire fighter" *(usa bombas de agua)*.
cuerpo de bomberos = *fire department (brigade)*
Los **bomberos** salvaron a la niñita. *The **fire fighters** saved the little girl. Bomber* is *bombardero (tirabombas)*. El **bombardero** destruyó la ciudad. *The **bomber** destroyed the city.*

bonanza / bonanza *Bonanza* is not "bonanza" but "fair weather, calm at sea," and in a figurative sense, "peacefulness, calm." Los marineros gozaron de **bonanza** por varios días. *The sailors enjoyed **calm at sea** for several days. Bonanza* in English means *fuente* (f.) *de riqueza, prosperidad* (f.), *"mina de oro."* La lotería es una **mina de oro** para muchos estados. *The lottery is a **bonanza** for many states.*

bonete / bonnet *Bonete* (m.) is the "cap" worn by the clergy in present times and by students and graduates in the past. [The modern clergy is more down-to-earth than in the old times. Usually its members don't want to be singled out in everyday life, and for this reason they wear the *bonete* only during formal ceremonies.] *Bonnet* means *gorro* (for children), *gorra* (for men), and *toca* (for women). Also, *capó* (of a car) and *campana* (of a fireplace) are equivalents of the British meanings for *bonnet*. Las mujeres menonitas siempre llevan una **toca**. *Mennonite women always wear a **bonnet**.* Pon el **gorro** al niño, que hace frío. *Put the **bonnet** on the child. It's cold.*

botica / boutique *Botica* is "pharmacy, drugstore" and also "medicament." The modern term is *farmacia*, but *botica* is still used in some countries. Hay de todo como en **botica**. *There is everything under the sun.* En el pueblo no hay una **botica**. *There is no **pharmacy** in town. Boutique* means *tienda pequeña (de ropa, etc.)*, usually with fashionable or special types of clothes. The term is becoming international. La **tienda** de María tiene rebajas para Navidad. *María's **boutique** has discounts for Christmas. Botiquín* (m.) translates as "medicine chest" and also "first-aid kit." En mi casa hay un **botiquín**. *There is a **first-aid kit** at home.*

botón / button *Botón* (m.) is "button" (on clothes, a flower bud, a badge). In some countries, *botón* is used for "knob" or "handle" (of a door). *Un botones* translates as "bellboy" and, in some countries, "errand boy."
como botón de muestra = *as a sample*
Cada candidato político tiene su **botón**. *Each political candidate has his or her own **button**.* El **botones** subió las maletas. *The **bellboy** took the luggage upstairs.*

brazalete / bracelet *Brazalete* (m.) (or *pulsera*) is "bracelet, band, chain" (on the wrist) and also "armband." Lleva un **brazalete** negro porque murió su padre recientemente. *He is wearing a black **armband** because his father died recently.* Le regalé un **brazalete** de oro para Año Nuevo. *I gave her a gold **bracelet** for New Year's. Bracelets* is also a slang term for *esposas* ("handcuffs"). Se lo llevaron con **esposas**. *They took him away in **"bracelets."***

bravo / brave *Bravo* means "brave" as "courageous" *(valiente)*, but in Latin America *bravo* is also used for "wild, fierce" (with animals) and "angry" (with people). *¡Bravo!* has been adopted in English for "Well done!"
toros bravos = *fighting (wild) bulls*
¡No te pongas **bravo** por tan poca cosa! *Don't get **angry** over such nonsense (such a small thing)!* Son dos toros **bravos** de Domecq. *They are two of Domecq's **wild** bulls.* *Brave* also means *galante, espléndido.*

breve / brief *Breve* is not exactly "brief" because the word *brief* emphasizes "conciseness" rather than "brevity." The best rendition of *breve* is simply "short."
en breve = *shortly, soon*
Brief is best translated as *conciso.* Sometimes *brief* means *muy corto,* as in a "brief" bathing suit *(un bañador muy corto).* *Brief* is also a noun and means *informe* (m.), *sumario, resumen* (m.). The plural *briefs* is used for "underwear" *(calzoncillos).* Debe ser una carta **concisa** (clara). *It should be a **brief** letter.* ¡Lleva **calzoncillos** rosados! *He's wearing pink **briefs**! To **brief** is rendered by informar, dar instrucciones a.* **Informó** al presidente sobre los últimos acontecimientos. *He **briefed** the president on the latest developments.*

bruto / brute *Bruto* is "brute, beast, brutish" in the real sense with wild animals, and in a figurative sense, it refers to "people with violent behavior." *Bruto* has a further meaning of "ignorant, stupid."
a viva fuerza = *by brute force*
peso bruto = *gross weight*
diamante en bruto = *rough diamond, diamond in the rough*
producto nacional **bruto** / *gross national product (GNP)* Es un **bruto**. No aprende nada. *He's **stupid**. He can't learn anything.* *Brutal* has the idea of "brutal, violent, cruel." In colloquial speech, *brutal* has upgraded its connotation to mean "terrific, colossal, formidable, huge." Fue una fiesta **brutal** (colosal). *It was a **terrific** party.* ¡Qué **brutal**! ¡Ganaste la lotería! *That's **great**! (That's **awesome**!) You won the lottery!*

bufete / buffet *Bufete* (m.) means "lawyer's office." Mi tío es abogado y casi duerme en su **bufete** de trabajo. *My uncle is a lawyer and practically sleeps at his **office**.* *Buffet* is rendered now by both *buffet* and *bufé* (m.) (both spellings are accepted by the *Real Academia*) to refer to a self-service dinner with a variety of entrées. *Buffet* is also used for the piece of furniture where the food is set. The Spanish term for it is *aparador* (m.).
coche bar = *buffet car*
No me gusta la comida de **bufé** porque soy muy comelón y me paso. *I don't like to eat **buffet** style because I am a big eater and I overdo it.*

bulbo / bulb *Bulbo* means "bulb" (as of a tulip) in botany and "bulb" (as a small, round organ) in anatomy. Holanda exporta **bulbos** de tulipán. *Holland exports tulip **bulbs**.* *Bulb*, as an electric bulb or a light bulb, has different translations according to different countries: *bombilla* (Spain, South America), *bombillo* (Mexico), *foco* (Cuba, Puerto Rico), *lámpara.* Edison inventó la **bombilla** eléctrica. *Edison invented the electric light **bulb**.*

C

cabaña / cabana *Cabaña* is not "cabana" but a small and primitive home: "cabin, shack, hut." *Cabaña* also means "livestock, cattle." El autor existencialista escribió sobre sus años de soledad en una **cabaña** en las montañas. *The existentialist author wrote about his years of loneliness in a mountain **cabin**.* *Cabana* translates as *caseta, cambiador* (m.) *de playa*. [This is a good example of English using a Spanish term, but with an entirely different meaning.] Los bañistas se cambian de ropa en la **caseta** de la playa. *The bathers change their clothes in the beach **cabana**.*

cabina / cabin *Cabina* means "cabin" (of a truck, plane, ship), as well as "booth" (telephone). El camionero tiene aire acondicionado en su **cabina**. *The truck driver has air conditioning in his cab (**cabin**).* *Cabin* is also translated as *cabaña, choza*.

cacerola / casserole *Cacerola* is used only as "casserole" in the sense of "saucepan, container," but not as the food. La viejita cocinaba en unas **cacerolas** más viejas que ella misma. *The little old lady cooked in some **casserole** dishes that were older than she was.* *Casserole* is better translated as *cazuela*, which means both the container and the food. [Actually, *casserole* is very specific because it refers to an earthenware container, and the food to cook in it seems to be taken from a recipe (*Webster's*).]

café / coffee, café *Café* (m.) is "coffee" (plant, bean, drink) and also "café" (bar, small restaurant). *Café* is also used to mean "brown" (color), the short form of *color café*. *Café* in English is borrowed from French with the limited sense of "restaurant, bar" in place of traditional terms like *coffee shop, coffeehouse*. El **café** era un lugar de reunión de escritores, pintores y otros artistas. *The **café** was the meeting place for writers, painters, and other artists.* Los solteros charlan por horas y horas en el **café** de la universidad. *The university singles chat endlessly in the campus **coffee shop**.*

cafetería / cafeteria *Cafetería* is almost the equivalent of "coffee shop, snack bar." This is a modern term in Spanish, as is the English term *cafeteria*, standing for the traditional *café*. *Cafeteria* is translated as *restaurante* (m.) *de autoservicio*, or simply, *autoservicio*. However, the *Real Academia* has recognized that in some Latin American countries, *cafetería* means the same as the English *cafeteria*. Un (restaurante de) **autoservicio** no tiene camareros; una **cafetería**, sí. *A **cafeteria** does not have waiters; a **coffee shop** (café) does.*

cálculo / calculus *Cálculo* means "calculus," as a division of mathematics, and means "calculation" in the everyday world. In medicine, *cálculo* means "stone, gallstone."
cálculo biliar = *gallstone*
cálculo renal = *kidney stone*
Tengo hechos mis **cálculos** para el viaje a Perú. *I have made my **calculations** for the trip to Peru.* Fue operado de **cálculos** biliares. *He was operated on for **gallstones**.*

calificación / qualification *Calificación* means "qualification" (regarding ability, competence), but *calificación* is also used in the sense of "school grade, mark." Recientemente las secundarias han mandado las **calificaciones** al trabajo de los padres. *High schools have recently begun sending **grades** to the parents' workplace. Qualifications*, in the plural, has a concrete sense of *títulos, requisitos, pruebas de aptitud*. Los candidatos deben tener sus **títulos**. *The candidates should have their **qualifications**.*

calificar / qualify *Calificar* is "to qualify" with the active sense of "to consider, label" and also "to grade (exams), assess." La crítica **califica** la obra de arte como atrevida. *The critics **describe** (qualify, assess) the work of art as daring. To qualify* is also used with the passive meaning of *estar calificado*. *Calificado* (or *titulado, capaz*) means "qualified, able, competent, with degrees," as well as "graded, corrected (exams, quizzes, etc.)." Ella es una experta **titulada**. *She is a **qualified** expert.* Tiene **títulos suficientes** para lograr esta posición. *He is **well qualified** for this position.*

cáliz / calyx *Cáliz* (m.) is "calyx" (part of a flower in the shape of a cup) and also "chalice, cup, goblet, cup used for Holy Communion." *Cáliz* is used in a figurative sense to refer to a difficult situation, a "bitter cup." [The plural of *cáliz* is *cálices*. The plural of calyx is *calyces* or *calyxes*.] El **cáliz** de la flor no es la parte colorida. *The **calyx** of a flower is not the colorful part.*   apurar el **cáliz** hasta las heces / *to drain the **cup** to the dregs*

calloso / callous *Calloso* is not "callous"; rather, it is "rough" or "hard of skin" in a material sense and has nothing to do with feelings. *Calloso* comes from *callo* which is "corn," and in medical terminology, "callus." ¿Tienes **callos** en los pies? *Do you have **corns** on your feet?* ¿Por qué no compras algo para suavizar los codos tan **callosos**? *Why don't you buy something to soften up those **rough** (hard) elbows? Callous* refers directly to feelings and means *insensible, desalmado, duro*. Es un padre **insensible** con sus hijos. *He is a **callous** father with his children.*

campar / camp *Campar* is not "to camp" but "to excel, stand out" *(sobresalir)*. El artista **campa** por el dinamismo de sus talentos. *The artist **stands out** because of the range of his talents. To camp* means *acampar*. [*Camping* (m.) is used in Spanish as much as *camping* is in English. This term has become an international word, similar to *parking, O.K.*, etc.]

campo / camp *Campo* means "camp" in the figurative sense of "faction, group" and also in the real sense of *campo de concentración* ("concentration camp") and *campamento* ("military, summer camp"). *Campo* primarily means "field, countryside, open country, court (tennis), course (golf)."
camposanto = *cemetery*
Prefiero el **campo** a la ciudad. *I prefer the **country** to the city.* Soy del **campo** republicano. *I am on the republican **side** (camp).* Se puede sacar a una joven del **campo**, pero no se puede sacar el **campo** de la joven. *You can take the girl out of the **country**, but you cannot take the **country** out of the girl.*

canal / canal, channel   *Canal* (m.) means "canal" (of water, like the Panama Canal), as well as "channel" (TV, official course, communication, body of water, ditch). *Canal* (f.) means "trough" and also "carcass." El **canal** de riego es un buen adelanto. *The irrigation channel is a sign of progress.* Hay demasiados **canales** de televisión. *There are too many television channels.* ¿De quién es el **canal** de Panamá? *Who owns the Panama Canal?* El ganado bebe agua en las **canales**. *The cattle drink water from the troughs.*

canapé / canapé   *Canapé* (m.) is "canapé" with the meaning of *bocadillo* ("snack"), but the most frequent usage of *canapé* in Spanish is "sofa, couch." Se me cayeron los **canapés** en el **canapé**. *I dropped the canapés on the couch.*

cancel / cancel   *Cancel* (m.) is not "cancel" but "storm door, screen partition, folding screen." El **cancel** del patio está roto. *The storm door to the patio is broken. Cancel* in English means *cancelación, anulación.* To *cancel* translates as *cancelar,* and more frequently as *anular.* **Cancelaron** el concierto. *They cancelled the concert.*

candela / candle   *Candela* is "candle" *(vela, cirio),* and also is used for "fire" in general and "light" for a cigarette. Figuratively, it is used with people to mean "mischievous, rascal, prankish." Las **candelas** (velas) se hacen de cera. *Candles are made of wax.* El muchachito es **candela** pura. *The little boy is a real rascal.*

cándido / candid   *Cándido* does not mean "candid" at all but "innocent, ingenuous, naive," and even has the somewhat negative meaning of "gullible."   la **cándida** mirada de un niño   /   *the innocent look of a child Candid* has very noble denotations: *franco, sincero, justo, abierto, imparcial.* Para serle **franco** a usted... *To be quite candid with you...* Es un candidato **justo,** imparcial. *He is a candid, open candidate. Cándidamente* translates as "innocently, naively." *Candidly* means *francamente, sinceramente.* Dígame **francamente** lo que Ud. opina. *Tell me candidly what you think.*

candor / candor   *Candor* (m.) is "innocence, naiveté, gullibility, credulity." *Candor* in English means *franqueza, sinceridad* (f.), *candidez* (f.), *imparcialidad* (f.).

caña, cana / cane   *Caña* is "cane, stem, reed" (as in "sugarcane"), and also "rod" (for fishing), and in colloquial speech, "shinbone, arm bone." In Spain, *caña* is used colloquially for a "glass of draft beer" because beer is served in a tall, narrow glass. [One asks the bartender for *una caña* (about six ounces) or *media caña* (about three ounces).] Me gusta pescar a **caña** si hay muchas truchas. *I like to fish with a rod if there are many trout.* ¡Cantinero, dame **media caña**! *Bartender, serve me a small glass of beer!* Le dio una patada en la **caña** del pie. *He kicked him in the shinbone. Cana* means "gray hair" ("white hair").
echar una cana al aire = *to have a fling*
Cane has other meanings in English such as *bastón* (m.; "walking cane or stick"), *mimbre* (f.; as in "wicker"), *palmeta* (a "stick" for punishment). ¿Ya necesitas **bastón?** *Do you need a cane already?*

cañón / canyon, cannon *Cañón* (m.) means "canyon" (a passage in the mountains) and "cannon" (weapon). Furthermore, *cañón* means "barrel (of a gun), shaft or flue (of a chimney)," and "pipe (of an organ)." El **cañón** de la pistola es corto. *The pistol barrel is short.* El Gran **Cañón** del Colorado es famoso. *The Grand Canyon of the Colorado (river) is famous.*

capa / cape, cap *Capa* is "cape, cloak," as well as "layer" (of air, dust, soil, of society) and "coat" (of paint, of makeup, etc.).
defender a capa y espada = *to defend with all one's might*
so capa de = *under the pretext of*
Hay una **capa** de tierra arenosa. *There is a layer of sandy soil.* Las **capas** pobres de la sociedad sufren mucho en tiempo de crisis. *The poor layers (strata) of society suffer greatly in time of crisis.* Puse dos **capas** de pintura. *I applied two coats of paint.* *Cape* also translates as *cabo* (in geography). *Cap* means *gorro* (children), *gorra* (men), *toca* (women), and *tapa* (of a bottle).

capón / capon *Capón* (m.) is used for "capon" ("a castrated rooster for eating") and also for "a rap on the head with the knuckles" *(golpe,* m.*)*. *Capón* is also used as an adjective to mean "castrated" *(castrado)*. Le dio un **capón** por testarudo. *He gave him a rap on the head for being stubborn.* Nos sirvieron **capón** a la italiana. *They served us capon Italian style.*

capote / capote *Capote* (m.) is "capote" (a long cape with a hood), used especially by soldiers and peasants. *Capote* is also a "bullfighter's cape," and usually is red. [The bull, however, is color blind, so the red means nothing to him. He charges when the matador moves the cape. The *capa* and *capote* were very popular in the Golden Age, and most of the comedies and plays had scenes in which the cape played an important part.]
dar capote = *to win all the tricks* (in a card game)
decir para su capote = *to say to oneself*
El toro ataca cuando el torero mueve el **capote**. *The bull charges when the bullfighter moves the cape.*

caracol / caracole *Caracol* (m.) is "caracole," which is "a half turn made by a horse with its rider." The everyday meaning of *caracol* is "snail" *(escargot)* and "seashell."
escalera de caracol = *winding staircase*
Es un plato delicioso de **caracoles** picantes. *It's a delicious dish of spicy snails (escargots).* El caballo hizo **caracoles** graciosos. *The horse made graceful caracoles.*

carácter / character *Carácter* (m.) means "character, nature, disposition, trait of a person; handwriting, typeface." *Carácter* is limited to the way a person is, with his or her features, disposition, etc. [The plural of *carácter* is *caracteres* without an accent mark but with a change of stress or emphasis.] un hombre de buen **carácter** / *a good-natured man* *Character* may have a similar meaning to the Spanish, but the term has upgraded its meaning in English to refer to the best moral values: *buena reputación, excelencia moral, superioridad* (f.), *virtud* (f.). For example, "a woman of good character" is not a woman who is *apacible* or *dulce*, but who is *de elevadas cualidades morales*. On the other hand, *character* has downgraded its meaning for *persona excéntrica* (eccentric person). *Character* is also used in plays, novels, etc. to mean *personaje* (m.) in Spanish. Don Quijote es un **personaje** famoso. Don Quixote is a famous **character**.

personajes; reparto = *cast of characters*
un hombre de **cualidades** morales **marcadas** / *a man of good* **character**

caramelo / caramel *Caramelo* means "caramel" as "melted and burnt sugar," but the most common meaning of *caramelo* is "candy, sweets." In colloquial Spanish the expression *de caramelo* translates as "excellent."

a punto de caramelo = *syrupy, tasty*
Los **caramelos** no son buenos para la dentadura. *Sweets are not good for your teeth.*
El flan se cubre de **caramelo**. *Flan is covered with* **caramel**.

carbón, carbono / carbon *Carbón* (m.) means "carbon paper" and also "coal" and "charcoal." The technical term *carbono* refers to the mineral element called "carbon" in English. El diamante es una variedad de **carbono**. *The diamond is a variety of* **carbon**. negro como el **carbón** / *black as* **coal**

cardinal, cardenal / cardinal *Cardinal* as an adjective means "cardinal" in the sense of "main, fundamental, essential," for example, in *puntos cardinales, virtudes cardinales*. *Cardenal* (m.) means the same as the English noun "cardinal"; however, its meaning also includes "bruise, black-and-blue mark." Los **Cardenales** es el equipo de béisbol de San Luis. *The* **Cardinals** *are the St. Louis baseball team.* Tiene unos **cardenales** del accidente. *He got a few* **bruises** *in the accident.* Los **cardenales** ayudan al Papa. *The* **cardinals** *help the Pope.* The English noun *cardinal* translates as *cardenal*, meaning "an official of the church; a bird."

cargo / cargo *Cargo* is not "cargo" but "post, job, duty, charge," as well as "accusation, charge." In business, it refers to a "charge" ("money owed").

hacerse cargo de = *to take charge of*
hacer cargos = *to press charges, to accuse*
Tiene un **cargo** excelente. *She has a wonderful* **job**. *Cargo* in English means *carga, cargamento*. El avión llevaba una **carga** de cocaína. *The plane was carrying a* **cargo** *of cocaine.* ¿Qué tiene esta bolsa tan pesada? ¡Parece llevar una **carga** de piedras! *What's inside this heavy bag? It seems like it's full of rocks (has a* **cargo** *or load of rocks)!*

carpeta / carpet *Carpeta* is not "carpet" but "folder, file, portfolio, briefcase, table cover."

cerrar la carpeta = *to close the file* (investigation)
Carpet translates as *alfombra, tapiz* (m.), *tapete* (m.). La casa tiene **alfombra** de pared a pared. *The house has wall-to-wall* **carpets** *(carpeting).* recibir a uno con todos los honores / *to roll out the red* **carpet**

carpintería / carpentry *Carpintería* is "carpentry," meaning "carpenter's work or trade," as well as "carpenter's shop." De niño mi hermano visitó una **carpintería** y la experiencia le decidió a ser carpintero. *As a boy my brother visited a* **carpenter's shop** *and the experience inspired him to become a carpenter.*

carrera / career *Carrera* means "career" *(profesión),* and also "a run (in baseball), running, jogging, a race (in sports), a run (in a stocking), a major (at school)."
a la carrera = *at full speed*
dar carrera a uno = *to pay for one's education*
Los Cachorros de Chicago ganaron por tres **carreras** a una. *The Chicago Cubs won by three runs to one.* Me gustan las **carreras** de coches. *I like car (auto) races.*

carro / car *Carro* is not only "car" *(automóvil* [m.], *coche* [m.]) but also "cart, cartload, carriage (of a typewriter), wagon."
carro blindado = *armored car*
Los **carros** (las carretas) de bueyes son muy lentos. *Ox carts are very slow.* parar el **carro** a alguien / *to put someone in his or her place*

carta / carte, card *Carta* means "carte" ("menu") as well as "letter" and "card" (in games).
carta blanca = *carte blanche (full powers)*
carta certificada = *registered letter*
carta credencial = *letter of reference; letter of credit*
a carta cabal = *thoroughly*
la última **carta** de la baraja / *the worst thing in the world (the last card in the deal)* Me mandaron una **carta certificada** y al recibirla tuve que firmar mi nombre. *They sent me a registered letter, and when I got it, I had to sign for it.* Card translates as tarjeta, ficha, carné (m.). [*Carné* is the actual spelling used by the *Real Academia.*]
tarjeta postal = *postcard*
Las **tarjetas** de crédito son dinero plástico. *Credit cards are plastic money.*

cartel / cartel *Cartel* (m.) means "cartel" (in politics, business) and also "poster, bill, wall chart." The expression *de cartel* translates as "famous, celebrated."
tener cartel = *to be reputable*
Un **cartel** comercial fija precios. *A commercial cartel fixes prices.* Prohibido fijar **carteles.** *No posters allowed. (Post no bills.)* Hay que tener permiso del presidente antes de poner un **cartel.** *You have to get the president's permission before putting up a poster. Cartelera* is "billboard" and also "entertainment section" (in newspapers, magazines).

cartón / carton *Cartón* (m.) is not "carton" (of milk, etc.) but "cardboard, cartoon (sketch, drawing)." In some countries different words are used to mean "cartoons": *caricaturas, dibujos animados, tebeos, muñequitos.*
cartón piedra = *papier-mâché*
Pusieron el gato en una caja de **cartón.** *They put the cat in a cardboard box.* Me gustan los **cartones** políticos. *I like political cartoons. Carton* (of milk, a box, etc.) is translated as *caja* (which is made of *cartón*).

casco / cask *Casco* is not "cask" but "helmet (of a soldier, fire fighter, mason, etc.), skin (of an onion), segment (of an orange), fragment (of a broken bottle), hull (of a boat)," and "hoof" (of an animal). In colloquial speech *casco* is used

for "head" or "brains" (usually with the plural *cascos*) and also "empty bottle, central area (of a city)."
casco protector = *crash helmet*
El **casco** puede salvar la vida del motociclista. *A **helmet** can save a motorcyclist's life.* ¿Tienen efectos curativos los **cascos** de cebolla? *Do onion **skins** have curative properties?* El **casco** de la ciudad es pequeño. *The **central part** of the city is small.* *Cask* means *tonel* (m.), *barril* (m.). El vino madura en **toneles** de roble. *Wine ages in oak **casks.***

caso / case   *Caso* means "case" (legal, medical, political, etc.). Both *caso* and *case* are used frequently in a wide variety of situations and idiomatic expressions.
hacer caso = *to take notice*
por si acaso = *just in case*
venir al caso = *to be relevant*
en último caso = *as a last resort*
Si un abogado toma un **caso**, trata de ganarlo. *If a lawyer takes a **case**, he will try to win it.* *Case*, however, has some concrete meanings not shared by the Spanish *caso: funda* ("pillowcase"), *caja* (of beer, wine, etc.), *maleta* (short for "suitcase"), *vitrina* or *escaparate* (m.; "show or display case"), *bastidor* (m.) or *marco* (around a door).

casquete / casket   *Casquete* (m.) (or *casco pequeño*) is not a common term in modern Spanish and certainly does not mean "casket." It translates as "toupée, skullcap, helmet (military)." *Casket* means *ataúd* (m.) (for a corpse) and also *estuche* (m.) or *cofrecito* ("chest"). El muerto se levantó del **ataúd** y se fue corriendo por el cementerio. *The dead man arose from the **casket** and ran away through the cemetery.*

castigar / castigate   *Castigar* is not "to castigate"; rather, it means "to penalize, punish, chastise, wound (a bull), ride hard (a horse)." ¿Cuál es la mejor manera de **castigar** a los hijos? *What is the best way to **punish** children?* La maestra ideal no **castiga** a sus alumnos cuando se equivocan. *The ideal teacher doesn't **punish** (penalize) her students when they make mistakes.* *To castigate* means *corregir* (i), *reprobar* (ue), *censurar* (especially in public). El senador fue **censurado** en público. *The senator was **castigated** publicly.*

casual / casual   *Casual* in Spanish and *casual* in English share the idea of "unexpected occurrence," something *accidental, fortuito, al azar*. *Casual* in English is also used for *deportivo* (clothing), *informal, ocasional*. Es un trabajo **eventual** de verano. *It's a **casual** (occasional) job for the summer.* ropa para ocasiones **informales** / *clothes for **casual** occasions* *Casualmente* means "by chance, by accident, as it happens." Me topé con ella **casualmente**. *I met her **by accident**.* *Casually* is *informalmente, de sport, de paso*.

casualidad / casualty   *Casualidad* (f.) is not "casualty" but "coincidence, chance, accident."
por (de) casualidad = *by chance*
Casualty means *víctima* (*muerto* or *herido* in an accident); *baja* (*muerto* in a war). Hay demasiadas **víctimas** en la carretera. *There are too many **casualties** on*

the highways. No puedo soportar las películas de guerra porque me entristece ver tantas **bajas.** *I cannot tolerate war movies because seeing all the **casualties** makes me sad.*

categoría / category *Categoría* shares with *category* the ideas of "class, kind, condition, rank, type." But *categoría* also means "prestige, social class, distinction."
de categoría = *first-class, luxury*
Hay varias **categorías** (clases) de personas. *There are several **categories** (kinds) of people.* Esta marca tiene **categoría.** *This brand has **prestige.***

católico / Catholic *Católico* is "Catholic," of course, but notice that the Spanish term is not capitalized. There are two common expressions with *católico:*
no sentirse (estar) muy católico = *to be under the weather*
no ser muy católico (el asunto) = *to be a bit fishy*

cava / cave *Cava* is not "cave, cavern" but "champagne" in modern Spain and "fosse" or "moat" in old castles. *Cava* is also an old word for "wine cellar"; *bodega* is used today. [*Cava* is a medical term in Latin, as in *vena cava*, and it is used in both Spanish and English.] La **cava** (el champán, champaña) siempre se sirve bien fría. *Champagne is always served very cold.* Cave translates as *cueva* if it is small and *caverna* if it is large. El tigre se escondió en la **cueva.** *The tiger hid inside the **cave.***

ceder / cede *Ceder* shares with *to cede* the meanings of "to yield, give away, give in," but *ceder* also means "to sell, lease, transfer."
ceda el paso = *yield* (street sign)
No **cedas** a la tentación de abandonar los estudios. *Don't **give in** to the temptation of leaving school.* **Se cede** la tienda. *Shop **for sale** (lease). Cesión* is the noun from *ceder* and translates as "transfer" (of a business).

celebrar / celebrate *Celebrar* means "to celebrate" in the sense of ceremonies, parties, festivities, concerts, parades, banquets, etc. *Celebrar* is one of those privileged terms used in Spanish for every occasion. It means "to praise, applaud, be glad, hold (meetings), reach (an agreement), welcome, say (mass), sing (deeds), fall on (a date)." **celebrar** su belleza / *to **praise** her beauty* **Celebraron** la mejoría del enfermo. *They **welcomed** the patient's recovery.* **Celebro** que no sea grave. *I **am glad** that it's not serious.* Navidad **se celebra** en lunes este año. *Christmas **falls on** a Monday this year.*

célebre / celebrated *Célebre* means "celebrated" in the sense of "famous, noted" and also means "funny, witty" (*gracioso*). Sus chistes son siempre **célebres.** *Her jokes are always **witty.*** Picasso era un pintor **célebre.** *Picasso was a **celebrated** painter.*

celestial / celestial *Celestial* is "celestial" with the (religious) meaning of "heavenly, perfect, of the heavens." música **celestial** / *celestial (heavenly) music* Celestial in English also has the material meaning of "of the sky": *celeste, del firmamento, astronómico* (of the stars). Apareció un cuerpo **celeste.** *A **celestial** body appeared.*

celoso / zealous *Celoso* is not "zealous" but "jealous." Es una esposa muy **celosa**. *She is a very **jealous** wife.* Zealous means *diligente, entusiasta, ferviente, religioso.* Es un **entusiasta** defensor de Gandhi. *He is a **zealous** supporter of Gandhi.* *Celo* (singular) translates as "zeal, fervor, piety" and also "heat" (in female animals) and "rut" (in male animals). The plural *celos* means "jealousy."
tener celos = *to be jealous*
estar en celo = *to be in heat*

cemento / cement *Cemento* is exactly "cement," but there is a slight difference in meaning. In Spanish, *cemento* is always *cemento*, before and after mixing it. The terms *concreto* and *hormigón* (m.) translate as "concrete" and "mortar," but only in the mouths of architects, not in everyday speech. Las autopistas son de **cemento**. *Freeways are made of **concrete**.* El **concreto** (cemento) dura más que el asfalto. *Concrete lasts longer than asphalt.* Cement, in English, is the term used for the material before it is mixed, and it becomes "concrete" or "mortar" after it has been mixed.

censurar / censure, censor *Censurar* is "to censure, condemn, criticize, disapprove," as well as "to censor": "to blacklist books, movies, papers, authors, etc." Es muy común **censurar** a los políticos. *It's common to **censure** (criticize) politicians.* Algunos países **censuran** Playboy. *Some countries **censor** Playboy.* *Censura* is both "censure" or "criticism" and "censorship."

central / central *Central* means "central" as an adjective: "in the center." As a noun, *central* (f.) means "headquarters, main office, plant, station, sugar refinery (*ingenio*)."
central telefónica = *telephone exchange*
central de correos = *main post office*
La **central** produce mucho azúcar. *The sugar **plant** produces a lot of sugar.* La **central** de Sears está en Chicago. *Sears' **headquarters** is in Chicago.*

certificar / certify *Certificar* is used for "to certify, to declare to be true in writing, to guarantee" and also "to register" (mail). **Certificamos** una carta importante. *We **register** an important letter.* *Certificado* means "certificate" ("verified") as a noun, as in *certificado médico*. It means "certified" and also "registered" (mail) as an adjective.   **certificado** de penales / *a copy of one's police record*

cigarro / cigar *Cigarro* is not "cigar" but "cigarette." Other terms for *cigarro* are *cigarrillo* and *pitillo*, depending on the country.
colilla = *cigarette butt (end)*
Una cajetilla tiene veinte **cigarros** (pitillos). *A pack contains twenty **cigarettes**.* Cigar is translated as *puro* (short for *cigarro puro*), *habano, tabaco* (in Cuba). ¿Los **tabacos** huelen mal? *Do cigars stink?* Me molesta el humo de los **cigarrillos**, pero ¡me pone enferma el de los **puros**! *Cigarette smoke bothers me, but cigar smoke makes me sick!*

cínico / cynic, cynical *Cínico* is "cynic, cynical," meaning "sarcastic, sneering, insincere." *Cínico* is one of those terms whose meaning in Spanish has become downgraded to refer to "shameless, brazen, impudent." No acepto esa conducta tan **cínica.** *I don't accept such* **shameless** *behavior.* **Cinismo,** similarly, translates as "cynicism, sarcasm, sneer, insincerity" and also "shamelessness, brazenness." **¡Qué cinismo!** = *What nerve!* Su **cinismo** me cae muy mal. *His* **cynicism** *rubs me the wrong way (is very displeasing to me).*

circular / circulate *Circular* is "to circulate" (air, blood, news, paper, water, money, ideas), but *circular* is used virtually for anything that moves: "to drive, walk about, run (trains, buses), move (traffic)." **¡Circulen, por favor!** = *Move along, please!* Los peatones **circulan** por la derecha. *Pedestrians* **walk** *on the right side.* Por esta vía ya no **circulan** trenes. *Trains no longer* **run** *on this line.* **Circulación** is "circulation" (of air, blood, etc.), as well as "traffic, walking, strolling." *Circulation* in English also means *difusión* (of news), *tirada* (of a newspaper, magazine, book). *U.S.A. Today* tiene la **tirada** más grande de todos los periódicos. *U.S.A. Today has the largest* **circulation** *of all the newspapers.*

circunstancial / circumstantial *Circunstancial* is "circumstantial" as a grammatical term. *Circumstantial* is used also to mean *circunstanciado* ("detailed"), *incidental,* and in legal terminology, *circumstantial evidence* translates as *pruebas indirectas.* No lo pueden condenar porque sólo tienen **pruebas indirectas.** *They cannot convict him because they only have* **circumstantial evidence.**

clamor / clamor *Clamor* (m.) means "clamor" with the denotation of "shout, noise, cry, scream." But in Spanish, *clamor* goes farther, toward the cause of the noise: "moan, knell, cheer," and in a figurative sense, "protest." Los **clamores** del gentío eran ensordecedores. *The* **cheers** *from the crowd were deafening.* El **clamor** de la gente anima a los bailadores del carnaval. *The people's* **shouts** *encourage the Carnival dancers.* Se oía bien el **clamor** de las campanas. *The* **tolling** *of the bells was heard all over.*

clasificado / classified *Clasificado* is "classified" ("arranged in order") as an adjective. "Classified ads" translates as *anuncios clasificados. Classified* has taken on a new meaning to refer to "classified material." The Spanish adjective for it is *secreto (reservado).* El Pentágono tiene muchos documentos **secretos.** *The Pentagon has many* **classified** *documents.*

clerical / clerical *Clerical* shares with "clerical" the religious meaning of "of the clergy, priestly." los deberes **clericales** del obispo / *the bishop's* **clerical** *duties Clerical* in English has the common meaning of *secretarial, oficinesco, de oficina.* **error de copia** = *clerical error* Es difícil conseguir buena ayuda **secretarial.** *It is difficult to find good* **clerical** *help.*

cliente / client *Cliente* (m.) translates as both "client" and "customer." [*Clienta* is used in most countries as the feminine form of *cliente.*] Son buenos **clientes** de este restaurante. *They are good* **customers** *of this restaurant.* *Client* in English is reserved almost exclusively for business, whereas *customer* is used to mean everyday patrons of stores and restaurants. *Clientela* applies to all kinds of *clientes*, and the best rendition is "customers." Este supermercado tiene mucha **clientela**. *This supermarket has many customers. Clientele* includes only *clientes especiales.*

clímax / climax *Clímax* (m.) appears in the latest dictionary of the *Real Academia* with all the meanings of the English word *climax: punto más alto o culminación de un proceso.* In Spanish, *clímax* used to be limited to literature and rhetoric. Synonymous terms are *punto culminante, desenlace* (m.), *crisis* (f.). [The plural of *clímax* is *clímaxes.*] La bolsa de Nueva York tuvo su **clímax** a las doce del día. Luego empezó a declinar. *The New York Stock Exchange hit its climax at noon. Then it started to decline.*

club / club *Club* (m.) is "club," meaning a "social circle or group." [The plural of *club* in Spanish is *clubes*, but *clubs* is frequently used.] *Club* in English also means *cachiporra* or *porra* ("nightstick, billy club"), *garrote* (m.), *palo* (of golf), *bastos* (in playing cards). El policía se defendió con la **porra**. *The police officer defended himself with his club.* El hombre primitivo usaba **garrotes**. *Primitive man used clubs.*

código / code *Código* and *code* are equivalent and common terms in the world of law and business.
código de honor = *code of honor*
Code also means *clave* (f.), "a system of signals or secrets."
prefijo (de teléfono) = *area code*
palabra clave = *code word*
Alfabeto Morse = *Morse Code*
El sistema de alarma tiene una **clave** secreta para prenderlo y apagarlo. *The alarm system has a secret code for turning it on and off.*

colectar / collect *Colectar* is "to collect," as in "to call for, to receive money for taxes, rent, etc." *To collect* also means *coleccionar* as "to gather, accumulate things as a hobby." ¿Quién **colecciona** monedas romanas? *Who collects Roman coins? Colecta* means "collection" as "goods or money received for taxes, in church, etc." *Colección* is "collection" when it refers to "things gathered or collected as a hobby." Di cinco dólares en la **colecta** de la iglesia. *I put five dollars in the church's collection plate.* Tengo una **colección** de dedales. *I have a thimble collection. Collector* in English is *cobrador* (m.; of money, taxes, etc.) and *coleccionador* (m.; of things as a hobby). No me gusta el **cobrador** de impuestos. *I don't like the tax collector.*

colega / colleague *Colega* (m., f.) is "colleague" as a "member of the same profession." But *colega* has extended its connotation in colloquial speech to mean "roommate, friend, crony, fellow." Debes cooperar con tus **colegas**. *You should share with your colleagues.* No puedo estudiar con mi **colega**. *I can't study with my roommate.*

colegial / collegial *Colegial* is not "collegial" but "schoolboy," and *colegiala*, "schoolgirl." As an adjective, *colegial* means "school" (elementary or high school). Recuerdo con placer mi vida **colegial**. *I remember school life fondly.*

Collegial ("collegiate") in English comes from *college* and is difficult to translate. Since the term suggests "cooperation, friendliness with colleagues," possible renditions are *cooperativo, buen compañero* (school), *buen colega*. El Dr. Peale es muy **cooperativo**. *Dr. Peale is very* **collegial**.

colegio / college *Colegio* is not "college" but "private school" (grammar school or high school), and by extension it is used for any school, whether public or private. *Colegio* is also used to mean a professional association, such as for lawyers or doctors, and translates as "college." In some countries, *colegio mayor* is "hall of residence." Los **colegios** de la América del Sur no son baratos. *Private schools are not cheap in South America.* colegio de abogados / *college of barristers (lawyers)* College translates as *universidad* (f.), no matter if it is an institution offering two, four, or more years. Estoy en mi segundo año de **universidad**. *I am a sophomore in* **college**.

colon, colón, colono / colon *Colon* (m.) is "colon" (i.e., "the last part of the intestine"). El cáncer del **colon** causa muchas muertes. *Colon cancer causes many deaths. Colon* in English is also a punctuation mark: *dos puntos* [:]. *Colón* (m.) (notice the written accent) is the monetary unit of Costa Rica and El Salvador, in honor of Cristóbal Colón (Christopher Columbus). *Colono* means "colonist" and "colonial," and in the modern world, "tenant farmer." Los **colonos** alquilan la tierra. *The* **tenant farmers** *lease the land.*

colorado / colored *Colorado* means "red," not "colored."
ponerse colorado = *to blush*
¿Es **colorado** el estado de Colorado? *Is the state of Colorado* **red**? *Colored* translates as *coloreado, de color, teñido, colorido*. Su pelo no es rubio; es **teñido**. *Her hair is not blond; it's* **colored** *(dyed).*

collar / collar *Collar* (m.) shares with *collar* the meaning of "band around the neck of animals." But in Spanish, *collar* also means "necklace" and "chain" (around the neck); in other words, Spanish does not differentiate people from animals in this respect.
collar de perro = *dog collar*
Lleva un **collar** de perlas. *She is wearing a pearl* **necklace**. *Collar* in English is also used to refer to *cuello* (in clothes).
trabajador de cuello blanco = *white-collar worker*
El **cuello** de la camisa está sucio. *The shirt* **collar** *is dirty.*

coma / coma, comma *Coma* means "coma" (plural, *comae*) as "a state of deep unconsciousness." *Coma* [,] also means "comma" (notice the double *m* in English). In a figurative sense, *coma* refers to "detail, minutia." [*Coma* is rendered by "point" to write decimal figures in the Hispanic world, except in Mexico where the U.S. system is generally used. The Spanish 2,50 becomes the U.S. 2.50.] Hace dos días que está en **coma**. *He has been in a* **coma** *for two days.* sin faltar una **coma** / *down to the last* **detail**

comedia / comedy *Comedia* is not only "comedy, a comic play" but also a "play" (in the theater). *Comedia* is also used for the "theater" in general. Figuratively,

comedia stands for "a put-on, make-believe, an act."
hacer la comedia = *to put on an act*
No hagan la **comedia**. Quiero que sean serios. *Don't put on an act. I want you to be serious.* Me gusta ir a la **comedia**. *I like to go to the theater.*

comentar / comment *Comentar* is both "to comment, to make remarks," and "to commentate" (i.e., "to write or deliver a commentary"). *Comentario* means "commentary," as well as "comment." Sus **comentarios** sobre el candidato se publicaron en el periódico local. *His **commentaries** on the candidate appeared in the local newspaper.*

comenzar / commence *Comenzar* (ie) is "to commence" ("to start"), but the everyday terms for *comenzar* are "to begin, to start." La corrida de toros siempre **comienza** puntualmente. *The bullfight always **starts** on time. Commence* in English is restricted to formal and literary style, for example, in a graduation ceremony ("commencement").

comercial / commercial *Comercial* translates as "commercial" ("related to commerce") as an adjective. *Commercial* in English is also used as a noun to refer to an advertisement on radio or television. *Anuncio* is the traditional Spanish term for it, but some Latin American countries are using the noun *comercial* (m.) instead of *anuncio*, perhaps because of the English influence. [The dictionary of the *Real Academia* does not accept *comercial* with the meaning of *anuncio*, but some other dictionaries do include the term. There is no doubt that in Mexico, for example, *comercial* is used on a daily basis on radio and television.] Hay muchos **anuncios** (comerciales) tontos en la televisión. *There are many silly **commercials** on television.*

comercio / commerce *Comercio* translates as "commerce, trade" as an abstract, noncountable noun, but *comercio* is also a concrete, countable noun that means "retail store."
libre comercio = *free trade*
Hay buenos **comercios** en este barrio. *There are some good **stores** in this district.* Mi padre es dueño de unos **comercios** en el centro. *My father owns a few **retail stores** downtown.*

cometa / comet *Cometa* (m.) stands for "comet" ("a kind of star") as a masculine noun. As a feminine noun, *cometa* means "kite" (the toy). Los **cometas** siguen una órbita parabólica alrededor del sol. *Comets follow a parabolic orbit around the sun.* Para volar la **cometa** necesitamos viento. *To fly a **kite**, we need some wind.*

cometer / commit *Cometer* means "to commit" (a crime, a mistake). *To commit* also means *confiar* ("to entrust"); *internar* (a patient, a madman). *To commit oneself* means *comprometerse a.* In English *to make a commitment* is used more frequently than *to commit oneself.*
aprender de memoria = *to commit to memory*
Se **comprometió** a aprender el material. *He **made a commitment** to learn the material.* Se **comprometió** a pasar el resto de su vida con ella. *He **made a***

commitment to spending the rest of his life with her. **Confiamos** su fama a la posteridad. *We* **commit** *his fame to posterity.* Para **aprender de memoria** el vocabulario hay que **comprometerse** a estudiar mucho. *To* **commit** *the vocabulary to memory requires* **committing** *oneself to studying a lot.*

comisario / commissary *Comisario* is "commissary" ("delegate, officer, commissioner") and also in some Hispanic countries "police inspector." *Commissary* also means *economato* ("government store"). El **economato** es más barato que otras tiendas. *The* **commissary** *is cheaper than other stores.* **Comisaría** *translates as "police station."* El **comisario** se llevó al ladrón a la **comisaría.** *The* **police officer** *took the thief to the* **police station.**

comisión / commission *Comisión* is "commission" with its multiple denotations: "percentage of sales, task, post, mission, delegation." *Comisión* also means "committee," for example, in Congress. *Comité* (m.) is used in many countries instead of *comisión* for "committee."
comisión permanente = *standing committee*
trabajar a comisión = *to work on commission*
Aceptó la **comisión** de trabajar en Londres. *She accepted the* **commission** *(post) to work in London.* *Commission:* the expression *out of commission* has two meanings: *inservible* (for things) and *fuera de servicio* (for people). Como el ascensor estaba **inservible,** subió por las escaleras hasta el piso siete. *Since the elevator was* **out of commission** *(out of order), she walked upstairs to the seventh floor.*

comodidad / commodity *Comodidad* (f.) does not mean "commodity"; it means "comfort, convenience, well-being." La **comodidad** del hotel nos relaja. *The* **comfort** *of the hotel puts us at ease.* la **comodidad** de los pasajeros / *the* **comfort** *of the passengers* *Commodity* means *artículo* or *producto, mercancía (mercadería).* Todos queremos mejores **productos.** *Everybody wants better* **commodities.**

cómodo / commodious *Cómodo* is not "commodious" but "comfortable, convenient, useful, handy, easy-going."
carácter cómodo = *easy-going nature*
Commodious means *espacioso, amplio.* Compraron una casa **amplia.** *They bought a* **commodious** *(spacious) house.* *Comodín* (m.) is a "wild card" in card games. *Cómoda* is a noun meaning "chest of drawers," similar to one meaning of *commode* in English.

compañía / company *Compañía* is "company" in its multiple meanings: "corporation, firm, friendship, group of actors." The two terms do differ somewhat. The plural *compañías* (of a person) is a concrete countable noun, meaning "friends, companions." Una **compañía** comercial es una firma. *A commercial* **company** *is a firm.* "Son ricos los que tienen amigos", o sea, una buena **compañía** vale mucho. *"Those who have friends are rich"; in other words, good* **friendship** *is worth a lot.* Las malas **compañías** no son buenas consejeras. *Bad* **companions** *are not good advisers.* *Company* also means *visita, invitado* ("guest").

perdonando el presente = *present company excepted*
buenos modales = *company manners* (best behavior)
estar esperando **visita** / *to be expecting* **company**

compás / compass *Compás* (m.) is "compass" (an instrument for drawing circles), but each term has additional meanings. *Compás* is used in music for "bar, time, beat." *Compass* means *brújula* (for determining direction), *límites* (m.), *alcance* (m.; "range"). Los marineros usan la **brújula** en el mar. *Sailors use a* **compass** *at sea.* Está fuera del **alcance** de mi tarea. *It's beyond the* **compass** *(range) of my task.*

compensación / compensation *Compensación* shares with *compensation* the idea of "indemnization, payment for damages." However, *compensación* is not necessarily a legal term; it is used in everyday life to mean "make up for, adjust." Recibió la **compensación** justa. *He received fair* **compensation**. En **compensación** por tu ayuda, te ofrezco una cerveza bien fría. *To repay you for your help, I'll buy you an ice-cold beer.* *Compensation* is used also to mean *salario, remuneración, recompensa, paga.* Esta semana me dieron doble **paga (salario).** *They gave me double* **compensation** *this week.* *Compensar por* means "to compensate (for), make up for, adjust."

competencia / competence *Competencia* is not "competence." It means "competition, scope, field (in a figurative sense)."
en competencia con = *in competition with*
Hay mucha **competencia** en los negocios. *There is a lot of* **competition** *in business.* ¡No hay **competencia** en este concurso! *There's no* **competition** *in this contest!* Eso no es de mi **competencia**. *That's beyond my* **scope (field)**. *Competence* stands for *capacidad* (f.), *aptitud* (f.). Tiene **capacidad** para matemáticas. *He shows* **competence** *(an aptitude) in mathematics.* La falta de **capacidad** profesional puede hacer que la compañía pierda clientes. *Lack of professional* **competence** *can lose clients for the company.*

competición / competition *Competición* translates as "competition" in the world of sports and in school contests. *Competition* translates as *competencia, oposición* ("opponent," as in a test for a job). Conseguí el empleo sin **oposición**. *I got the job without any* **competition**.

complacencia / complacency *Complacencia* is almost the opposite of *complacency (complacence)*. *Complacencia* stands for "pleasure, satisfaction, indulgence." Siento **complacencia** al ayudar a otros. *I feel* **satisfaction** *when helping other people.* *Complacency* or *complacence* has the negative connotation of *apatía, indolencia, dejadez* (f.). *Complaciente* means "obliging, eager or ready to please, helpful." El maestro es **complaciente**. *The teacher is* **eager to please**. Tengo un alumno **complaciente**. *I have one* **helpful** *student.* *Complacent* stands for *indiferente, apático.* La clase está llena de muchachos **indiferentes**. *The class is full of* **complacent** *boys.*

complemento / complement, compliment *Complemento* does not mean "compliment"; rather, it means "complement" ("something that completes or fills up"). Un buen vino es el **complemento** de una buena comida. *A good wine is* *the* **complement** *of a good meal.* Compliment means *cumplido, atención, piropo, enhorabuena.* Mi **enhorabuena** al maestro cocinero. *My* **compliments** *to the master chef.* Los andaluces son los maestros del **piropo** a la mujer en el mundo hispano. *The Andalusians are the masters of the* **compliment** *to the ladies in the Hispanic world.* **Complementario** means exactly "complementary," but not "complimentary." *Complimentary* translates as *halagador; gratis* or *gratuito* (free, as a courtesy). [*See also* **cumplimiento / compliment.**]

completar / complete   *Completar* is "to complete" ("to make full, to finish"). *To complete* is also *llenar (formularios)* ("to fill out forms"). Llenen los espacios en blanco. *Complete (fill in) the blanks.* *Completo* is used for "complete," although the Spanish term is not used as frequently as the English. *Complete* is also translated as *acabado, perfecto, concluido.*
una sorpresa total = *a complete surprise*
El trabajo no está concluido. *The work is not complete.*

complexión / complexion   *Complexión* is not "complexion" but "disposition, nature, physical constitution." *Complexión* refers to the physiological and moral traits of a person. [*Complexión* used to be a very common term from the Golden Age to the last century; now it is used infrequently.] Don Quijote era de **complexión** recia. *Don Quijote was of a strong* **constitution.** *Complexion,* however, is limited to the appearance of a person, especially the skin. Good translations are *tez* (f.), *cutis* (m.), *piel* (f.; especially of the face), and in a figurative sense, *aspecto, cariz* (m.; "look"). Tiene la **piel (tez)** morena. *He has a dark* **complexion.**

complicado / complicated   *Complicado* means "complicated," as in "complex, elaborate, difficult to understand, solve, or analyze." But *complicado* has additional denotations: "implicated, involved (in something illegal), accessory (to a crime)." ¡Qué examen más **complicado**! *What a* **difficult** *exam!* *Complicar* is "to complicate, to make complicated" and also "to get involved or mixed up (in something illegal)." ¿Por qué **complicas** una cosa sencilla? *Why do you* **make** *a simple thing* **complicated?** ¡Esto se complica! *This is getting serious!* Está **complicado** en un robo. *He is* **involved** *in a theft.*

componer / compose   *Componer* is "to compose," ("to form, make, or write music, art, etc.") and also "to repair, fix, mend, settle a matter." **componer** un ramillete de flores   /   *to make up a bouquet of flowers* Nadie sabe quién **compuso** "La bamba". *No one knows who* **composed** *"La Bamba."* *To compose* also has its own meaning, different from *componer: calmar, sosegar* (ie), *tranquilizar.* ¡Cálmate! *Compose yourself!*

compositor / compositor   *Compositor* (m.) means "composer," not "compositor." *Compositor* translates as *tipógrafo, cajista de imprenta.*

compostura / composure   *Compostura* means "composure" ("moderation, restraint, dignity, calm") and also "repair, mending, tidiness, agreement." la **compostura** de un reloj   /   *the* **repair** *of a watch* No pudo conservar su **compostura**. *She couldn't keep her* **composure.**

comprensivo / comprehensive *Comprensivo* does not mean "comprehensive"; rather, it means "understanding." Es una madre **comprensiva**. *She is an **understanding** mother.* *Comprehensive* can be translated by quite a few terms in Spanish, such as *amplio, extensivo, global, general.* [In Spain and some other countries, there is a "comprehensive examination," which is the *reválida.*]
seguro contra todo riesgo = *comprehensive insurance*
El término *política* es muy **amplio**. Politics *is a **comprehensive** term.*

comprometer / compromise *Comprometer* is "to compromise" ("to risk, endanger") and also "to commit, implicate (in a crime), impair (health)." **comprometer** sus intereses / to **jeopardize** one's interests To compromise also means *llegar a un acuerdo, hacer concesiones, transigir.*

compromiso / compromise *Compromiso* does not mean "compromise," but "obligation, commitment, engagement, date *(cita),* difficult situation." No me ponga en ese **compromiso**. *Don't put me in that **difficult situation**.* ¡Qué **compromiso**! *What a **nuisance**!* hacer honor a sus **compromisos** / to meet one's **obligations** *Compromise* means *arreglo, acomodo, término medio, acuerdo mutuo.*

compulsión / compulsion *Compulsión* is "compulsion" ("being compelled, constraint, coercion"). Tiene **compulsión** por el juego. *He has a **compulsion** to gamble. Compulsorio* would only be used by a judge to mean "compulsory." *Compulsory,* as used outside a courtroom, is translated as *obligatorio, forzoso.* El servicio militar es **forzoso** en España. *Military service is **compulsory** in Spain.*

conclusivo / conclusive *Conclusivo* is "conclusive" in the sense of "finished, final, about to end." Necesita un toque **conclusivo**. *It needs a **final** (conclusive) touch. Conclusive* goes farther because it involves the people responsible for concluding the matter. The Spanish terms are *concluyente, convincente, definitivo.* No hay evidencia **concluyente**. *There is no **conclusive** evidence.*

concreto / concrete *Concreto* is "concrete" as the opposite of *abstracto.* But *concreto* also means "actual, definitive, particular." *Concreto* is "concrete" ("mixed cement") as a noun, but in everyday speech, *cemento* is used before and after mixing the "cement." [See also **cemento / cement**.] La cantidad **concreta** no es alta. *The **actual** amount is not high.* Dame los detalles **concretos**. *Give me the **particular** (specific) details. Concretamente* means "concretely" ("specifically, not abstractly") and also "to be exact, exactly." **Concretamente** murieron los dos en la guerra. *To be exact, the two died in the war. Concretar* translates as "to pinpoint, sum up, boil down (a statement).
concretarse a = to concentrate on, keep to
Concreta tus ideas en pocas palabras. ***Sum up** your ideas in a few words.* To concrete stands for *cubrir con cemento* (concrete).

concurrencia / concurrence *Concurrencia* means "concurrence" as "coincidence, conjunction." The primary meaning of *concurrencia* is "audience, crowd." La **concurrencia** fue de 30.000 personas. *The **audience** (attendance) was 30,000 people. Concurrir* means "to attend, go to, get together." Algunos **concurrieron** en el café. *A few people **got together** at the café.* To concur means *estar de* *acuerdo, coincidir, asentir* (ie, i). Creo que **coincidimos** en una cosa. *I think we concur on one thing.* **Concurrido** means "busy, crowded, well-attended." Las calles de Nueva York siempre están **concurridas.** *The streets of New York are always crowded.*

concurso / concourse *Concurso* is "concourse," meaning "contest, competition." Hay varios **concursos** literarios en la universidad. *There are several literary contests (concourses) at the university.* *Concourse*, as its primary denotation, translates as *concurrencia, vestíbulo* (in stations), *confluencia.* El **vestíbulo** de la estación de trenes estaba muy concurrido. *The concourse of the railroad station was very crowded.*

condición / condition *Condición* is almost exactly the same as "condition" ("nature, stipulation, quality, state, sort, circumstance"), except when *condición* applies to people with the meaning of "character, disposition."
en condición de = *in the capacity of (as)*
Juan es áspero de **condición.** *John has a surly disposition.* ¿Está en buena **condición** el carro? *Is the car in good condition?* En mi **condición** de Ministro de Educación, tómense dos días de vacaciones. *In my capacity as Secretary of Education, you can take two vacation days.*

condonar / condone *Condonar* shares with *to condone* the ideas of "to forgive, pardon, cancel." *To condone* also means *permitir, tolerar, dejar pasar* ("to overlook"). Ella **tolera** (deja pasar) muchas cosas a su marido. *She condones many things in her husband.*

conducir / conduct *Conducir* is "to conduct," meaning "to act, behave, take to," as well as "to drive" (a car, in Spain), "to lead" (people). Siempre debes **conducir** con mucho cuidado. *You must always drive very carefully.* To conduct also translates as *dirigir* (an orchestra, a business). Es emocionante **dirigir** una orquesta. *It's exciting to conduct an orchestra.* Una visita **acompañada** puede ser muy educativa. *A conducted tour can be very educational. Conductor* (m.) means "conductor" (of electricity, a leader) and also "driver." *Conductor* in English also means *director* (m.; of an orchestra), *cobrador* (m.; of a bus), *revisor* (m.; of a train or subway).

confección / confection *Confección* is not "confection" but "manufacture, making" and especially "tailoring, ready-made clothes." The plural *confecciones* applies to "clothing, the clothing industry." Trabaja en la **confección** de zapatos. *He works in shoe manufacturing.* confecciones de trajes / *suit tailoring Confection* means *confitura, dulce* (m.), *confite* (m.). La **confitura** te engorda mucho. *Confections (candies) make you very fat. Confeccionar* means "to confect, to prepare" and also "to make up (lists, clothes)." ¿Sabes **confeccionar** una nómina? *Do you know how to make a payroll list?*

conferencia / conference *Conferencia* translates as "conference" in the sense of a "press or political meeting." The primary denotation of *conferencia* is "lecture, talk, long-distance call." Mañana voy a una **conferencia** sobre la contaminación del aire. *Tomorrow I'm going to a lecture on air pollution. Conference* also stands for *consulta, entrevista, congreso* ("meeting"). Dio una conferencia en el **congreso** de lingüística. *He gave a lecture at the* **conference** *on linguistics.*

confiar / confide *Confiar* is "to confide," meaning "to tell in confidence, be confident," and also "to trust, entrust, rely on, hope."
Confiamos en Dios. = *In God we trust.*
confiar un trabajo a alguien / *to* **entrust** *someone with a job* **Confiado** translates as "confident, trusting" in its best denotation, but it can be very negative, such as "gullible" (*crédulo*) and even "conceited." Estamos muy **confiados** en el resultado. *We are very* **confident** *about the result.* No seas **confiado** en los negocios. *Don't be* **gullible** *in business.*

confidencia / confidence *Confidencia* does not mean "confidence" but "personal secret, private information." No comuniques a nadie esta **confidencia**. Será nuestro secreto. *Don't tell anybody about this* **private information.** *It will be our secret. Confidence means confianza. Confidente means "confidant (man), confidante (woman), faithful." Confident stands for convencido, seguro (of oneself),* and sometimes it takes on a negative shade as *confianzudo, presuntuoso.* Estoy **convencido** de que ella me ama apasionadamente. *I am* **confident** *that she loves me passionately. Confianza is a common word used in many situations such as "confidence, trust, friendliness, intimacy, familiarity." Sometimes it takes* on the negative connotation of "conceit" *(presunción).*
en confianza = *confidentially*
de confianza (confiable) = *reliable*
Es un secreto de **confianza**. *It's an* **intimate** *secret.*

confinar / confine *Confinar* is not only "to confine, to keep within limits" but also "to border, be contiguous; to banish, exile." Napoleón fue **confinado** a la isla Elba. *Napoleon was* **banished** *to the isle of Elba.* Francia **confina** con España. *France* **borders** *on Spain.*

confirmado / confirmed *Confirmado* is "confirmed, established, proved" and also "experienced, mature," when it applies to people.
un soltero inveterado = *a confirmed bachelor*
Quedó **confirmado** de que se trata de un criminal bien **confirmado**. *It was* **confirmed** *(proved) that he is an* **experienced** *criminal.*

conformidad / conformity *Conformidad* (f.) translates as "conformity," in the sense of "similarity, consent, approval, agreement," and also "resignation, patience." Siento **conformidad** ante la muerte. *I am* **resigned** *to accept death. Conformar(se) is "to conform," meaning "to adjust, comply, agree, adapt," and* also "to resign oneself, have patience."
¡Conforme! = *Agreed!*
conforme a = *in accordance with*
No **me conformo** con esa decisión. *I don't* **agree (conform)** *with that decision.*

confortable / comfortable *Confortable* has been included in the latest dictionary of the *Real Academia* with the same meaning as its English cognate *comfortable,* referring to physical comfort. Mi sillón favorito es muy **confortable**. *My favorite* *armchair is very **comfortable**. **Confort** (m.) was not included in the dictionary, although it is used in many countries and is included in other dictionaries with the meaning of "luxury, luxe" (*lujo*). [Some Spanish writers have used **confort** for *lujo* since the last century.] *"Vivir a la moderna con algún **confort** y elegancia."* (Juan Valera) *To live in modern style with some **comfort** and elegance.* **Confortar** is "to comfort" in the sense of "to console, cheer, strengthen."

confrontar / confront *Confrontar* is "to confront" ("to face" is *enfrentarse a*), and also "to compare, to collate." *Nos **confrontamos** con una dificultad insuperable. We are **confronted** (faced) with an insurmountable difficulty. Hay que **confrontar** los dos manuscritos para ver si coinciden. It's necessary **to compare** the two manuscripts to see if they agree.*

confundir / confound *Confundir* stands for "to confound, confuse, bewilder," and also for "to mistake, to embarrass." *Confundirse*, the reflexive form, means "to be mistaken, to be embarrassed."
Me he confundido. = *I have made a mistake.*
El profesor me **confundió** con sus teorías sobre la sociedad. *The professor **confused** (confounded) me with his theories on society.* **Confundí** una calle por otra y me perdí. *I **mistook** one street for another and got lost.* To confound also takes a downturn to mean *frustrar* and even *maldecir* (i) "to curse, to damn."
¡Maldito sea! = *Confound him!*
¡Caray! = *Confound it! (Damn it!)*

congelar / congeal *Congelar* is the everyday word for "to freeze." It is also used in a figurative sense for "to freeze" (money, salaries, etc.). *No me gusta congelar la carne porque pierde el sabor. I don't like to **freeze** meat because it loses its flavor.* To congeal is more of a technical term and applies only to liquids, meaning "to solidify by cooling or freezing." The formal term in Spanish for *to congeal* is *coagularse* and is used only referring to blood (*sangre*, f.). *La sangre **se coagula** a menos de 90 grados Fahrenheit. Blood **congeals** (coagulates) below 90 degrees Fahrenheit.*

congestión / congestion *Congestión* was included in the latest dictionary of the *Real Academia* with the meaning of "(traffic) congestion": *concurrencia excesiva de personas, vehículos, etc., que ocasiona un entorpecimiento del tráfico.* The medical term *congestión* also translates as "congestion" (of the lungs or sinuses). *Congestion*, referring to traffic, has many other terms in the Spanish world: *embotellamiento, atasco, tapón* (m.), *tranque* (m.). *A la hora punta siempre hay **congestión** (tranques) de tráfico. At rush hour there is always traffic **congestion**. Congestionar* is exactly "to congest, to overcrowd, to clog." *Congestionado* translates as "congested, overcrowded." *Las autopistas están **congestionadas** durante muchas horas. Freeways are **congested** for many hours.*

congratular / congratulate *Congratular* means "to congratulate," but it is rarely used nowadays. It has been replaced by *felicitar, dar la enhorabuena.* The reflexive, *congratularse* is used sometimes to mean "to be glad, to be pleased." *Te **felicito** por tu nuevo ascenso y subida de salario. I **congratulate** you on your new promotion and salary increase. Congratulación* is rarely used for

"congratulation." It has been replaced by *felicitación, felicidades* (f.), *enhorabuena.*
¡Felicidades! = *Congratulations!*

conjugar / conjugate *Conjugar* means "to conjugate" (verbs) in grammar, but *conjugar* is used in real life to mean "to combine, pair, alternate." Es necesario **conjugar** el trabajo con el placer en la vida moderna. *It's necessary to combine work and pleasure in modern life.*

conjuración / conjuration *Conjuración* is not "conjuration" but "conspiracy, plot." *Conjuration* means *conjuro, exorcismo. Conjurar* stands for "to conjure up, to exorcise," as well as "to plot, conspire." El ladrón **conjuró** contra el millonario para robar su casa. *The thief plotted against the millionaire to rob his house.* El mago **hace aparecer** un conejo de un sombrero. *The magician conjures a rabbit out of a hat.*

conmoción / commotion *Conmoción* barely means "commotion." Both terms share the idea of some kind of "disturbance, confusion," but in Spanish, *conmoción* usually is more serious: "upheaval, shock (nervous)," and in geography, "tremor, earthquake." La noticia me produjo una gran **conmoción.** *The news was a great shock to me.*

consecuencia / consequence *Consecuencia* means "consequence, result."
en consecuencia = *consequently*
Las **consecuencias** del SIDA son fatales. *The consequences of AIDS are fatal. Consequence* has upgraded its meaning in some contexts also to refer to *importancia, transcendencia.*
sin importancia = *of no consequence*
Consecuente translates as "consequent" (in logic) and also "consistent." No es **consecuente** en su conducta. *He is not consistent in his behavior.*

consentir / consent *Consentir* (ie, i) not only is "to consent, permit, say yes, tolerate" but also is applied to people to mean "to spoil, pamper."
consentir en = *to consent to*
Consentí en pagarlo en seguida. *I consented to pay for it right away.* No es bueno **consentir** a los hijos. *It's not good to spoil children.*

conservativo / conservative *Conservativo* is not "conservative" but "preservative, preserving." La sal es un elemento **conservativo.** *Salt is a preservative element. Conservative* means *conservador, moderado, prudente.*
cálculo moderado = *conservative estimate*
inversión prudente = *conservative investment*
Es un candidato muy **conservador.** *He is a very conservative candidate. Conservatorio* means "conservatoire" or "conservatory," referring to an academy of music or art.

consideración / consideration *Consideración* translates as "consideration" with all its meanings, including "esteem, respect" *(aprecio, estima).* One expression, however, does not translate literally: *de consideración* ("great, considerable").

Recibió daños **de consideración** en el accidente. *He suffered **considerable** damages in the accident.*

consistencia / consistency, consistence   *Consistencia* shares with *consistency (consistence)* the meanings of "density (of liquids), agreement, harmony, conformity." But *consistencia* also refers to "firmness, strength" *(firmeza)* of a person.
sin consistencia = *insubstantial*

consistente / consistent   *Consistente* means "consistent," as "firm, solid, consisting of," but it also refers to "stable, substantial, durable" regarding an opinion or the behavior of a person. *Sus decisiones siempre fueron* **consistentes.** *Her decisions were always* **consistent.** *Consistent,* on the other hand, stresses the idea of "agreement, compatibility" and as such stands for *consecuente, lógico, de acuerdo. Su conducta no está* **de acuerdo** *con sus promesas. His conduct is not* **consistent** *with his promises.*

constipado / constipated   *Constipado* (m.) is not "constipated" but is a noun meaning "a cold" as in "I have a cold." [*Constipado* is used in Spain for the common cold. Actually, in everyday speech, the term is shortened to *costipado* and the corresponding verb is *costiparse.* In Latin America the most frequent term for a cold is *resfriado.*] *Tengo un* **constipado** *terrible. I have a terrible* **cold.** *Constipated,* on the other hand, is an adjective, meaning *estreñido. Es bueno comer ciruelas pasas para evitar estar* **estreñido.** *It is good to eat prunes to avoid becoming* **constipated.** *Constipación* means "a cold." *Constipation* translates as *estreñimiento. Constiparse* means "to catch a cold." **Me constipé** *con la lluvia por no llevar paraguas. I* **caught a cold** *in the rain because I didn't take an umbrella. To constipate* stands for *estreñir(se).*

consumición / consumption   *Consumición* is not "consumption" but "drink" (in a bar, club, restaurant).
consumición mínima = *cover charge*
Consumption, on the other hand, translates as *consumo. Consumido* means "consumed" in the sense of "eaten" or "drunk," and it means "tormented" when applied to people. In a figurative sense, *consumido* means "emaciated, exhausted, undermined (health)." *Su salud fue* **consumida** *por la fiebre. His health was* **undermined** *by the fever.*

consumir / consume   *Consumir* translates the multiple meanings of "to consume" (products) and also "to drink" (in a bar, restaurant). The reflexive form, *consumirse,* is used to refer to one's health, as in "to waste away, wear out," and "to boil away" (a liquid) or "to burn out" (a candle). **Se consumió** *en esfuerzos inútiles. She* **wore** *herself* **out** *in useless efforts.*

contar / count   *Contar* (ue) is not only "to count" (numbers, things) but also "to tell" or "to talk about."
contar con = *to rely on, to count on*
Mi abuelo siempre me **contaba** *cosas de su infancia. My grandfather always* **used to tell** *me things about his childhood. Contable* is translated as "countable" ("able

to be counted") and also as "relatable" ("able to be told, related"). In the business world, **contable** (m.) is a noun and means "bookkeeper."

contemplación / contemplation   *Contemplación* means "contemplation, looking, study, meditation." The plural *contemplaciones* means "ceremony, indulgence, leniency."   no andar con **contemplaciones** / *to not stand on ceremony*   *Contemplation* also means *perspectiva, proyecto.*   No hay cambios en **perspectiva.**   *There are no changes* **contemplated.**

contemplar / contemplate   *Contemplar* is "to contemplate, gaze, meditate."   *To contemplate* now has the primary denotation of *proyectar, planear, tener* (ie) *la intención de, prever* ("to expect"). No **proyectamos** hacer grandes cambios. *We do not* **contemplate** *making great changes.*

contención / contention   *Contención* and *contention* share the idea of "strife, struggle, contending" in the best sense of the word *(contienda, emulación).* Sometimes *contención* conveys the idea of "restraint, holding, retaining." **muro de contención** = *retaining wall* *Contention* in English has downgraded its meaning also to refer to *disputa, desacuerdo, controversia.* Hubo una **disputa** entre los candidatos. *There was* **contention** *between the candidates.*

contener / contain   *Contener* (ie) stands for "to contain, hold, include, enclose, have," as well as "to restrain, control, refrain." No pude **contener** la risa cuando oí el chiste. *I couldn't* **refrain** *from laughing when I heard the joke.*

contento / content   *Contento* (adjective) suggests an active state of mind, and a good translation is not "content" but "happy, joyful, glad, cheerful." As a noun, *contento* means "happiness, joy," and in literary use, "contentment." Está muy **contento** con su trabajo. *He is very* **happy** *with his job.* Su **contento** se refleja en la sonrisa. *Her* **joy** *is reflected in her smile.* *Content,* as an adjective, suggests a passive state and is more a literary term than a commonly used term. It conveys the idea of *satisfecho* ("pleased, satisfied"). As a noun, *content* translates as *contenido.* **índice** = *table of contents*

contestar / contest   *Contestar* is not "to contest" but "to answer, reply, return (a greeting)." **Contesté** su carta inmediatamente. *I* **replied** *to (answered) his letter immediately. To contest* means *disputar, argüir, impugnar, rebatir, presentarse* (as a candidate). El abogado **disputó** su razonamiento. *The lawyer* **contested** *his reasoning. Contestación* is "reply, answer, plea (in court)." **contestación a la demanda** = *defendant's plea* *Contestation* is translated as *disputa, altercado, controversia, impugnación.*

continuo / continuous, continual   *Continuo* is translated as two different adjectives: "continuous" ("without interruption") and "continual" ("repeated often"). movimiento **continuo** / *continual motion* una línea **continua** / *a continuous line Continuamente* is also translated as two adverbs: "continuously" ("without stopping") and "continually" ("happening over and over").

contrario / contrary *Contrario* means "contrary" in the real sense of "opposite, opposing," but in a figurative sense, it means "harmful, adverse." *Contrario* as a noun means "opponent, rival" *(adversario, enemigo).*
llevar la contraria = *to oppose, to contradict*
de lo contrario = *otherwise*
Lo **contrario** de bueno es malo. *The opposite (contrary) of good is bad.* El tabaco es contrario a la salud. *Tobacco is harmful to good health.*

contribución / contribution *Contribución* means "contribution" as "help, aid" in a material sense as well as an intellectual sense. But *contribución* is also "tax, taxes," although currently the term *impuestos* is more common. Todos tenemos que pagar **contribución** (impuesto) territorial. *We all have to pay property taxes. Contribution,* on the other hand, is also used to refer to *artículo, colaboración* in newspapers, magazines, and journals. Tuvo un buen **artículo** en la revista médica. *He made a good contribution to the medical journal.*

control / control *Control* (m.) means "control" as recognized in the most recent dictionary of the *Real Academia. Control* is not as common in Spanish as its true cognate in English. *Control* in English is one of those handy terms used (and perhaps misused) in multiple situations, both as a noun and as a verb. The following list of words is suggested as possible translations of *control* in English:

dominio	autoridad (f.)	dirección
mando(s)	medidas	limitación
reglas	prevención	gobierno
potestad (f.)	manejo	inspección
administración	freno	represión

mando a distancia = *remote control*
tablero de mando = *control board*
limitación de nacimientos = *birth control*
La epidemia está fuera de nuestra **potestad**. *The epidemic is beyond our control.* Consiguió **dominar** la situación. *He got the situation under control. Controlable* translates as "controllable" and as "verifiable."

controversial / controversial *Controversial* finally has been included in the dictionary of the *Real Academia* with the same meaning as *controversial* ("relative to controversy") in English. Other terms to convey the same idea are *polémico, controvertible, discutible.* El aborto es siempre un tema muy **controversial** (polémico). *Abortion is always a highly controversial issue.*

conveniencia / convenience *Conveniencia* is not "convenience" but "conformity, agreement (of taste, opinions), compatibility." [The *Real Academia* states that *comodidad* (f.) is one of the meanings of *conveniencia,* but this use is very rare in modern writings, and even rarer in conversational Spanish.] *Convenience* means *comodidad* (f.), *ventaja, confort* (m.). The plural *conveniences* suggests *servicios* (toilets), *baños, váteres* (m.) or *retretes* (m.; in Spain). In old English, *conveniences* were *beneficios* (of servants).
cuando guste = *at your convenience*
Las casas nuevas tienen más **comodidad** (confort) que las antiguas. *New homes*

*have more **conveniences** than old ones.* tan pronto como sea **posible** / *at your earliest **convenience***

conveniente / convenient *Conveniente* is not "convenient" but "appropriate, suitable, proper, advisable." No es la respuesta **conveniente**. *That is not the **proper** response*. *Convenient* is better rendered by *cómodo, oportuno, útil, práctico, bien situado*. Este banco está muy **bien situado** para Ud. *This bank is very convenient for you.*

convenir / convene *Convenir* (ie, i) means "to agree, suit, be convenient, be advisable."
sueldo a convenir = *salary to be agreed on*
el día convenido = *the appointed day*
To convene means *reunirse, convocar, juntarse, citar*. El director **convocó** a los maestros. *The principal **convened** the teachers.*

convento / convent *Convento* means both "convent" and "monastery." In Spanish both *convento* and *monasterio* have been used without a difference in meaning, but in modern Spanish, *convento* has prevailed over *monasterio*. [In the old times the *convento* used to be in the city and the *monasterio* in the countryside, with vast lands for cultivation. Some *monasterios* in Spain were very rich, almost like palaces, for example, the Real Monasterio de San Lorenzo del Escorial or the Monasterio de las Huelgas in Burgos.] El rey Felipe III visitaba el **convento** de las Clarisas de Carrión todos los meses. *King Phillip III used to visit the **convent** of Clarisas at Carrión every month. Convent* in English is generally for nuns (*monjas*) and *monastery*, for monks (*monjes*).

convertible / convertible *Convertible* (m.) means "convertible" (open car) in Latin America. The term used in Spain is *descapotable* (m.). The *Real Academia* accepts both terms. [To save space, Europeans make furniture that "hides" in the wall and possibly serves as a bookshelf during the day and as a bed at night. This type of furniture is called *convertible*. In Spanish there are *mesas* and *camas convertibles*.] Los **convertibles** (descapotables) eran muy populares por los años sesenta. *Convertibles were very popular in the sixties.*

convicción / conviction *Convicción* is "conviction" in the sense of "strong belief." *Conviction* is a key word in legal terminology to refer to *condena, declaración* or *sentencia de culpabilidad*. El juez declaró la **condena** del reo (criminal). *The judge declared the **conviction** of the accused. Convicto* is an old term for "convicted." The modern rendition is *condenado, sentenciado, preso, presidiario*. El **preso** lleva ya dos años de cárcel. Le quedan 99 más. *The **convict** has been in prison for two years. He has to serve 99 more.*

convocación / convocation *Convocación (convocatoria)* is not "convocation" but "a call to a meeting, convening, summoning." *Convocation* is *asamblea, junta, congreso*. [It is interesting to note that in Spanish *convocación* points toward "the steps or measures" needed to get together the *asamblea*. In English the emphasis is on the practical result, the "meeting" itself. Perhaps this suggests a cultural trait of Hispanic people: "it is not easy to convene them."] Habrá una **asamblea** de catedráticos en

Miami. *There will be a* **convocation** *of professors in Miami.* ***Convocar***, on the other hand, translates fully as "to convoke": "to summon, call together, convene, call (for a strike)." El dueño **convocó** a sus empleados para anunciarles una subida de salario. *The owner* **convoked** *(convened, called together) his employees to announce the salary increase.*

convoy / convoy *Convoy* (m.) is exactly "convoy": "a protecting escort as for troops, a group of vehicles." Currently the ordinary terms are *escolta* in Spanish and *escort* in English. [The plural of the Spanish *convoy* is *convoyes*.] Se veía venir de lejos un **convoy** de camiones. *A* **convoy** *of trucks could be seen coming from far away.*

copa / cup *Copa* is "cup" only as a "trophy, a part of a brassiere." *Copa* has many denotations, such as "wine glass (stemmed glassware), goblet, drink, top (of a tree), crown, top (of a hat)."
Copa Mundial = *World Cup*
sombrero de copa = *top hat*
Vamos a tomar una **copa** en el bar. *Let's have a* **drink** *in the bar.* Esas **copas** son bien caras. *Those* **goblets** *are very expensive.* *Cup* translates as *taza, cáliz* (m.; of a flower, for Communion). In a figurative sense, *cup* (of pleasure, of sorrow) means *copa (de placer, de dolor).* El fútbol americano **no me gusta** mayormente. *American football is not* **my cup of tea.** purar la **copa** del dolor / *to drain the* **cup** *of sorrow*

copia / copy *Copia* is "copy" as "a reproduction, imitation of an original." [The *Real Academia* states that *copia* also means *abundancia*, as in *cornucopia*, but this usage is out of date in written and oral Spanish.] Mandé hacer una **copia** de una fotografía antigua. *I ordered a* **print** *(copy) made of an old photograph. Copy* means *ejemplar* (m.), as "any of a number of books, magazines, newspapers." Quisiera tener un **ejemplar** del *Don Quijote* original. *I would like to own a* **copy** *of the original* Don Quijote. *Copioso* is an adjective and means "copious, plentiful" (*abundante, numeroso*).

coqueta / coquette *Coqueta* translates as "coquette, flirt" to refer to a woman, but *coqueta* is also used to mean "dressing table" (*tocador*, m.). As an adjective, *coqueto (coqueta)* as well as *coquetón (coquetona)* means "coquettish, flirtatious," and in a figurative sense, "cute, charming" (for things or people). El baño tiene una **coqueta** de caoba. *The bathroom has a mahogany* **dressing table.** Ella tiene un apartamento **coquetón.** *She has a* **charming** *apartment.*

coraje / courage *Coraje* (m.) is not "courage" but "anger, rage, passion, irritation." Sintió **coraje** cuando perdió el juego de tenis por tercera vez. *He felt* **angry** *when he lost the tennis match for the third time. Courage* means *valor* (m.), *valentía.* Recibió una medalla por su gran **valentía.** *He received a medal for his great* **courage.**

cordón / cordon, cord *Cordón* (m.) means "cordon" as in "a line of police, a decorative cord," and also "string, cord, lace (for shoes), ribbon, bell-pull."
cordón eléctrico = *electric cord*

cordón umbilical = *umbilical cord*
Los **cordones** nunca duran tanto como los zapatos. *Shoelaces never last as long as the shoes.*

corporación / corporation *Corporación* is "corporation, company" *(sociedad anónima).* María es la primera ejecutiva de la **corporación.** *María is the first female executive of the corporation. Corporation,* figuratively, also means *panza, barriga* ("fat stomach, potbelly"), but this usage is rare. Nuestro vecino tiene una enorme **panza.** *Our neighbor has a large potbelly (corporation).*

corpulencia / corpulence *Corpulencia* does not exactly mean "corpulence," but "stoutness, burliness." *Corpulence* is better translated as *obesidad* (f.), *gordura, adiposidad* (f.). *Corpulento* means "stout, burly, bulky." Ese hombre es **corpulento.** *That man is big and stout. Corpulent* suggests the idea of *muy gordo, obeso, grueso.* Es una señora **muy gruesa.** *She is a corpulent lady.* [In Spanish, *corpulencia* and *corpulento* seem to refer to the strength that one expects from a "large" person. In English, *corpulence* and *corpulent* stress the idea of volume and weight that generally is associated with a "large" person. Behind this language usage lies a reality: the overweight person in the United States weighs *many more pounds* than an overweight person in a Hispanic country. This cultural difference carries over into the language.]

corral / corral *Corral* (m.) in Spanish has been used traditionally as "an area or pen for poultry and sheep." *Corral* also means "playpen" (for children). [*Corral, corrala,* and *corralón* were the natural theaters (a poor reflection of the Greek theaters) where classical plays were presented in the Golden Age. Recently, some of these *corrales* have been restored in Madrid.] El **corral** de Pedrito está lleno de juguetes. *Little Peter's playpen is full of toys.* En el **corral** hay muchas gallinas. *There are many chickens in the yard. Corral* is a word that English borrowed from Spanish, and as usually happens with loan words, the meanings are not the same in both languages. A *corral* usually holds horses and cattle, rather than poultry and sheep.

correcto / correct *Correcto* is almost exactly "correct," meaning "exact, just, not mistaken, certain." However, *correcto* also applies to people to refer to "polite, proper, courteous, well-mannered." Estuvo muy **correcta** con los invitados. *She was very courteous to the guests.* Su conducta fue **correcta.** *His behavior was correct. Corrección* translates as "correction" (i.e., "changing from wrong to right") and also "correctness, politeness, good manners; reprimand." Practico la **corrección** del lenguaje. *I practice correctness of language.* No quiero recibir una **corrección** del maestro. *I do not want to receive a reprimand from the teacher.*

correspondencia / correspondence *Correspondencia* is "correspondence" with the meanings of "agreement with something or somebody, conformity, similarity, mail." However, *correspondencia* also means "connection" or "transfer" (for a bus, a subway). curso por **correspondencia** / *correspondence course* Este metro tiene **correspondencia** con dos líneas. *This subway train makes connections with two lines. Corresponder* means "to correspond" ("to match, conform, be similar") and also "to repay, to be one's turn, to belong to." Hoy me **corresponde** trabajar tarde. *It's my turn to work late today.* La llave no **corresponde** a la cerradura. *The key doesn't belong with (fit) the lock.* Le **correspondí** con otro regalo. *I repaid him with another gift.* To *correspond* has other denotations such as *escribirse con, tener* (ie) *correspondencia con. Corresponsal* (m.) translates as "correspondent" (of the press, TV, etc.). **corresponsal** de periódico / *newspaper* **correspondent** *Correspondiente* is an adjective, meaning "corresponding, related."

corriente / current *Corriente* as an adjective means "current, flowing, running, valid (money), going on now." It also means "common, usual, ordinary, average." *Corriente* (f.) as a noun means "current, stream, electric power" and also "draft (of air), trend (in fashions).

actualidades = *current affairs*
cuenta corriente = *checking account*
agua corriente = *running water*
el corriente = *this month* (in commercial letters)
estar al corriente = *to be up-to-date*
El español **corriente** fuma demasiado. *The **average** Spaniard smokes too much.* Es un hombre **corriente**. *He is an **ordinary** man.* Hay mucha **corriente** en este cuarto. *There are too many **drafts** in this room.* Ella me tiene **al corriente**. *She keeps me **up to date** (informed).*

corte / court *Corte* (f.) translates as "court (of the king and his retinue, of justice), courting, wooing." As a masculine noun, *corte* means "cutting, cross-section, haircut, cut (of meat, cake)."
Las Cortes = *Parliament* (in Spain)
corte y confección = *dressmaking*
Me gusta ese **corte** de carne de res. *I like that **cut** of meat (beef).* Juan hace la **corte** a su novia. *John is **courting** his sweetheart (girlfriend).* Court also means *patio, plaza, palacio, tribunal* (m.; Spain), *pista* or *cancha* (tennis court).
tribunal supremo = *high court*
La iglesia tiene una **plaza** muy linda. *The church has a beautiful **court(yard)**.*
tribunal de menores / *juvenile **court***

cortejo / cortege *Cortejo* shares with *cortege* the meaning of "ceremonial procession" (at a funeral, for example). However, *cortejo* also means "courting, wooing, entourage, suite, train" *(séquito).*
cortejo nupcial = *wedding party (cortege)*
El **cortejo** de los amantes fue corto. *The **courtship** of the lovers was short.* el **cortejo** del Presidente / *the President's **entourage***

costar / cost *Costar* (ue) stands for "to cost" (money, effort, etc.) and also means "to be difficult or hard, to find it difficult." El anillo de la boda me **costó** un ojo de la cara. *The wedding ring **cost** me an arm and a leg.* Me **cuesta** mucho confesarlo. *It **is very difficult** for me to confess it.* Esa tontería le **costará** cara. *He'll **pay** dearly for that nonsense.* *Coste* (m.) and *costo* are two nouns used with the meaning of "cost" (money, effort, etc.), but sometimes they are better translated as "price, expense, charge." [Some countries use *costa* instead of *coste* or *costo*. These terms are interchangeable in colloquial Spanish. Strictly speaking, *coste* refers

directly to the price (*coste de un disco*). *Costo* applies to large projects and is used more in economics (*costo* of a bridge, a home, a trip to the moon).]
a toda costa = *at any price*
a costa de = *at the expense of*
costo de la vida = *the cost of living*
coste, seguro y flete (c.s.f.) / *cost, insurance, freight (c.i.f.)*

criatura / creature *Criatura* means "creature" as in "everything created: things, people." It also means "baby, infant, kid" in colloquial speech. [*Crío* and *cría* are used frequently in Spain for "baby."] La pobre muchacha lloraba como una **criatura.** *The poor girl was crying like a baby.* Las arañas son **criaturas** de Dios. *Spiders are God's creatures.*

crimen / crime *Crimen* (m.) (*asesinato*) translates only as "crime" in the sense of "murder." Matar es un **crimen.** *To kill is a crime.* *Crime* in English is better translated as *delito,* meaning "any breaking of the law," from murder to a misdemeanor. *Crime* also stands for *criminalidad* (f.). Robar es un **delito.** *To steal is a crime.* *Criminal* means "murderer." In colloquial Spanish, *criminal* is used for "terrible, difficult" (colloquially, "murder"). Ayer trabajé 12 horas. Fue un día **criminal** para mí. *Yesterday I worked 12 hours. It was a terrible day for me. (It was murder.)* *Criminal* in English is often rendered as *delincuente* (m., f.).
derecho penal = *criminal law*
antecedentes penales = *criminal record*

crisis / crisis *Crisis* (f.) means "crisis" in the sense of "crucial situation or time, great danger, an attack of a disease." In Spanish, *crisis* also means "shortage, scarcity." Cuando hay una **crisis** de gasolina los precios suben rápidamente. *When there is a gasoline shortage, the prices rise sharply.* Muchos países pasan por una **crisis** económica. *Many countries are going through an economic crisis.*

cristal / crystal *Cristal* (m.) means "crystal" from a scientific point of view, as "clear, transparent quartz." *Cristal* also means "glass" (*vidrio*) and "window-pane." The plural *cristales* translates as "windows."
puerta de cristales = *glass door*
bola de cristal = *crystal ball*
cristal tallado = *cut glass*
cristal ahumado = *smoked glass*
Se rompieron dos **cristales** con el terremoto. *Two windowpanes were broken in the earthquake.* *Crystal* is used as an adjective, meaning *cristalino, de cristal, transparente.* Allí hay las copas de **cristal** muy caras. *There are the expensive crystal goblets.*

cristiandad / Christianity *Cristiandad* (f.) is translated as two English words: *Christianity* ("the state of being a Christian") and *Christendom* ("all the Christian countries"). Toda la **cristiandad** sigue a Cristo. *The whole of Christendom follows Christ.* *Cristiano* means "Christian" in a literal sense, but in a figurative sense, it means "soul, person, nobody (in negative sentences)." *Cristiano* is also used in a number of idiomatic expressions. *Hablar en cristiano* means "to speak clearly," according to the *Real Academia*, and "to speak Spanish," according to other sources. *Vino cristiano* suggests "watered-down wine" (*vino aguado*). No hay **cristiano** que lo entienda. *No one could understand it.* Por la calle no pasaba ni un **cristiano** en aquel momento. *Nobody (Not a soul) was walking down the street at that moment.*

crítica / critique, critic *Crítica* essentially has two meanings. One is positive, meaning "critique" ("an oral or written comment, review, notice"). The other is negative, meaning "criticism," which becomes "faultfinding" and even "censure." Between the positive and negative meanings is "criticism" ("an evaluation of qualities"). As a masculine noun, *crítico* means "critic" ("a person who makes or writes a critique"). Hay mucha **crítica** contra el gobierno. *There is a lot of criticism against the government.* Leí la **crítica** sobre esa novela. *I read the critique (review) of that novel.* Es el **crítico** de arte y música. *He is the art and music critic.* *Crítico* in Spanish and *critical* in English both come from the term *crisis* and have the same meaning: "dangerous, risky, serious, demanding, crucial."
en el momento crítico = *at the crucial moment*
La condición del enfermo es **crítica** (muy grave). *The condition of the sick man is critical.*

crucial / crucial *Crucial* means "crucial," and the *Real Academia* has included the term in its latest dictionary. Bilingual speakers use *crucial* in Spanish as much as its English cognate. *Crucial* in English is a handy term used (and possibly misused) in too many situations. The following is a list of equivalent terms in Spanish that have similar meanings, but with connotations that vary according to the situation:

decisivo	supremo
crítico	de prueba
vital	terminante
peligroso	relevante

La economía del país es un tema **vital** (crítico). *The economy of the country is a crucial (critical) issue.* Vivimos un momento **decisivo** (de prueba) en el mundo. *We are living in a crucial (decisive) moment in the world.*

crudo / crude *Crudo* is translated as "crude" only in expressions such as *petróleo crudo* ("crude oil"). *Crudo* has the real meaning of "raw, unripe, untreated," and in a figurative sense, it stands for "severe, harsh (weather), coarse (words, jokes), inexperienced (artist, athlete, etc.)." As a feminine noun, *una cruda* is used in some countries to mean "hangover"; other countries use terms such as *resaca, juma.* Este torero está **crudo**. *This bullfighter is inexperienced.* No comemos carne **cruda**. *We don't eat raw meat.* *Crude*, on the other hand, also means *bruto, sin refinar, basto, ordinario, vulgar, tosco, rudo.*
azúcar sin refinar = *crude sugar*
Su respuesta fue muy **ordinaria** (vulgar). *His reply was very crude (vulgar).* Esa mesa es muy **tosca** (basta). *That's a very crude (rough) table.*

cruz / cross *Cruz* (f.) is "cross" in real and figurative senses: "the symbol [+]," as well as "sorrow, pain, burden." *Cruz* also means "tails (of a coin), hilt (of a sword), crotch (of pants)."
cruz y raya = *no more of this*
cruz gamada = *swastika*
hacerse cruces = *to be speechless*
Todo el mundo lleva su **cruz** (carga). *Everyone has a **cross** (burden) to bear. Cross* in English has a few meanings not shared by *cruz*: *cruce* (m.; "street crossing, cross of lines, animals"), *golpe cruzado* (in boxing), *estafa* or *timo* ("swindle"). *Cross* is also an adjective, meaning *enojado, irritado*. En este **cruce** siempre hay accidentes. *There are always accidents at that **crossing**.* Mi perro es un **cruce** de varias razas. *My dog is a **cross** of several breeds.* Ella está muy **enojada** conmigo. *She is very **cross** with me.*

cualidad / quality *Cualidad* (f.) means "quality" as "a characteristic of a person, a property of a thing." El patrón tiene buenas **cualidades**. *The boss has good **qualities** (features). Quality* also means *calidad* (f.; "the value of things, the capacity of a person"). [*Calidad* is a noncountable noun (i.e., without plural), as the sum of values and qualities. On the other hand, *cualidad* is a countable noun, hence the phrase *más de una cualidad*. In English, if "the *qualities* of a person or product" are added, the result is "the end *quality*."]
en calidad de = *in the capacity of, as*
Necesitamos productos de buena **calidad**. *We need good **quality** products.*

cubo / cube *Cubo* means "cube" only in geometry. *Cubo* also means "pail, bucket, (waste)basket, hub (of a wheel), drum (of a watch)."
terrón de azúcar (azucarillo) = *sugar cube*
cubitos de hielo = *ice cubes*
Uso un **cubo** de agua para lavar el coche. *I use a **bucket** of water to wash the car.* Tira la basura al **cubo**. *Throw the garbage into the **basket** (wastebasket).*

cuestión / question *Cuestión* is not "question" as a primary meaning, but "matter, affair, topic, issue, debate," and sometimes takes the negative meaning of "dispute, quarrel." Es **cuestión** de vida o muerte. *It's a **matter** of life or death. Question,* on the other hand, basically means *pregunta,* but sometimes it is translated as *cuestión* ("important"). Good Spanish terms for *question* are *problema* (m.), *debate* (m.), *interrogante* (m.). la **cuestión** de la pena capital / *the **question** of capital punishment* Ya me hiciste esa **pregunta**. *You already asked me that **question**.* ¿De qué se trata? *What is the **question**?* Aquí está el **problema**. *That is the **question**.* someter el **problema** a votación / *to put the **question** to a vote* No, ni hablar. *No, it's out of the **question**.*

culto / cult *Culto* is both "cult" and "worship" ("a system of religious rituals"), as well as "cultism." In a figurative sense, it is used for "admiration" (*admiración*) toward a person or an abstract idea such as "beauty." As an adjective, *culto, culta* translates as "learned, educated" as applied to people, words, etc. Los aztecas rendían **culto** al sol. *The Aztecs used to **worship** the sun.* Esa profesora es muy **culta**. *She is a very **learned** professor. Cult* in English has a downgraded connotation, meaning "extravagant admiration or worship of a person or an idea," such as a "satanic *cult*." The Spanish term for this is *culto.* ¿Sientes **culto** a la belleza o al nudismo? *Do you have a cult of beauty or nudity? Cultismo* has nothing to do with religion or worship; it means a "learned (educated) word or expression." *Cultismo* es un **cultismo** (una voz culta). Cultism *is a learned word.*

cumplimiento / compliment *Cumplimiento* is not "compliment" but "fulfillment, execution, carrying over," and in a figurative sense, "ceremony, courtesy, politeness."
en cumplimiento de = *in compliance with*
por cumplimiento = *out of courtesy*
El **cumplimiento** de la ley es para todos. *The fulfillment of (compliance with) the law is meant for all.* Compliment in English means *cumplido, piropo, atención,* and the plural *compliments* translates as *saludos, enhorabuena.* Dé mis **saludos** a su mujer (señora). *Pay my compliments to your wife. Complimentary* means *elogioso, halagador,* as well as *gratis* or *de regalo* (as a courtesy) for books, tickets, products, etc. [*See also the entry for* **complemento.**]

cúmulo / cumulus *Cúmulo* is "cumulus" as the technical word for a "thick, fluffy cloud." *Cúmulo* also means "pile, heap" (of things), and figuratively, "a load, a lot of."
un cúmulo de circunstancias = *a concurrence of circumstances*
Su discurso fue un **cúmulo** de disparates sobre la agricultura. *His speech was a load of rubbish about agriculture.*

cuplé / couplet *Cuplé* (m.) [the spelling of the *Real Academia*] is not "couplet" *(copla)* but "variety song, pop song." Sarita Montiel fue la reina del **cuplé** en España. *Sarita Montiel was the queen of the pop song in Spain. Couplet* is used in poetry to mean a "two-line stanza" and is translated as *pareado, dístico. Cupletista* translates as "variety singer, pop singer."

cupón / coupon *Cupón* (m.) is "coupon," meaning "bond, stub, ticket for redemption." It also means "lottery ticket." Si no compras **cupones** de lotería nunca podrás ganar. *If you don't buy lottery tickets, you will never win.*

cura / cure *Cura* (f.) means "cure, care, treatment of wounds or diseases." Both *cura* and *cure* are used in a figurative sense to mean "care of the soul." However, *cura* as a masculine noun is used to refer to "a Catholic priest" *(sacerdote,* m.*).* [In Hispanic countries, *cura* is used for a "Catholic priest," whereas *pastor* (m.) or *ministro* is used for a "Protestant pastor or minister."]
no tener cura = *to be incorrigible* (regarding faults)
no tener cura = *to be incurable* (regarding disease)
primera cura = *first aid*
No hay verdadera **cura** ni para el cáncer ni para el SIDA. *There is no true cure for either cancer or AIDS. Curita,* as a feminine noun, is used in some countries for "band-aid"; as a masculine noun, it is used to refer to a priest as "short" (in height), "dear" (as a person), or "bad" (as a priest). *Curar* means "to cure" (ailments, wounds, souls) and also "to cure" (meat, fish, etc.), but the latter

meaning is typically translated as *salar* (from salt). El **cura** del pueblito tuvo que **curar** a los enfermos de la epidemia. *The **priest** of the village had to **cure** the sick during the epidemic.*

curiosidad / curiosity *Curiosidad* (f.) means "curiosity" as a "desire to learn" and as "anything strange or novel, a curio (as in a curio shop)." *Curiosidad* also means "cleanliness, neatness, care." Ese carpintero trabaja con **curiosidad**. *That carpenter works **neatly** (with neatness).* Todos los niños tienen una **curiosidad** innata. *All children have an innate **curiosity**.*

curioso / curious *Curioso* means "curious," referring to a person who is "eager to learn, inquisitive," and for things that are "odd, peculiar, unusual." *Curioso* also means "clean, neat, tidy," applied to things or people. Sometimes *curioso* is used as a noun to mean "onlooker, spectator" *(mirón, m.)*, and also "a busybody, a nosy person" *(un indiscreto, un metiche)*. Había dos **curiosos** en la fiesta. *There were two **onlookers** at the party.* Tiene la casa muy **curiosa**. *She has a very **tidy** house.* Mi suegro se mete en todo. Es demasiado **curioso**. *My father-in-law wants to know everything. He is too **nosy**.*

curso / course *Curso* means "course" as "progress in space or time" and also "school year" (not just a particular course or class) and "tender, money, currency."
moneda de curso legal = *legal tender*
en curso = *under way, in progress*
El **curso** escolar dura nueve meses. *The school **year** lasts nine months.* Course has additional meanings, such as *ruta, rumbo, programa* (m.), *ciclo, plato, pista, tratamiento, cotización.*
en debido tiempo = *in due course*
un ciclo de conferencias = *a course of lectures*
Está en un **tratamiento** de medicina. *She is on a **course** of treatment (medical care).* Sirvieron cinco **platos** y tres postres en el banquete de graduación. *They served five **courses** and three desserts at the graduation banquet.* *Cursar* means "to take a course, to study, to deal with, to dispatch (letters, messages)." La secretaria **cursó** las solicitudes. *The secretary **dispatched** the applications.* ¿Qué **cursas** en la universidad? *What do you **study** at the university?* To course is an infrequently used verb, meaning *cazar, hacer correr* (to pursue), *correr* (to run, flow). The most common usage is in the expression "to feel the blood *coursing* through one's veins" *(sentir hervir* [ie, i] *la sangre).*

CH

champán, champaña / champagne *Champán* (m.) and *champaña* (m.) both mean "champagne." [The two spellings appear in the dictionary of the *Real Academia*. Notice that both are masculine, as are other types of wine: *el jerez* (sherry), *el rioja* (from the Rioja region), *el tinto* (red wine), *el málaga* (port), and *el chablís* (chablis), etc.]

chance / chance *Chance* (m.) is used in many Latin American countries with the meaning of "chance" in English ("luck, opportunity, risk, fortuity"). [*Chance* was not included in the latest dictionary of the *Real Academia*, but the term appears in other reliable dictionaries, such as Larousse and Morínigo.]
tener chances = *to stand a chance*
Vamos a darle otro **chance**. *Let's give him another chance.* *Chance* in English is translated as *chance, suerte* (f.), *riesgo, destino, azar* (m.), *casualidad* (f.).
por mera casualidad = *by sheer chance*
La **probabilidad** es que suban los impuestos. *Chances are that they will raise taxes.* Es muy poco probable. *It's a remote chance.* *To chance,* meaning "to take chances," is *arriesgarse, aventurarse, probar* (uc) *(una fortuna).* Se **arriesgó** en un negocio sospechoso. *He took chances on a suspicious business.*

charlatán / charlatan *Charlatán* (m.) does not mean "charlatan"; rather, it means "talkative, garrulous, chatterbox, gossipy." [The feminine form of *charlatán* is *charlatana.*] La maestra le castigó por **charlatán**. *The teacher punished him for being talkative. Charlatan* comes from the Italian, but it has downgraded its original connotation to mean *impostor* (m.), *embaucador* (m.; "fake") and even *curandero* ("quack"), according to Webster's Dictionary. No es médico; es sólo un **embaucador**. *He's not a doctor; he's just a charlatan (quack). Charlatanería* translates as "loquacity, verbosity" and "gossip" *(chismorreo). Charlatanry* is used infrequently, but it means *engaño, embaucamiento.*

cheque / check *Cheque* (m.) [*talón* (m.) in Spain] means "check" or "cheque" only as a "banknote." Ella pagó con un **cheque** personal. *She paid with a personal check. Check* is a handy word with many meanings, such as *restricción, inspección, contratiempo, comprobación, cuenta* (in restaurants), *contraseña* (for luggage), *marca, señal* (f.), and *jaque* (m.; in chess).
traje de cuadros = *check (checked) suit*
Necesito la **contraseña** para darle la maleta. *I need the check (stub) in order to give you the suitcase.* Hay una **inspección** en la autopista. *There is a check (checkpoint) on the highway.* Traté de pagar la **cuenta** del restaurante. *I tried to pay the restaurant check (bill).*

chequear, checar / check *Chequear* or *checar* means "to check." Ella **chequea** (vigila) con cuidado a su marido. *She is checking on her husband carefully.* El mecánico mexicano está **checando** el carro. *The Mexican mechanic is checking the car. To check* is a term used for many different actions: *facturar, reprimir, detener* (ie), *vigilar, revisar, cotejar* ("to compare"), *verificar, refrenar, contener* (ie), *registrarse.*

registrarse = *to check into* (a hotel)

sacar (retirar) = *to check out* (books from a library)

Hay que **facturar** el equipaje. *We have **to check** the luggage.* ***Chequeo*** is "check" as a noun, with all the meanings listed in the entry for ***cheque***. [The latest dictionary of the *Real Academia* does not include *chequear* or *checar* (which is used by more than 80 million Mexicans), but it does include *chequeo* as "a medical examination." Some other dictionaries do include *chequear* and *chequeo* as terms used more frequently in Latin America than in Spain.] Voy a hacer un **chequeo** de los frenos del carro. *I am going to have my brakes **checked**.* Los hombres que estaban en la playa le dieron un **chequeo** a los bañadores muy cortos. *The men on the beach **checked out** the skimpy bathing suits.*

chimenea / chimney *Chimenea* means more than "chimney" ("a structure with a flue, smokestack"); it also means "fireplace, mantelpiece, shaft (in a mine)."

fumar como una chimenea = *to smoke like a chimney*

Antes se usaban las **chimeneas** de campana. *In the old days, they used canopy **chimneys**.* En invierno enciendo la **chimenea**. *I light the **fireplace** in the winter.*

china / china *China* does not mean "china"; it means "pebble, a game (with pebbles), a Chinese girl." In some Latin American countries, *china* is used as an affectionate name for "a mestiza" or "an Indian girl."

tocarle la china a uno = *to win the draw*

Rompió la ventana con una **china**. *He broke the window with a **pebble**. China* in English is translated as *porcelana, loza.*   un toro en la tienda de **porcelana** / *a bull in a **china** shop*

chocar / choke, shock *Chocar* means neither "to choke" nor "to shock." *Chocar* means "to collide, crash, bump into, surprise, shake (hands)." El borracho **chocó** con un camión. *The drunk **collided** with a truck. To choke* means *ahogar, asfixiar, estrangular.*

silenciar a uno = *to choke someone off*

El humo del incendio nos **asfixió**. *The smoke from the fire **choked** us. To shock* is translated as *escandalizar, horrorizar, indignar, sobresaltar.* Su conducta **escandalizó** al pueblo. *His behavior **shocked** the town.* Me **horrorizó** averiguar que el choque fue causado a propósito. *I was **shocked** to find out that the crash was caused on purpose.*

choque / choke, shock *Choque* (m.) does not mean "choke," but it does mean "shock" (electric or nervous), and also "collision, crash, clash (material or abstract)." *Shock* also translates as *terremoto, temblor* (m.; earthquake). A *shock* absorber is *amortiguador* (m.). El último **temblor** no fue serio. *The last **shock** (tremor) was not serious. Choke,* on the other hand, means *ahogo, estrangulamiento, obturador* (m.), *mariposa de motor.* La muerte por **estrangulamiento** es terrible. *Death by **choking** is horrible. Chocante* is an adjective meaning "surprising, striking, funny, odd, strange." Ese chiste me pareció muy **chocante**. *That joke seemed very **funny** to me.* Su uso de color fue **chocante**. *Her use of color was **striking**. Shocking* means *escandaloso, vergonzoso,* *espantoso, horrible, aterrador.* Lo que hizo es **vergonzoso.** *What he did is* **shocking** *(shameful).*

chocolate / chocolate *Chocolate* (m.) means "chocolate" as a food substance and as a hot drink: *un chocolate* ("a cup of hot chocolate"). *Chocolate* in English refers to the substance as a whole and also to the countable, individual units, for example, "the *chocolates* in a box." The substance as a whole is translated as *chocolate* in Spanish; the "countable units" are *chocolatinas, bombones* (m.).
caja de bombones = *box of chocolates*
La niñita escogió la **chocolatina** más linda. *The little girl chose the most scrumptious* **chocolate.**

chofer / chauffeur *Chofer* or *chófer* (m.) [both spellings are accepted by the *Real Academia*] refers to "any driver," not just a "chauffeur" ("hired driver"). *Chauffeur* can be translated best as *chofer particular.* Un **chofer** pobre puede ser **chofer particular** de un millonario. *A* **driver** *who is poor can become a* **chauffeur** *for a millionaire.*

D

dama / dame *Dama* does not mean "dame" but "lady, noblewoman, lady-in-waiting *(de cámara)*, lady-love, mistress (title), bridesmaid (in weddings), king (in checkers), queen (in chess)."
juego de damas = *checkers*
tablero de damas = *checkerboard*
Dulcinea es la **dama** de don Quijote. *Dulcinea is Don Quijote's **lady-love**. Dame*, aside from the British title of nobility, is a colloquial term for *mujer, matrona (mujer mayor)* and in a pejorative sense, *fémina*. Esa **fémina** no tiene buena reputación. *That **dame** has a poor reputation.*

danza / dance *Danza* means "dance" only as "a ritual, traditional, or folkloric dance." *Danza* sounds like an old Spanish term, but it is used also to mean "deal, affair" in a figurative sense. [*Danzón* (m.) is a kind of dance that is typical of Cuba.] ¿Por qué te metiste en esa **danza**? *Why did you get mixed up in that **deal**? Dance* is most frequently translated as *baile* (m.).
pista de baile = *dance floor*
sala de baile = *dance hall*
La lambada fue un **baile** muy sensual y popular, pero pasó de moda pronto. *The lambada was a popular, sensual **dance**, but it went out of style quickly. Danzar* means "to dance" only in a ritual or folkloric dance. *To dance* is *bailar* in everyday language. **Bailar** es un buen ejercicio. *Dancing is good exercise.*

datar / date *Datar* means "to date" in the sense of "to put a date on" *(fechar). To date* also means *citar, dar cita, salir con*. **Sale con** él desde hace un mes. *She **has been dating** him for a month.*

dato / data, date *Dato* translates as "fact" (technically "datum," plural "data"). The plural *datos* means "data, facts."
informática = *data processing*
Ese **dato** es una buena clave. *That **fact** (datum) is a good key. Date* has additional meanings such as *fecha, dátil* (m.; fruit), *cita* (appointment), *compañero de cita, novio* or *novia*.
anticuado = *out-of-date*
fecha tope = *closing date*
El **dátil** es una fruta que se come seca. *The **date** is a fruit that you eat dried.* ¿Tienes **compañera** para la **cita**? *Do you have a **date** for the **date**?*

deán / dean *Deán* (m.) translates as "dean" ("the senior member of a church"). El **deán** dirige un grupo de sacerdotes. *The church **dean** heads a group of priests. Dean* also means *decano* (of a college or university). El **decano** dirige un grupo de profesores. *The college **dean** heads a group of professors.*

década / decade *Década* does not exactly mean "decade" as a period of "ten days" or "ten years." *Década* is counted from zero to zero by tens:

la década del 20 al 30 = *the twenties*
primera década del mes = *first decade of the month*
Hubo una guerra durante la **década** de 1910. *There was a war in the 1910s (the decade of 1910).* la primera **década** de febrero / *the first ten days in February* Decade is also translated as *decenio*, meaning "ten years," starting with any year. Decade is translated as *decena* to mean "ten beads" of a rosary. Pasé dos **decenios** de mi vida en la cárcel. *I spent two decades (20 years) of my life in jail.* Rezamos cinco **decenas** del rosario. *We prayed (said) five decades of the rosary.*

decantar / decant *Decantar* and *to decant* are technical words for winemakers, meaning "to pour off gently without stirring up the sediment." *Decantar* goes beyond the winery to mean "to praise, laud, ponder." Un buen jerez es **decantado** unas 200 veces de un tonel a otro. *A good sherry has been decanted about 200 times from one cask to another.* El profesor **decantó** las proezas del pintor encarcelado. *The professor praised the deeds of the imprisoned painter.* Decanter as a container is a little more sophisticated than a *garrafa*.

decente / decent *Decente* and *decent* have a lot in common: "not obscene, modest, seemly, fitting and proper, respectable, reasonable, good, fair, kind." *Decente*, however, stresses the idea of *honradez* (f.) or honesty in people and should be rendered as "honest, honorable, upright" and it also includes the idea of *limpieza* or cleanliness in things and places, meaning "clean, tidy."
un sueldo decente = *decent wages*
un bañador decente = *a decent, modest bathing suit*
Mis vecinos tienen una casa **decente**. *My neighbors have a tidy house.* un nivel de vida **decente** / *a decent standard of living* El mecánico es un **buen** chico. *The mechanic is a decent fellow.* Use Ud. un lenguaje **decoroso**. *Please use decent language.*

decepción / deception *Decepción* does not mean "deception"; rather, it means "disappointment, disenchantment." [The natural sequence of *deception* is *disappointment*, so we can see how the two languages are related. The dictionary of the *Real Academia* states that *decepción* is *engaño*, but that idea has faded away. It is the only dictionary to give that meaning.] La obra sobre el fin del mundo fue una **decepción** muy grande. *The play about the end of the world was a great disappointment.* Deception means *engaño*, which is more strongly negative than *decepción*. Deceptive translates as *engañoso*. [Note that there is no such word in Spanish as "*deceptivo*."] Hay miles de palabras **engañosas** (falsos cognados). *There are thousands of deceptive words (false cognates).*

declaración / declaration *Declaración* means "declaration" as "a formal statement, a proposal of love," and it also means "evidence, testimony, deposition (of a witness)." The plural *declaraciones* is better rendered in English in the singular: "statement, comment."
declaración de renta = *income tax declaration (return)*
declaración jurada = *testimony under oath*
El testigo hizo su **declaración** ante el juez. *The witness gave his testimony before the judge.* Se negó a hacer **declaraciones**. *She refused to make a statement.*

declarar / declare *Declarar* is "to declare, to let know, to state formally" and also "to testify" (in court). The reflexive form, *declararse,* conveys a different meaning of "to propose (marriage), to break out (a fire, an epidemic, etc.)." **declarar culpable** = *to find guilty* El senador **declaró** su candidatura. *The senator **declared** his candidacy.* ¿Cuándo **te le declaraste** a María? *When did you **propose** to Mary?*

declinar / decline *Declinar* means "to decline" with the denotations of "to diminish, draw to a close, go down, fade, decay, get weaker." El poder romano **declinaba** (decaía). *Roman power was **declining** (decaying).* *To decline* also conveys the idea of *renunciar a, rechazar* (an offer), *negarse* (ie) *a* (to do something). **Rechazó** el trabajo que le ofrecían. *He **declined** the job they offered him.*

decorar / decorate *Decorar* covers "to decorate, adorn, paint, embellish," as well as *condecorar* ("to decorate with medals, crosses, etc."). La casa estaba bien **decorada**. *The house was well **decorated**.* **Fue condecorado** por el Presidente. *He was **decorated** by the President.*

deducible / deducible, deductible *Deducible* means "deducible" ("inferable, able to be concluded or surmised"), as well as "deductible" ("able to be deducted or subtracted"). Los gastos de viajes de negocios parcialmente son **deducibles** para los impuestos. *Business trip expenses are partially **deductible** on your taxes.*

deducir / deduce, deduct *Deducir* means "to deduce" ("to infer, follow, conclude") and also "to deduct" ("to subtract"). Esa conclusión **se deduce** de sus declaraciones sobre Irak. *That conclusion is **deducible** from his statement about Iraq.*

defectivo / defective *Defectivo* means "defective" as a term in grammar, such as the "defective verb" *ought. Defective* also means "faulty" (people or things) and is translated as *defectuoso.* Nació con un pie **defectuoso**. *He was born with a **defective** foot. Defecto,* a noun, exactly means "defect." *To defect,* however, has no parallel term. It is best expressed by *desertar.* **Desertó** del partido republicano. *He **defected** from the Republican Party. Defection,* likewise, is best translated as *deserción.*

defender / defend *Defender* (ie) means exactly "to defend" ("to guard, protect, support," etc.). However, *defenderse* not only means "to defend oneself" but also "to manage, handle, get along" in colloquial speech. **Se defiende** bastante bien en alemán después de vivir un año en Austria. *He **gets along** pretty well in German after living one year in Austria.* Sabe **defenderse** bien como gerente de la tienda de videos. *She knows how to **handle** things well as manager of the video store.*

definitivo / definitive *Definitivo* and *definitive* share the idea of "coming to an end." But *definitivo* seems to stress the idea of time: "permanent, final." **en definitiva** = *really, in short* Están haciendo una carretera provisional mientras construyen la **definitiva**. *They are building a temporary road while they construct the **permanent** one. Definitive,* on the other hand, stresses the reasons to get to the end: *decisivo, concluyente.* **Definitivamente** means "permanently, for good, finally." Las obras están **definitivamente** terminadas. *The road work has finally ended.* Se marchó **definitivamente.** *He went away for good. Definitively* means *decisivamente, concluyentemente.*

defraudar / defraud *Defraudar* and *to defraud* share the meaning of "to cheat, to swindle" *(estafar).* However, the basic meaning of *defraudar* can also convey a less immoral meaning: "to disappoint, frustrate." From a legal point of view, *defraudar* is very important: "to evade taxes."
defraudar al fisco = *to evade taxes*
La secretaria nueva nos **defraudó** a todos por su inexperiencia. *The new secretary **disappointed** all of us because of her inexperience.* **Defraudó** a sus acreedores. *He **defrauded** his creditors.* Ella **defraudó** mi confianza. *She **betrayed** my confidence.*

delicado / delicate *Delicado* and *delicate* share the ideas of "mild, fragile, frail, refined, dainty, exquisite, polite." *Delicado,* however, also downgrades its meanings to refer to "fastidious, fussy, particular, hard to please, squeamish, touchy, scrupulous." [This seems to be one of several cases in the language where a "beautiful" word such as *delicado* can be used to convey either an "exquisite" concept or a very negative idea. It is necessary to examine the context in which the word is used in order to determine if the speaker or writer is referring to one or the other.]
manjar delicado = *delicacy*
Hace como diez años que ella está **delicada** de salud. *She has been in **delicate** (frail) health for about ten years.* Es un jarrón italiano muy **delicado** (fino) y muy caro. *It is a very **delicate** (fine) Italian vase and is very expensive.* La muchachita es muy **delicada** a la hora de comer. *The young girl is very **particular** (fussy) at mealtime.*

delicioso / delicious *Delicioso* and *delicious* both refer to the senses of taste *(gusto)* and smell *(olfato)* and reflect the best in flavors and aromas, the "exquisite." In Spanish, however, *delicioso* extends its scope to include meanings such as "charming, delightful" *(encantador)* and in colloquial speech, "funny, witty" *(gracioso).* Sirvieron una comida **deliciosa.** *They served a **delicious** meal.* Es una mujer **deliciosa.** *She is a **charming** woman.* Es una persona **deliciosa** para contar chistes verdes. *He is a **funny** person for telling dirty jokes.*

delincuencia / delinquency *Delincuencia* and *delinquency* refer to "breaking the law." In Spanish, though, *delincuencia* applies only to people. La **delincuencia** juvenil es un problema serio. *Juvenile **delinquency** is a serious problem. Delinquency* refers to things, as well as to people. The word conveys two different concepts: *delincuencia* for people and *violación, ilegalidad* (f.) for things. Hay muchas **violaciones** en el uso de las tarjetas de crédito. *There is much **delinquency** in the use of credit cards. Delinquent* also translates two concepts: *delincuente* for people and *moroso, atrasado* for things (such as bills, accounts, etc.). Ud. no pagó a tiempo, por eso su cuenta está **morosa.** *You didn't pay on time, so your account is **delinquent.***

demanda / demand *Demanda* shares with *demand* the ideas of "petition, claim, request, asking for." *Demanda* also means "lawsuit." La ley de la oferta y la demanda. *The law of supply and* **demand**. *Demand* also means *exigencia*.

demandar / demand *Demandar* and *to demand* mean "to request, ask for." *Demandar* also means "to sue, file a lawsuit." María va a **demandar** al médico que la operó. *Mary is going to sue the doctor who operated on her.* To demand is also *exigir, insistir en.* El dueño **exige** demasiado a los dependientes. *The owner* **demands** *too much of (from) the clerks.*

demonio / demon *Demonio* means "demon" and *diablo* means "devil." The terms in English and Spanish all refer to the same entity. Yet, *demonio* is "the devil" and *diablo* is "a demon." In Spanish, *diablo* is one of many possible *diablos,* but *el demonio* is one, the opposite of *Dios. Devil* in English is only one, the opposite of "God"; whereas, there are many *demons.* In other words, *diablo* and *demon* are countable nouns, but *demonio* and *devil* are noncountable nouns.
¿Cómo demonios...? = *How the devil...?*
¡Demonio de niño! = *You little devil!*
ser el mismo demonio = *to be a real devil*
ese demonio de hombre = *that devil of a man*
Ese muchacho es un **diablo** porque tiene **el demonio** en su cuerpo. *That boy is* **a demon** *because he has* **the devil** *in his body (he is possessed by* **the devil**).

departamento / department *Departamento* means "department" as "section, division." In some countries, *departamento* is used to mean "apartment" (*apartamento, piso* in other countries). *Departamento* also means "compartment" (of a train). En este **departamento** de tren caben ocho personas. *Eight people can fit in this train* **compartment.** **Departamento** de Lenguas Romances / **Department** of Romance Languages

departir / depart *Departir* does not mean "to depart"; it means "to chat, speak." The term is rather literary. [*Departir* is one of those terms that is bound to die. The *Real Academia* gives as many as seven meanings of this term, but all of them are considered archaic.] Los dos amigos **departen** en ruso por horas. *Both friends* **chat** *in Russian for hours.* To depart means *marcharse, irse, salirse, apartarse.* Figuratively, it means *morir (ue, u), irse* (to the next life).
pasar a mejor vida = *to depart this life*
Se está **apartando** de la verdad. *He is* **departing** *from the truth.*

dependencia / dependence, dependency *Dependencia* means "dependence" or "dependency" in the sense of "reliance, subordination." *Dependencia* also means "section, department, branch (office)." The plural *dependencias* refers to "outbuildings, outhouses." las **dependencias** de un palacio / *the* **outbuildings** *of a palace* **Dependiente** means "dependent" ("relying on another person"), but in everyday speech, it is used to mean "clerk, salesclerk." [Most countries use *dependienta* to refer to a "female salesclerk."] Los hijos son **dependientes** de los padres. *Children are their parents'* **dependents.** Esta tienda tiene treinta **dependientes.** *This store has thirty* **salesclerks.** **Depender de** exactly means "to depend on." [Note the preposition *de.*]

bastarse a sí mismo = *to depend on oneself*
Dependo de mis padres. *I depend on my parents.*

depósito / deposit   *Depósito* means "deposit" regarding money, things, trust, sediment, etc. *Depósito* also means "tank (for gas), warehouse, dump."
depósito de cadáveres = *morgue*
en depósito = *in bond*
¿Il liciste un **depósito** de 20.000 dólares? *Did you make a deposit of 20,000 dollars?*
Me gusta llenar el **depósito** de gasolina. *I like to fill up the gas tank. Depositar* translates exactly as "to deposit." *Depositario* is used especially in legal business as "depositary" ("a person or firm entrusted with safekeeping"). It should not be confused with "depository," which is translated as *almacén* (m.).

derogatorio / derogatory   *Derogatorio* does not mean "derogatory." *Derogatorio* means "abolishing, annulling, repealing."   un decreto **derogatorio** de la ley del aborto / *a decree **abolishing** the abortion law   Derogatory* means *despreciativo, peyorativo, indigno.* Se expresó con términos **indignos** de su cargo. *He spoke in terms **derogatory** of his rank.* No hables en términos **peyorativos.** *Don't speak in **derogatory** terms. Derogar* means "to abolish, annul, repeal." Lincoln **derogó** (abolió) la esclavitud. *Lincoln **abolished** slavery. To derogate* translates as *atentar contra* (rights, liberty), *rebajarse* ("to lose face").

desastre / disaster   *Desastre* (m.) means "disaster" when it refers to "an accident that is serious," for example, a car crash, a fire, an earthquake, etc. If the *desastre* is not serious, it means "accident, mishap." Figuratively, *desastre* suggests "calamity, hopelessness, absolute mess." Este borracho es un verdadero **desastre.** *This drunk is **absolutely hopeless.*** Esa alcoba es un **desastre.** *That room is an **absolute mess.*** La cocinera tuvo un **desastre** con el pollo. Se le quemó completamente. *The cook had a **mishap** (accident) with the chicken. She burned it completely.*

descargar / discharge   *Descargar* and *to discharge* share the idea of "to unload, to shoot." Los obreros **descargaron** el camión. *The workers **unloaded** (discharged) the truck.* ¿Por qué **descargaste** el fusil? *Why did you **discharge** the rifle? To discharge* has additional meanings such as *despedir* (i) (an employee), *saldar* or *pagar* (debts), *poner en libertad* (convicts), *dar de alta* (patients), *dar de baja* (soldiers). El gerente **despidió** a la secretaria. *The manager **discharged** the secretary.* El médico **dio de alta** al enfermo. *The doctor **discharged** the patient.*

descubrir / discover   *Descubrir* means "to discover" in the sense of "to be the first to find or find out, to realize." *Descubrir* also means "to disclose or reveal, uncover, be able to see *(divisar)*." The reflexive *descubrirse* means "to take off one's hat, to clear (the sky), to confide, to come out (a crime, a secret, etc.)." ¿Quién **descubrió** los antibióticos? *Who **discovered** antibiotics?* El presidente **descubrió** la estatua. *The president **unveiled** the statue.* Ella **se descubrió** al entrar. *She **took off her hat** when she came in.* Desde la ventana **se descubre** todo el valle. *From the window **one can see** the whole valley. Descubierto* means "discovered," as well as "open, exposed, bare." Se le cayó la toalla y dejó al

descubierto (desnudo) su bello cuerpo. *The towel fell away and her beautiful body was **exposed** (bare).*

desesperado / desperado, desperate *Desesperado* does not mean "desperado" but "desperate, hopeless, furious, despairing." Está **desesperado** porque perdió el trabajo. *He's **desperate** because he lost his job.* una situación **desesperada** / *a **hopeless** situation* *Desperado* means *bandido, forajido, criminal*. [*Desperado* is derived from an old Spanish term (or Portuguese, according to other authors) from the verb *desperar*, which has disappeared from use.] Muchos vaqueros se convirtieron en **bandidos** el siglo pasado. *In the last century, many cowboys became **desperados** (desperadoes).*

desesperar / despair *Desesperar* is not "to despair" but "to cause to despair, to exasperate." The reflexive *desesperarse* means "to despair, to lose hope." Su manera de actuar me **desespera**. *His way of acting **makes me despair**.* Me **desespero** por no saber de él. *I am **desperate** from not hearing from him.*

desgracia / disgrace *Desgracia* is not "disgrace" but "misfortune, tragedy, blow, mishap."
por desgracia = unfortunately
Tuvo la **desgracia** de perder el avión. *She had the **misfortune** of missing the flight.* Las **desgracias** nunca vienen solas. *It never rains but it pours. Disgrace* means *deshonra, vergüenza* ("shame"), *ignominia*. Es una **vergüenza** que haya tanta pobreza. *It's a **disgrace** that there is so much poverty. **Desgraciado** is neither "disgraced" nor "disgraceful." **Desgraciado** means "unfortunate, unlucky, unhappy."* Sometimes its meaning takes a downturn: "wretched, poor" and in some Latin American countries, "bastard." ¡**Desgraciado**! ¡No vuelvas por aquí! *Bastard! Don't you ever come back here!* Lleva una vida muy **desgraciada**. *She leads a **wretched** life. Disgraced*, on the other hand, means *desacreditado, deshonrado. **Desgraciar** means "to damage, spoil, cripple (lisiarse)." To disgrace* translates as *deshonrar, desacreditar.* **Deshonró** a su patria. *He **disgraced** his country.*

deshonesto / dishonest *Deshonesto* is not "dishonest" but "indecent, immodest, improper" *(obsceno)*. Fue culpable de conducta **deshonesta**. *She was guilty of **improper** conduct.* No se permiten palabras **deshonestas**. *Indecent (obscene) language is not permitted. Dishonest* means *fraudulento, embustero, tramposo, falta de honradez*. Hiciste **trampa** en el examen. *You were **dishonest** on the test.* Ese negocio es **fraudulento**. *That is a **dishonest** business. **Deshonestidad** (f.) means "indecency, immodesty, impropriety."* En este traje de baño, te pueden acusar de **deshonestidad**. *In this bathing suit, they can charge you with **indecency**. Dishonesty* means *fraude* (m.), *trampa, embuste* (m.). ¿Te preocupa la **falta de honradez** en un político? *Does **dishonesty** in a politician bother you? **Deshonestamente** means "indecently." Dishonestly* means *fraudulentamente*.

desinteresado / disinterested *Desinteresado* means "disinterested" ("without a vested interest; indifferent"). However, *desinteresado* seems to emphasize the lack of interest in material goods, meaning "unselfish, altruistic." Es un joven muy **desinteresado**. *He is a very **unselfish** young man. Disinterested*, on the other hand, emphasizes personal feelings: *imparcial* ("unbiased"), *sin prejuicio* ("unprejudiced"). Un maestro debe ser **imparcial** al corregir exámenes. *A teacher must be **disinterested** when grading tests.*

desistir / desist   *Desistir (de)* means "to desist, give up, stop"; but the English term is rarely used today, only in literary style. On the other hand, *desistir de* is an everyday term for "to withdraw (a candidate), to waive (a right in court)." **Desistió de** su candidatura por falta de apoyo de público. *He **withdrew** his candidacy for lack of public support.* **Desistió de** fumar hace dos años y nunca ha vuelto a hacerlo. *She **stopped** smoking two years ago and has not smoked since.*

desmayar / dismay   *Desmayar(se)* is not "to dismay" but "to faint, swoon, lose heart." La noticia inesperada lo **desmayó**. *The unexpected news **made** him **faint**.* Hacía tanto calor que **se desmayó**. *It was so hot that he **fainted**.* To dismay means *espantar, desalentar, aterrar. Desmayo* means "faint, swoon, unconsciousness."
sin desmayo = *unfaltering*
tener un desmayo = *to faint*
Dismay, on the other hand, means *desaliento, consternación, espanto.* Le entró el **desaliento** por falta de cooperación de sus colegas. *He was **dismayed** by the lack of cooperation from his colleagues.*

desmontar / dismount   *Desmontar* means "to dismount," as well as "to remove, take down, dismantle, clear or level (woods, land)." [*Apearse del caballo* is used more frequently than *desmontar del caballo* to mean "to dismount from a horse."] **Desmontó** del caballo sin ayuda. *She **dismounted** from the horse with no help.* **Desmontó** el motor rápidamente. *He **dismantled** the engine quickly.* Los soldados **desmontaron** parte del bosque para acampar. *The soldiers **cleared** part of the woods in order to make camp.*

desnudar / denude   *Desnudar* is not "to denude" but "to undress," and in the real or figurative sense, "to strip." No es legal **desnudarse** en público. *It's not legal to **undress** in public.* To denude is used in ecology to mean *erosionar, destruir, despojar.* Las lluvias **erosionan** muchos terrenos. *The rain **denudes** many lands.*

desolado / desolate   *Desolado* shares with *desolate* the idea of "lonely, deserted, uninhabited." *Desolado* also means "upset, sorry, heartbroken, distressed, disconsolate." La viuda está **desolada** tras la muerte de su querido esposo. *The widow is **heartbroken** after the death of her beloved husband. Desolar* means "to desolate" ("to ravage") and also "to distress, upset." Los soldados **desolaron** la región. *The soldiers **desolated** (ravaged) the region. Desolación* means "desolation" ("loneliness, a desolate or ravaged place"), as well as "distress, grief." La **desolación** es mala compañera. *Grief is a bad companion.*

desorden / disorder   *Desorden* (m.) shares with *disorder* the idea of "lack of order, untidiness, confusion." *Desorden* may also refer to people's behavior with the meaning of "disorderliness." The plural *desórdenes* stands for "riots, disturbances." No aprobamos el **desorden** de la conducta del senador. *We don't approve of the **disorderliness** of the senator's behavior.* Provocó varios **desórdenes** callejeros. *He incited (provoked) several street **disturbances**. Disorder* also refers to people's health, meaning *enfermedad* (f.), *trastorno.* El alcohol trae **trastornos** al hígado. *Alcohol causes **disorders** of the liver.*

despachar / dispatch   *Despachar* and *to dispatch* both mean "to send off, to finish quickly," but *despachar* also means "to wait on or help (customers), to dismiss," and in the worst sense of the word, "to kill, get out of the way." *Es importante* **despachar** *esta carta hoy. It's important to dispatch this letter today. La mesera* **despacha** *a los clientes. The waitress is helping the customers.* **Despaché** *la clase antes de la hora. I dismissed the class before it was time. Despacho* is "dispatch" (of letters, documents, merchandise), as well as "office, store, shop, official report."
despacho de billetes = *box office*
Tengo una ordenadora en mi **despacho.** *I have a computer in my office. En la esquina hay un* **despacho** *de vinos que vende muy barato. There is a wine store around the corner that sells wine very cheap.*

desplazar / displace   *Desplazar* and *to displace* both mean "to move from the usual place, discharge, replace." However the reflexive *desplazarse* means "to travel, get around," as well as "to move." *El general* **desplazó** *al dictador. The general displaced the dictator.* **Nos desplazamos** *por toda España. We travel all over Spain.*

destino / destiny   *Destino* shares with *destiny* the meaning of "fate, lot, fortune *(hado)*." But *destino* has additional meanings such as "destination, use, job, post, station."
con destino a = *bound for*
dar destino a = *to put to use*
Nadie sabe su **destino** *final. No one knows his or her final destiny. El* **destino** *de esta máquina es ... The use of this machine is ... El avión va* **con destino** *a Roma. The flight is bound for Rome. Destinar* means "to destine" ("to intend, head for") and also "to appoint, to send (to a place with a job), to post or station, to be addressed." *El presidente lo* **destinó** *a Texas. The president sent him to Texas. un paquete* **destinado** *a ti / a package addressed to you* *Está* **destinado** *a ser un líder. He is destined to be a leader.*

destitución / destitution   *Destitución* does not mean "destitution" but "removal, dismissal (from a job)." *Nos sorprendió la* **destitución** *del director. The dismissal of the principal surprised us. Destitution* means *pobreza, miseria, indigencia, carencia. Hay mucha* **miseria** *en la India. There is much destitution in India. Destituido* means "removed, dismissed (from a job)." *Destitute* stands for *pobre, necesitado, indigente. Ese niño está* **necesitado.** *No ha comido en tres días. That boy is destitute. He hasn't eaten in three days. Destituir* translates as "to dismiss, remove (from a job)." *El general* **destituyó** *al presidente del país. The general removed the president of the country. To destitute* has faded from usage, but is used to mean *privar de, empobrecer.*

destreza / distress   *Destreza* is not "distress" but means "skill, mastery, dexterity." *Tiene una gran* **destreza** *en carpintería. He has great skill in carpentry. Distress* is one of those "sad" words that covers many situations such as *pena, angustia, aflicción, desolación, miseria* ("poverty"), *peligro, apuro, socorro.*
señal de socorro = *distress signal*

estar en apuro = *to be in distress*
Siento mucha **angustia** por su muerte. *I feel great **distress** over his death.*

desvestir / divest   *Desvestir* (i) is not "to divest" but "to undress, strip, lay bare."
Se **desvistió** en un dos por tres. *He **got undressed** in a jiffy.* *To divest* means
desposeer, despojar (of goods, honors), *quitar.*   **renunciar** a sus derechos / *to
divest oneself of one's rights* ¿Se puede **despojar** al rico de sus riquezas para
enriquecer al pobre? *Is it moral to **divest** the wealthy of their riches to make the
poor rich?*

desviación / deviation   *Desviación* means "deviation" as "deflection, detour, de-
parture from principles."   una **desviación** moral de la religión tradicional / *a
moral **deviation** from traditional religion*   *Deviation* has downgraded its original
meaning to refer also to *extravío, alejamiento* (from the truth), *inversión* (sexual).
Deviate is not *desviado*, but *invertido sexual, extravagante.* ¿Hay muchos
invertidos sexuales en los Estados Unidos? *Are there many **deviates** in the United
States?*

detener / detain   *Detener* (ie) stands for "to detain" ("keep in custody, confine,
hold up, stop"), but *detener* also means "to arrest." **Detuvieron** al ladrón en el
banco. *They **arrested** the thief in the bank.* Quedamos **detenidos** por la nieve. *We
were **detained** by the snow.* *Detención,* similarly, is "detention" as "keeping in
custody, confinement," and also "temporary arrest."

deteriorar / deteriorate   *Deteriorar* is "to deteriorate" in the sense of "to wear
out, get worse," both in the real and figurative senses (such as morals). *Deteriorar*
seems to take on an active connotation, meaning "to damage, impair, spoil (food,
meat, etc.)." Las manzanas **se deterioraron** en las cajas. *The apples **got spoiled**
in the boxes.* Mis libros llegaron **deteriorados**. *My books arrived **damaged**.* La
moral del país **se deteriora** con los malos ejemplos de los turistas. *The country's
morality **deteriorates** with the bad examples of the tourists.* *Deterioración
(deterioro)* means "deterioration" ("wearing out, getting worse") and also "damage, spoiling." *Deterioration* is also translated as *degeneración* (of a breed or
race).

determinado / determined   *Determinado* and *determined* mean "decided, reso-
lute, unwavering" *(decidido, resuelto, enérgico).* *Determinado* also describes
things, with the meaning "appointed, given, definite (prices, dates, business,
etc.), specific."
en un momento determinado = *at a definite moment*
Es un hombre **determinado** (decidido). *He is a **determined** man.* Tenemos precios
determinados. *We have **fixed** (definite) prices.* *Determined,* however, usually
applies only to people.

devoción / devotion   *Devoción* and *devotion* share the meaning of "religious
worship, piety, prayers." Tiene mucha **devoción** en la iglesia. *She has great
devotion to the church.* *Devotion,* unlike *devoción,* is not limited to religion.
Devotion applies to a profession, a job, a person, etc., and means *dedicación*
(to work, studies), *lealtad* (f.; to a person or group), *afición* (to a hobby, sport).

Como tiene una gran **dedicación** a los estudios saca notas excelentes. *Due to his great devotion to his studies, he receives excellent grades.* Juan tiene gran **lealtad** con su familia. *John is greatly devoted to his family.*

devolver / devolve *Devolver* (ue) is not "to devolve" but "to return (things), repay, refund, send back, give back" and, when applied to an upset stomach, "to vomit, throw up."
devolver la palabra = *to give back the floor*
devuélvase al remitente = *return to sender*
¿Cuándo piensas **devolverme** el libro que te presté hace un año? *When do you intend to return the book I loaned you a year ago?* To devolve, on the other hand, is not a frequently used term, but it means *transmitir, delegar* (powers), *recaer sobre, incumbir.* La responsabilidad de comprar la pistola **recayó sobre** Juan. *Responsibility for buying the pistol devolved upon John.*

deyección / dejection *Deyección* is not "dejection" but "defecation, excrement." The plural *deyecciones* in geology means "debris." *Dejection* means *desaliento, postración, abatimiento.* La muerte de su amigo le causó **abatimiento** por mucho tiempo. *His friend's death left him dejected for a long time.*

diablo [*See entry for* **demonio / demon.**]

diario / diary *Diario* shares with *diary* the meaning of a "daily written record," but *diario* also means "newspaper," and in the business world, "journal" or "daybook." As an adjective, *diario* means "daily."
diario matutino = *morning paper*
diario vespertino = *evening paper*
El **diario** de Ana Frank es famoso, especialmente después de la película. *The diary of Anne Frank is famous, especially after they made a movie about it.* En Madrid hay seis **diarios** importantes. *There are six important newspapers in Madrid.*

diferir / differ *Diferir* (ie, i) means "to differ" in the sense of "to be different," but *diferir* also means "to defer, postpone, put off." **Diferimos** la boda para el verano. *We postponed the wedding until summer.* Sus trabajos **difieren.** *Their jobs differ. To differ,* on the other hand, also stands for *no estar de acuerdo* or *disentir* (ie, i) ("disagree"). No **están de acuerdo** en ese punto. *They differ on that point.* Siento **disentir** con ustedes. *I beg to differ with you.*

difunto / defunct *Difunto* only applies to people, meaning "dead, deceased, late." The use of *difunto* or *muerto* with organizations would sound very funny in Spanish. El **difunto** era hombre de muchas virtudes. *The deceased was a man of many virtues. Defunct* only applies to organizations, corporations, clubs, etc., and is translated as *desaparecido, extinto.* La organización está **desaparecida.** *The organization is now defunct.*

dignidad / dignity *Dignidad* (f.) is "dignity" ("self-respect, honor, worthiness"), as well as "office, post, rank."
hacerse respetar = *to stand on one's dignity*
La **dignidad** de la presidencia debe respetarse por todos. *The office of president*

must be respected by all. Todos buscan **dignidades** cada vez más altas para ganar más. *Everyone searches out the highest **rank** to earn more money.*

dilapidar / dilapidate *Dilapidar* is not "to dilapidate" but "to squander, waste." Después de **dilapidar** su dinero por un año, dejó de ser rico. *After a year of **squandering** his money, he was no longer rich.* To dilapidate means *deteriorar, desmoronarse, arruinarse.* La casa se **deterioró** rápidamente. *The house **dilapidated** very fast (quickly became **dilapidated**).* **Dilapidación** means "squandering, waste." *Dilapidation* means *deterioro, estado ruinoso.* **Dilapidado** means "wasted, squandered." *Dilapidated* means *derruido, estropeado, ruinoso.* [It is interesting to note that in this case, the Spanish terms indicate a strong activity, "squandering," on the part of people; whereas the English terms stress the sad result of that activity on property, "deterioration."] Encontramos la casa muy **ruinosa**. *We found the house very **dilapidated** (in a **dilapidated** condition).*

diligencia / diligence *Diligencia* means "diligence" ("being diligent, careful effort, perseverance") and also "errand, speed," and in a figurative sense, "step, measure." [*Diligencia* used to be the "stagecoach."]
hacer diligencias = *to take the necessary steps*
Tengo que hacer dos **diligencias**. *I have to run two **errands**.* Lo hizo con suma **diligencia**. *She did it with great **speed**.* Ella siempre ha trabajado con **diligencia** para subir de rango. *She has always worked with **diligence** to reach a high rank.*

diputado / deputy *Diputado* exactly means "deputy" ("delegate, representative, assistant"). In some Latin American countries *diputado* is every member of the Congress: "Congressman, Congresswoman."
Teniente alcalde = *Deputy Mayor*
Juez suplente = *Deputy Judge*
La mayoría de los **diputados** votaron en contra de la guerra. *The mayority of the **congressmen** voted against the war.*

dirección / direction *Dirección* is translated as "direction" ("directing, management, order, way, trend"). *Dirección* also means "address, steering wheel, board of directors."
dirección general = *head office*
dirección única = *one-way street*
dirección asistida = *power steering*
Le confiaron la **dirección** de la obra. *They entrusted him with the **direction** of the project.* Se reunió la **dirección** de la compañía. *The company's **board of directors** held a meeting.* ¿Cuál es su **dirección**? *What is your **address**? Direction* in the plural, *directions,* means *instrucciones* (for example, for assembling something). Siga las **instrucciones** del mapa. *Follow the **directions** on the map.*

director / director *Director* (m.) is "director" ("leader, head, manager"), as well as "conductor (of an orchestra), principal (of a school), editor (of a newspaper)."
director de escena = *producer* (theater)

directorio / directory *Directorio* means "directory" ("rules, set or list of names, instructions"), as well as a "board of directors."
guía telefónica = *telephone directory*

discípulo / disciple *Discípulo* shares with *disciple* the original meaning of "pupil or follower of any teacher." [*Disciple* has always retained the original meaning; however, *discípulo* has changed to refer to any student—*alumno, estudiante* (m., f.), *escolar* (m., f.)—of any school. Nowadays, *discípulo* is used more in formal situations than in everyday speech.] Los **discípulos** (alumnos) de Kant se vestían elegantemente. *Kant's disciples used to dress very elegantly.*

disco / disk, disc *Disco* means "disk" or "disc" in several contexts: in computers, in brakes, as part of the spine. *Disco* has additional meanings, such as "record (music), dial (of a telephone), signal (railroad), discus (in the Olympic event)." In Spain, *disco* is the *semáforo* ("streetlight, traffic signal"). *Disco flexible* is "floppy disk," *mini disco* is "diskette," and *disco compacto* is "compact disk."
disco rayado = *broken record*
lanzamiento de disco = *discus throwing*
El mercado de **discos** y casetes es un gran negocio hoy día. *Today the record and cassette market is a big business.* Siempre estás con el mismo **disco**. *You're always singing the same old tune. (It's the same old story.)* Te llevaste el **disco** rojo. *You ran the red light.*

discreto / discreet, discrete *Discreto (reservado)* and *discreet* share the same basic idea: "prudent, cautious, silent, careful." But *discreto* has additional meanings such as "wise, sensible, sober (color), modest, subdued, reasonable, average, witty." El muchacho tiene una inteligencia **discreta**. *The boy has average intelligence.* La abuela es una persona **discreta**. *The grandmother is a wise person.* A los jóvenes de hoy no les gusta llevar ropa de colores **discretos**. *The young people today don't like to wear subdued colors.* *Discrete* is a different adjective but with a similar spelling. It means *distinto, separado, discontinuo.*

discusión / discussion *Discusión* does not mean "discussion" but "(strong) dispute, argument." La **discusión** casi termina en pelea. *The dispute almost ended in a fight.* Discussion means *charla, conversación, intercambio de ideas, argumentación.*

discutir / discuss *Discutir* and *to discuss* have something in common: "to exchange ideas in conversation." The only difference is that in Spanish the action can be carried to a "risky" point; then the meaning changes to "to argue about (over)."
¡No discutas! = *Don't argue!*
Vamos a **discutir** como gente civilizada. *Let's discuss (talk) like civilized people.* No **discutas** más sobre eso. *Don't argue about that anymore.*

disertación / dissertation *Disertación* shares with *dissertation* the idea of "a written treatise or thesis for a doctorate." But *disertación* also means "lecture, discourse" *(conferencia)* and even a "school monograph or paper." *Disertar* means "to lecture, to discourse." El Dr. Jasso va a **disertar** sobre la semejanza de la guitarra y la mandolina. *Dr. Jasso is going to lecture on the similarities between the guitar and the mandolin.* To dissert is a defunct term in English.

disgustar, degustar / disgust *Disgustar* is not "to disgust" but "to annoy, dislike, displease." *Disgustarse,* the reflexive form, means "to get angry." Se **disgustó**

con ella por una tontería. *He got **angry** with her over a trifle.* **Degustar** translates as "to taste, sample, relish (food or drinks). ¿Te gusta **degustar** vinos nuevos? *Do you like to **sample** new wines?* To disgust, on the other hand, has the negative meaning of *dar asco, repugnar, indignar.* La borrachera me **da asco.** *Drunkenness **disgusts** me.* **Disgustado** means "annoyed, displeased, angry." Estoy **disgustado** de los resultados. *I am **displeased** with the results.* Disgusted means *hastiado, asqueado, indignado.* Me siento **asqueado** con el humo. *I feel **disgusted** with the smoke.* **Disgusto** means "displeasure, misfortune, argument, minor quarrel."

estar a disgusto = *to be ill at ease*
Su vida ha estado llena de **disgustos.** *Her life has been full of **misfortunes.*** **Degustación** means "sampling, relishing, tasting (of food or drinks)." *Disgust* is very negative, referring to *asco, repugnancia, aversión.*
¡Qué asco! = *How disgusting!*

disipar / dissipate *Disipar* shares with *to dissipate* the idea of "to dispel, disperse, make disappear." But *disipar* also means "to squander, waste." Las nubes se **disiparon** y salió el sol. *The clouds **dissipated** and the sun came out.* **Disipó** su fortuna en inversiones sospechosas. *He **wasted** his fortune on suspicious investments.*

disolver / dissolve *Disolver* (ue) shares with *to dissolve* the idea of "to change from a solid to a liquid, to end a marriage, to tear apart a society, to disband parliament." *Disolver* also means "to break up (meetings, riots), to annul (a contract)." La pastilla **se disuelve** en el café. *The tablet **dissolves** in coffee.* La policía **disolvió** la manifestación. *The police **broke up** the demonstration.* El divorcio **disuelve** el matrimonio. *Divorce **dissolves** marriages.* To dissolve also means *disipar* (illusions, dreams). No dejes **disipar** tus ilusiones en el aire. *Don't let your dreams **dissolve** (disappear) into thin air.*

dispensar / dispense *Dispensar* and *to dispense* both mean "to give out, to distribute medicine, etc.," but the primary idea of *dispensar* is "to pardon, excuse, confer or grant (honors), exempt."
deshacerse de = *to dispense with*
¡Dispénseme! = *Excuse me!*
Dispensaron medicinas a los pobres y a los enfermos. *They **dispensed** medicine to the poor and the sick.* Le **dispensaron** de pagar impuestos por ser extranjero. *They **exempted** him from paying taxes because he was a foreigner.*

disponer / dispose *Disponer* and *to dispose* share the meaning of "to arrange, place, set out." *Disponer* also means "to order, command, prescribe (as of laws)." *Disponer de* means "to have available, to own, to be free to use." The reflexive *disponerse a* translates as "to get ready, to prepare."
Disponga de mí. = *I am at your disposal.*
Ese señor **dispone de** una fortuna inmensa. *That gentleman **has** (owns) an immense fortune.* To dispose of means *tirar, desechar.* No se deben **tirar** las latas vacías. *One must not **dispose of** empty cans.* Disposable is translated as *desechable, para tirar.* Los pañales **desechables** no son buena idea, según los ecologistas. *Disposable diapers are not a good idea, according to ecologists.*

disposición / disposition   *Disposición* and *disposition* mean "arrangement, layout, article, order." *Disposición* also means "disposal, talent, gift, bent, steps (measures)."
tomar disposiciones = *to take steps*
a la disposición de Ud. = *at your disposal*
últimas disposiciones = *last will*
La **disposición** de los cuartos de mi casa es bastante variada. *The **layout** of the rooms in my house is quite varied.* Tiene **disposición** para la música. *She has a **talent** for music.* *Disposition* also means *temperamento, forma de ser, carácter* (m.). Me gusta su **temperamento** alegre. *I like his cheerful **disposition.***

distinto / distinct   *Distinto* and *distinct* mean "different." However, when *distinto* is used in the plural *(distintos)* before a noun, it means "various"; after a noun, "different."
distintos libros = *various books*
dos libros distintos = *two different books*
Distinct also means *claro, marcado, señalado.*
a diferencia de = *as distinct from*
Ese café tiene un sabor **marcado**. *That coffee has a **distinct** flavor. Distintivo* means "distinctive" ("characteristic") as an adjective, but as a noun, it translates as "badge, emblem, symbol." El águila es el **distintivo** de los Estados Unidos. *The eagle is the **symbol** of the United States.*

distracción / distraction   *Distracción* and *distraction* share the same positive idea of "amusement, pastime, recreation." But each term has additional meanings with negative overtones. *Distracción* also means "absentmindedness." Hay muchas **distracciones** en la gran ciudad. *There are many **distractions** (amusements) in the big city. Distraction* sometimes means *confusión, perplejidad* (f.). *Distraído* suggests "absentminded, untidy, entertaining (book, movie, etc.), amusing." Esa película de Cantinflas es muy **distraída**. *That movie with Cantinflas is very **entertaining.*** ¿Hay profesores **distraídos** en realidad? *Are there really **absentminded** professors? Distracted* means *confuso, perplejo, aturdido.*

diversión / diversion   *Diversión* means "diversion" as "amusement, entertainment" as a noncountable noun with no plural, but *diversión (pasatiempo)*, as a countable noun stands for "pastime, distraction, hobby." El cine es una **diversión** y una escuela para algunas personas. *Movies are both a **diversion** (amusement) and a school for some people.* Mi **diversión** favorita es la computadora. *My favorite **pastime** is the computer. Diversion*, on the other hand, means *desviación, desvío* (of a river, a road, a mind, etc.).

divertir / divert   *Divertir* (ie, i) is not "to divert" but "to entertain, amuse." The reflexive, *divertirse*, translates as "to have a good time, to enjoy." **Nos divertimos** a costa de José. *We **enjoyed ourselves** at Joe's expense. To divert* means *desviar.*

divisa / devise, device   *Divisa* means neither "devise" nor "device." It means "foreign currency, emblem, badge." La **divisa** más valuada es el dólar en los negocios internacionales. *The dollar is the most valued **foreign currency** in international business.* El águila es la **divisa** de EE. UU. *The eagle is the **emblem** of* the U.S. *Devise* stands for *testamento, legado. Device* means *invento, plan* (m.), *aparato, truco, estratagema.* Tengo un **plan** para ganar la lotería. *I have a **device** for winning the lottery.* Hacerse el enfermo era un **truco** para ganarse nuestra compasión. *Playing sick was a **device** to win our sympathy.*

divisar / devise *Divisar* is not "to devise" but "to perceive, see, discern, make out." Se puede **divisar** la luna entre las nubes. *One can **discern** (make out) the moon among the clouds.* To devise means *inventar, idear, concebir* (l), *imaginar.* ¿Quién **inventó** la rueda? *Who **devised** (invented) the wheel?*

doblar / double *Doblar* shares with *to double (duplicar)* the notion of "to multiply by two; to fold." *Doblar* also means "to bend, turn (the corner), dub (in film-making), line (a garment)." The reflexive form *doblarse* translates as "to stoop, bend down." El coche **dobló** por la calle Bolívar. *The car **turned** on Bolivar Street.* **Se dobló** para recoger el libro del piso. *He **bent down** to pick the book up from the floor.*

doble / double *Doble* is an adjective meaning "double" ("twice as much"), as well as "thick" (for example, *tela doble* means "thick material"). Figuratively, it is used for people who are "deceitful, two-faced." *Doble* (m.) is also a noun, meaning "double" ("twice as much"), as well as "fold, crease (in clothes)."
costar el doble = *to cost twice as much*
ocupación doble = *double occupancy*
habitación para dos = *double room*
montar dos = *to ride double*
con toda rapidez = *on the double*
No me gustan las personas **dobles**. *I don't like **two-faced** people.* Soy **dos veces** mayor que tú. *I am **twice (double)** your age.*

doctor / doctor *Doctor* (m.) is exactly "doctor," but the two terms are not used in the same situations. In Spanish, *doctor* applies to any field: philosophy, history, mathematics, medicine, etc. Except in academic circles, *doctor* in English is now limited to physicians and dentists, and when the word is used, *médico* is generally understood. Este herido necesita un **médico** con urgencia. Se está desangrando. *This wounded man needs a **doctor** right away. He is bleeding to death.*

documentación / documentation *Documentación* is exactly "documentation" (for the car, a passport, etc.). El policía le pidió la **documentación** del carro. *The police officer asked her for the **papers** for the car.* Documentation is a "formal" term; in colloquial English it is frequently supplanted by *papers*. Similarly, in Spanish, *papeles* (m.) is sometimes used in this sense. *Documento,* similarly, translates as "document" in formal style and "papers" in everyday English.

doméstico / domestic *Doméstico* shares with *domestic* the idea of "home, family." As a noun, *doméstico* means "(male) servant" and *doméstica* means "(female) servant." [Synonyms are *criado* and *criada,* respectively.]
animal doméstico = *pet, domestic animal*
Los problemas **domésticos** se ventilan en la casa, no en la calle. *Domestic problems*

must be discussed at home, not in the street. **Domestic** in English, unlike **doméstico** in Spanish, has extended its meaning outside the family and home to mean "of the country." For this reason, it is best translated as *nacional, interno.* Los problemas **internos** son importantes. *Domestic problems are important.* vuelos **nacionales** e internacionales / *domestic and international flights*

dominar / dominate   *Dominar* is "to dominate," meaning "to rule, control, over-power." However, *dominar* is also used for "to master (a topic, a language); to rise over, overlook (a place); to get over, recover from (a pain); to predominate." Franco **dominó** España por cuarenta años hasta su muerte. *Franco dominated Spain for forty years until his death.* La casa **domina** toda la bahía. *The house overlooks the whole bay.* La profesora **domina** cinco lenguas. *The professor is fluent in (has mastered) five languages.* *Dominio* means "domain, dominion" ("rule, control, power, territories"), as well as "mastery, restraint (of passions)." **dominio público** = *public property, public domain*

dormitorio / dormitory   *Dormitorio* and *dormitory* are both "places to sleep," but the term *dormitorio (alcoba)* is reserved for "bedroom." *Dormitory* is used for a place where many people, such as students, can live and sleep. This is called a *residencia* in Spanish and, in some countries, *dormitorios* (plural). La **residencia** estudiantil de la universidad está llena. *The student dormitory of the university is full.*

dragar / drag   *Dragar (excavar)* is not "to drag" but "to dredge" ("to dig and clean out rivers, bays, etc.") and also "to sweep" (for mines). Esta máquina **draga** la bahía. *This machine dredges the bay.* To drag means *arrastrar* and, in a figurative sense, "to be a drag" is *dar la lata, fastidiar, fregar (ie), molestar.* Los presos modernos no **arrastran** cadenas. *Modern prisoners do not drag chains.*

drama / drama   *Drama* (m.) shares with *drama* the idea of "tragedy in theater" and, in a figurative sense, "a vivid or interesting event." In Spanish, *drama* does not include comedy in theater; whereas the English term does. *Drama* may also take on a derogatory meaning such as "fiction, play." **¡Qué tragedia!** = *What a drama!* *Dramático* and *dramatic* are used in theater to refer to drama, but they are frequent words in everyday life, used descriptively to mean "vivid, exciting, with action, moving." El encuentro de los esposos fue **dramático** (conmovedor). *The meeting of the couple was dramatic (moving).*

droguista / druggist   *Droguista* and *druggist* seem to share a meaning that deals with "drugs." However, *droguista* refers to illegal drugs, regarding the selling of drugs. It is best translated as "drug trafficker, drug dealer." El **droguista** puede hacerse millonario y terminar su vida en la cárcel. *The drug dealer can become a millionaire and spend the rest of his life in jail.* *Druggist*, on the other hand, is someone who deals in legal drugs or medicine. The Spanish terms are *farmacéutico* ("pharmacist") and the older term *boticario.* El **farmacéutico** despacha las recetas del médico. *The druggist fills the doctor's precriptions.*

ducha / douche   *Ducha* is translated as "douche" (for women), but the basic idea of *ducha* is "shower" ("bath"). In Mexico, the word for *ducha* is *regadera.*

Figuratively, *una **ducha** fría* means "bad news, damper." *Todo el mundo canta en la **ducha**. Everybody sings in the **shower**. La noticia me cayó como una **ducha** fría. The news put a **damper** on everything. Douche* translates as *ducha higiénica*. ***Ducharse*** means "to take a shower." *To douche* means *aplicarse una ducha higiénica*.

duelo / duel *Duelo* is "duel" as a "formal fight between two people," an activity that has been banned in most countries. In Spanish *duelo* has additional meanings such as "grief, sorrow, mourning *(luto)*, mourners, funeral procession *(cortejo)*." Figuratively, it is used for "toils, trials, labors."

batirse en duelo = *to fight a duel*

*En algunos países todavía es legal **batirse en duelo**. In some countries it's still legal to fight a duel. Ella está de **duelo** porque murió su querido esposo. She is in **mourning** because her beloved husband died. El **duelo** caminaba lentamente por las calles silenciosas del pueblo. The **mourners** were walking slowly through the silent streets of the village.*

dueña / duenna *Dueña* is not "duenna" but "owner" *(propietaria)* of something, with different translations, according to circumstances: "(female) owner, mistress (of the house), landlady, matron, lady." [*Dueña* was used in old Spanish with the sense of the English *duenna*. Nowadays, all the dictionaries consider that meaning to be archaic.] *¿Quién es la **dueña** de este perrito? Who is the **mistress** (owner) of this little dog? María es la **dueña** de este coche. Mary is the **owner** of this car. Duenna*, which is not commonly used today, means "governess" and is translated as *chaperona, dama, señora de compañía. La **chaperona** cuida de las hijas de la familia como si fueran suyas. The **duenna** (governess) takes care of the family's daughters as though they were her own.*

duplicar / duplicate *Duplicar* means "to duplicate," in the sense of "to copy, to do something again"; but *duplicar* also means "to double" ("multiply by two").

por duplicado = *in duplicate*

*Es necesario **duplicar** la producción de zapatos para satisfacer la demanda. It's necessary to **double** shoe production in order to satisfy the demand. Tienes que llenar el formulario **por duplicado**. You have to fill out the form **in duplicate**. No es legal **duplicar** las llaves de la universidad del estado. It's not legal to **duplicate** the state university's keys. Duplicación* is "duplication" as "copy" and also means "doubling."

dureza / duress *Dureza* is not "duress" but "hardness (of water, of metal, of hearing), toughness (of food), harshness, difficulty." *La **dureza** del oro es mayor que la del plomo y la de la plata. The **hardness** of gold is greater than that of lead and silver. Nos sorprendió la **dureza** del padre con sus hijos. We were surprised by the father's **harshness** toward his children. Duress*, on the other hand, is used in legal terminology to mean *coacción, coerción, prisión. El acusado atestiguó que cometió el crimen por **coacción**. The defendant testified that he committed the crime under **duress**.*

E

económico / economic, economical *Económico* is translated as two different terms and concepts in English: "economic" ("financial") and "economical" ("cheap, inexpensive").
crisis económica = *economic (financial) crisis*
ropa económica = *cheap (inexpensive) clothes*
Muchos países tienen una crisis **económica** seria. *Many countries have a grave economic crisis.* La gente de Monterrey tiene fama de ser **económica** (agarrada). *The people of Monterrey are famous for being economical (stingy).* **Economizar** translates fully as "to economize."

edificar / edify *Edificar* has a real sense of "to build" and a figurative sense of "to give a good example." Hoy día no se **edifican** catedrales góticas ni románicas. *Nowadays they don't build gothic nor romanesque cathedrals.* Los buenos predicadores **edifican** con su vida más que con sus palabras. *Good preachers edify with their lives better than with their words.* To *edify* only shares with *edificar* the figurative sense of setting a good example. *Edificación* means "edification" as "good example," as well as the concrete sense of "construction."

edificio / edifice *Edificio* refers to any kind of construction. *Edifice*, on the other hand, refers only to important, large buildings. *Edifice*, as well as *edificio*, may be used to refer to ideas, studies, science. La catedral de Notre Dame es un **edificio** impresionante. *The cathedral of Notre Dame is an impressive edifice.*

editar / edit *Editar* is not "to edit" but "to publish." ¿Quién **editó** ese libro? *Who published that book?* To *edit* means *dirigir* (a newspaper), *redactar* (articles), *preparar* or *corregir* (i) (text, books). una versión **preparada** del discurso / *an edited version of the speech*

editor / editor *Editor* (m.) in Spanish means "publisher." *Editor* in English means *director* (m.; of a newspaper), *anotador* (m.) or *compilador* (m.; of books). Don Carlos es el **director** del periódico. *Don Carlos is the editor of the newspaper.* Don Wadley es **anotador** de libros. *Don Wadley is a book editor.*

editorial / editorial *Una editorial* (f.) is a "publishing house." *Editorial* (m.) *(artículo de fondo)* means "editorial" in the sense of "leading article" or "opinion article." [The latest dictionary of the *Real Academia* recognizes the term *un editorial* as an alternative to *artículo de fondo*, the "editorial" of a newspaper.]
casa editora (editorial) = *publishing house*
El **editorial** (artículo de fondo) es un ataque contra el terrorismo. *The editorial (leading article) is an attack on terrorism.*

educación / education *Educación* shares with *education* the idea of "instruction, schooling, learning." However, *educación* goes beyond school to mean "manners, politeness, breeding." Es importante invertir dinero en la **educación** para un futuro mejor. *It's important to invest money in education for a better future.* La buena **educación** hace al hombre. *Good manners make the man.* ¡Qué falta de **educación!** *How rude!* No tienen **educación.** *They have no manners.* **Educado** translates as "educated" ("learned, schooled"), as well as "well-mannered, refined, polite." *Educar,* similarly, means "to educate" (in school) and also "to raise or rear, to bring up, to train (a voice), to develop (taste)." La viuda **educó** bien a sus hijos. *The widow raised her children well.*

efectivo / effective *Efectivo* does not mean "effective"; rather, it means "true, real, actual, permanent (job)." As a noun, *efectivo* means "cash, assets."
hacer efectivo = *to cash*
pagar en efectivo = *to pay in cash*
No sabemos la causa **efectiva** del SIDA. *We do not know the **true** cause of AIDS.* *Effective* means *eficaz, impresionante, vigente* (in force), *disponibles* (troops). la fecha **vigente** de una factura / *the **effective** date of an invoice* Hay muchas tropas **disponibles.** *There are many **effective** (available) troops.* Esas píldoras son muy **eficaces.** *Those pills are very **effective.*** La ley entró **en vigor.** *The law became **effective** (went into effect).* *Efectivamente* means "really, actually, in fact." *Effectively* means *eficazmente, con provecho.*

eficiente, eficaz / efficient *Eficiente* means "efficient," but it is only used with people. *Eficaz* means "efficacious" with things and "efficient" with people. [The difference between *eficaz* and *eficiente* is that the first refers to people and things, and the latter refers only to people. Furthermore, *eficaz* stresses the effect or result, whereas *eficiente* stresses the cause producing an effect.] Me gusta porque es una secretaria **eficaz.** *I like her because she is an **efficient** secretary.*

egregio / egregious *Egregio* does not mean "egregious." *Egregio* means "eminent, illustrious, extraordinary"—all as positive values in a person.
una obra egregia = *an illustrious work*
Benjamín Franklin fue un hombre **egregio** en los Estados Unidos. *Benjamin Franklin was an **eminent** man in the United States.* *Egregious* used to have the same meaning as *egregio,* but it has downgraded its denotation to mean the opposite: *notoriamente malo, atroz* or *enorme* (error), *notable* (wicked person). El sargento cometió errores **notables** y fue degradado. *The sergeant committed **egregious** errors and was demoted.*

ejecutor / executor *Ejecutor* (m.; *verdugo*) is not "executor" but is "executioner." El **ejecutor** dejó caer la guillotina. *The **executioner** let the guillotine fall. Executor* is a term used in law for *albacea* or *testamentario* ("person in charge of carrying out a will"). El juez lo nombró **albacea** del niño. *The judge named him **executor** for the child.*

ejemplar / exemplar *Ejemplar* (m.) is not "exemplar" but "copy, sample" (of a book, magazine, a specimen, an example). As an adjective *ejemplar* means "exemplary." una tirada de diez mil **ejemplares** / *a run of ten thousand copies* un **ejemplar** magnífico de mariposa / *a magnificent **example** (specimen) of a butterfly* un marido **ejemplar** / *an **exemplary** husband Exemplar,* on the other hand, means *ejemplo, modelo.* Es un buen **modelo.** *He is a good **exemplar** (model).*

ejercer / exercise *Ejercer* shares with *to exercise* the idea of "to use one's right, authority," but *ejercer* also means "to practice (a profession), to exert (power)."
ejercer el derecho del voto / *to exercise* the right to vote Es médico, pero no **ejerce** porque se dedica a la literatura. *He is a doctor, but he doesn't practice because he dedicates himself to literature.* To exercise has the additional meaning of *hacer ejercicio, ejercitar.*
ejercitar la caridad = *to exercise charity*
Ella **hace ejercicio** por la mañana. *She exercises in the morning.*

elaboración / elaboration *Elaboración* shares with *elaboration* the meaning of "manufacture, making, preparation, production."
elaboración de la miel = *honey production*
Elaboration also stands for *explicación detallada, trabajo detallado, decoración.* Ese tema necesita una **explicación** más completa. *That point requires a more thorough elaboration. Elaborar,* similarly, means "to elaborate" in the sense of "to manufacture, process, prepare, make." En Brasil **elaboran** muchos zapatos. *In Brazil they manufacture many shoes. To elaborate means explicar, desarrollar, ampliar. Elaborado* translates as "manufactured, processed, prepared, made."
elaborado en España = *made in Spain*
Elaborate means *detallado, suntuoso, acicalado* (style). Es un trabajo muy **detallado.** *It's a very elaborate piece of work.*

elación / elation *Elación (altivez, f.)* is not "elation" but "pride, haughtiness, pomposity (of style)." [Note that *elación* is a rather literary term in Spanish and is not used much in everyday speech.] Todos odian al supervisor por su **elación** (altivez). *Everybody hates the supervisor for his haughtiness. Elation,* on the other hand, conveys a very positive feeling: *alegría, júbilo, regocijo.* Siente gran **júbilo** porque ganó las elecciones. *He feels great elation because he won the election.*

elección / election *Elección* is "election" (for public office), as well as "selection, choice." The plural *elecciones* is used for "election" (singular).
elecciones generales = *general election*
Me gusta la **elección** de carrera que hiciste porque tiene futuro. *I like the career choice you made because there is a future in it.* Tenemos **elecciones** generales cada cuatro años. *We have a general election every four years.*

elemental / elemental *Elemental* shares with *elemental* the meaning of "elementary, basic, fundamental."
Eso es elemental. = *That's basic (elementary).*
Es una gramática **elemental,** pero bastante completa. *It's a basic (fundamental) grammar, but quite complete. Elemental* also translates as *ecológico, de la naturaleza,* in the sense of "a force of nature, of the elements." En las montañas hay que combatir las fuerzas **de la naturaleza.** *In the mountains, it's necessary to combat the elemental forces.*

elevador / elevator *Elevador* (m.) has been "elevator" in parts of Latin America since the time the machine was invented; however, in Spain and other Latin American countries, *ascensor* (m.) is the commonly used term. [The *Real Academia* has not included *elevador* in its latest dictionary, but the term appears in many other dictionaries.] En casos de emergencia no se puede usar el **elevador** (ascensor). *The elevator cannot be used in case of emergency.*

embarazada / embarrassed   *Embarazada* is not "embarrassed" but "pregnant." Hace dos meses que está **embarazada**. *She has been pregnant for two months. Embarrassed* is translated as *confuso, desconcertado, turbado.* Quedé **confuso** al hacer el error. *I was embarrassed when I made the mistake.* José está mal de dinero. *Joe is financially embarrassed. Embarazar* means "to make pregnant." *To embarrass* translates as *poner en un aprieto, turbar, pasar vergüenza, tener* (ie) *apuros.* ¡No me **pongas en apuros**! *Don't embarrass me!*

embarcación / embarcation   *Embarcación* is not "embarcation" but "boat, ship." *La pinta* era una **embarcación** pequeña. *The Pinta was a small ship. Embarcation* means *embarco* (persons) or *embarque* (m.; things or people).
tarjeta de embarque = *boarding (embarcation) pass*
El **embarco** en el ferry duró media hora. *The embarcation of the ferry lasted half an hour.*

embargo / embargo   *Embargo* stands for "embargo" as "an official prohibition for ships, articles, etc." In Spanish, *embargo* is used for the official action of "seizure, sequestration, distraint (of goods)."
sin embargo = *however*
Hay un **embargo** internacional de drogas. *There is an international embargo on drugs.* El capitán ordenó el **embargo** de ese carro. *The captain ordered the seizure of that car.*

emergencia / emergence, emergency   *Emergencia* means "emergence" ("rising from, coming out from") and "emergency" ("a sudden situation requiring immediate action"). *Emergencia* and *emergency* share the same meaning of "critical situation": *salida, estado, solución.* [The *Real Academia* states that *emergencia* means a simple *ocurrencia,* not necessarily a critical situation. In this case, *emergencia* is translated as "incident, happening." In Spanish *urgencia* is used for *emergencia* in hospitals.]
aterrizaje de emergencia = *emergency landing*
Llegué tarde porque me ocurrió una **emergencia** inesperada. *I arrived late because I had an unexpected incident*   sala de **emergencia** (urgencia) del hospital / *hospital emergency room*   en caso de **emergencia** / *in case of emergency*

emisión / emission   *Emisión* is "emission" ("the escape of gases, etc."), but in Spanish, *emisión* also means "broadcasting" in general, "broadcast" ("a program") and "issue" (of paper, money, stamps, bonds). Muchas fábricas tienen que eliminar la **emisión** de gases tóxicos. *Many factories have to stop the emission of toxic gases.* ¿De qué año es la **emisión** de los billetes de dos dólares? *What year was the issue of the two-dollar bills?* La **emisión** de noticias por televisión es muy importante. *Broadcasting the news on television is very important.*

emoción / emotion   *Emoción* is exactly "emotion" ("feeling"). Hispanics take this feeling to a high degree, so *emoción* should be translated as "thrill, excitement."

¡Qué **emoción** volver a ver a mi abuelo! *What a **thrill** to see my grandfather again!* Los comediantes juegan con **emociones.** *Comedians play with human **emotions.*** ***Emocionante*** means "emotional" as "touching, moving" *(conmovedor)*, and good translations are "thrilling, exciting." El juego de fútbol fue muy **emocionante.** *The soccer game was very **exciting.*** *Emotional*, whenever the idea of *emoción* applies to people, is translated as *emotivo, impresionable, sensible* (to emotions). Ella es una persona muy **emotiva.** *She is a very **emotional** person.*

emplear / employ *Emplear* shares with *to employ* the idea of "to use people and time," but *emplear* also has the meanings of "to use (tools, machines, words), to invest (money)."
emplear mal = *to misuse*
Empleo (uso) la computadora para escribir cartas comerciales. *I **use** the computer to write business letters.* ¿**Empleas** tu dinero en la banca o en la bolsa de valores? *Do you **invest** your money in banking or in the stock market? **Empleado*** is equivalent to "employee," but in English *clerk* is commonly used for office and bank employees.
empleado del estado = *state employee, civil servant*
Ha sido **empleado** fiel de este banco por veinte años. *He has been a faithful **clerk** (employee) of this bank for twenty years.*

encantar / enchant *Encantar* is "to enchant," meaning "to bewitch, cast a spell," as well as "to delight, like, charm." Me **encanta** viajar por México. *I **love** (like) to travel in Mexico. **Encanto,*** similarly, means "enchantment" and also "charm, delight, magic."
como por encanto = *as if by magic*
La casa es un **encanto.** *The house is a **dream.*** ¡Qué **encanto** tiene esta mujer! *What **charm** this woman has! **Encantado*** means "enchanted" ("haunted"), as well as "delighted, pleased" (for example, on being introduced to a stranger). Estoy **encantado** con tu regalo. *I am **delighted** with your gift.*

encontrar / encounter *Encontrar(se)* (ue) is not "to encounter" but "to find, come across, meet, think of (seem)." **Encontré** un dólar a la entrada del banco. *I **found** a dollar bill at the bank entrance.* Acabo de **encontrar** a Juan en el club. *I just **met** John at the club. To encounter* means *tropezar* (ie) *con* ("to meet by chance"), *enfrentarse a, luchar contra.* En todos los negocios uno **se enfrenta** con dificultades. *One **encounters** problems in all kinds of businesses.*

endosar / endorse *Endosar* (there's no *r* in Spanish before the *s*) is "to endorse" (checks or documents). Para cobrar el cheque tienes que **endosarlo.** *You have to **endorse** the check to cash it. To endorse* is also used with people to mean *respaldar* or *apoyar* (a candidate, a proposition), *avalar* (a bill), *aceptar, escribir* (a license), *visar* (a passport). El cónsul **visó** el pasaporte. *The consul **endorsed** the passport.* El sindicato **respalda** al candidato demócrata porque promete ayudar a los obreros. *The union **endorses** the democratic candidate because he promises to help workers. **Endoso*** is "endorsement" (checks). *Endorsement* also means *respaldo* or *apoyo, aval* (m.), *aprobación, visado.*

energía / energy *Energía* is "energy" (electric, atomic, of a person, etc.), but *energía* usually indicates a greater degree of *energy* in reference to people. Good translations are "vigor, stamina, spirit *(ánimo)*." Aunque es viejo tiene mucha **energía.** *He has* **stamina** *in spite of his age.* **Enérgico** is "energetic" and sometimes more than that: "forceful (decision); vigorous, strenuous; firm." El gerente de la compañía debe ser **enérgico** para tener éxito. *The company manager must be firm (forceful) to succeed.* **Energético** is used as a noun with the meaning of "fuels, energy, power." Los **energéticos** son muy importantes ahora. *Fuels are very important nowadays.*

énfasis / emphasis *Énfasis* (m.) and *emphasis* both refer to "phonetic stress, importance, insistence." The *Real Academia* only accepts *énfasis* as "phonetic emphasis," but other dictionaries identify *énfasis* with *importancia, insistencia, hincapié* (m.), in other words, the "accepted" meaning of *emphasis* in English. Fidel usa demasiado **énfasis** en sus discursos para impresionar. *Fidel tries to impress in his speeches by using too much* **emphasis.** **Enfático** is translated as "emphatic" with all its connotations. El candidato es muy **enfático** (categórico) en sus ideas. *The candidate is very* **emphatic** *in his ideas.* **Enfatizar** is used for "to emphasize." [There is no doubt that *emphasis, emphatic,* and *to emphasize* are used very much in English, much more than their Spanish cognates. Other terms in Spanish that convey the same meaning include *hincapié, hacer hincapié, categórico, decidido.*]

enfermo / infirm *Enfermo* is not "infirm" but "sick, ill." Están **enfermos** por comer demasiado. *They are* **sick** *because they ate too much. Infirm* means *enfermizo, débil* (physically), and in a figurative sense, *indeciso, irresoluto.* El niño es **enfermizo** de nacimiento. *The child has been* **infirm** *since birth.*

engrosar / engross *Engrosar (engruesar)* is not "to engross" but "to increase, enlarge, get fatter, put on weight, swell (a river)." Si comes mucho vas a **engrosar** demasiado. *If you eat a lot, you will* **become** *too fat. To engross* means *absorber* (attention) and, less commonly, *copiar, pasar a limpio* (letters, papers). La lectura de la novela le **absorbió** la atención. *Her attention was* **engrossed** *in reading the novel.*

enrollar / enroll *Enrollar* does not mean "to enroll"; rather, it means "to roll up, wind, coil, wrap up." Me **enrollé** las mangas de la camisa. *I* **rolled up** *my shirtsleeves. To enroll* stands for *inscribir* or *apuntar* (in a list), *matricularse* (in school), *alistarse* (in the army). Ella **se matriculó** en cinco asignaturas. *She* **enrolled** *in five courses.* Muchos hispanos **se alistan** en las fuerzas armadas de EE.UU. para poder estudiar. *Many Hispanics* **enroll** *(enlist) in the U.S. armed forces to be able to study.* [According to the *Real Academia, enrolar* is used only "to enroll the crew of a ship" and *enrolarse* is "to enroll in the army or politics." Other dictionaries do not mention this verb.]

ensayo / essay *Ensayo* translates as "essay" ("composition") and also "test (tube), rehearsal."
tubo de ensayo = *test tube*
En el teatro se necesitan muchos **ensayos** para tener éxito. *You need many* **rehearsals** *to succeed in the theater.* Muchos profesores piden **ensayos** para sus asignaturas.

*Many professors require **essays** for their courses. Essay* is also used in school to refer to *composición, redacción,* and in everyday life, *tentativa, intento.* ***Ensayar*** shares all the meanings of *to essay,* and it also means "to rehearse."

entender / intend   *Entender* (ie) is not "to intend" but "to understand, mean (to say)."

entender mal = *to misunderstand*
dar a entender = *to hint*
no entender ni jota = *not to understand a thing*
Entiendo perfectamente tu opinión. *I **understand** your opinion perfectly.* ¿Qué **entiende** usted por esa palabra? *What do you **mean** by that word? To intend* means *querer* (ie) *hacer, tener la intención de, pensar* (ie) or *esperar* (+ verb). *Espero graduarme de español en dos años si todo va bien. I **intend** to graduate (with a major) in Spanish in two years if everything goes right.*

entero / entire   *Entero* means "entire" in the real sense of "full, complete, all, whole." *Entero* also applies to people, meaning "honest, upright, strong, fair," and in some countries, "look-alike, identical." *Entero* means "uncastrated" when applied to animals. In a humoristic sense, *entero* means "virginal" (a person).

por entero = *entirely*
el mundo entero = *the whole world*
número entero = *whole number* (in mathematics)
*Siempre se portó como un hombre **entero**. He always behaved like an **honest** man. La abuela tiene un carácter **entero**. The grandmother has a **strong** character.* Leo un libro **entero** cada día. *I read an **entire** book every day. Entire* also means *intacto* in certain expressions, such as "the stock is entire" (*las existencias están intactas*). **Toda** la población lo sabe. *The **entire** population knows it.*

entidad / entity   *Entidad* (f.) means "entity" in philosophy as "being, anything real." *Entidad* also stands for "association, organization, company, firm."
persona jurídica = *personal entity*
*Mesa es una **entidad** contable y oro es una **entidad** no contable. Table is a countable **entity** and gold is an uncountable **entity**.* La Cruz Roja es una **entidad** benéfica mundial. *The Red Cross is a worldwide nonprofit **organization**.*

entonar / intone   *Entonar* is "to intone" ("to sing, chant") and also "to pitch or give (a musical note)," and figuratively, "to tone up, put right, match (colors)." *La copa de ponche **me ha entonado**. The glass of punch **has put me right**.* Tienes que **entonarme** un do alto. *You have **to give** me a high "do." (musical note)* Este azul no **entona** con el rosado. *This blue doesn't **go with (match)** the pink. **Entonado*** means "intoned" ("in tune") and, in a figurative sense, "arrogant, haughty, conceited." When speaking about health, *entonado* means "on form." *La gente **entonada** no agrada a nadie. Nobody likes **arrogant** people.*

entrada / entry, entrance   *Entrada* means "entry" or "entrance" (of a building), but *entrada* is a very common word with many possible meanings, according to the context:

admission, ticket (movies, games)	beginning (of a season)
audience, house (show))	downpayment (for a car, house)
entrance (in a scene)	hall (vestibule)
entrée (in a meal)	inning (in baseball)

The plural, **entradas** is used in business to mean "earnings, receipts."

entrada general = *standing room*

entrada bruta = *gross receipts*

dar entrada a = *to lead into*

Las **entradas** para el teatro son cada día más caras. *Theater **tickets** are more expensive every day.* La película tuvo una **entrada** fantástica. *The movie had an incredible **audience.*** Hubo como cinco **entradas** en el banquete. *There were about five **entrées** at the banquet.* **entrada** del verano / *the **beginning** of summer* Se prohíbe la **entrada.** *No **admittance.***

entrar / enter *Entrar en* and *entrar a* mean the same thing: "to enter." In Spain, *entrar en* is commonly used; in Latin America, *entrar a* is used. [Note that no preposition is used in English with *to enter.*] **Entramos en** clase. **Entramos a** clase. *We **entered** the class.*

entrenar / entrain *Entrenar* is not "to entrain." *Entrenar* means "to train, coach." Lombardi **entrenó** muy bien a los Green Bay Packers para ser los campeones. *Lombardi **trained** the Green Bay Packers very well to become the champions.* *Entrain* has a very limited meaning of "to put on a train": *poner en un tren* (troops), *tomar el tren* (troops).

entretener / entertain *Entretener* stands for "to entertain," as "to amuse" *(divertir,* ei, i), but it is also used for "to keep occupied, distract, put off, delay, linger, dally." Si te **entretienes** con los libros llegarás tarde. *If you **putter around** with those books, you'll be late.* La lectura de novelas me **entretiene** más que ir al cine. *Reading novels **keeps** me better **occupied** than going to movies.* To *entertain,* in addition to its shared meaning with *entretener,* means *convidar, invitar, agasajar.* Me gusta **convidar** a los amigos. *I like to **entertain** my friends.* *Entretenimiento* is "entertainment" in the sense of *diversión, pasatiempo.* *Entertainment* also stands for *hospitalidad* (f.), *agasajo.*

envidioso / invidious *Envidioso* is not "invidious" but "envious, jealous." Los pobres suelen estar **envidiosos** de los bienes de los ricos. *The poor are usually **jealous** of rich people's wealth.* *Invidious* means *odioso, injusto, detestable.* Debe ser terrible ser **odioso** sin saberlo. *It must be terrible to be **invidious** (hateful) without knowing it.*

envolver / involve *Envolver* (ue) shares with *to involve* the idea of "to implicate, engage, include, entail." However, *envolver* also means "to wrap, surround, cover, coat." Las fresas están **envueltas** con chocolate. *The strawberries are **coated** with chocolate.* Tengo que **envolver** el regalo. *I have **to wrap** the present.* Tu amigo está **envuelto** en el robo y la va a pasar mal. *Your friend is **involved** in the robbery, and he is in big trouble.*

época / epoch *Época* shares with *epoch* the idea of "an important period in history," but *época* is also an everyday word for "time, period, season." Me gusta la **época** de Navidad porque tengo vacaciones. *I like the Christmas season because I'm on vacation.*

equidad / equity *Equidad* (f.) means "equity" ("justice, fairness"). *Equity* is also an important term in the business world, meaning *valor* (m.) *de una propiedad* (minus the mortgage) and also *acciones* ("stocks"). [In some countries, *plusvalía* is used to refer to the *equity* of a house or property.] He pedido un préstamo con el aval del **valor de mi propiedad.** *I have requested a loan against the equity of my property.*

equilibrio / equilibrium *Equilibrio* is "equilibrium" in the scientific sense used in physics, chemistry, etc. But *equilibrio* is an everyday term for "balance," for example, when walking, or "harmony." Figuratively, it means "calmness, composure."
equilibrio político = *balance of power*
hacer equilibrios = *to perform miracles* (with money)
Mantuvo **equilibrio** sobre la cuerda. *She kept her balance on the highwire.* Pudo mantener **equilibrio** en medio de la crisis. *He was able to keep his composure during the crisis.*

equipo / equipment *Equipo* means "equipment" (for lab work, sports, etc.), as well as a "team" of people, for example, in sports.
compañero de equipo = *teammate*
El **equipo** de fútbol americano es muy pesado. *Equipment for American football is very heavy.* El **equipo** ganador se llevó la copa del torneo. *The winning team walked away with the tournament cup.*

equivocación / equivocation *Equivocación* is not "equivocation" but "mistake, error, misunderstanding." Una **equivocación** puede ser cara. *A mistake can be expensive. Equivocation* is translated as *ambigüedad* (f.), *engaño*. Hay mucha **ambigüedad** en sus palabras. *There is much equivocation in his words. Equivocarse* is "to make a mistake, to be mistaken." Todo el mundo **se equivoca** alguna vez. Lo importante es reconocerlo. *Everybody makes mistakes sometimes. What matters is to recognize it. To equivocate* means *usar equívocos, confundir.*

era / era *Era* means "era" ("age, epoch"), as well as "threshing floor." In some countries *era* is used to refer to a "bed" (for flowers, etc.) *(cantero)*. La **era** de los bueyes y los trillos en la **era** ya se acabó. *The era of oxen and of harrows on the threshing floor is gone.*

ermita / hermit *Ermita* does not mean "hermit" but "hermitage, hideaway." *Ermitaño* means "hermit." El **ermitaño** vivía en el desierto cerca de una **ermita.** *The hermit used to live in the desert near a hermitage.*

errar / err *Errar* means "to err" ("to make a mistake") and also "to roam, wander, rove." In a figurative sense, it means "to miss" (the road, the target). El borracho **estuvo errando** toda la noche. *The drunk was wandering around all night long.*

errático / erratic   *Errático* is not "erratic" but "wandering, transient." *Erratic* translates as *irregular, desigual,* referring to things; *excéntrico, voluble,* referring to people.

asistencia irregular = *erratic attendance*
Sus escritos son muy buenos pero **desiguales**. *His writings are very good but erratic.* Esa señora parece un poco **excéntrica**. *That woman seems to be a little erratic.*

escabroso / scabrous   *Escabroso* shares with *scabrous* the negative denotations of "crude, dirty, risqué." *Escabroso* is also used commonly to mean "rough, uneven, rugged (terrain)," which is an uncommon usage in English and in a figurative sense, "difficult, tough, thorny." Las montañas Rocosas tienen un terreno **escabroso**. *The Rocky Mountains have a rugged terrain.* Nadie quiere enfrentar un problema **escabroso** (espinoso). *No one wants to face a tough (thorny) problem.*

escala / scale   *Escala* and *scale* share several meanings: in music, they mean "notes within an octave," and they also mean "a graduated ruler" as in a thermometer. In a figurative sense, *escala* and *scale* apply to social layers: *escala social = social scale.* In addition, *escala* means "ladder" and "stop" (during a trip). Me gustan los vuelos sin **escalas**. *I like nonstop flights.* *Scale* also refers to *balanza* (for weighing), *escama* (of a fish), *tarifa* (of prices). La **balanza** sirve para pesar. *The scale is used to weigh things.* Aunque parezca increíble, las **escamas** de sardina se usan para hacer lápiz labial. *Although it may seem incredible, sardine scales are used to make lipstick.*

escalador / escalator   *Escalador* (m.) does not mean "escalator" but "climber, scaler." *Escalator* stands for *escalera automática.* La **escalera automática** es práctica. *Escalators are practical.*

escalar / scale   *Escalar* means "to scale, climb." **Escalar** montañas es un deporte difícil. *Climbing (scaling) mountains is a difficult sport.* *To scale* also means *escamar* (fish).

escándalo / scandal   *Escándalo* and *scandal* both mean a "reproachable act, an act that shocks moral feelings." However, *escándalo* also means "noise, uproar, racket."

armar un escándalo = *to make a racket, to make a scene*
Scandal also has the meaning of *chisme* (m.), *chismorreo, habladurías.* ¿Quién empezó el **chisme**, él o ella? *Who started the scandal, he or she? Escandaloso* refers to "scandalous" and also "noisy, rowdy." Los muchachos son **escandalosos** con sus radios. *The boys with their radios are noisy. Scandalous* can also mean morally *vergonzoso.* Su conducta es muy **vergonzosa**. *His behavior is very scandalous. Escandalizar* "to scandalize, shock" (morally) and "to make a fuss, make a racket." No **escandalice** a los lectores. *Don't shock the readers.*

escapada / escapade   *Escapada* is not "escapade" but "escape, flight, breakaway (of a cyclist)." *Escapade* means *aventura.* Todo el mundo tiene sus **aventuras**. *Everybody has his or her own escapades.*

escapar / escape   *Escapar* and *to escape* mean "to flee, get out, break loose." Alguien **se escapó** de la prisión de Alcatraz. *Someone escaped from Alcatraz prison.*

To *escape* also means *evitar, eludir, rehuir.* **No recuerdo** su nombre. *His name escapes me.*

escape / escape *Escape* (m.) and *escape* mean "flight, evasion." In Spanish, *escape* also means a "leak (of gas), exhaust (fumes)."
a escape = *at full speed*
tubo de escape = *exhaust pipe*
Un **escape** de gas siempre es peligroso. *A gas **leak** is always dangerous.*

escena / scene *Escena* and *scene* share the ideas of "part of a play" and "an incident." *Escena* also means "stage" (in a theater) and, in a figurative sense, "theater" (dramatic arts).
poner en escena = *to stage a play*
El accidente fue una **escena** terrible. *The accident was a terrible **scene**.* Le gusta trabajar en la **escena**. *He likes to work on the **stage**.*

escenario / scenario *Escenario* is not "scenario" but "stage." *Scenario* means *guión* (m.; in movies) and *situación* (political, commercial, etc.). La **situación** financiera no parece buena a causa de la guerra. *The financial **scenario** doesn't look good because of the war.*

escolar / scholar *Escolar* is not "scholar" but "student, pupil, school." (*Escolar* applies both to a boy and a girl.) El profesor no es un **escolar** aunque parece muy joven. *The professor is not a **student** even though he looks very young. Scholar,* on the other hand, means *erudito, docto, sabio, investigador* (m.). La profesora es una **erudita** de renombre. *The professor is a renowned **scholar**.*

escritura / scripture *Escritura* and *scripture* are terms used to refer to the Bible, usually in the plural form. In Spanish *escritura* also refers to "handwriting, writing" and in legal terminology "deed, title deed." Tu **escritura** no es muy legible. *Your **handwriting** is not very legible.* La **escritura** de mi casa está en el banco. *The **deed** to my house is in the bank.*

escuálido / squalid *Escuálido* and *squalid* share the denotation of "filthy, foul, wretched, sordid." However, *escuálido* also means "skinny, thin." Da pena ver los niños **escuálidos** de África. *It's pitiful to see the **skinny** children in Africa.*

espada / spade *Espada* and *spade* only share their meaning in the card game. *Espada* means "sword, swordsman."
el as de espadas = *the ace of spades*
Los toreros usan la **espada** para matar el toro. *Bullfighters use a **sword** to kill the bull. Spade* is used by farmers and gardeners: *pala, laya.* llamar al pan pan y al vino vino / *to call a **spade** a **spade***

especial / especial, special *Especial* and *especial* refer to "outstanding, exceptional." *Especial* means both "especial" and "special." *Especial* and *special,* to translate accurately, become *particular, íntimo* in Spanish. *Special* is usually used for something "different, particular, unique," as well as "outstanding." Cada especia tiene su sabor **particular** (especial). *Each spice imparts its own **special** flavor.* Son amigos **íntimos** (especiales). *They are **special** friends.* ¿Qué tiene de **particular**? *What's so **special** about it?*

especie / species *Especie* (f.) and *species* are used in natural sciences to indicate "classes of plants and animals." *Especie* is also a common word for "sort, type, kind, matter." Hay varias **especies** de iguana. *There are several species of iguanas.* Se trata de otra **especie** de problema. *We are dealing with another kind of problem.*

espectáculo / spectacle *Espectáculo* exactly means "spectacle" as a "public show, pageant."
hacer un espectáculo = *to make a scene*
El fútbol es un gran **espectáculo** en los Estados Unidos. *Football is a great spectacle in the United States. Spectacles,* the plural form, is an old term for "eyeglasses": *gafas, lentes* (m.), *anteojos, espejuelos.*

esperar / expect *Esperar* and *to expect* share the idea of "to hope for" *(contar* [ue] *con, creer). Esperar* also means "to wait for, await."
estar esperando (bebé) = *to be expecting (a baby)*
Esperamos a muchos espectadores para el partido. *We **expect** a lot of spectators at the game.* **Espero** sacar un premio de la lotería. *I **hope** to win a prize in the lottery.* Te **espero** en casa. *I'll **wait for** you at home. To expect* also means *suponer.* Ella se lo **suponía** alto y rubio. *She **was expecting** him to be tall and blond.*

espina / spine *Espina (vertebral)* and *spine* are terms in anatomy: "backbone, spinal cord" *(espinazo, columna vertebral). Espina* is also an everyday word for "thorn, fish bone" and, figuratively, "difficulty." No hay rosas sin **espinas.** *There are no roses without **thorns.*** Este pescado tiene pocas **espinas.** *This fish has few **bones.*** Eso me da mala **espina.** *I don't like the **look** of that.* En la vida siempre hay **espinas.** *There are always **difficulties** in life. Spine* also means *lomo* (of a book).

espléndido / splendid *Espléndido* and *splendid* both mean "magnificent, beautiful" to describe things, entities. However, *espléndido* also refers to people with the meaning of "generous, lavish." La ceremonia de la boda resultó **espléndida.** *The wedding ceremony was **splendid.*** Los abuelos son **espléndidos** con sus nietos. *The grandparents are **generous** with their grandchildren.*

esposa / spouse *Esposa* is the female *spouse:* "wife." In Spanish, the plural *esposas* is used to mean "handcuffs." El policía puso las **esposas** al ladrón. *The police officer put the **handcuffs** on the thief. Spouse* also means *esposo* ("husband").

esposar / espouse *Esposar* means "to handcuff." Los niños traviesos **esposaron** a su tío. *The mischievous children **handcuffed** their uncle. To espouse* has two meanings: *casarse con* and, figuratively, *apoyar* (an idea), *abrazar* (a cause). Jorge **se casó** con Josefina. *George **espoused** (married) Josephine.* El patrón **apoyó** la idea del salario básico. *The boss **espoused** the idea of a minimum salary.*

estación / station *Estación* and *station* are places for catching trains, buses, etc., and also the buildings for radio and television, as well as for gasoline. *Estación,* in addition, means "season, time" *(temporada)* and "resort."
estación veraniega = *summer resort*

estación balnearia = *seaside resort*
estación emisora = *broadcasting station*
Mi **estación** preferida es el invierno. *My favorite season is winter.* Ya llegó la **estación** del béisbol. *Baseball season has arrived.* **Estacionar** stands for "to station" (troops, police) and also "to park" (cars, buses). En muchas calles no se puede **estacionar** el coche. *You cannot park your car on many streets.*

estado / estate   *Estado* is not "estate" but "state, country, government, condition" and also "status, statement (in business)." The plural *estados* translates as "lands."
estar en estado = *to be pregnant*
hombre de estado = *statesman*
El banco me mandó el **estado** de mi cuenta. *The bank sent me the statement of my account.* Su **estado** civil es soltero. *His marital status is single.* El carro no está en mal **estado** (malas condiciones), pero es muy viejo. *The car is not in bad condition (a bad state), but it is very old.* Estate, on the other hand, means *propiedad* (f.), *bienes* (m.) *raíces, finca, herencia, fortuna.*
bienes raíces = *real estate*

estampa / stamp   *Estampa* is not "stamp" but "print, engraving, picture" *(grabado)* and, in a figurative sense, "appearance, figure" (with people). The diminutive form *estampilla* means "rubber stamp" and in Latin America, "postage stamp." [The *Real Academia* recognized this meaning of *estampilla* in its latest dictionary]. Los libros modernos tienen muchas **estampas**. *Modern books have many pictures.* La novia tiene buena **estampa**. *The bride has a nice appearance.* Stamp means *sello, timbre* (m.) and *estampilla* (in the Americas). It also means *marca, huella, señal* (f.), *cuño* (of a rubber stamp). Las cartas necesitan **sellos** (estampillas) para llegar a su destino. *Letters need stamps to get to their destination.*

estándar / standard   *Estándar* (m.) has been included in the latest dictionary of the *Real Academia* with the meaning of *tipo, patrón* (m.), *modelo, nivel* (m.). In other words, it has been accepted as meaning "standard" in those senses. Todos trabajamos para alcanzar un **estándar** de vida más alto. *We all work to have a higher standard of living.* Standard also has the denotation of *estandarte* (m.; "small flag"). *Standard* is used frequently as an adjective and has different translations according to the context.
oro de ley = *gold standard*
teclado universal = *standard keyboard*
peso legal = *standard weight*
velocidad normal = *standard speed*

estimación / estimation, estimate   *Estimación* is almost exactly "estimation" in the sense of "value, esteem, regard, opinion, thinking." The main difference is that the primary meaning of *estimación* is "esteem" and the least frequent meaning is "value."
estimación propia = *self-esteem, self-respect*
Hicieron una **estimación** de mis propiedades para darme el préstamo. *They made an estimation (estimate) of my properties in order to grant me the loan.* ¿Sientes

mucha **estimación** a tus padres? *Do you feel much **respect** toward your parents?* *Estimation,* on the other hand, has the primary meaning of "value" and the least frequent meaning of "esteem." It is as though the priorities were reversed.

a mi juicio = *in my estimation*

Estimate is a noun and means *estimación* (value), *presupuesto, cálculo.*

estimar / estimate *Estimar* and *to estimate* mean "to calculate, value, esteem, respect." As in the case of the nouns, the primary meanings are reversed. El banco me **estimó** la casa en 200.000 dólares. *The bank **estimated** (assessed) my house at 200,000 dollars. Estimado* is an adjective and means "esteemed, respected." It is used in the salutation of letters to mean "dear."

Estimado señor: = *Dear Sir.*

Es uno de mis amigos más **estimados.** *He is one of my most **esteemed** friends.*

estofar / stuff *Estofar* is not "to stuff" but "to stew, to quilt." Me gusta la carne **estofada** con papas. *I like beef **stew** with potatoes. To stuff* has other denotations: *llenar* or *rellenar, meter, disecar* (animals), *atracarse* (with food).

aceitunas rellenas = *stuffed olives*

Metí mis cosas en una maleta. *I **stuffed** my things into a suitcase.*

estólido / stolid *Estólido* does not mean "stolid"; rather, it means "stupid." *Stolid* is translated as *impasible, insensible, imperturbable.* Hay personas **insensibles** al hambre. *There are persons who are **stolid** (insensitive) in the face of hunger.*

estrechar / stretch *Estrechar* is not "to stretch" but "to narrow, tighten, take in, shake (hands)." La carretera **se estrecha** en el puente. *The road **narrows** at the bridge.* Estreché la mano al banquero como si valiera un millón. *I **shook** hands with the banker as though he were worth a million dollars. To stretch* means *estirar, extender* (ie), *alargar.* Necesito **estirar** las piernas un poco. *I need **to stretch** my legs a little bit.*

estudio / studio *Estudio* and *studio* both mean "a small apartment, a room or place for filming movies or television programs or for taking pictures." In Spanish, *estudio* also means "study, survey, research."

estudio del mercado = *market survey*

estar en estudio = *to be under consideration*

¿Dónde hiciste tus **estudios** de bachillerato? *Where did you complete your high-school **studies**?*

estudioso / studious *Estudioso* and *studious* both mean "dedicated, engaged in study." *Estudioso* also means "scholar, specialist." Los **estudiosos** descubren mundos nuevos en su campo. *Scholars discover new worlds in their fields. Studious* also means *minucioso, detallado, atento* (regarding *estudio, trabajo, esfuerzo*). El profesor dio una conferencia muy **minuciosa** sobre las plantas. *The professor gave a very **studious** lecture on plants.*

estupendo / stupendous *Estupendo* and *stupendous* share the feeling of surprise: "wonderful, marvelous." *Estupendo,* however, stresses the idea of beauty with the meanings of "fantastic, great, terrific." Tengo una secretaria **estupenda.** *I have a **terrific** secretary. Stupendous,* on the other hand, seems to emphasize size or greatness, with the meanings of *prodigioso, formidable*. Tuvo que hacer un esfuerzo **formidable**. *He had to make a **stupendous** effort.*

estúpido / stupid *Estúpido* does not exactly mean "stupid." In Spanish, the term is very strong (often it's a word heard before a fight!) and is an insult. In short, it is one cognate to be avoided. *Stupid* is best translated as *tonto, absurdo,* conveying the idea of "silly." El cocinero siempre sale con sus ideas **absurdas**. *The cook always comes out with **stupid** ideas.*

etiqueta / etiquette *Etiqueta* and *etiquette* share the meaning of "social manners, rules, ceremonies." In Spanish, *etiqueta* also means "label, sticker, tag." **de etiqueta** = *formal* (dress, dance, etc.) Recibieron al presidente con mucha **etiqueta** (gala). *They entertained the president with great **ceremony** (etiquette, formality).* La **etiqueta** de la ropa te dice la talla, el precio, etc. *The **label** on clothes tells you the size, price, etc.*

evento / event *Evento* and *event* both refer to "happening" *(suceso).* [The *Real Academia* has accepted this meaning in its most recent dictionary.] In Spanish *evento* refers to everyday occurrences and should be rendered as "happening, contingency." There are other terms used for important events such as *prueba* (in sports), *encuentro* (in boxing), *suceso social* (such as a wedding), *acontecimiento*. Me ocurrió un **evento** inesperado al salir del teatro. *An unexpected **occurrence** happened when I was leaving the theater.* *Event* in English is associated with an important "happening," for example, in sports or regarding social functions. In those cases, *event* should be translated with the appropriate Spanish term (see discussion of *evento*). Ir a la ópera es un gran **acontecimiento** (evento) para nosotros. *Going to the opera is quite an **event** for us.*

eventual / eventual *Eventual* is not "eventual" but "possible, temporary, provisional, fortuitous." Debes comprar un seguro para cubrir una pérdida **eventual**. *You should buy an insurance policy to cover a **possible** loss.* *Eventual* in English means *final, definitivo*. *Eventualmente* means "fortuitously, occasionally, by chance." Lo encontré en el club **eventualmente**. *I met him at the club **by chance**.* *Eventually* translates as *finalmente, a la larga, en definitiva*. **Finalmente** llegó la lluvia tan esperada. ***Eventually** the long-awaited rain came.*

evidencia / evidence *Evidencia* and *evidence* share their meaning in the court of justice: "proof, testimony, witness." In everyday life, *evidencia* is translated as "certainty, obviousness, clearness." Llamaron a su esposa como **testigo**. *They called his wife to give **evidence**.* Puso en **evidencia** que tenía razón. *He made it **obvious** that he was right.* *Evidence* in English means *prueba, hechos, justificante* (m.). Los **hechos** prueban que tengo razón, aunque nadie quería creerme. *The **evidence** proves I'm right, although nobody wanted to believe me.* *Evidentemente* means "obviously, clearly." **Evidentemente** está enferma. ***Obviously** she is sick.* *Evidently* means *por lo visto, naturalmente, por supuesto*. **Por lo visto** no pudo venir. ***Evidently** he couldn't make it.*

exacto / exact *Exacto* means "exact, correct," as well as "punctual, sharp, right, OK." Nos encontramos en el café a las dos **exactas**. *We met at the café at two* *o'clock **sharp**.* ¿Sacó A en español? ¡**Exacto!** *Did you get an A in Spanish?* ***Great!*** *Exactamente* meant "exactly," as well as "right, OK."

exagerar / exaggerate *Exagerar* and *to exaggerate* both mean "to speak, write, act as though something is greater than it really is." The difference between the two terms is based on a cultural trait. In general, Hispanics like to *exagerar* more than Anglos do. For this reason *exagerar* actually means "to go too far with, overdo, overstate." No **exageres** el entrenamiento para los Olímpicos. *Don't **overdo** your training for the Olympics.* Exageró demasiado la importancia del uniforme. *He **overstated** the importance of the uniform.* ***Exagerado*** means "exaggerated," as well as "excessive, exorbitant, outrageous (prices)." **confianza exagerada** = *overconfidence*

exaltado / exalted *Exaltado* and *exalted* share the meaning of "praised, extolled." However, *exaltado* refers to strong passions and is better translated as "overexcited, hotheaded, excitable," and even "extremist (in politics), fanatic." Ese muchacho es muy **exaltado** en las fiestas. *That boy is very **excitable** at parties.* Entre los palestinos hay muchos **exaltados**. *There are many **extremists** among the Palestinians.* *Exalted* has a more positive denotation, such as *elevado* (style), *eminente* (person), *jubiloso, orgulloso*. Es una profesora **eminente** en su campo. *She is an **exalted** professor in her field.*

examen / exam *Examen* (m.) and *exam* (short for *examination*), similarly, are tests for students and drivers. [*Examinación* is an archaic term in Spanish.] *Exam* and *examination* in English are also translated as *reconocimiento* (by a doctor), *interrogatorio* (of a defendant), *registro* (in customs), *revisión* (of accounts), *investigación* ("inquiry"). Está haciendo **investigación** sobre las causas de pobreza. *He is conducting an **examination** of the causes of poverty.* Necesito un **reconocimiento** médico. *I need a medical **examination**.*

examinar / examine *Examinar* and *to examine* share the meaning of "to test" (in school, at the department of motor vehicles, etc.). *To examine* is widely used in English outside the school environment and includes the following meanings: *reconocer* (by a doctor), *registrar* (in customs), *revisar* (accounts), *interrogar* (a defendant), *investigar* (by a scholar). En México no siempre **registran** las maletas en la aduana. *In Mexico they don't always **examine** suitcases in customs.*

excitado / excited *Excitado* and *excited* both mean "happy, enthusiastic, warm." Está **excitado** porque se va de vacaciones. *He is **excited** because he is going on vacation.* *Excited* also means *nervioso, agitado, acalorado, emocionante*. Está **nerviosa** por la boda. *She's **excited** about the wedding.*

excitar / excite *Excitar* and *to excite* similarly share the idea of "to stimulate, arouse, get worked up (with joy)." *To excite* also means *emocionar, poner nervioso, provocar* (admiration, jealousy). La película **provocó** la admiración de todos. *The movie **excited** everyone's admiration.*

exclusivo / exclusive *Exclusivo* shares with *exclusive* the idea of "sole, one and only." José es el agente **exclusivo** de Ford en esta ciudad. *Joe is the **exclusive** (sole) Ford agent in this city.* *Exclusive* also means *selecto, cerrado, exclusivista*.   barrio

selecto / *exclusive* neighborhood sociedad **cerrada** / *exclusive society* club **exclusivista** / *exclusive club*

excusa / excuse *Excusa* does not mean "excuse" but "apology, reason." *Excuse*, on the other hand, translates as *pretexto, justificación*. Inventó un **pretexto** para hablar con ella. *He invented an excuse to speak with her.*

excusar / excuse *Excusar* and *to excuse* both mean "to try to exonerate, to apologize" *(disculpar)*. However, *excusar* is also "to avoid, dodge; to exempt (from taxes)." **Excúsame** con tu madre. *Give my apologies to your mother.*

exhibición / exhibition *Exhibición* shares with *exhibition* the idea of "a public show, display." But *exhibición* also means "showing (in movies), making visible." ¿Cuántas **exhibiciones** ha tenido esa película? *How many showings has that movie had? Exhibir* means "to exhibit" in the sense of "to show in public," as well as "to show" (a movie, anything) and figuratively, "to show off." **Exhibió** su pasaporte. *He showed his passport.* A los yupis les gustaba **exhibir** sus trajes lujosos, sus carros, todas sus cosas. *Yuppies liked to show off their elegant suits, their cars, all their belongings.*

existencia / existence *Existencia* means "existence" exactly, but the plural *existencias* stands for "stock, goods, merchandise." Las **existencias** de ropa están en el almacén. *The stock of clothing is in the warehouse.*

éxito / exit *Éxito* is not "exit" but "success, hit, outcome *(resultado)*."
exitazo = *smash hit*
Todos buscamos el **éxito** en la vida, no necesariamente dinero. *We all look for success in life, not necessarily money. Exit* is *salida*.
salida de emergencia = *emergency exit*
Exitoso means "successful" and is used frequently in most of Latin America. [The *Real Academia* did not include *exitoso* in its latest dictionary, but other dictionaries such as Larousse and Morínigo accept this term.] Las novelas de García Márquez son muy **exitosas**. *The novels of García Márquez are very successful.*

exonerar / exonerate *Exonerar* and *to exonerate* mean "to free from charges, to declare blameless," but *exonerar* also means "to dismiss, to remove (from a job)." Fue **exonerado** de su trabajo por llegar borracho. *He was dismissed from his job for arriving drunk.*

expectación / expectation *Expectación* is not "expectation" but "anticipation, excitement, suspense." La llegada del Rey Juan Carlos creó gran **expectación** en Oaxaca. *The arrival of King Juan Carlos created great anticipation in Oaxaca. Expectation*, on the other hand, means *esperanza, expectativa, previsión*. Hay grandes **esperanzas** con el nuevo presidente. *There are great expectations for the new president.*

expedición / expedition *Expedición* and *expedition* share the meaning of "journey, voyage, travel." In Spanish, *expedición* also means "dispatch, sending." La **expedición** de estas cajas debe hacerse inmediatamente. *The dispatch (sending) of these boxes must be done immediately.*

expediente / expedient *Expediente* (m.) is a noun that means "file, record, dossier." Toda la información está en tu **expediente**. *All the information is in your file.* *Expedient* is an adjective that means *conveniente, oportuno, ventajoso.* El FAX es una solución moderna muy **ventajosa** en los negocios. *The FAX is a very expedient modern solution for business.*

expedir / expedite *Expedir* (i) is not "to expedite" but "to send off, dispatch, issue." Es importante **expedir** los paquetes hoy mismo. *It's important to send the packages today.* To expedite is translated as *acelerar, facilitar, apresurar.* Es necesario **apresurar** (acelerar) ese asunto. *It's necessary to expedite that matter.*

experiencia / experience *Experiencia* and *experience* refer to "practice, knowledge." *Experiencia* is also "experiment" (in a lab, in psychology, etc.). Hacen **experiencias** con animales en el laboratorio. *They do experiments with animals in the laboratory.*

experimentar / experiment *Experimentar* means "to experiment, test, try out," as well as "to experience" (in everyday life). Estamos **experimentando** dificultades técnicas. *We are experiencing technical difficulties.*

explanar / explain *Explanar* and *to explain* have the same origin: "to make level, to make plain." However, *explanar* has kept the original meaning of "to level, make level (terrain)" and the meaning of "to explain, clear up." Tienen que **explanar** el terreno antes de construir. *They have to level the ground before they build.*

explicar / explicate *Explicar* is not "to explicate" but "to explain, to lecture." *To explicate* means *desarrollar* (an idea, a theme), *aclarar, exponer.* Permítame **desarrollar** ese concepto. *Allow me to explicate that concept.*

explotar / explode *Explotar (estallar)* and *to explode* are actions that occur with arms, tires, bombs. But *explotar* is also "to exploit (mines, fields, people), to take advantage of (people), to farm, to manage (a business)." Es muy feo **explotar** a una persona. *It is reprehensible to exploit a person.* Es necesario **explotar** la tierra. *It's necessary to farm the land.*

expreso / express *Expreso* and *express* share the meaning of "specified, said," for example, in expressions such as *por orden expresa del jefe* ("by express order of the boss"). When applied to trains, *un tren expreso* is not an *express train*; rather, it is a train with a long route that is usually far from fast. The closest equivalent of *express train* is *rápido,* which is the name of the fast train in Spain. El **rápido** llega a Barcelona en 7 horas, el **expreso** en 10. *The express train arrives in Barcelona in 7 hours, the regular train in 10.*

extemporáneo / extemporaneous *Extemporáneo* is not "extemporaneous" but "unseasonable, untimely, ill-timed, inappropriate." La respuesta del gerente fue **extemporánea**. *The manager's reply was ill-timed. Extemporaneous* means *improvisado, espontáneo.* La respuesta del gerente fue **improvisada**. *The manager's reply was extemporaneous.*

extender / extend   *Extender* (ie) and *to extend* mean "to stretch, enlarge, spread." *Extender* also means "to issue, write out, draw up." *To extend* also means *prorrogar, tender* (ie) (one's hand), *dar* (welcome or greetings). Me **prorrogaron** las vacaciones. *They* **extended** *my vacation.*

extensión / extension   *Extensión* and *extension* mean "continuation, prolongation." But *extensión* also means "area, duration, extent, expanse (of land), range (of a voice)." la **extensión** de un país   /   *the* **area** *of a country*   *Extension,* on the other hand, means *anexo* (to a building), *prórroga, aumento.* Mi despacho es un **anexo** a mi casa. *My office is an* **extension** *of my house.*   mesa **extensible**   /   *extension table*

extenuar / extenuate   *Extenuar* is not "to extenuate" but "to exhaust, weaken." *To extenuate* means *atenuar, disminuir* (a sentence or conviction). El abogado trató de **atenuar** la condena. *The lawyer tried* **to extenuate** *the sentence.* **Extenuado** describes the person who is "exhausted, weak, emaciated." El corredor estaba **extenuado** después de la carrera. *The runner was* **exhausted** *after the race.* *Extenuante* means "exhausting." *Extenuating* means *atenuante.*

extinguir / extinguish   *Extinguir* is "to extinguish" in terms of a fire, but this verb also applies to other situations. *Extinguir* also means "to wipe out (a race, an epidemic), to put down (a rebellion)." The reflexive *extinguirse* means "to die out (a fire, a rebellion), to go out (a light)." Los bomberos **extinguieron** el fuego en cuatro horas. *The fire fighters* **extinguished** *the fire in four hours.* Adolfo Hitler trató de **extinguir** al pueblo judío. *Adolph Hitler tried to* **wipe out** *(eliminate) the Jewish people.*

extra / extra   *Extra* and *extra* are both adjectives, meaning "of superior quality, best quality." *Extra* in English has become a handy word that is used for different meanings such as *de más* or *de sobra, adicional, no incluido, aparte, de recambio* or *de repuesto, suplementario.*
paga extraordinaria = *extra pay*
recargo = *extra charge*
sobrecarga = *extra weight*
He tenido varios gastos **adicionales.** *I have had several* **extra** *expenses.* Si quieres ganar **más** dinero, trabaja horas **extras.** *If you want to earn* **extra** *money, work* **extra** *hours (overtime).* Las clases de canto **no están incluidas.** *Singing lessons are* **extra.**

extravagancia / extravaganza, extravagance   *Extravagancia* is neither "extravaganza" nor "extravagance." *Extravagancia* means "oddness, wildness, nonsense, eccentricity."   La **extravagancia** del millonario no tiene explicación.   *The millionaire's* **eccentricity** *has no explanation. Extravaganza* means *variedades* (f.), *fantasía, producción musical.*   El espectáculo de aniversario era una **fantasía** musical. *The anniversary show was a musical* **extravaganza.** *Extravagance* means *derroche* (m.), *despilfarro, demasía.* Su **derroche** de dinero va más allá de la lógica. *His* **extravagance** *with money goes beyond logic.*

extravagante / extravagant   *Extravagante* is not "extravagant" but "strange, eccentric, weird." Aunque no tiene ni un centavo, su conducta es **extravagante.**

*Although he doesn't have a penny, his behavior is **weird.*** *Extravagant* has different meanings, depending on whether it applies to people or to things. Applied to people, *extravagant* means *gastador, pródigo, manirroto, derrochador.* When applied to things, it means *excesivo, exorbitante, costoso, desmedido.* Algunos millonarios son **derrochadores** de su fortuna. *Some millionaires are **extravagant** with their fortunes.* Imelda Marcos tenía la cantidad **exorbitante** de tres mil pares de zapatos. *Imelda Marcos had the **extravagant** amount of three thousand pairs of shoes.*

F

fábrica / fabric   *Fábrica* does not mean "fabric" but "factory, mill, plant."
de fábrica = *stonework*
marca de fábrica = *trademark*
Una maquiladora es una **fábrica** de EE.UU. cerca de la frontera dentro de México. *A maquiladora is a U.S. factory near the border in Mexico.* Fabric means *tejido, tela, estructura* (of a building), and in a figurative sense, *clase* (f.) or *índole* (f.; of people). Me gusta el color de esa **tela**. *I like the color of that fabric.* Hay gente de toda **índole**. *There are people of all fabrics (of society).*

fabricar / fabricate   *Fabricar* and *to fabricate* share the idea of "to build, construct." *Fabricar* also means "to manufacture, make" and, in a figurative sense, "to make up, fabricate (stories)."
fabricar una fortuna = *to make a fortune*
fabricado en España = *made in Spain*
fabricar en serie = *to mass-produce*
Se **fabrican** muchos carros en Detroit. *Many cars are manufactured in Detroit.* Es experta en **fabricar** historias. *She is an expert at fabricating stories.* To fabricate, on the other hand, has another, negative meaning: *falsificar, inventar, forjar* (documents, money). **Falsificar** dinero es contra la ley. *It's against the law to fabricate (to forge, to counterfeit) money.*

facción / faction   *Facción* and *faction* share the idea of "a group or band of people in politics, organizations, clubs, etc." In addition, the plural *facciones* means "facial features." Ganó la **facción** de la derecha. *The right-wing faction won.* La novia tiene hermosas **facciones**. *The bride has beautiful features.*

facial / facial   *Facial* and *facial* are adjectives meaning "of the face." *Facial,* in English, is also used as a noun to mean *masaje* (m.) or *limpieza facial (maquillaje,* m.). Le hicieron una **limpieza facial** para quitar las arrugas. *They gave her a facial to take the wrinkles away.*

fácil / facile   *Fácil* and *facile* both mean "easy, ready, superficial." But *fácil* is used much more frequently and with other meanings such as "likely, simple, compliant, easygoing, loose, of easy virtue." Es **fácil** que llueva mañana. *It's likely to rain tomorrow.* Eso es **fácil** de hacer. *That is easy to make.*   una persona **fácil** / *an easygoing person*

facilidad / facility   *Facilidad* (f.) and *facility* share the idea of "easiness," but *facilidad* also means "fluency (in languages), talent, simplicity, easygoing nature."
facilidad de palabra = *fluency of speech*
Tiene mucha **facilidad** para las lenguas. *He has a great talent for languages.* *Facilidades* and *facilities* are countable nouns and have different meanings. *Facilidades* stands for "means, opportunities."

facilidades de pago = *easy payments*
Facilities means *comodidades* (f.), *servicios* (public). No hay **comodidades** para comer en este tren. *There are no eating **facilities** on this train.*

facilitar / facilitate *Facilitar* is "to facilitate, to make easier," but it also means "to provide, supply, get." Le **facilité** información sobre el trabajo. *I **provided** him with information about the job.*

factoría / factory *Factoría* means "factory" according to the most recent dictionary of the *Real Academia*. Historically, *factoría* also means "trading post." Las **factorías** eran importantes en el Oeste de los Estados Unidos. ***Trading posts** were important in the Old West of the United States.*

facultad / faculty *Facultad* (f.) and *faculty* share the idea of "ability, power of the mind, authority." When the two words refer to people, their meanings differ. *Facultad* is also translated as "college" or "school" of a university and also refers to the members of that school.
Facultad de Derecho = *Law School*
No tienes **facultad** (autoridad) para hacer eso. *You don't have the **faculty** (authority) to do that. Faculty*, on the other hand, refers to the *profesorado, claustro* (of professors) of the entire university. Esta universidad tiene buen **profesorado**. *This university has a good **faculty**.*

facultativo / facultative *Facultativo* and *facultative* are adjectives for "optional, elective." In Spanish, *facultativo* is also a noun, meaning "doctor" *(médico)*, but this use is rather literary. Hay muchas asignaturas **facultativas** en la carrera. *There are many **elective** courses in the major.* El **facultativo** visita la aldea una vez al mes. *The **doctor** visits the village once a month.*

falacia / fallacy *Falacia* is not "fallacy" but "deceit, fraud." El pintor descubrió su **falacia**. *The painter discovered their **deceit**. Fallacy* means *falsedad* (f.), *sofisma, idea falsa, error* (m.). Sus sermones sobre la caridad son una **falsedad**. *His sermons on charity are a **fallacy**. Falaz* is not "fallacious" but "deceptive, deceitful, treacherous." Es obvio que el candidato hizo promesas **falaces**. *It is obvious that the candidate made **deceptive** promises. Fallacious* means *falso, erróneo, sofístico*. Ella apoyó su argumento con razonamientos **erróneos**. *She supported her argument with **fallacious** reasoning.*

falso / false *Falso* and *false* both mean "not true," but each term has additional meanings. *Falso* also means "counterfeit" (money), "fake" or "imitation" (jewels), "incorrect" (measure).
paso en falso = *false step*
falsa alarma = *false alarm*
puerta falsa = *hidden door*
Este diccionario tiene más de 2.000 **falsos** amigos (cognados). *This dictionary has more than 2,000 **false** friends (cognates). False* also means *postizo* (hair, teeth), *mal entendido* (false pride, misunderstood). salida **nula** / *false start*

falta / fault *Falta* and *fault* share the idea of "error, defect." In addition, *falta* has the basic meaning of "lack, shortage, need, absence," and in legal

terminology, "misdemeanor" *(infracción)*.
falta de víveres = *food shortage*
sin falta = *without fail*
a falta de = *lacking*
Esta composición casi no tiene **faltas** (errores). *This composition has hardly any* **faults** *(mistakes).* En el sur de California siempre hay **falta** de agua. *In southern California, there is always a water* **shortage.** *Fault* has the basic meaning of "moral error" such as *culpa, defecto* (moral), *imperfección.* Yo no tengo la **culpa** de ser gordo. *It's not my* **fault** *that I'm fat.*

faltar / fault   *Faltar* is an everyday term that is used to mean "to need, be absent, be missing." Faltó a clase como de costumbre. *He* **missed** *school as usual.* **Faltan** dos libros en la biblioteca. *Two books* **are missing** *from the library. To fault* is not used much, but it has the meaning of *criticar, tachar, echar la culpa.* No puedes **criticarlos** por querer ganar la lotería. *You can't* **fault them** *for wanting to win the lottery.*

fallar / fail   *Fallar (fracasar)* is "to fail" in the sense of "to miss, be inadequate, be a failure, be a disappointment." However, *fallar* also means "to pronounce (a sentence in court), to award (a prize)."
sin fallar = *without fail*
La electricidad **falla** a menudo en invierno. *The electricity often* **fails** *in winter.* El juez **falló** la sentencia. *The judge* **pronounced** *the sentence. To fail* is used more frequently than its Spanish cognate with connotations such as *no lograr, acabarse, debilitarse, quebrar* (ie) (in business). *To fail* (an exam) is translated as *fallar, suspender, catear,* according to different countries. **Se quebró** (rompió) el ascensor. *The elevator* **failed.** Es un músico **fracasado.** *He is a* **failed** *musician.*

familiar / familiar   *Familiar* and *familiar* share the meaning of "family, something known." In Spanish, *familiar* (m.) is also a noun, meaning "relative, member of the family," and an adjective, meaning "family, colloquial, informal."
parecido familiar = *family resemblance*
expresión familiar = *colloquial expression*
Mis **familiares** viven en España. *My* **relatives** *live in Spain. Familiar,* in English, is translated as *íntimo* or *de confianza* ("friendly"). Ella es una amiga **íntima** (de confianza). *She is a* **familiar** *friend.* [*Familiar* and *familiar* mean "known" in both languages, but the syntactic structures are different. In English *familiar* agrees with the person who is the "knower," whereas in Spanish *familiar* agrees with the thing that is "known" by the "knower": **John** is **familiar** with those books. / *Esos* **libros** *le son familiares a Juan.*]

famoso / famous   *Famoso* means "famous" as "celebrated." In colloquial speech it means "fantastic, fabulous, great." Su **famosa** respuesta fue recibida con carcajadas. *His* **fabulous** *answer was greeted with loud laughter.* Cada estrella del bulevar de Hollywood representa un personaje **famoso.** *Each star on Hollywood Boulevard represents a* **famous** *personality. Famous* colloquially means *excelente, de categoría* ("first rate").

fascinante / fascinating   *Fascinante (fascinador)* means "fascinating" as "charming, captivating." *Fascinating* in English sometimes takes on a sexual shade of meaning: *apasionante, seductor.* Esa escena de la película es **apasionante.** *That movie scene is **fascinating.*** *Fascinar* is exactly "to fascinate" in the sense of "to attract, charm, captivate." In some Latin American countries, *fascinar* is used for *gustar* ("to like, love"). Me **fascina** el helado de chocolate. *I love chocolate ice cream.* *Fascinación* likewise translates as "fascination" ("charm, allure"). [Note that in both English and Spanish, the words have lost the original meaning of "spell" *(hechizo)*, "spellbound." The *Real Academia* states that *fascinar* means "deception" in a figurative sense, but the term is almost never used with that meaning.]

fastidioso / fastidious   *Fastidioso* is not "fastidious" but "annoying, tiresome, obnoxious, irritating, tedious." un niño **fastidioso** / *an **obnoxious** child* No me gusta hacer trabajos **fastidiosos.** *I don't like to do **tedious** work. Fastidious,* on the other hand, has more positive meanings such as *delicado, exigente,* but at times it takes a downturn to mean *melindroso* or *quisquilloso.* Es un jefe **melindroso.** *He is a **fastidious** boss.* El niño es muy **delicado** en la comida. *The child is very **fastidious** with food.*

fasto / fast   *Fasto (fausto)* is a rather literary term for "important (or happy) occasion (or day)." La celebración de sus bodas de oro fue un **fasto** memorable. *The celebration of their golden wedding anniversary was a memorable **day.*** *Fast* in English means *ayuno* as a noun and *rápido* as an adverb or adjective.

fatal / fatal   *Fatal* and *fatal* share the idea of "most unfortunate, disastrous, fateful." In Spanish, *fatal* is used in colloquial speech to mean "terrible, lousy, rotten." una película **fatal** / *a **rotten** movie* mujer **fatal** / *femme **fatale** (vamp)* Estoy **fatal.** *I feel **terrible.*** Tuve un día **fatal** en la oficina. *I had a **terrible** (lousy) day at the office. Fatal,* on the other hand, also means *mortal* ("deadly").

fatalidad / fatality   *Fatalidad* (f.) is not "fatality" but "misfortune, bad luck, fate" and in a figurative sense, it conveys the idea of "disaster" *(desastre,* m.*).* Tuve la **fatalidad** de perder la cartera. *I had the **misfortune** of losing my wallet. Fatality* means *muerto, muerte* (f.), *víctima.* En la guerra siempre hay **muertos.** *There are always **fatalities** in war.*

fatiga / fatigue   *Fatiga* is almost exactly "fatigue" ("tiredness, weariness, breathing difficulty"; *cansancio*). Después de correr mucho sentimos **fatiga** (cansancio). *After running a lot, we feel **fatigued** (tired). Fatigue* also applies to the military, meaning *faena* or *fajina;* and in the plural, *fatigues* is the military uniform for the *faena.* La tela de ropa de **faena** ha pasado al mundo de la moda. *Fatigue dress material has entered the fashion world.*

fatuo / fatuous   *Fatuo* and *fatuous* are not as simple as "silly" or *necio.* In Spanish, *fatuo* seems to stress the aspect of false pride. A good translation is "conceited, too full of pride." Una persona **fatua** no razona. *A **conceited** person cannot reason. Fatuous,* on the other hand, stresses the idea of "silliness": *tonto, vano, loco.* Es un juego **vano** de palabras. *It's a **fatuous** play on words. Fatuidad* (f.), similarly, means "conceit, vanity." *Fatuity* (or *fatuousness*) refers to *tontería, necedad* (f.), *estupidez* (f.).

favor / favor *Favor* (m.) is exactly "favor," but it is also used in idiomatic expressions.
a favor de la oscuridad = *under cover of darkness*
Favorecer means "to favor." *To favor*, however, also means *apoyar, preferir* (ie, i), *regalar (obsequiar), parecerse a.* El senador **apoya** su nombramiento. *The senator **favors** her appointment.* El hijo menor **se parece a** su madre. *The younger son **favors** his mother.*

felón / felon *Felón* is not "felon" but "treacherous, villainous, perfidious." No me gustaría tener un amigo falso, **felón.** *I wouldn't like to have a false, **treacherous** friend. Felon* means *criminal* (m.), *ladrón* (m.).

felonía / felony *Felonía* is not used in a court of law but in everyday life with the meaning of "betrayal, treachery, perfidy." Esa telenovela trata de una **felonía** entre amigos. *That soap opera deals with a **betrayal** between friends. Felony* is used basically in court to mean *crimen* (m.), *delito grave.* Una felonía puede resultar en un **delito grave.** *A treachery may result in a **felony.***

férula / ferrule, ferule *Férula* or *palmeta* used to be the "cane" or "ferule" used by school-teachers to punish their students. Nowadays, the term is used in the figurative sense of "authority, rule." El muchacho está bajo la **férula** estricta de su padre. *The boy is under the strict **rule** of his father. Ferrule* means *regatón* (m.; "the metal tip of a cane or umbrella"), *abrazadera* or *virola* ("a ring on a tool or a pole").

feudo / feudal, feud *Feudo* and *feudal* both are historical and very old terms. The Spanish is not used anymore, except to refer to the old feudal system. *Feud*, however, is more than a historical term. It is used nowadays to mean *odio* or *enemistad hereditaria.*
peleado a muerte con = *at feud with*
Las dos familias tienen una vieja **enemistad** a causa de límites de las fincas. *Both families have an old **feud** because of the ranch boundaries.*

fiero / fiery *Fiero* is not "fiery" but "ferocious, wild, cruel." Los coyotes son muy **fieros.** *Coyotes are very **ferocious.** Fiery* has several meanings, such as *ardiente, apasionado, encendido* (eyes), *picante* (food), *acalorado* (discussion), *fogoso* (temper), *abrasador* (sun). ¡Qué ojos más **encendidos!** *What **fiery** eyes!* Ella tiene un carácter **fogoso.** *She has a **fiery** temper.* Hoy hace un sol **abrasador.** *Today we have a **fiery** sun.*

fiesta / fiesta, feast *Fiesta* and *fiesta* refer to a "religious festival, a holiday." In Spanish, *fiesta* has other denotations such as "party, ceremony" and in a figurative sense, "treat." The plural *fiestas* is "celebrations, festivities, holidays" and in a figurative sense, "flattering words."
aguar la fiesta = *to be a party pooper*
En Madrid se celebran las **fiestas** de San Isidro por dos semanas. *In Madrid they celebrate the **festival** of San Isidro for two weeks.* Tu carta fue una **fiesta** para mí. *Your letter was a **treat** for me. Feast* not only means *fiesta* but also *banquete* (m.), *festín* (m.). Los convidados tuvieron un **banquete** tradicional. *The guests had a traditional **feast** (banquet).*

figura / figure   *Figura* and *figure* share the meaning of "picture" (of a person). *Figura* also means "shape" or "form," "personality." La **figura** de Don Quijote es universal. *The figure of Don Quijote is universal.* ¿Qué **figura** tiene ese animal raro? *What shape is that strange animal?* Figure also means *cifra* or *número, suma* or *cantidad* (f.; in business), *línea* (of the body).

guardar la línea = *to keep one's figure*

Los **números** no engañan, pero los mentirosos pueden figurarlo. *Figures don't lie, but liars can figure.*

figurar / figure   *Figurar* means "to figure" in the sense of "to act, be, appear on, imagine." But *figurar* also means "to simulate, feign, be important, show off" *(presumir).* Su nombre no **figura** en la nómina. *Your name doesn't figure (appear) on the payroll.* Le gusta **figurar** en las fiestas. *He likes to show off at parties.*

figurativo / figurative   *Figurativo* and *figurative* both are used for a type of concrete art as opposed to abstract art. *Figurative* also means *figurado* in the expression *sentido figurado* ("figurative sense").

figurín / figurine   *Figurín* (m.) is not "figurine" but "fashion, design, small model, sketch" and in a figurative sense, "dandy, fop" *(elegantón,* m.). Le gusta ser siempre el **figurín** de la fiesta. *He always likes to be the dandy at the party.* Me gusta ese **figurín.** *I like that fashion design. Figurine,* on the other hand, means *estatuilla, figurilla.* Las **figurillas** de Lladró son famosas en todo el mundo. *Lladro's figurines are famous all over the world.*

fila / file   *Fila* and *file* share the meaning of "a line or row (of people)." *Fila* also means "rank" (military). In Spain, the plural *filas* is a colloquial term for "military service."

fila india = *Indian file*

ponerse en fila = *to line up*

Se sentó en la primera **fila** del teatro. *He sat in the first row of the theater.*   estar en **filas** / *to be in the army* File means *lima* (for fingernails, for metal), *carpeta, expediente* (m.), *archivo, fichero, archivador* (m.; "file cabinet").

ficha personal = *personal file*

Tu **expediente** no está completo. *Your file is not complete.*   **archivos** de la policía / *police files*

final / final   *Final* and *final* share the basic idea of "last." In Spanish, *final* (m.) is a noun, meaning "end" *(fin,* m.*),* and can be used in everyday speech to mean the "end" of anything. *La final* (f.) is used in sports to mean "the last game" of any tournament.

la final de copa = *the cup final*

¿Quién ganó **la final** de fútbol? *Who won the final soccer game?*   el **final** de la película / *the end of the movie*   Final in English also means *decisivo, terminante* as an adjective and *fin* or *final* as a noun, but it is used only in sports and to refer to the last edition of a daily newspaper. The plural *finals* refers to *exámenes finales.* In English, *finale* translates as *final* (m.) or *escena final* (in the theater, musicals).

y **sanseacabó** = *and that's final*
Su decisión es **terminante**. *His decision is final.*

finalidad / finality *Finalidad* (f.) is not "finality" but "goal, objective, purpose, aim." ¿Con qué **finalidad** trabajas tanto? *What's the purpose of your hard work?* *Finality* stands for *determinación, carácter definitivo.* Lo declaró con **determinación**. *He declared it with finality.* El proyecto tiene **carácter definitivo**. *The project has finality.*

fineza / finesse *Fineza* and *finesse* have something in common—"delicacy" *(delicadeza).* In Spanish *fineza* means "delicacy" as "compliment, kindness, courtesy," and sometimes as "gift, present." Debemos tratar siempre a los clientes con **fineza**. *We must always treat the customers with kindness.* Finesse means *diplomacia, tacto,* but the term has downgraded its connotation to mean *estratagema* or *treta* ("trick") and even *astucia* ("cunning").

fino / fine *Fino* and *fine* mean "good quality, polite, thin, pure" but their meanings differ according to context. *Fino* also means "keen, sharp (senses), subtle (humor), elegant, choice (material), dry (sherry)."
piedra fina = *semiprecious stone*
oído fino = *keen hearing*
Fine also means *agradable* (feeling), *magnífico, ligero* or *sutil* (difference).
¡Estupendo! = *Fine!*
Hizo un trabajo **excelente** en la cocina. *He did a fine job in the kitchen.* El muchacho es **buen** mozo. *The young man is a fine fellow.*

firma / firm *Firma* and *firm* are both important terms in business for "company" (a commercial enterprise). However, *firma* also means "signature, (the act of) signing." The adjective *firme* translates the English "firm."
firma en blanco = *blank signature*
Una **firma** comercial es una empresa. *A commercial firm is a company.* Esta **firma** es ilegible. *This signature is not legible.*

fiscal / fiscal *Fiscal* and *fiscal* are adjectives to refer to "public treasury" *(fisco).* In Spanish, the noun *fiscal* (m.) also means "district attorney." In colloquial speech *fiscal* is used to refer to a "snooper" *(entremetido).*
año económico = *fiscal year*
El **fiscal** es un hombre muy ocupado. *The district attorney is a very busy man.* María es **la fiscal** del barrio. *Mary is the neighborhood snoop.*

físico / physique, physical, physician *Físico* and *physique* both mean "form, appearance of the body" as nouns. *Físico* also means "physicist" and, as an adjective, it means "physical" (either related to the body or to physics). ¿Qué **físico** ganó el premio Nobel este año? *What physicist won the Nobel prize this year?* El muchacho tiene un **físico** agradable, por eso me gusta. *The boy has a nice physique (appearance), that's why I like him.* *Physical* is *examen físico* (medical) as a noun, but it has downgraded its meaning as an adjective to refer to *violento, agresivo.*
fisioterapia = *physical therapy*

El juego se puso **violento** al final y hubo dos heridos. *The game turned **physical** toward the end, resulting in two injuries. **Physician** is another term for médico.*

flamante / flaming *Flamante* is an old term for "flaming" ("blazing"). Nowadays it means "splendid, magnificent." Acabo de comprar un coche **flamante**. *I just bought a **magnificent** car.* Flaming is translated as *llameante, abrasador,* and in a figurative sense, *apasionado, ardiente.* Tienen un romance **apasionado**. *They are having a **flaming** affair. Flamear* stands for "to flame, blaze, burn" and also for "to flutter" (a flag). Actually, *flamear* is used in the culinary arts to mean "to flame." La bandera **flamea** al viento. *The flag is **fluttering** in the wind. Flameado* translates as "flambé" (in the kitchen). Comí una tarta **flameada**. *I ate a tart **flambé**.*

flauta / flute *Flauta* means "flute" (the musical instrument) and also "baguette" (of bread) in Spain. Si vas a la panadería, me traes dos **flautas**. *If you go to the bakery, bring me two **baguettes**. Flute* also means *estría* (of glass).

flete / fleet *Flete* (m.) is not "fleet" but "freight, cargo" and also "charter" (vehicle). El importador generalmente paga el **flete**. *Generally the importer pays for the **freight**.* El avión de **flete** llevaba a los turistas a la costa. *The **charter** plane was carrying the tourists to the coast. Fleet* means *flota* as a noun and *ligero, veloz* as an adjective.

flota / float *Flota* is not "float" but "fleet" (of boats, vehicles). *Float* means *carroza* (in a parade), *paso* (in a religious procession), *flotador* (m.; in liquids). Pasadena es famosa por sus **carrozas** enormes de flores y rosas. *Pasadena is famous for its huge **floats** of flowers and roses.*

fluido / fluid *Fluido* and *fluid* are adjectives and nouns, and they have the same meaning. However, *fluido* also means "fluent, flowing" to refer to languages, style, etc. Se lee bien porque tiene un estilo **fluido**. *He is easy to read because of his **flowing** style.*

foco / focus *Foco* and *focus* mean "center of attention or activities." In Spanish *foco* is also "spotlight, light bulb." (In some countries, *bombillo* and *bombilla* are used for "light bulb.") The verb "to focus" translates as *enfocar, concentrar.* Hollywood es siempre el **foco** de atención de periodistas. *Hollywood is always the **focus** of attention for reporters.* Necesito un **foco** pequeño para el horno. *I need a small **bulb** for the oven.* **Enfocó** el problema desde otro punto de vista. *He **focused** on the problem from another angle.*

follaje / foliage *Follaje* (m.) and *foliage* are both defined as a "mass of leaves, leafage." In Spanish, *follaje* sometimes means "gaudy ornaments" and figuratively "verbiage, verbosity." Me gusta el **follaje** tropical. *I like tropical **foliage**.* Esa novela tiene demasiado **follaje**. *That novel has too much **verbiage**.*

forjar / forge *Forjar* is "to forge" (as a blacksmith does) and also "to make, build up (dreams), coin (words, expressions)," and in a figurative sense, "to fabricate, make up (lies, excuses)."
hierro forjado = *wrought iron*

Rubén Darío **forjó** muchas palabras. *Rubén Darío coined many words.* *To forge,* on the other hand, also means *falsificar* (money, a signature, etc.). Alguien ha **falsificado** esta firma. *Someone has forged this signature.*

forma / form *Forma* almost exactly means "form."
no hay forma = *there is no way*
Form is also used to mean the paper or document that one fills out for almost everything: *formulario, modelo, planilla, impreso.* Favor de rellenar este **formulario** con letra de molde. *Please print when filling out this form.*

formación / formation *Formación* and *formation* both refer to "form" in general. In Spanish, *formación* also refers to "education, training, personal development." Sin **formación** universitaria no es fácil triunfar. *It is not easy to succeed without a college education.*

formal / formal *Formal* does not mean "formal" but "reliable, dependable, serious-minded, correct"; and the term only applies to people. Es una muchacha **formal** y aplicada. *She is a serious and studious girl.* *Formal* in English describes both people and things. With people, it means *formalista, ceremonioso, grave, solemne.* With things, it means *solemne, ceremonioso, de cumplido, de etiqueta.*

formalidad / formality *Formalidad* (f.) means "formality" as a "routine" and it also means "reliability, seriousness, good behavior." Todos cuentan con la **formalidad** del gerente. *Everyone counts on the reliability of the manager.* *Formality* also means *ceremonia, etiqueta, trámite* (m.). Hay que pasar por muchos **trámites** para entrar. *One must go through a lot of formalities to get in.*

formidable / formidable *Formidable* and *formidable* share the idea of "fearful enormity." But each culture interprets this idea in its own way. In Spanish *formidable* stresses the feeling of surprise and quality: "marvelous, terrific, fantastic."
¡Formidable! = *Great!*
Es un jugador **formidable** de fútbol. *He is a fantastic soccer player.* *Formidable* in English emphasizes fear and difficulty: *terrible, alarmante, aterrorizante, impresionante.* El terremoto causó unos daños **terribles.** *The earthquake caused formidable damage.*

fósforo / phosphorus *Fósforo* and *phosphorus* both stand for the same chemical. In Spanish *fósforo* is used in some countries to mean "match" ("light"). In other countries the words *cerilla* (Spain), *cerillo* (Mexico), and *mixto* (Spain) are used.

fracaso / fracas *Fracaso* is not "fracas" but "failure." Los **fracasos** son lecciones para el futuro para quienes quieran aprender. *Failures are lessons for the future for those who want to learn.* *Fracas* (plural, *fracases*) means *pelea, riña, alboroto.* Los iraquíes armaron una **pelea** terrible. *The Iraquis started a terrible fracas.*

franco / frank *Franco* and *frank* share the idea of "sincere, candid, open." In Spanish, *franco* also means "free, exempt (from taxes)."
franco a bordo = *free on board*
puerto franco = *free port*

El candidato parece **franco** cuando habla. *The candidate seems to be **frank** when he speaks.* ***Franqueza*** translates as "frankness, openness, candor." Me gusta su **franqueza.** *I like his **openness.***

franquicia / franchise   *Franquicia* means "franchise" in the sense of "exemption, immunity" (from customs, postage charges). Los diplomáticos tienen **franquicia** aduanera. *Diplomats have a customs **franchise** (exemption). Franchise* also means a "right or special privilege" such as *derecho de voto,* and in business it translates as *concesión, licencia.* Para comprar una **concesión** como McDonald's necesitas mucho dinero. *To buy a **franchise** such as McDonald's, you need a lot of money.*

fraternidad / fraternity   *Fraternidad* (f.) is "fraternity" and "brotherhood." *Fraternity* also refers to an association of male university students and means *hermandad* (f.), *cofradía, club* (m.). Las universidades de Estados Unidos tienen **hermandades.** *Universities in the United States have **fraternities.** Fraternal* is translated as both *fraternal* and *fraterno. Fraternal* refers to the typical qualities of a brother (brotherhood) and *fraterno* means "belonging to brothers." The concepts are not differentiated in English. Los gemelos se quieren con amor **fraternal.** *The twins love each other with **fraternal** (brotherly) love.*

frente / front   *Frente* (f.) means "forehead" as a feminine noun, but *frente* (m.) stands for "front" (of battle, of a house, of the class) as a masculine noun. Tiene la **frente** ancha. *He has a wide **forehead.*** El **frente** de la casa es sencillo. *The **front** of the house is plain.* Las ventanas **del frente** de la casa tienen rejas. *The **front** windows of the house have bars.*

fresco / fresh, fresco   *Fresco* is almost exactly "fresh" ("cool, calm, impudent" *[descarado]*). *Fresco* as a noun means "fresh air." Ese chico es muy **fresco** con las muchachas. *That boy is very **fresh** with the girls.* ¡Qué **fresco** eres! *You've got some **nerve!** Fresh* also means *dulce* (water), *nuevo* (life, second chance), *recién.* Casi todos los lagos son de agua **dulce.** *Almost all lakes have **fresh** water.*   empezar una vida **nueva**   /   *to make a **fresh** start Fresco* and *fresco* both refer to a type of painting on fresh plastered surfaces.

fricción / friction   *Fricción* means exactly the same as the word *friction:* "rubbing, massage" *(roce,* m.*).* Figuratively, both terms mean "trouble, discord" *(discordia, desavenencia).* In Spanish, the plural *fricciones* is preferred to the singular for the meaning of "discord." Las dos familias han tenido **fricciones** por años. *There has been **friction** between the two families for years.*

frontal / frontal   *Frontal* and *frontal* both are adjectives used to refer to "the forehead" *(la frente).* In Spanish, the meaning is limited to "of the forehead." *Frontal* in English extends its meaning to the battlefront, the front of the house, etc. In these cases, *frontal* is translated as *de frente.*
un ataque **de frente** = a **frontal** attack
una vista **de frente** = a **frontal** view

fruición / fruition   *Fruición* and *fruition* both mean "enjoyment, delight, pleasure." Todos sentimos **fruición** al cumplir el deber. *We all feel **pleasure** when we fulfill our duties. Fruition* also means *fructificación* (of plants) and, figuratively,

113

cumplimiento, realización. Logró la **realización** de sus sueños. *She brought her dreams to fruition.*

fuente / fountain *Fuente* (f.) and *fountain* share the meaning of "spring, source (of anything)." *Fuente* also means "platter" (serving dish). [There are other terms for both *fuente* and *fountain,* according to different situations. For example, *fuente* can also be *manantial* (m.; a "spring"), *surtidor* (m.; a "jet" of water, liquid). In English, *font* translates as *fuente* or *pila bautismal.* From this comes the Spanish expression *nombre* (m.) *de pila* ("first name").] La señora sirvió una **fuente** enorme de arroz con pollo. *The lady served a huge platter of chicken and rice.* Los libros son una gran **fuente** de sabiduría. *Books are a great fountain of knowledge.*

fuerte / fort, forte *Fuerte* (m.) means both "fort" and "forte." *Fuerte militar* is "military fort" ("stronghold"). In a figurative sense, *fuerte* means "forte" ("strong point"). However, *fuerte* is also an adjective meaning "strong, loud (sound), heavy (rain, snow), intense (heat), severe, hard." Figuratively, *fuerte* means "good," for example, *fuerte en latín* ("good at Latin"). Mi **fuerte** es la música. *Music is my forte.* **fuerte** como un roble / *strong as an oak; strong as an ox* ¿Te gusta la música **fuerte**? *Do you like loud music?* ¡Más **fuerte**! *Speak up!*

fuga / fugue *Fuga* is "fugue" in music, but *fuga* is used in everyday Spanish for "escape." La **fuga** de los prisioneros causó terror en toda la región. *The prisoners' escape caused terror throughout the area.*

fumar / fume *Fumar* is not "to fume" but "to smoke" (cigars, cigarettes). **Fumar** es peligroso para la salud. *Smoking is dangerous to your health.* To fume means *rabiar, estar furioso* in a figurative sense, and *humear, echar humo* in a real sense. Se fue **rabiando** porque perdió el juego. *He left fuming because he lost the game.* Fumes, the plural noun, translates as *vapores* (m.), *gases* (m.). Los **vapores** de la gasolina pueden causar cáncer. *Gasoline fumes can cause cancer.*

función / function *Función* is almost exactly "function": "act, celebration, job, purpose." In Spanish, *función* is also used for "show, performance" and in some countries, "party." **funciones** del corazón / *functions of the heart* estar en **funciones** / *to be in office* **función** de gala / *gala performance* Hay dos **funciones** diarias de teatro. *There are two daily performances at the theater.*

fundamento / fundament *Fundamento* is not "fundament" but "foundation, reason, grounds, seriousness."
sin fundamento = *unfounded*
Los edificios necesitan buenos **fundamentos**. *Buildings need good foundations.* *Fundament,* in addition to meaning *fundamento* in the sense of "an underlying principle," refers to the body: *trasero, nalgas* ("buttocks"), *ano* ("anus").

fundar, fundir / fund *Fundar* is not "to fund" but "to found, base on, set up." ¿Quién **fundó** Los Angeles? *Who founded the city of Los Angeles? Fundir* means "to smelt, to fuse." Para **fundir** el oro se necesita mucho calor. *A lot of heat is needed to smelt gold. To fund* means *invertir* (ie, i), *consolidar* (debt), *proveer fondos, pagar.* Mi padre **está pagando** mis estudios universitarios. *My father is funding my college education.*

funeral / funeral   *Funeral* (m.) is "funeral" as "burial ceremonies," although the plural *funerales* is more commonly used than the singular form. *Los funerales de Mamá la Grande es un libro de García Márquez. Big Mama's Funeral is a book by García Márquez. Funeral* is also an adjective in English, meaning *fúnebre. Funeraria* is translated as "funeral parlor" or "funeral home." En los Estados Unidos hay muchas **funerarias**. *There are many funeral parlors in the United States.*

furioso / furious   *Furioso* and *furious* both show a mental state of "anger, rage." In Spanish, *furioso* stresses the loss of reasoning and is more accurately translated as "insane, out of one's mind." Se puso **furioso** en el accidente. *He was out of his mind during the accident. Furious* emphasizes the violence that "anger" presupposes. Good translations are *furibundo, airado, violento, frenético.* Durante el ciclón los vientos eran **violentos**. *The winds were furious during the hurricane.*

fútbol, futbol / football   *Fútbol* or *futbol* (m.) means "soccer," not "football." Hispanics refer to American "football" as *fútbol norteamericano,* as opposed to *fútbol europeo* for "soccer" or simply *fútbol.* The original term for soccer, *balompié* (m.), is not widely used nowadays. In some countries *fútbol* is used; in others, *futbol.* [The *Real Academia* has included both spellings in its latest dictionary.] [*Fútbol* is a loan word from English (*football*), the British name for soccer. The irony is that *football* is not exclusively played with the feet as the term suggests.]

fútil / futile   *Fútil* and *futile* share the idea of "pointless, trifling" *(trivial).* In Spanish *fútil* has kept that meaning and translates as "trivial, insignificant, unimportant, pointless." El detalle mencionado por la criada es **fútil**. *The detail mentioned by the maid is pointless. Futile* stresses the practical aspect that goes with "triviality" and emphasizes the lack of "usefulness." Good translations in Spanish are *vano, inútil, estéril, frívolo.* Todos sus esfuerzos resultaron **inútiles**. *All their efforts were futile.*

futilidad / futility   *Futilidad* (f.) means "triviality, trifle." According to the *Real Academia,* the term does not apply to people.   hablar de **futilidades**   /   *to talk about trivialities   Futility,* on the other hand, is translated as *inutilidad* (f.; "worthlessness"), *frivolidad* (f.).   la **inutilidad** del argumento   /   *the futility of the argument*

G

gabinete / cabinet *Gabinete* (m.) and *cabinet* both refer to "a body of official advisors." *Gabinete* also means a "study, office (room), consulting room." El **gabinete** francés se reunió con urgencia. *The French **cabinet** had an urgent meeting. Cabinet* is translated as *armario, vitrina, mueble* (m.). A kitchen cabinet is *amario de cocina.* La **vitrina** es de madera de encina. *The **cabinet** is made of oak.*

gala / gala *Gala* and *gala* have one expression in common: *baile* (m.) *de gala* ("gala ball"). In Spanish *gala* also means "best dress (clothing), elegance, poise, choicest" or "cream." The plural form, *galas,* translates as "ornaments, bridal attire, regalia."
hacer gala de = *to boast of*
La presidenta mostró su **gala** en la fiesta. *The president showed her **elegance** at the party.* María es la **gala** de la sociedad camagüeyana. *Mary is the **cream** of society in Camagüey. Gala* in English is translated as *fiesta de gala* or *fiesta de etiqueta.*

galante / gallant *Galante* and *gallant* both mean "courteous" (especially with women). *Galante* also means "flirtatious, agreeable." Don Juan era muy **galante** con las damas. *Don Juan was very **flirtatious** with the ladies. Gallant* means *valiente, elegante, espléndido.* Viajamos con un capitán **valiente**. *We traveled with a **gallant** captain.*

galón / gallon *Galón* (m.) and *gallon* both are used to measure liquids, including gasoline, and are the equivalent of 3.8 liters in the United States and 4.55 liters in England. *Galón* also means "stripe" or "chevron" (in the military) and "braid" (ribbon for clothes). El **galón** de Inglaterra es más grande que el de los Estados Unidos. *The English **gallon** is larger than that of the United States.* El general lleva muchos **galones** y medallas. *The general wears many **stripes** and medals.*

gas / gas *Gas* (m.) means "gas" as a "natural chemical used for cooking and heating." *Gas* is also used to refer to "fizziness" or carbonation in drinks. When ordering mineral water, for example, it is necessary to specify *con gas* ("fizzy, carbonated") or *sin gas.* (In Spain the natural gas used for cooking or heating is called *butano.* Also some taxicab engines run on *butano* instead of *gasolina.*) Quiero una botella de agua mineral con **gas**. *I want a bottle of **fizzy** mineral water.* El **butano** se vende en bombona. *Butane (natural gas) is sold in a bottle, or carboy.*

generoso / generous *Generoso* and *generous* both refer to people who are "willing to give or share money, time, etc." Both terms also apply to wines with the meaning of "full-bodied." However, in Spanish *generoso* also means "fertile (soil, life), valiant, courageous." Siempre ha sido **generoso** con los pobres de Haití. *He has always been **generous** with the needy people of Haiti. Generous* also conveys the idea of *grande, abundante.* Me sirvió una ración **abundante** de arroz con pollo. *He served me a **generous** portion of chicken and rice.*

genial / genial   *Genial* is not "genial" but "talented, brilliant, full of genius" and in a figurative sense, "fantastic, witty."
¡Genial! = *Fantastic!*
Ayer pasé un día **genial** en la playa. *Yesterday I had a **fantastic** day at the beach.* El gerente tuvo una idea **genial**. *The manager had a **brilliant** idea. Genial* means *simpático, cordial, afable, jovial, suave* (weather). Mi abuelo era un viejito muy **jovial**. *My grandfather was a **genial** old man. **Genialidad** (f.) is translated as "talent, stroke of genius, brilliant idea." *Geniality* is translated as *simpatía, afabilidad* (f.), *cordialidad* (f.).

genio / genius   *Genio* and *genius* both refer to "talent, a talented person." The basic meaning of *genio,* however, is "temper, disposition, nature (character)."
genio de una lengua / *peculiarities of a language*   Goya era un **genio** como pintor. *Goya was a **genius** as a painter.* Mi sobrina tiene mal **genio**. *My niece has a bad **disposition**.*

gentil / gentile, gentle, genteel   *Gentil* and *gentile* are both historical terms for "a pagan" (not a Christian, not a Jew). *Gentil,* however, is neither "gentle" nor "genteel" but "kind, pleasant, charming, comely, attractive." Me trató de una manera muy **gentil**. *She treated me in a very **pleasant** manner. Gentle* is translated as *dócil, suave, cortés, ligero, cuidadoso, lento*. Es más **dócil** que una borreguilla. *He is **gentler** than a lamb. Genteel* means *fino, distinguido, gallardo,* and sometimes it takes a downturn to mean *cursi* ("affectedly polite"). La viuda quiere casarse con un caballero **distinguido** y acomodado. *The widow wants to marry a **genteel**, wealthy gentleman. **Gentilmente** means "politely, kindly, gracefully." *Gently* means *despacio, suavemente, con cuidado*. Un huevo de canario debe manejarse **con mucho cuidado**. *A canary's egg must be handled very **gently**.*

gentileza / gentleness   *Gentileza* means "kindness, pleasantness." *Gentleness* means *docilidad* (f.), *dulzura, suavidad* (f.).

globo / globe   *Globo* and *globe* both mean "sphere, the earth." But *globo* is also the everyday term for "balloon" (both the toy and the hot-air balloon to ride in).
en globo = *in bulk, as a whole*
globo terrestre = *globe, earth*
Había muchos **globos** de colores en la fiesta. *There were many colorful **balloons** at the party.*

glorioso / glorious   *Glorioso* and *glorious* both mean "full of glory." In a religious context, *glorioso* is translated as "blessed" and applies especially to the Virgin Mary. La Pascua es un día **glorioso**. *Easter Sunday is a **glorious** day. Glorious,* on the other hand, has many shades of meaning, such as *espléndido, magnífico, radiante* (day), *colosal, enorme*.
lío colosal = *glorious mess*
Desde el balcón hay una vista **magnífica**. *There is a **glorious** view from the balcony.*

gol / goal   *Gol* (m.) comes from the English word *goal* and means "one point" *(un tanto)* in *fútbol* (m.), or soccer, as well as in hockey. (The plural of *gol* is

goles.) Metió dos **goles** en cinco minutos. *He made two **goals** in five minutes. Goal* in English goes beyond sports to mean *meta, objetivo, fin* (m.). *Goalie* (goalkeeper) translates as *portero, guardameta.* Su **meta** es llegar a ser médico. *His* **goal** *is to become a doctor. Golear* means "to score a series of goals." *Goleador* (m.) is the person who scores a goal.

goma / gum   *Goma* shares with *gum* the meaning of "sticky substance." *Goma,* however, also means a "tire" *(llanta)* for a car or truck, an "eraser," and "rubber" (the material for tires or boots, etc.). [In different Spanish-speaking countries, *goma, llanta,* and *neumático* are terms for "tire."] Me gustan los zapatos con suela de **goma.** *I like shoes with **rubber** soles. Gum* means *chicle* (m.; "chewing gum") and the plural *gums* means *encías* ("the tissue in the mouth that holds teeth"). Mastico **chicle** para no fumar. *I chew **gum** to keep from smoking.*

gota / gout   *Gota* and *gout* both refer to the same illness, a type of arthritis or inflammation of the joints. Nevertheless, the basic meaning of *gota* is "a drop" (of liquid). In a figurative sense, *gota* refers to "a little bit, a small amount."
ni gota = *nothing at all*
Hace un año que no fumo **ni gota.** *I haven't smoked **at all** for the past year.* Si toma unas **gotas** de vino se emborracha. *If he drinks a few **drops** (a little bit) of wine, he gets drunk.*

gotera, gotero / gutter   *Gotera* means "leak" (of a liquid). El radiador del carro tiene una **gotera.** *The car radiator has a **leak.** Gotero* means "eyedropper." *Gutter,* however, is translated as *canal* (m.) or *canalón* (m.; of a roof), *arroyo, cuneta* (of streets, roads), *ranura* (a "groove"). Mi tejado no tiene **canalones.** *Mi roof has no **gutters.***

gracia / grace   *Gracia* and *grace* both mean "God's favor, gracefulness" *(donaire,* m.). *Gracia* also means "charm, wit, sense of humor," and *gracias* means "thanks."
tener gracia = *to be funny*
Siempre habla con **gracia.** *He always speaks with a **sense of humor.*** No es guapa pero tiene cierta **gracia.** *She isn't pretty but she has a certain **charm.*** Los niños siempre aprenden a decir **gracias.** *Children always learn to say **thank-you.** Grace* also means *elegancia, esbeltez* (f.), *cortesía, perdón* (m.), *bendición* (before meals), *plazo, demora.*
bendecir la mesa = *to say grace*
Tuvo la **cortesía** de disculparse. *He had the **grace** to excuse himself.*   un plazo de **perdón** / *a **grace** period*

gracioso / gracious   *Gracioso* is "funny, witty, amusing." Lo **gracioso** del caso es que no se casaron. *The **funny thing** about it is that they didn't get married. Gracious* is used to describe people or things. To describe people, it means *amable, cortés, gentil, indulgente* ("lenient"). To describe things, it means *grato, elegante, de buen gusto.*

grado / grade   *Grado* and *grade* both mean "degree in rank, quality, school." *Grado* is also used for "degree (of temperature), stage, step."

de buen grado = *willingly*
diferentes **grados** de la evolución de las especies / *different **stages** of evolution of the species* Un buen vino debe tener doce **grados** de alcohol al menos. *A good wine must have an alcohol content of at least twelve **percent** (degrees).* Grade also means *nota* or *calificación* (in school), *pendiente* (f.; "gradient, slope"), *nivel* (m.).
paso a nivel = *grade crossing*
Espero unas buenas **notas** este semestre. He trabajado mucho. *I expect good **grades** this semester. I have worked hard.*

granada / grenade *Granada* and *grenade* both refer to the same "weapon." *Granada* is also a round-shaped fruit that is called a *pomegranate* in English. *Granada* also means "shell" (of a cannon, mortar). Los soldados tiran **granadas** de mano. *The soldiers throw hand **grenades**.* El escudo de España tiene una **granada**. *The shield of Spain has a **pomegranate**.*

grande / grand *Grande* is not "grand" but "large, tall, great, big," and in the Americas, "middle-aged." [*Grande* becomes *gran* when it is placed before a singular masculine or feminine noun: *gran señor; gran señora*. *Gran* before the noun means "great" and after the noun, *grande* means "large": *gran libro* ("great book"); *libro grande* ("large book").]

personas grandes = *grown-ups*
pasarlo en grande = *to have a great time*
gran velocidad = *high speed*
en grande = *on a grand scale*
un gran hombre = *a great man*
Mi padre ya es una persona **grande**. *My father is already a **middle-aged** person.* Grand is used for *grandioso, majestuoso, estupendo*.
jurado de acusación = *grand jury*
piano de cola = *grand piano*
total general = *grand total*
La fiesta quedó **grandiosa**. *It was a **grand** party.*

gratificación / gratification *Gratificación* is not "gratification" but "tip, reward, gratuity, bonus *(sobresueldo)*, bounty *(subvención)*." *Gratification* means *gusto, placer* (m.), *satisfacción*. ¡Qué gran **placer** encontrar al niño perdido! *What great **gratification** it was to find the lost child!*

gratificar / gratify *Gratificar* is "to reward, tip, give a bonus or gratuity." Gratificó al simpático botones con cinco dólares. *He **tipped** the cheerful bellboy five dollars. To gratify* stands for *satisfacer, dar gusto, agradar*. Sus palabras elogiosas le dieron **gusto** a mi vanidad. *Her words of praise **gratified** my vanity (ego).*

gratuito / gratuitous *Gratuito* and *gratuitous* share the figurative meaning of "uncalled-for, unwarranted." *Gratuito (gratis)* also means "free" (of charge). [*Gratis* means "free, for nothing"; although grammar books state that the word is an adverb, speakers use it as an adjective as well.]
afirmación gratuita = *gratuitous remark*
La entrada al parque zoológico es **gratuita** (gratis). *Admission to the zoo is **free**.*

Sus palabras fueron completamente **gratuitas** (gratis). *His words were completely gratuitous. Gratuitous* also means *innecesario, voluntario.*

grave / grave   *Grave* and *grave* share the idea of "serious." In Spanish, *grave* is used more frequently with the meaning of "serious," but it also means "low, deep" (voice) and "solemn" (style). Tiene una enfermedad **grave**. *She has a grave (serious) illness.* Me gustan las notas **graves** del órgano. *I like the low notes of the organ.*

guardar / guard   *Guardar* and *to guard* both mean "to protect, defend, watch." *Guardar* has additional denotations such as "to store away, keep, put away, save, observe (laws)."
guardársela a uno = *to hold a grudge against*
El dinero se **guarda** en la caja de seguridad. *The money is kept in the safe.* **Guardó** el encendedor en el bolsillo. *He put the lighter away in his pocket.* To guard sometimes means *escoltar* ("to escort"), and it also stresses the idea of *custodiar, vigilar.*
protegerse contra = *to guard against*
El dueño **vigila** su restaurante para que los empleados no le roben. *The owner guards his restaurant so that the employees won't rob him.*

guardia / guard   *Guardia* (m., f.) is "police officer" whether for traffic or to maintain public order. In other cases, *guardia* translates as "guard." The Spanish *guarda* (m., f.) suggests "security guard" (for private business), whereas *guardia* is a cover term for both public and private situations. As a feminine noun, *guardia* means "troops, police or military force."
guardia de asalto = *shock troops*
Algunas tiendas tienen **guardas** (guardias) todo el día. *Some stores have 24-hour security guards.*

guardián / guardian   *Guardián* (m.) refers to "guardian, keeper, watchman" *(custodio). Guardian* in English also refers to *tutor* (m.; of a minor). El tío ha sido el **tutor** del muchacho por seis años. *The uncle has been the boy's guardian for six years.*

guerrilla / guerrilla   *Guerrilla* is not "guerrilla" but "guerrilla band, guerrilla warfare." *Guerrilla* (also spelled *guerilla*) is translated as *guerrillero*. [This is another case of a loan word taken from Spanish but with a different meaning. In this case, the confusion is between one person (*guerrillero* = "guerrilla") and the group or the warfare (*guerrilla*).] Los **guerrilleros** idealistas pelean en las montañas. *The idealistic guerrillas are fighting in the mountains.* La **guerrilla** tenía treinta **guerrilleros** bien entrenados. *The guerrilla band had thirty well-trained guerrillas.*

guisa / guise   *Guisa,* although it is an infrequently used term in Spanish, retains the old meaning of the word *guise* in English: "way, fashion."
de tal guisa = *in such a way*
a guisa de = *as, for*
Guise, on the other hand, also means *apariencia, aspecto* and usually *falsa apariencia* or *pretexto.* Quiso engañarme bajo la **falsa apariencia** de la amistad. *He tried to deceive me under the guise of friendship*

H

hábil / able   *Hábil* is not exactly "able." *Hábil* assumes "manual skill" *(destreza manual)* and translates as "skillful, dexterous, proficient, expert, good for, working (day)." *Generalmente los sábados y domingos no son días hábiles. Generally, Saturdays and Sundays are not **working** (work) days.*   ser **hábil** en / *to be **good** at*   un cirujano **hábil** / *a **skillful** surgeon*   una sala **hábil** para conferencias / *a **good** room for meetings*   *Able*, on the other hand, indicates "mental capability" and translates as *listo, inteligente, capaz, competente. Ese abogado es muy **capaz**. That lawyer is very **able** (capable).* [The difference between *hábil* and *able* results in very different meanings. For example, in a Hispanic country *un político hábil* really means "a tricky politician." The opposite is true in the United States where "an *able* politician" actually means *un político capaz.*] **Habilidad** (f.) is not "ability" but "skill, dexterity, expertise." *Ability* is *capacidad* (f.), *aptitud* (f.), *talento, inteligencia.*

habitación / habitation   *Habitación* is not "habitation"; rather, it means "room, bedroom, habitat." The Spanish term reflects the practical and concrete way of life of the people. *¿Cuántas **habitaciones** tiene tu casa? How many **rooms** does your house have?* *Habitation* seems to stress the abstract idea of living place. Good translations are *morada, vivienda. El desierto no es la mejor **morada** humana. The desert is not the best **habitat** for humans.*

hacienda / hacienda   *Hacienda* and *hacienda* both stand for a "large ranch with a house." The basic meaning of *hacienda* in Spanish is "wealth, possessions, property." [Different terms are used for *hacienda* in different Hispanic countries to mean "farm": *finca, rancho, granja, estancia, quinta.*]
hacienda pública = *public treasury*
*Mi **hacienda** no está en el campo sino en el banco. My **wealth** is not in the country but in the bank.* *Hacienda* has become an English word borrowed from Spanish and takes only a part of the original meaning of "a large ranch or farm."

halo / halo   *Halo* and *halo* share the idea of a "ring of light around the sun, moon, etc." *La luna tiene un **halo** muy bello. The moon has a very beautiful **halo**.* *Halo* in English also refers to the "ring of light or glory" around the head of a saint or an angel, which is *aureola* or *nimbo* in Spanish. *Cada santo se ha ganado su **aureola**. Each saint has earned his **halo**.*

héroe / hero   *Héroe* (m.) exactly means "hero." *Hero*, however, also means *protagonista* (m., f.), *galán* (m.), *personaje* (m.) *principal* (of a novel). [In Spanish *héroes* are people who do heroic things, but the person who plays the hero's role in a movie or play is the *galán*, and in literature, the character is the *personaje principal*. In English *heroes* are always *heroes*, in real life or in movies.]

historia / history *Historia* and *history* both refer to "relevant facts or events in the past." *Historia* also means "story, tale, past" and in a figurative sense, "gossip, fabricated story."
pasar a la historia = *to go down in history*
Nos contó la **historia** de su vida. *He told us the story of his life.* No me vengas con **historias.** *Don't come to me bearing tales.*

histórico / historic, historical *Histórico* is translated as "historic" and "historical." *Historic* indicates the "making of history" because of importance and is translated as *importante*. *Historical* refers to "history in general," whether important or not. It is translated as *histórico*. La victoria de Juárez contra los franceses fue un momento **histórico** importante. *The victory of Juárez over the French was an important historical moment.*

honestidad / honesty *Honestidad* (f.) and *honesty* have nothing in common except their Latin origin. *Honestidad* means "decency, modesty, decorum." *Honesty* means *honradez* (f.), *rectitud* (f.), *sinceridad* (f.). La **honradez** es la mejor política. *Honesty is the best policy. Honesto* is "decent, virtuous, decorous, modest." *Honest* means *honrado, recto, franco, sincero.* El hombre **honrado** es siempre respetado. *An honest man is always respected.* un juez **recto** / *an honest judge* No lo hice yo, **te lo juro.** *I didn't do it, honest.* la **pura** verdad / *the honest truth Honestamente* means "decently, modestly." *Honestly* is used more frequently and is translated as *francamente, honradamente.* con toda **sinceridad** / *honestly speaking* [Note that in this group of words, the Spanish terms aim directly at the behavioral or sexual aspect, whereas the English terms stress the idea of morality and justice.]

honorario / honorary *Honorario* and *honorary* are adjectives for "given as an honor only." The plural in Spanish, *honorarios,* means "honorarium" ("professional fee"). Los **honorarios** del profesor son altos, tal vez demasiado altos. *The professor's honorarium is high, perhaps too high.*

hora / hour *Hora* and *hour* are both "sixty minutes." *Hora* also means "time" and, in the Americas, "appointment."
en mala hora = *at a bad time, at the wrong time*
fuera de hora = *after hours*
por horas = *by the hour*
hora punta = *rush hour*
horas libres = *spare time*
Ha llegado su **hora.** *His time (hour) has come. Hour,* on the other hand, sometimes means *momento* in a figurative sense. The plural *hours* is often translated as *horario.* acostarse temprano / *to keep good hours*

humano / human, humane *Humano* means both "human" and "humane." *Humano* and *human* both refer to "human nature," which is distinct from that of animals and God. *Humano* and *humane* both deal with "the best of human feelings." Other terms for this meaning include *humanitario, compasivo, filántropo.* Tiene un trato muy **humano** con los empleados. *He has a very **humane** relationship with his employees.*

húmedo / humid *Húmedo* and *humid* both apply to weather: "moist, damp." In Spanish, *húmedo* is used to describe many things: "damp" (clothes, floor), "wet" (refering to anything, except paint). [Note that in English *humid* is used when it is hot and *damp* is used when it is cold. In Spanish, *húmedo* is used in both situations.] Los helechos se dan muy bien en climas **húmedos.** *Ferns grow very well in humid climates.* Tu suéter está **húmedo** todavía. *Your sweater is still damp. Humedad* (f.) is not only "humidity" but also "dampness, moisture." La gente dice que la **humedad** da artritis. *People say that humidity gives you arthritis.*

humor / humor *Humor* (m.) and *humor* share the comic idea of "wit, sense of humor." In Spanish, *humor* also means "mood, disposition, character."
sentido de humor = *sense of humor*
humor de todos los diablos / *very bad temper* No entendió lo **cómico** de la situación. *He didn't catch the humor of the situation.*

I

idioma / idiom *Idioma* (m.) is not "idiom" but "language." Idiom is translated as *modismo, locución, expresión idiomática.* Muchos **modismos** españoles nacieron en el campo. *Many Spanish idioms came from the countryside. Idiomático,* on the other hand, exactly means "idiomatic."

idiosincrasia / idiosyncrasy *Idiosincrasia* and *idiosyncrasy* mean exactly the same thing: "the peculiar ways of a person or an institution." [These two terms are frequently misspelled. Note that both are spelled with an *s* (not a *c*): *-sia; -sy.*] El pastel de manzana es parte de la **idiosincrasia** de los Estados Unidos. *Apple pie is part of the American idiosyncrasy. Idiosincrásico* and *idiosyncratic,* the corresponding adjectives, share the same meaning.

idiota / idiot, idiotic *Idiota* (m., f.) means both "idiot" and "idiotic." The Spanish term has a stronger connotation than the English cognates and can be a strong insult, equivalent to "fool, moron." Milder terms are preferred, such as *tonto* and *bobo.* La gente **tonta** (idiota) no piensa en el futuro. *Idiotic people don't plan for the future. Idiotez* (f.) means "idiocy, foolishness" and also "nonsense" as a countable noun.
decir idioteces = *to talk nonsense*
¡No hagas **idioteces**! *Don't fool around!*

ignorar / ignore *Ignorar (desconocer)* is not "to ignore" but "to be unaware of, not to know." **Se ignora** el paradero del supuesto criminal. *The whereabouts of the alleged criminal are not known. To ignore* means *no hacer caso, pasar por alto, hacer caso omiso.* La persona valiente **no hace caso** del peligro. *A valiant person ignores danger.* [Note that *ignorar* is the opposite of *conocer* and both verbs convey an "unintentional" meaning. On the other hand, *to ignore* is the opposite of *to find out* and both expressions convey a "willing" or "intentional" meaning *(dinámico).*] *Ignorado* means "unknown." *Ignored* translates as *rechazado, discriminado, postergado.* Se siente **postergado** por todos. *He feels ignored by everyone.*

iliterato / illiterate *Iliterato (iletrado)* is not "illiterate" but "ignorant, unschooled, without studies." Una persona **iliterata** no sabe leer literatura, pero sí el periódico. *An unschooled person cannot read literature but can read the newspaper. Illiterate,* on the other hand, means *analfabeto* ("unable to read or write"). ¿Cómo puede votar un **analfabeto**? *How can an illiterate person vote?*

ilusión / illusion *Ilusión* and *illusion* share the idea of "false conception, not in accord with reality." In Spanish, *ilusión* also means "dream, delusion, wishful thinking," and in a figurative sense, "pleasure, thrill, hopefulness."
trabajar con ilusión = *to work with a will*
con ilusión = *hopefully*
Me hace mucha **ilusión** ir a Cancún. *I am really looking forward to going to Cancún.*
Todos tienen **ilusiones** en la vida. *Everybody has dreams in life.* ¡Qué **ilusión** ir

a pescar el domingo! *What a **pleasure** to be going fishing on Sunday! Illusion,* however, sometimes means *engaño, espejismo.* [Note that *ilusión* in Spanish is much more positive than *illusion* in English. The difference is similar to comparing "a nice dream" with "an impossible dream."] ¡Vives de **espejismos**! *You are living on **illusions!***

ilustración / illustration *Ilustración* exactly means "illustration," according to the the latest dictionary of the *Real Academia.* Now the accepted meanings are not only *conocimiento* but also *grabado* or *dibujo de un libro.* Este diccionario no tiene **ilustraciones** (grabados). *This dictionary does not have **illustrations.** Illustration* is also used in the figurative sense of *ejemplo.* Voy a mencionar un solo caso como un **ejemplo**. *I will mention just one case as an **illustration.** **Ilustrado** and illustrated* mean exactly the same thing.

imbécil / imbecile *Imbécil* is almost exactly "imbecile," but the Spanish term is a strong word and can be an embarrassing insult, similar to *idiota* (m., f.) and *estúpido.* Yet native speakers sometimes use these words colloquially among friends in jest, without meaning an insult. Nonnative speakers are advised to exercise caution and use terms such as *tonto* or *bobo* instead. *Imbecile* also applies to a mentally retarded or disabled person and is translated as *atrasado mental.* However, such terms are rarely used nowadays owing to a more enlightened approach to physical and mental limitations. El niño no es normal. Es **atrasado mental.** *The child is not normal. He's an **imbecile.** **Imbecilidad** (f.)* means "imbecility," and the plural form *imbecilidades* translates as "nonsense." ¡No digas **imbecilidades**! *Don't talk **nonsense!***

impartir / impart *Impartir* and *to impart* share the meaning of "to grant, allow." La universidad **impartió** algunas becas. *The university **granted** a few scholarships. To impart* also means *comunicarse, hacer saber.* Sabe **comunicar** sus conocimientos. *He knows how **to impart** his knowledge.*

impedir / impede *Impedir* (i) does not mean "to impede"; rather, it means "to stop, prevent." La lluvia le **impidió** que saliera de paseo. *The rain **prevented** her from going for a walk. To impede* is not *parar* ("to stop") completely but *estorbar, obstruir, molestar* (for example, traffic). La ropa le **estorbaba** para salvar al niño que se ahogaba. *His clothes **impeded** him from rescuing the drowning boy.*

imperfecto / imperfect *Imperfecto* and *imperfect* both refer to something "incomplete, unfinished." *Imperfect*, in addition, means *defectuoso.* El ejemplar del libro que compré está **defectuoso.** *The copy of the book I bought is **imperfect** (faulty).*

imperioso / imperious *Imperioso* is not "imperious" but "urgent, needed, imperative." Tengo que hacer una tarea **imperiosa**. *I have an **urgent** task to do. Imperious* means *arrogante, dominante.* No me gusta la gente **arrogante**. *I dislike **imperious** people.*

implemento / implement *Implemento* was included in the latest dictionary of the *Real Academia* as a term borrowed from English with the meaning of "implement" *(herramienta, utensilio).* La máquina viene con los **implementos** para arreglarla. *The machine comes with the **implements** (tools) to fix it. Implements,* the plural form, means *enseres* (m.), *muebles* (m.), *aperos* (countryside). *To implement* translates as *cumplir, ejecutar, llevar a cabo, aplicar* (the law). [Note that in Spanish, there is no such word as *"implementar."*] Es importante **aplicar** las leyes en todo el país. *It is important to implement the laws throughout the country.*

implicación / implication   *Implicación* and *implication* share the idea of "involvement in crime." In addition, **implicación** also means "contradiction." No se puede justificar su **implicación** en el robo. *There is no justification for his **implication** in the robbery. Implication also means consecuencia, resultado.* ¿Te das cuenta de las **consecuencias** de esa decisión? *Do you realize the **implications** of that decision?*

imponer / impose   *Imponer* and *to impose* share the idea of "to place a burden; to levy taxes, fines; to place obligations." *Imponer* is also used in a figurative sense to mean "to impress." The reflexive form, *imponerse,* suggests the meaning of "to show authority, to command, respect, prevail." San Pedro de Roma **impone** mucho. *Saint Peter of Rome **impresses** greatly.* El dólar **se imponía** sobre las otras monedas extranjeras. *The dollar **used to prevail** over other foreign currencies. To impose on* (or *upon*) translates as *abusar de* ("to take advantage of"). No quiero **abusar de** ustedes. *I don't want to **impose on** you.*

importar / import   *Importar* and *to import* both stand for "to buy from abroad." However, *importar* has three other meanings: (1) "to cost, to add up"; (2) "to matter"; (3) "to be important." México **importa** maquinaria de los Estados Unidos. *Mexico **imports** machinery from the United States.* ¿Cuánto **importa** este libro? *How much **does** this book **cost?*** No me **importa** esa obra. *That work doesn't **matter** to me.* **Importa** que te quedes. *It's **important** that you stay.*

impresión / impression   *Impresión* has all the meanings of the word *impression,* but it also means "printing, edition, recording (taping)." Este libro ya tiene cinco **impresiones**. *This book has already had five **printings**. Impresionante* means "impressive, amazing." *Impresionar* means "to impress, to touch, move (with emotion, feeling)." La guerra **impresiona** a mucha gente. *War **moves** (touches) many people.*

impúdico / impudent   *Impúdico* does not mean "impudent." It means "immodest, shameless" *(desvergonzado).* Es una joven **impúdica**. *She is a **shameless** young woman. Impudent* means *atrevido, insolente, descarado.* ¡Qué muchacho tan **insolente**! *What an **impudent** boy! Impudencia* means "shame, indecency." *Impudence* means *insolencia, descaro, desfachatez* (f.). Tiene la **insolencia** de llamarme. *He has the **impudence** to call me.*

inauguración / inauguration   *Inauguración* is used only to "inaugurate shops, monuments, statues, etc." but is not used in the sense of a ceremony "to inaugurate a person in a post or position." La **inauguración** del Capitolio fue un acontecimiento histórico. *The **inauguration** of the Capitol was a historic event. Inauguration* means *inauguración* (of things) and *toma de posesión, investidura* (of people). La **toma de posesión** de la presidencia ocurre en enero. *The **inauguration** of the president*

takes place in January. **Inaugurar** means "to inaugurate" (houses, buildings, etc.). It does not refer to people.
inaugurar una casa = *to have a housewarming*
To inaugurate (people) is translated as *tomar posesión.*

incensar / incense   *Incensar* means *to incense* in a church or elsewhere by burning incense. *Incensar* is also used figuratively for "to flatter, overpraise." No se cansa de **incensar** a su jefe. *He never tires of flattering his boss. To incense* in English has negative connotations such as *irritar, exasperar, sacar de sus cabales.* Sus preguntas tontas me **exasperaban.** *I was incensed at their silly questions.*

incidental / incidental   *Incidental* and *incidental* both stand for "happening as a result of something more important." *Incidental* in English also means *fortuito, accesorio.* The plural *incidentals* is a noun, meaning *gastos* or *puntos menores, puntos imprevistos.* El divorcio siempre conlleva problemas **accesorios.** *Divorce always brings **incidental** problems.* Tuvimos algunos **gastos imprevistos** en el viaje de negocios. *We incurred some **incidental expenses** during the business trip.*

incineración / incineration   *Incineración* means both "incineration" and "cremation." [*Cremación* was included in the latest dictionary of the *Real Academia* with the meaning of "the burning of corpses." However, the verb *cremar* was not included.] *Incinerar,* likewise, means "to incinerate" and "to cremate." En muchos países se acostumbra **incinerar** los cadáveres. *In many countries the custom is **to cremate** corpses.*

incitar / incite   *Incitar* and *to incite* share the idea of "to urge, to stir," but *incitar* also means "to encourage" *(animar).* México trata de **incitar** a los norteamericanos a visitar el país. *Mexico tries **to encourage** Americans to visit the country.*

incógnito / incognito   *Incógnito* and *incognito* are both adjectives that literally mean "unknown." The terms are also used as adverbs. The feminine noun form *incógnita* means "mystery, hidden motive."
viajar de incógnito = *to travel incognito*
Esas son regiones **incógnitas.** *Those regions are **unknown.*** El futuro de una persona es una **incógnita.** *A person's future is a **mystery.***

incondicional / unconditional   *Incondicional* and *unconditional* both mean "without conditions, absolute." However, *incondicional* is an "in" word that means "staunch (friend, follower), wholehearted." Todo el mundo necesita un amigo **incondicional.** *Everybody needs a **staunch** (wholehearted) friend.*

inconsciente / unconscious   *Inconsciente* and *unconscious* both mean "unconsciousness, unaware, unintentional," reflecting passive, involuntary states of mind. However, in Spanish, *inconsciente* can be used in an active, voluntary sense, meaning "irresponsible, thoughtless."
inconsciente del peligro = *unaware of the danger*
Quedó **inconsciente** (sin sentido) a consecuencia del accidente. *He was **unconscious** because of the accident.* No daré ese empleo a una persona **inconsciente.** *I will not give that job to an **irresponsible** person. Inconsciencia* similarly means "unconsciousness," as well as "irresponsibility, thoughtlessness, rashness, folly."

inconsistencia / inconsistency *Inconsistencia* and *inconsistency* both suppose "instability, lack of agreement with logic or principles." *Inconsistency* goes even farther to mean *inconsecuencia,* and even *contradicción.* Hay **contradicción** en este testigo. *There is inconsistency in this witness.*

inconsistente / inconsistent *Inconsistente* is "inconsistent" as "unstable, insubstantial." *Inconsistente* also refers to "flimsy (material), loose (ground)." Caminamos sobre un terreno muy **inconsistente**. *We are walking on very loose ground. Inconsistent* also means *inconsecuente, contradictorio.* Son actos **inconsecuentes** con su religión. *They are acts inconsistent with his religion.*

incontinente / incontinent *Incontinente* and *incontinent* share the idea of "unchaste, without control." *Incontinente* also has a literary use as an adverb meaning "instantly, immediately." Muchos ancianos son **incontinentes**. *Many elderly people are incontinent.* Comió la tortilla e **incontinente** salió. *He ate the (Spanish) omelet and left immediately.*

inconveniencia / inconvenience *Inconveniencia* does not mean "inconvenience"; it means "impropriety, inadvisability." *Inconvenience* means *molestia, incomodidad* (f.). Es una gran **incomodidad** no tener carro en California. *It's a great inconvenience not to have a car in California.*

inconveniente / inconvenient *Inconveniente* means "unsuitable, improper, inadvisable." *Inconveniente* (m.) is also a noun meaning "objection, obstacle, disadvantage."
no tener inconveniente = *to have no objection*
¿Hay algún **inconveniente** en eso? *Is there any objection to that? Inconvenient* is an adjective, meaning *molesto, incómodo.* Es muy **incómodo** leer con una vela. *It's very inconvenient to read by candlelight.*

incorporar / incorporate *Incorporar* and *to incorporate* both mean "to join, to include, to admit into a corporation." *Incorporar* also means "to sit someone up" and the reflexive form *incorporarse* means "to get up" (after having been lying or sitting down). Se **incorporó** a la compañía el diez de mayo. *He was incorporated in the company on the tenth of May.* Se cayó tontamente, pero se **incorporó** inmediatamente. *She fell clumsily, but she got up right away.*

incorrecto / incorrect *Incorrecto* and *incorrect* both mean "wrong, improper, inadequate." *Incorrecto* also means "impolite, rude, discourteous." No justifico su conducta **incorrecta**. *I am not justifying his incorrect (improper) behavior. Incorrectamente* stands for "rudely, impolitely," as well as "incorrectly." El dependiente la trató muy **incorrectamente**. *The clerk treated her very rudely. Incorrección* is "incorrectness" (for example, of style) and "inaccuracy," as well as "bad manners, bad behavior, rudeness." Hay una **incorrección** en la cuenta. *There is an inaccuracy (error) on the bill.* Es una **incorrección** comer tan rápido. *It's bad manners to eat so fast.*

incurrir en / incur *Incurrir en* is exactly "to incur," but the Spanish term must have the preposition *en,* whereas the English term has no preposition. **Incurrió en** (cometió) un delito mayor. *He incurred (committed) a serious crime. To incur* also means *contraer* (debts, obligations). **Contrajo** varias obligaciones. *He incurred several obligations.*

indiano / Indian   *Indiano* does not usually mean "Indian" but "a Spaniard who returns to Spain after living in America." [Historically, the *indianos* became rich in the Americas, following the tradition of the *conquistadores* (m.).] La tradición asegura que todos los **indianos** son ricos. *Tradition assures that all indianos are rich. Indian* (also called Native American) translates as *indio* or *indígena*. [Do not confuse this with "Indian" by nationality (of India), which translates as *hindú, or, colloquially, as indiano.*]

indicación / indication   *Indicación* means "indication" as "sign, suggestion, clue, hint." The plural **indicaciones** stands for "instructions" (for example, for fixing something). No hay **indicaciones** sobre el manejo del reloj. *There are no directions for using the clock. Indicado* is translated as "suitable, good for, recommended, suited." un traje **indicado** para la ocasión / *dress suited for the occasion* Tú eres la persona más **indicada** para la tarea. *You are the most suitable person for the job.* el momento menos **indicado** / *at the worst possible moment*

indignante / indignant   *Indignante* does not exactly mean "indignant" ("angry, causing anger"); instead, it means "infuriating, outraged, outrageous." In other words, *indignante* shows a greater degree of "anger" than its English cognate. Me gritó palabras **indignantes**. *He yelled infuriating words at me. Indignant* is more accurately translated as *enfadado, enojado*. Estaba **enojado** porque perdió. *He was indignant because he lost.*

indiscreto / indiscreet, indiscrete   *Indiscreto* exactly means "indiscreet" ("tactless, lacking good judgment"). Dijo varias cosas **indiscretas** en la reunión. *She made several indiscreet remarks at the meeting. Indiscrete* is a false cognate for *indiscreto. Indiscrete* means *homogéneo, continuo*. Justicia es una unidad **homogénea;** no se puede dividir. *Justice is an indiscrete unit; it cannot be divided.*

individuo / individual   *Individuo* is translated as the adjective *individual* ("by a single thing or person"). *Individuo* is also a noun equivalent to *individual* in English, and sometimes in colloquial speech takes on the derogatory tone of "fellow, guy." Un **individuo** pregunta por Ud. *Some fellow is asking about you.* ¿Quién es ese **individuo** tan alto? *Who is that tall guy? Individual* is used more frequently in English than its Spanish cognate. It takes on different shades of meaning, according to its context: *propio, personal, particular, cada uno*. Suma **cada una** de las notas. *Add up the individual marks (grades).* Cada invitado tiene su **propio** teléfono. *The guests all have individual telephones.*

indoctrinado / indoctrinated   *Indoctrinado* is not "indoctrinated"; rather, it means "ignorant, uneducated." Es una persona **indoctrinada**. *He is an uneducated person. Indoctrinated* means *adoctrinado, instruido*. Fue **adoctrinado** en las teorías de Marx. *He was indoctrinated in Marx's theories. To indoctrinate* means *adoctrinar, instruir.* [Note that there is no such word as *indoctrinar.* The reason is logical because there is no way "to make someone ignorant" nor to "take away the education that someone has."]

industrial / industrial *Industrial* and *industrial* both mean "related to industry." However, as a noun, *industrial* (m.) means "industrialist." *Los dos* **industriales** *fundaron una empresa privada. The two* **industrialists** *founded a private company. Industrial* (especially the plural form, *industrials*) also is a noun that refers to business and is translated as *valores* (m.) or *acciones industriales* ("industrial stocks").
accidente de trabajo = *industrial accident*
Los **valores industriales** *subieron dos puntos ayer.* **Industrials** *went up two points yesterday.*

industrioso / industrious *Industrioso* does not mean "industrious" but "skillful, ingenious." *Ese carpintero es muy* **industrioso.** *That carpenter is very* **skillful.** *Industrious* means *aplicado, laborioso, diligente, estudioso. Es muy* **aplicado** *en la escuela. He is very* **industrious** *at school. Industria* means "industry" in the modern sense of the word; however, it is still used sometimes in the original sense of "skill, expertness."

inédito / unedited *Inédito* means "unpublished" and often suggests "original, unheard of." *Tengo unos poemas* **inéditos** *de Luis Borges. I have a few* **unpublished** *poems by Jorge Luis Borges. Unedited* is translated as *sin redactar. Mi libro está* **sin redactar** *todavía. My book is still* **unedited.**

ineducado / uneducated *Ineducado* is not "uneducated" but "ill-mannered, impolite." *¡Qué muchacho tan* **ineducado!** *What an* **ill-mannered** *boy! Uneducated* is translated as *inculto, analfabeto, iletrado. La criada es* **inculta.** *The maid is* **uneducated.**

infante / infant *Infante* (m.) means "infantryman, prince (i.e., son of a king)."
infantes de la marina = *marines*
Infant, however, means *criatura, bebé* (m.), *nene* (m.), *guagua* (in some American countries), *crío* (in Spain). *¡Qué* **criatura** *más preciosa! Parece un ángel. What a beautiful* **infant!** *He looks like an angel.*

infantil / infantile *Infantil* means "infantile" in the sense of "relating to children."
parque infantil = *playground, "children's park"*
No me gustan las ideas **infantiles** *del supervisor. I don't like the supervisor's* **infantile** *ideas. Infantile* has downgraded its meaning to refer to *pueril, aniñado. Tiene un sentido de humor* **pueril.** *She has an* **infantile** *sense of humor.*

infatuación / infatuation *Infatuación* means "conceit, presumption, vanity"; it does not mean "infatuation." *El general militar está lleno de* **infatuación.** *The military general is full of* **conceit.** *Infatuation* is an exaggerated, often foolish, feeling of love: *apasionamiento, encaprichamiento, enamoramiento loco.*

infatuado / infatuated *Infatuado* means "conceited, vain." *Infatuated* means *loco de amor, encaprichado por, chiflado, locamente enamorado. El muchacho está* **locamente enamorado** *de la maestra. The boy is* **infatuated** *with his teacher.*

inferior / inferior *Inferior* is almost exactly "inferior" ("lower in order or rank, of poor quality or value"), but *inferior* also applies to people who work under supervision ("subordinate").

el lado inferior = *the underside; underneath*
cursos **inferiores** de la universidad / *lower division courses in college* Los **inferiores** siguen las órdenes del jefe. *The subordinates follow the boss's orders.*

inferir / infer *Inferir* (ie, i) means "to infer" in the sense of "to conclude, to cause." *Inferir* also means "to inflict (wounds), to impose (punishment) on." De tus palabras **infiero** que eres republicano. *From your words, I infer that you are a Republican.* Sus palabras me **infirieron** un gran daño. *His words inflicted great damage on me.*

infernal / infernal *Infernal* means "infernal" in the sense of "hellish, diabolical," but *infernal* also is used figuratively to mean "terrible, very bad, detestable." Los chicos hacían un ruido **infernal** en la fiesta. *The boys were making a hellish noise (an infernal din) at the party.* Pasamos un día **infernal** entre la nieve en las montañas. *We spent a terrible day because of the snow in the mountains.*

informador / informer *Informador* (m.) is a positive concept: "informant, informing." Hubo cincuenta **informadores** en la encuesta. *There were fifty informants in the survey.* *Informer*, on the other hand, is a negative concept and can even become a risky profession: *delator* (m.), *denunciante* (m., f.), *confidente* (m., f.; of the police). Todos los **delatores** son traidores. *Every informer is a traitor.*

informal / informal *Informal* is not "informal" but "unreliable, undependable, incorrect (conduct)." Esa muchacha es **informal**. *That girl is undependable. Informal,* however, refers to a light side of life in a practical sense. It is a handy term that is used in many different contexts:
1. party, occasion: *íntima, de confianza, sin etiqueta*
2. clothes: *ordinario, de sport, de calle*
3. people: *sencillo, sin ceremonia, familiar*
4. attitude: *franco, sencillo*
Me gusta su conducta **sencilla**. *I like her informal behavior.*

informalidad / informality *Informalidad* (f.) means "unreliability, frivolity." La secretaria perdió el trabajo por su **informalidad**. *The secretary lost her job because of her unreliability. Informality* is translated as *sencillez* (f.), *falta de ceremonia*.

ingeniero / engineer *Ingeniero* is "engineer" in the sense of a "person working in an engineering profession who has training or schooling." Los **ingenieros** han llevado el hombre a la luna. *Engineers have taken mankind to the moon. Engineer* is used for many different tasks or jobs, some of which are far from being professional and requiring schooling. In general, the term is used to mean *mecánico* ("a workman, a mechanic"), *maquinista* (m., f.; a "railroad engineer"), and it is used figuratively to refer to an *autor* (m.; "author, maker"). ¿Quién ha sido el **autor** de esta obra de arte? *Who has been the engineer of this masterpiece?*

ingenuidad / ingenuity *Ingenuidad* (f.) is not "ingenuity" but "candor, frankness, openness." ¿Hay algún político con **ingenuidad** en el mundo? *Is there such a thing as a frank politician in the world? Ingenuity* means *ingenio, inventiva, ingeniosidad* (f.). Wren mostró gran **inventiva** en la construcción de campanarios.

*Wren showed great **ingenuity** in the construction of steeples.* **Ingenuo** and *ingenuous* mean the same thing: "frank, open, naive." *Ingenue* is translated as *dama joven* (in the theater).

ingrato / ingrate, ungrateful *Ingrato* translates the noun *ingrate* and the adjective *ungrateful*. However, *ingrato* has downgraded its connotation to mean "disagreeable, unpleasant" (with people) and "unrewarding, thankless, unproductive" (with things). [Note that *ingrato* takes the preposition *con* or *para con* followed by a noun.] *Es muy **ingrato** para con su familia. He is very **ungrateful** toward his family. Tenemos un tiempo muy **ingrato**. We are having very **disagreeable** weather. Estos terrenos son **ingratos**, por eso les llaman las "tierras flacas". This terrain is **unproductive**, which is why it is called "skinny lands."*

inhabitable / inhabitable *Inhabitable* means "uninhabitable"; it does not mean "inhabitable." *Inhabitable* means *habitable*. [This contradiction between the terms is due to the fact that the Spanish prefix *in-* is always negative, whereas the English prefix *in-* is sometimes affirmative for "in, within."] *Inhabitado* means "uninhabited." *Sueño con encontrar una isla **inhabitada**. I dream of finding an **uninhabited** island. Inhabited* is translated as *habitado, poblado. La colonia de Pennsylvania fue **habitada** por los cuáqueros. The colony of Pennsylvania was **inhabited** by the Quakers.*

injuria / injury *Injuria* is not "injury"; instead, it means "insult, affront, offense." *No soportamos las **injurias** de nuestros enemigos. We do not tolerate **insults** from our enemies. Injury* is *herida, daño, lesión. Sufrieron **heridas** graves en el accidente. They suffered grave **injuries** in the accident.* hacerse **daño** / *to **injure** oneself* *Injuriar* means "to insult, offend, abuse." *To injure* means *herir* (ie, i), *lastimar, hacer daño.*

estar **lesionado** = *to be injured*

*Se lastimó (se lesionó) la pierna. He **injured** his leg. Injurioso* is translated as "insulting, offensive, abusive." *No pude aguantar sus palabras **injuriosas**. I couldn't stand his **offensive** language. Injurious* means *perjudicial, pernicioso, dañino, nocivo.*

inmaterial / immaterial *Inmaterial* and *immaterial* both mean "incorporeal, spiritual." *Immaterial* is used frequently in the figurative sense of *indiferente, sin importancia, no pertinente.*

no importa = *it's immaterial*

*Para mí **no tiene importancia** que te quedes o no. As for me, it's **immaterial** whether you stay or go.*

inmediato / immediate *Inmediato* means "immediate" in the sense of "next in time, right away."

de inmediato = *immediately*

Immediate is used much more frequently than *inmediato*. Some of the additional meanings of *immediate* include *contiguo, cercano, próximo, urgente, primero. Ella vive en la casa **contigua** del lado izquierdo. She lives in the house **immediately** to the left.* peligro **inminente** / *immediate* danger **primera** necesidad / *immediate* need inmediaciones / *immediate* area (neighborhood)

inocente / innocent   *Inocente* and *innocent* share the same idea about a person who is "free from guilt." In addition, both terms are used in colloquial speech to mean a person who is "naive, simple, ignorant, gullible" *(simple, cándida, crédula).* una broma **inocente** /   an **innocent** joke   No seas **inocente**. *Don't be* ***naive*** *(innocent). Innocent* is also used in a figurative sense to describe things which are not serious: *benigno, sin importancia.*

insensible / insensible   *Insensible* in a medical sense means "insensible, numb" (referring to a part of the body). However, *insensible* also refers to a mental state: "insensitive, unfeeling, callous." El ladrón profesional es **insensible** ante el peligro. *The professional thief is* ***callous*** *in the face of danger. Insensible* keeps the original and material meaning in English of *inconsciente, sin sentido.* Estuvo **sin sentido** por veinte minutos cuando se cayó. *He was* ***insensible*** *(unconscious) for twenty minutes when he fell down.*

insinuar / insinuate   *Insinuar* and *to insinuate* both mean "to hint, suggest indirectly." The reflexive *insinuarse* means "to make advances" (usually, to a woman). **Se insinuó** a la muchacha. *He* ***made advances*** *to the girl. To insinuate* has downgraded its meaning to mean "to make a sly hint" and is more accurately translated as *maliciar.* ¿Estás **maliciando** que soy un ladrón? *Are you* ***insinuating*** *that I am a thief? Insinuación* is translated as "insinuation, hint, suggestion." *Insinuation,* similar to its verb, may have a negative connotation of "sly hint." In this sense, the translation is the noun *indirecta.* No me vengas con otra de tus **indirectas**. *Don't bring up another of your* ***insinuations.***

instancia / instance   *Instancia* is not "instance" but "request, petition." [*Instancia* translates as "instance" only as a legal term: *tribunal* (m.) *de primera* ***instancia,*** which means "small claims court" in the United States and "court of first instance" in Britain.] **en última instancia** = *as a last resort*
presentar una **instancia** /   *to present a* ***request***   **a instancias de** mi amigo /   *at* ***the request of*** *my friend   Instance* means *ejemplo, caso.*
por ejemplo = *for instance*
En muchos **casos** el acusado es inocente. *In many* ***instances,*** *the accused is innocent.*

instante / instant   *Instante* (m.) and *instant* are nouns, meaning "moment." *Instant,* as an adjective in English, means *urgente, inminente, inmediato;* and when it refers to food, *instantáneo, al instante.*
al instante = *instantly, right away*
café **instantáneo** (al instante) /   ***instant*** *coffee*   Llámame **en cuanto llegues**. *Call me* ***the instant you arrive.*** Es un mensaje **urgente**. *This is an* ***instant*** *(urgent) message.*

instrucción / instruction   *Instrucción* means "instruction" as "education," but the Spanish term is also used for "knowledge"; in common legal language, it means "preliminary investigation"; and in military talk, it means "drill, training, order." The plural form *instrucciones* stands for "directions," as well as "orders."
instrucciones para el uso de la computadora /   ***directions*** *for using the computer*

instrucción primaria y secundaria / *primary and secondary* **education** El profesor tiene mucha **instrucción**. *The professor is a person with much* **knowledge**. Es una **instrucción** de mi jefe. *It's an* **order** *from my boss.*

instrumental / instrumental *Instrumental* exactly means "instrumental." *Instrumental* is used in the following idiomatic expression that is not translated as *instrumental: to be instrumental in (contribuir a).* Ese jugador **contribuyó** mucho **a** la victoria. *That player* **was instrumental in** *the victory.*

insuficiencia / insufficiency *Insuficiencia* shares with *insufficiency* the idea of "inadequacy," but in Spanish *insuficiencia* also means "inefficiency, shortage" and in medical terminology, "failure." Hay **insuficiencia** de sangre. *There is a* **shortage** *of blood.* Murió de **insuficiencia** cardíaca. *He died of heart* **failure**.

insular / insular *Insular* means "insular" as "islander, of or referring to an island." España tiene tres provincias **insulares**. *Spain has three* **island** *provinces. Insular* in English has other meanings such as *aislado* ("isolated") and in a figurative sense *estrecho de miras* ("narrow-minded"). Tiene una mente **estrecha de miras**. *She has an* **insular** *mind (is narrow-minded).*

integral / integral *Integral* is "integral" in mathematics, and it also translates as "whole," as in *pan* **integral** ("whole wheat bread"). *Integral* in English also means *integrante, parte esencial.* una parte **integrante** de sus estudios / *an* **integral** *part of his studies* **Íntegro** is used to describe people who are "honest, upright" and things that are "whole, entire, complete." No todos los políticos son personas **íntegras**. *Not all politicians are* **honest** *people.* en versión **íntegra** / *in an* **unabridged** *edition* un día **íntegro** sin comer / *an* **entire** *day without food*

inteligencia / intelligence, intelligentsia *Inteligencia* means "intelligence" as "the ability to learn / think / act."
cociente de **inteligencia** = *intelligence quotient (IQ)*
No subestime la **inteligencia** de un perro. *Don't underestimate the* **intelligence** *of a dog. Intelligence* is also used for *información secreta.* Trabaja para el servicio de **información secreta**. *He works for an* **intelligence** *agency. Intelligentsia* is an English term of Russian origin that refers to *intelectuales* (collectively, "intellectuals").

intentar / intend *Intentar* is not "to intend" but "to try, attempt, mean." Con **intentarlo** no se pierde nada. *Nothing is lost by* **trying**. *To intend* stands for *proponerse, querer* (ie, i) *hacer, pensar.* Ella no **quería hacer** daño. *She* **intended** *no harm.*

interesado / interested *Interesado* means "interested" in the best sense of the word—"concerned." Both terms have downgraded this meaning, but in different ways. In Spanish *interesado* also means "selfish, greedy." No me gustan las personas **interesadas** en el dinero. *I don't like people who are* **greedy** *for money. Interested* has the downgraded meaning of *con prejuicio* ("biased"), *parcial.* Esa decisión no es buena porque fue hecha por partidarios **parciales**. *The decision is not good because it was made by* **interested** *parties. Interesante* exactly means "interesting" in Spanish, but it also is used colloquially to refer to "worthwhile, attractive (prices)."

interferencia / interference   *Interferencia* is "interference" regarding radio or television transmissions, in business, in games, and in languages or communication. *Interference,* however, has the primary meaning of *intromisión, intervención, ingerencia.* No nos gusta la **intervención** del gobierno. *We do not like government interference.*

interferir / interfere   *Interferir* (ie, i) means "to interfere" (in radio or television, in business, etc.). *To interfere* also means *intervenir* (ie, i), *entrometerse, dificultar.* ¡Deja de **entrometerte**! *Stop interfering!*

ínterin / interim   *Ínterin* (m.) and *interim* both refer to "a period of time in between" *(entretanto).* El **ínterin** de la presidencia duró dos meses. *The interim presidency lasted two months. Interim* is also used as an adjective to mean *interino, provisional.*
presidente interino = *interim president, acting president*
el concejo **interino** de la ciudad   /   *the city's interim council*

interior / interior   *Interior* is "interior," meaning "inside, inner," as well as "internal, domestic." As a masculine noun it means "inland" in countries with a seacoast.
ropa interior = *underwear*
decir para su interior = *to say to oneself*
La política **interior** es tan importante como la exterior. *Domestic policy is as important as foreign policy. Interioridad* (f.) is "interiority" ("inwardness"; the opposite of exteriority). The plural *interioridades* refers to "personal affairs, ins and outs" *(pormenores,* m.*).* No te metas en las **interioridades** de los demás. *Don't interfer in other people's personal affairs.*

interrogación / interrogation   *Interrogación* is "interrogation" with the meaning of "questioning" and is also the punctuation mark *(signo de interrogación;* "question" or "interrogation mark"). *Interrogation* is also a legal term that translates as *interrogatorio.* El **interrogatorio** duró una hora. *The interrogation lasted one hour. Interrogar,* similarly, is more of a legal term than the everyday word *preguntar* ("to ask") as a translation of *to interrogate.* El abogado **interrogó** al testigo. *The lawyer interrogated the witness.*

intervención / intervention   *Intervención* is "intervention" and also means "tapping (of telephones), auditing (accounts), participation (in a conversation), control (of prices)," and "operation" (or "surgery"). Su **intervención** en la conversación no fue bienvenida. *His participation in the conversation was not welcomed.* Muchos países tienen **intervención** gubernamental de los productos básicos. *Many countries have government control (of prices) on basic products.*

intervenir / intervene   *Intervenir* (ie, i) is "to intervene" as "to mediate in a dispute." However, *intervenir* also means "to participate, plead (for another), confiscate, interfere, audit, operate on (i.e., perform surgery)." Es bueno **intervenir**

en una clase de lenguas. *It's good to participate in a language course.* El gobierno **intervino** las drogas. *The government confiscated the drugs.* To intervene also means *mediar* (time, distance). **Mediaron** dos meses entre los asesinatos. *Two months intervened between murders.*

intoxicación / intoxication *Intoxicación* is "intoxication" with poison. *Intoxication* is also the everyday word for *borrachera, embriaguez* (f.), *ebriedad* (f.). *Intoxicado* means "intoxicated, poisoned." Fue **intoxicado** con arsénico y murió. *He was intoxicated with arsenic, and he died. Intoxicated* also means *borracho, ebrio, embriagado.* Un **borracho** con carro es un arma peligrosa. *An intoxicated person with a car is a dangerous weapon.* El chofer **emborrachado** fue detenido. *The intoxicated driver was arrested. Intoxicar* is "to intoxicate" (with poison). *To intoxicate* also translates as *emborracharse, embriagarse.*

introducir / introduce *Introducir* is "to introduce" ("to insert, bring in) and also "to create, cause, interfere." Los terroristas **introdujeron** estragos en todo el país. *The terrorists created havoc throughout the country. To introduce,* on the other hand, also means *presentar* (a person), *lanzar* (a new product), *prologar* (a book).
abordar un tema = *to introduce a question*
Le **presento** a mi amiga Rita. *May I introduce you to my friend Rita?* **lanzar** una nueva pasta de dientes / *to introduce a new toothpaste*

inusitado / unused *Inusitado* is not "unused" but "unusual, uncommon." No me agrada su conducta **inusitada.** *I don't like her unusual behavior. Unused* means either *sin usar (nuevo)* or *libre (desocupado)* ("vacant"). Mi condominio de Vallarta está **libre** ahora. *My condominium in Vallarta is unused (vacant) at the moment.*

inválido / invalid *Inválido* is "invalid" as a "disabled person." *Inválido* is used specially for a "disabled soldier." [Since modern society stresses positive values over negative values, the term *inválido* has been replaced in some countries by *minusválido* and in others by *limitado* or *impedido*. Likewise, in Spain, *invidente* ("sightless") has replaced the term *ciego* ("blind").] Este asiento está reservado para **inválidos.** *This seat is reserved for disabled persons. Invalid* (with the stress on the first syllable) sometimes refers to people who are *enfermizo* ("sickly"). *Invalid* (with the stress on the second syllable) means *nulo,* for example, applied to documents.
caducar = *to become invalid*
Ése es un contrato **nulo.** *That is an invalid contract. Invalidar* means "to invalidate" ("to deprive of legality, legal force"). *To invalid* (stress on the first syllable) means *dejar inválido* ("to disable").

inversión / inversion *Inversión* means "inversion" in the sense of "reversal, turning." However, *inversión* is a key word in business, meaning "investment" (of money, time, or energy). La **inversión** es la base de la economía moderna en el mundo capitalista. *Investment is the foundation of modern economy in the capitalistic world. Invertir* (ie, i) is translated as "to invert" ("to reverse, change, put upside down") and also "to invest" (money, energy), "to spend" (time). Con el resultado de las elecciones **se invirtieron** los papeles. *Roles were reversed (changed) as a result of the elections.* Para ganar mucho dinero hay que **invertir** mucho dinero. *To make a lot of money, you have to invest a lot of money.*

ira / ire *Ira* is translated as "ire" ("anger, wrath"). The plural form *iras* is a concrete noun meaning "fits of anger." en un arrebato de **ira** / *in a fit of* **anger** John Steinbeck escribió *Las uvas de la ira. John Steinbeck wrote* The Grapes of **Wrath.** *Ire* has become an archaic term that has been replaced by *anger, wrath.*

iris / iris *Iris* (m.) and *iris* are part of the anatomy of the eye that gives it color. (In Spanish, *iris* is both the singular and the plural form.) *Iris* is also used in the phrase *arco iris* or *arcoíris* (m.; "rainbow"). [The *Real Academia* and many other dictionaries spell *arco iris* as two words, but as a reflection of the constantly changing nature of language, many modern writers such as Octavio Paz and José Agustín spell it as one word—*arcoíris.* The spelling as one word follows Spanish phonetics, since the first part *arco* has no stress at all, which is the case with the first part of any compound word in Spanish.] Si tienes los ojos azules se lo debes al **iris.** *If you have blue eyes, you owe it to your* **iris.** El **arco iris** (arcoíris) es el símbolo de la paz. *The* **rainbow** *is a symbol of peace. Iris* in English also stands for the flower *lirio.* (In English, the plural of *iris* is *irises* or *irides.*) Hay muchas clases de **lirios.** *There are many kinds of* **irises.**

J

jarro, jarra, jarrón / jar *Jarro* is translated as "jar" ("jug" made of glass, stone, earthenware). The shape and size of a *jarro* may change from region to region. In Spain it is usual to say *jarro de vino* and also *jarro de cerveza* ("beer mug"). Nos sirvió un **jarro** de vino tinto. *He served us a jug of red wine.* ***Jarra*** comes from an Arabic word for "earthenware jar" *(de loza)*. A *jarra* is larger than a *jarro* and is translated most accurately as "pitcher." Nowadays, the *jarras* are made of glass and are used for wine, water, or beer. Pidieron una **jarra** de cerveza. *They ordered a **pitcher** of beer.* ***Jarrón*** (m.) translates as "vase" or "urn" (used for flowers or simply for decoration). Puse las rosas en un **jarrón** grande. *I put the roses in a large **vase**.* Jar in English translates as *tarro* for honey, jam, etc. Jar also means *chirrido, sacudida.* La mermelada se vende en **jarros** de una libra. *Jam (preserves) is sold in one-pound **jars**.*

jersey / jersey *Jersey* (m.) is exactly the same as *jersey* ("sweater") in Britain, where the Spanish term comes from. The plural form in Spanish has two spellings, according to different countries: / *jerséis* and *jerseyes*. [In the United States, *jersey* usually refers to a knitted fabric *(tela tejida)*.]

jornada / journey *Jornada* has something in common with *journey* in that one of its meanings is "one day's journey." Nevertheless, the basic meaning of *jornada* is "working day." In classical plays, it means "act" and in the movies, it means "part" or "episode." In a figurative sense, *jornada* means "lifetime." En esta oficina tenemos una **jornada** de ocho horas. *In this office we have an eight-hour **working day** (workday).* Hice el viaje en tres **jornadas**. *I made the trip in three **stages**.* Journey, on the other hand, means *viaje* (m.).
¡**Buen viaje**! = *Have a nice journey!*
Se fue al **otro mundo**. *He went on his **last journey**. (He passed away.)*

jornal / journal *Jornal* (m.) does not mean "journal"; instead, it means "a day's wage, a day's work."
trabajar a jornal = *to be paid by the day*
¿Cuánto ganas de **jornal** por recoger fresas? *How much is your **day's wage** for picking strawberries?* Journal has several denotations in English: *periódico, revista; diario* (in literature as well as in bookkeeping); and *boletín* (m.; of a club or society). Hispania es la **revista** de la American Association of Teachers of Spanish and Portuguese. *Hispania is the **journal** of the American Association of Teachers of Spanish and Portuguese.* El tenedor de libros asienta todas las cuentas en el **diario**. *The bookkeeper enters all the invoices in the **journal**.*

jubilación / jubilation *Jubilación* is not "jubilation" but "retirement, pension (money)." [In parts of Latin America *retiro* is used instead of *jubilación* to mean "retirement."] El día de su **jubilación** fue una ocasión de gran regocijo. *The day of his **retirement** was an occasion of great joy.* Tiene una **jubilación** de 900 dólares mensuales. *She has a **pension** of 900 dollars a month.* Jubilation means *júbilo,* *regocijo, alborozo, exultación.* La fiesta de cumpleaños causó gran **júbilo** entre los convidados. *The birthday party was the cause of great **jubilation** among the guests.* **Jubilarse,** as well as *retirarse* (in some Latin American countries), means "to retire."

jungla / jungle *Jungla* has been included in the most recent dictionary of the *Real Academia* with the meaning of "jungle," but for no apparent reason, the term was limited to Asia and the Americas (as though Africa and Australia had no jungles!). *Jungle* traditionally has been translated as *selva, bosque* (m.), *monte* (m.), *manigua* and now is acceptably translated as *jungla.* Tarzán y Jane vivían en las **junglas** (selvas) de África. *Tarzan and Jane lived in the **jungles** of Africa.* La palabra *jungla* viene del hindú *jangal* (desierto o bosque). *The word* jungle *comes from the Hindu word* jangal *(desert or forest).*

junta / junta *Junta* in Spanish means "meeting, assembly, session, board (of directors), council, junction." Se reunió la **junta** directiva. *The **board** of directors had a meeting.* Es miembro de la **junta.** *He is a member of the **council** (board).* Los profesores tuvieron una **junta** general. *The professors had a general **meeting.** Junta,* of course, has been borrowed from Spanish, but it has taken only one denotation: a "Spanish administrative body, a military group in power." La **junta** militar tomó el poder. *The military **junta** took power.*

jurado / jury *Jurado* means "jury" (in a court of law) as a noun, but as an adjective from the verb *jurar,* it means "sworn, sworn-in."
enemigo jurado = *sworn enemy*
El **jurado** necesitó dos días completos para deliberar y decidir. *The **jury** needed two full days to deliberate and decide.* Ha **jurado** decir la verdad y sólo la verdad. *He has **sworn** to tell the truth and nothing but the truth.*

justicia / justice *Justicia* means "justice, fairness." The Spanish term is also used to refer to the "execution" of a person condemned to death.
hacer justicia = *to do justice (to)*
La **justicia** está cumplida. *Justice has been done. Justice* also applies to *juez* (m.) or judge, for example, of the Supreme Court *(corte suprema).*
juez de paz = *justice of the peace*
Fue nombrado **juez** supremo hace cuatro años. *He was appointed a supreme court **justice** four years ago.* hacer **honor** a la comida / to do **justice** to a meal

justo / just *Justo* shares with *just* the idea of "fair, right, with justice." However, *justo* also means "tight, exact, correct, sufficient, deserved (punishment), sound (reasoning)." más de lo **justo** / *more than **enough*** lo **justo** y lo injusto / *right and wrong* vivir muy **justo** / *to eke out a living* Estos zapatos me molestan porque están muy **justos.** *These shoes bother me because they are so **tight.** Just* sometimes carries the nuance of *justificado, fundado* (complaint). *Justamente* shares the meaning of *justly,* and also means "tightly, exactly, precisely." Los tribunales deben tratar **con justicia,** incluso a los grandes. *The courts should deal **justly,** even with the great.*

juvenil / juvenile *Juvenil* means "juvenile" in the sense of "related to young people." In Spanish, *juvenil* refers only to teenagers and young adults *(jóvenes)*. Sometimes, according to context, *juvenil* is better translated as "young, youthful." delincuencia **juvenil** / *juvenile delincuency* en los años **juveniles** / *in one's youth* aspecto **juvenil** / *youthful appearance* *Juvenile* includes children, as well as teens and young adults. Often the sense of *juvenile* is translated as *infantil* or *de menores,* as well as *juvenil.*

tribunal de menores = *juvenile court*

libros **para niños** / *juvenile books*

L

labor / labor *Labor* (m.) and *labor* share the basic idea of "work in general, task." In Spanish, *labor* has many meanings: "farming (plowing, tilling); needlework, sewing, or knitting; household chores." *Ella no descuida sus* **labores** *de punto. She does not neglect her knitting* **work** *(needlework)*. *Labor* is used more frequently in English than its Spanish cognate. It has many meanings, according to context: *trabajo, faena, esfuerzos, parto, dolores* (m.) *de parto, mano* (f.) *de obra, trabajadores* (m.), *clase obrera.*
sindicato = *labor union*
Siempre se necesita **mano de obra** *en la fábrica de juguetes. There is always a need for* **labor** *in the toy factory.* *Hace dos horas que tiene* **dolores de parto.** *She has been in* **labor** *for two hours.* *Hubo un conflicto* **laboral** *y el* **sindicato** *trató de resolverlo. There was a* **labor** *dispute and the* **labor union** *tried to resolve it.*

laborioso / laborious *Laborioso* is "laborious" in the sense of "industrious, hardworking." *El gerente fue un peón* **laborioso** *por varios años. The manager was an industrious laborer for several years.* *Juanito es* **laborioso** *en el colegio. Johnny is industrious (hardworking) at school.* *Laborious* seems to emphasize the difficulty of working hard. Good translations for it are *arduo, difícil, pesado, penoso.* *Nadie quiere hacer una tarea* **penosa.** *No one wants to undertake a* **laborious** *task.*

labrador / laborer *Labrador* (m.) does not mean "laborer" but "farmer, peasant." *El* **labrador** *es el rey de sus campos, pobres o ricos. The* **farmer** *is the king of his fields, whether poor or rich.* *Laborer* means *peón* (m.), *jornalero, bracero* (Mexico), *obrero.* *Muchos mexicanos trabajan legalmente de* **braceros** *en los Estados Unidos. Many Mexicans work legally as* **laborers** *in the United States.* [The basic idea of *labrador* is the peasant who owns or leases the land he works (tills). The basic idea of *laborer* is a paid worker in a factory or in the fields.] *Labrar* means "to labor" ("to work") in general, but it also means "to carve (wood), to plow, to build, to cut (precious stones)." *To labor,* on the other hand, suggests *esforzarse* (ue), *estar de parto, avanzar difícilmente.*

lamentable / lamentable *Lamentable* means "lamentable" in the sense of "deplorable," but it also means "pitiful, regrettable, mournful," and in a figurative sense, "poor, bad, pathetic (work, result, etc.)." *El muchacho tuvo unas notas* **lamentables** *porque jugó más que estudió. The boy received* **pathetic** *grades because he played more than he studied.* *Su muerte repentina en el accidente es muy* **lamentable.** *Her sudden death in the accident is very* **regrettable.** *Lamentar,* on the other hand, exactly means "to lament" ("to feel sorry, to regret").

lámpara / lamp *Lámpara* and *lamp* both are "devices to produce light." However, *lámpara* also means "light bulb" *(bombilla, bombillo, foco)* and in colloquial speech in Spain, it means "grease stain" (on clothes). *Tengo una* **lámpara** *movible en el pupitre. I have a portable* **lamp** *on my desk.* *Necesito una* **lámpara** *de cien vatios. I need a one-hundred-watt* **light bulb.** *Lamp* also means *farol* (m.) or

farola, faro (headlight of a car), *linterna* ("flashlight").
pantalla = *lamp shade*
farol, farola = *street lamp (streetlight)*

lance / lance   *Lance* (m.) does not mean "lance"; instead, it means "adventure, event, episode, critical moment, throw or cast (in fishing), move or stroke (of fortune)."
lance de honor = *duel, challenge*
De joven tuve varios **lances** amorosos. *When I was young, I had several amorous* **adventures**. *Lance* is translated as *lanza, lancero, arpón* (m.; for fishing). Los caballeros peleaban con **lanzas** en sus caballos. *Knights used to fight on horseback with their* **lances**.

largo / large   *Largo* is not "large" but "long, lengthy, good."
una hora larga = *a good hour*
vestido largo = *evening dress*
a la larga = *in the long run*
a lo largo = *along, by*
Esta carretera es **más larga** que un día sin pan. *This road is* **longer** *than a day without bread (food).* Esta falda te está **larga**. *This skirt is* **long** *on you.* dos millones **largos** / *a good two million Large* has several meanings, according to its context: *grande, importante, abundante, copioso, grueso, considerable, voluminoso, numeroso, extenso.*
en libertad, suelto = *at large*
un paquete **voluminoso** / *a large package (parcel)* Robaron una cantidad **considerable** de dinero. *They stole a* **large** *amount of money. Largueza* exactly means "largesse" ("generosity").

latitud / latitude   *Latitud* (f.) and *latitude* are terms used in geography: "distance from a point to the equator." *Latitud* also means "width, breadth, extent, area." Madrid y Washington tienen casi la misma **latitud**. *Madrid and Washington are almost at the same* **latitude**. *Latitude* is also used figuratively to mean *libertad* (f.), *amplitud* (f.), *laxitud* (f.). Las personas buscan la **libertad** de opinión y de acción. *People look for* **latitude** *of opinion and of action.*

lavatorio / lavatory   *Lavatorio* and *lavatory* share the meaning of a religious ceremony at mass. However, *lavatorio* also means "washstand," and in some countries, "sink." (In other countries, the terms *lavabo, pila,* or *fregadero* are used to mean "sink.") Los **lavatorios** (lavabos) de metal son duraderos. *Metal* **washstands** *(sinks) are long-lasting. Lavatory* is frequently used for *cuarto de baño* or simply *baño* or *servicio*. In Spain, it is translated as *retrete* (m.) or *váter* (m.) (from the British term *watercloset*). Los aviones tienen **baño** de unisexo. *Airplanes have unisex* **lavatories**.

lazo / lasso, lace   *Lazo* and *lasso* both stand for the rope that cowboys use "to lasso animals." *Lazo,* however, has many more meanings: "knot, bow (of ribbon), snare or trap (in hunting), bend (in the road), rope" *(cordel, m.),* and in some countries, "laces" (for shoes). In a figurative sense, *lazo* means "tie, bond, link."

lazos de amistad = *bonds of friendship*
Los zorros se pueden cazar con **lazos**. *Foxes can be hunted with snares.* tender un **lazo** / *to set a trap* **lazo** corredizo / *slipknot* *Lace* shares the same origin as *lazo*, but *lace* means *encaje* (m.), *cordón* (m.; for shoes), *cinta, trencilla* ("braid"). Los **encajes** siempre están de moda. *Lace is always in style.*

lector / lecturer *Lector* (m.) is not "lecturer" but "reader" and, in some countries, "assistant (professor)." *Lecturer* means *conferenciante* (m., f.), *conferencista* (m., f.; in the Americas), *disertante* (m., f.), *profesor* (m.). El **conferenciante** estuvo muy gracioso. *The lecturer was very funny.*

lectura / lecture *Lectura* means "reading, reading matter."
dar lectura a = *to read*
Mi pasatiempo favorito es la **lectura**. *My favorite pastime is reading.* *Lecture* is translated as *conferencia, disertación, charla, curso.* dar una **conferencia** / *to give a lecture* sala de **conferencias** / *lecture room*

lenguaje / language *Lenguaje* (m.) is "language" in the sense of "a particular form of speaking of a person, group, or region." This meaning of *lenguaje* is roughly equivalent to the word *dialect* in English. No conozco el **lenguaje** de los jóvenes de hoy. *I don't know the language of today's youth.* *Language* in general is most commonly translated as *lengua.* ¿Cuál es la **lengua** oficial de Irlanda? *What is the official language of Ireland?*

letra / letter *Letra* and *letter* both stand for symbols of the alphabet: "a-b-c-d." *Letra* also means "handwriting, lyrics (of a song), bill of exchange, draft (in business)." The plural form *Letras* translates as the "Arts."
letra mayúscula = *capital (uppercase) letter*
al pie de la letra = *to the letter*
letra de molde = *printing* (in penmanship)
Tengo que pagar la **letra** del coche. *I have to pay the bill for the car.* Mi **letra** es difícil de leer. *My handwriting is hard to read.* *Letter* also means *carta.*
carta certificada = *registered letter*

liberar, libertar / liberate *Liberar, libertar* and *to liberate* mean "to free legally or financially from prison or captivity." When speaking of the liberation of a country, the Spanish term is *libertar* rather than *liberar*. Bolívar **libertó** muchos países de Sudamérica. *Bolivar liberated many countries of South America.* *To liberate* (from obligations) is *librar(se).* La mujer del siglo diecisiete raramente **se libró** de los deberes familiares. *The woman of the seventeenth century was rarely liberated from family duties.*

librería / library *Librería* is not "library" but "bookstore" and also "bookcase."
librería de ocasión = *secondhand bookstore*
Library means *biblioteca.*
hemeroteca = *newspaper library*
biblioteca de consulta (de préstamo, pública) / *reference (lending, public) library*
biblioteca circulante / *mobile library (bookmobile)* *Librero* means "bookseller," as well as "bookcase" and "bookshelf."

licencia / license *Licencia* and *license* share the ideas of "permission, leave, permit, liberty." The term *licencia* also roughly translates as "master's degree." [Some countries use *licencia* and other use *licenciatura* to refer to the degree obtained at a university, as in *licencia en derecho.*] **licencia** por enfermedad / *sick leave* Para pescar necesitas **licencia** de pescar. *In order to fish, you need a fishing license.* Tengo **licencia** de mi jefe. *I have my boss's **permission.*** Tiene una **licencia** en filosofía y letras. *He has a **master's degree** in liberal arts. License* in the sense of a driver's license is *carné* (m.; *de conducir)* in Spain and parts of South America and *licencia* or *permiso (de manejar)* in the rest of the Americas. [Note that *carné* is the new spelling that has been approved by the *Real Academia* for *carnet.*] *Licenciado* is the equivalent of a "graduate with a master's degree." The degree itself is called *licenciatura* or *licencia.*

liceo / lyceum *Liceo* is not "lyceum" but "high school, special school (for music, languages, etc.)." [In Spain and in some Latin American countries, *instituto* is "high school," but in other countries, the term is *liceo.* Culturally, *El Liceo* is the opera house in Barcelona.] Mi hijo estudia en el **liceo** Bolívar de Caracas. *My son is a student at Bolivar **High School** in Caracas. Lyceum* means *auditorio* or *sala de conferencias; sociedad literaria; ateneo; cursillo.* Celebramos un **cursillo** de dos días sobre Miguel de Cervantes. *We held a two-day **lyceum** on Miguel de Cervantes.*

lid / lid *Lid* (f.) is a sophisticated term for *fight, struggle, strife,* whereas the English "lid" means *tapa, tapadera.* "Eyelid" is *párpado.* Las **lides** del espíritu no son fáciles de ganar. *Spiritual **struggles** are difficult to overcome.*

líder / leader *Líder* (m.) comes from the English word *leader,* and both terms share the idea of "heading a group of people." [The *Real Academia* "finally" included *líder* in its latest dictionary.] *Lidiar* means "to fight" in general and the term is used especially to mean "to fight bulls." On the other hand, "to lead" translates as *guiar, conducir* (a group, an orchestra, etc.). Fidel Castro ha sido un gran **líder** comunista. *Fidel Castro has been a great communist **leader.** Leader* is an everyday word for different concepts: *guía* (m., f.), *cabecilla* (of rebels, of a gang), *caudillo* (of the military), *primero* or *primera,* and in a court of law, *abogado principal.* Ese joven nació para mandar. *That young man is a born **leader.*** El **cabecilla** rebelde fue detenido. *The rebel **leader** was arrested.*

línea / line *Línea* and *line* share the same ideas regarding geometry, communications, way of conduct, class. *Línea* also means "figure" (of a person), synonymous with *esbeltez* (f.). El borracho no caminaba en **línea** recta. *The drunk was not walking in a straight **line.*** Firme arriba de la línea de puntos. *Sign on the dotted line.* Escriba las respuestas en las líneas que siguen. *Write your answers on the lines below.* **línea** de saque en tenis / *service **line** in tennis* **línea** férrea / *railway **line*** en **líneas** generales / *in a broad **outline** (overview) Line* also means *cola* (a "line" or "queue" of people), *verso* (in a poem), *clase* (f.; of business), *vía* (railroad track), *alineación* (of a street). ¡No cuelgue! *Hold the **line!** (Don't hang up!)*

linterna / lantern   *Linterna* is not "lantern" but "flashlight, torch." La luz de la **linterna** ahuyentó a los ladrones. *The light from the flashlight scared away the thieves.* Lantern translates as *farol* (m.), *fanal* (m.; in a lighthouse). Caminaba con un **farol** en la mano. *He was walking with a lantern in his hand.* [Note that both cognates are used in the following expression: **linterna mágica** = *magic lantern.*]

literalmente / literally   *Literalmente* and *literally* mean "to the letter, literal manner or sense." Traducir **literalmente** puede ser peligroso. *Translating literally (word for word) can be risky. Literally* also is used to mean *verdaderamente, materialmente, como suena.* Llueve **materialmente** cada día un diluvio de libros. *Literally a flood of books pours out every day.*

literato / literate   *Literato* does not mean "literate"; instead, it means "writer, author" of literature. Jorge Luis Borges es un **literato** de importancia de este siglo. *Jorge Luis Borges is an important literary **writer** of this century. Literate* means *letrado* or *erudito* in the most elevated sense of the word. Its everyday meaning, however, refers to a person *que sabe leer y escribir, que no es analfabeto, con educación básica.* There is no specific adjective in Spanish for the concept of *literacy.* Para poder votar con conocimiento usted debe **saber leer y escribir.** *You must be **literate** in order to vote knowledgeably.*

literatura / literature   *Literatura* is "literature" with the meaning of "artistic writing." *Literature* has downgraded its "artistic" emphasis to refer to any written information: *folleto, panfleto, información escrita.* Los bancos tienen muchos **folletos** sobre sus operaciones. *Banks have plenty of **literature** about their facilities.*

lívido / livid   *Lívido* and *livid* share the concept of "discolored; pale (person)." *Livid* has changed its connotation to refer to "anger," the cause of the fading color in the face. Equivalents in Spanish are *furioso, enojado.* Cuando leyó la carta se puso **furioso** de rabia. *When he read the letter, he became **livid** with rage.*

local / local   *Local* and *local* are both adjectives, meaning "relating to a place." In Spanish, *local* (m.) is also a noun, meaning "room, building, premises." Alquilé un **local** para poner una zapatería. *I leased a **place** to establish a shoe store.*   abandonar el **local** / *to leave the **premises***

localidad / locality   *Localidad* (f.) is "locality" ("place") and also "town, village" and, in the world of public spectacles, "seat, ticket" (for a theater, auditorium, etc.) una **localidad** de mil almas / *a **town** of one thousand people (souls)*   Todas las **localidades** están vendidas. *All the **tickets** are sold out. Locality,* on the other hand, means *orientación, domicilio.* No conozco su **domicilio** actual. *I don't know his present **locality.*   mal sentido de **orientación** / *poor sense of **locality***

longitud / longitude   *Longitud* (f.) and *longitude* are terms used in geography for "the distance east or west of meridian zero (Greenwich)." However, *longitud* is the everyday word for "length." [Note that *long* is translated as *largo.*] Su **longitud** es de cinco metros. *Its **length** is five meters.*   salto de **longitud** / *long jump*

lote / lot *Lote* (m.) originally meant "each part of a lottery" *(lotería)*. *Lote* and *lot* share the idea of "portion, share, piece of land." Compré un **lote** para construir un chalé. *I bought a lot to build a chalet.* *Lot* also means *destino, suerte* (f.), and in a figurative sense, *tipo* or *individuo* ("fellow, guy"); *colección, serie* (f.), or *grupo*.

mucho = *lots, a lot of*

una barbaridad = *an awful lot*

Ese vaquero es un **tipo** peligroso. *That cowboy is a dangerous lot.* [British] La muerte es el **destino** de todos. *Death is the common lot.* Es un **grupo** de gente simpática. *It's a fine lot of people.*

lujo / luxe *Lujo* and *luxe* only share the expression *de lujo* ("deluxe"). *Lujo* is accurately translated as "luxury."

lujo de = *too much, too many (a wealth of)*

Hay que pagar impuestos en artículos de **lujo**. *One has to pay taxes on luxury items.* No puedo permitirme ese **lujo**. *I cannot afford that luxury.* Te compraste un Cadillac **de lujo**. *You bought a deluxe Cadillac.* *Lujoso* means "luxurious." [*See also the entry for* **lujuria / luxury**.]

lujuria / luxury *Lujuria* is not "luxury" but "lust, sensuality, lewdness, lechery." Lujuria es uno de los siete pecados capitales. *Lust is one of the seven deadly sins.* *Luxury* means *lujo, placer* (m.), *gusto.* Siempre vivieron con mucho **lujo**. *They always lived in luxury.* ¡Qué **gusto** poder descansar en la playa! *What a luxury to be able to rest at the beach!* *Lujurioso* means "lustful, lewd, lecherous." Fue acusado de conducta **lujuriosa**. *He was accused of lewd conduct.* *Luxurious* translates as *lujoso, de lujo, fastuoso.* *Lujuriante* means "luxuriant" in reference to vegetation, but it also means "lewd, lustful" when applied to people. vegetación **lujuriante** / *luxuriant* vegetation No te fíes. Es un viejo **lujuriante** (lujurioso). *Don't trust him. He is a lewd ("dirty") old man.* *Luxuriant* means *exuberante, frondoso.*

luminoso / luminous *Luminoso* means "luminous" ("filled with light"), as well as "bright, illuminated." letrero **luminoso** / *illuminated* sign fuente **luminosa** / *illuminated* (lighted) fountain idea **luminosa** / *bright* idea

lunar / lunar *Lunar* and *lunar* are both adjectives meaning "of or related to the moon" *(luna)*. *Lunar* (m.) is also a noun, meaning "mole" (on the skin), "beauty mark or spot," and in a figurative sense, "flaw, blemish." año **lunar** / *lunar* year **lunar** postizo / *beauty mark* vestido de **lunares** / *polka-dot dress* "Ese **lunar** que tienes, cielito lindo, junto a tu boca" (Canción, "Cielito lindo") *"That mole you have, my sweet love, next to your mouth" (Song, "Cielito Lindo")*

lunático / lunatic *Lunático* is not "lunatic" but "whimsical, capricious, moody, temperamental." Tengo un amigo **lunático** que cambia de idea como de camisa. *I have a moody friend who changes his mind as often as he changes his shirt.* *Lunatic* perhaps derives from one who has been exposed to the full moon because it means *loco* (insane), *descabellado* (out of one's mind). No me gusta ese proyecto **descabellado.** *I don't like that* **lunatic** *(crazy) plan.* Ese cuadro lo ha pintado un **loco.** *That picture was painted by a* **lunatic.**

lustre / luster   *Lustre* (m.) shares with *luster* the idea of "shine, brilliance, gloss, glory, distinction." In some countries, *lustre* is used to mean "shoe polish" *(betún,* m.*).* Esa pintura tiene mucho **lustre.** *That paint has a lot of* **luster** *(gloss).* Tus zapatos necesitan **lustre.** *Your shoes need* **polish.** *Luster* also means *araña* ("chandelier"), *colgante* (m.; "glass pendant"), *barniz* (m.; on pottery), *cerámica vidriada* ("lusterware"). *Luster* or *lustrum* are literary terms in English for *lustro* ("a five-year period"). Esa **araña** es maravillosamente elegante. *That* **luster** *(chandelier) is wonderfully elegant.* Hace dos **lustros** que terminó la guerra. *The war ended two* **lusters** *ago.*

Ll

llama / llama *Llama* and *llama* both refer to the same animal. The word comes from the Quichua language, not from the Latin *flamma* ("flame" in English; *llama* in Spanish). *Llama* in Spanish also means "flame" and, in a figurative sense, "a burning passion." [The story about the spit or saliva of the llama being hot or burning is false.] **llama** auxiliar / *pilot* **light** estallar en **llamas** / *to burst into* **flames** en **llamas** / *on* **fire***, ablaze*

M

maduro / mature   *Maduro* and *mature* are both used to describe people as "fully developed or fully grown." Both terms also mean "ripe, mellow" (fruit, etc.), although *ripe* is used more frequently than *mature* in English. El muchacho actúa como una persona **madura**. *The boy acts as a mature person.* Los mangos ya están **maduros**. *The mangoes are ripe (mature) already. Mature* is also used in business to mean *vencido* ("due, payable") in reference to bond notes, loans, etc. El bono ya está **vencido**. *The bond is already mature.*   después de **largas** deliberaciones / *after mature deliberations*   **Madurar** means "to mature," as well as "to ripen, to grow old." Las uvas **maduran** en agosto. *Grapes ripen (mature) in August.*
madurar un plan = *to think about*
una decisión **madurada** / *a mature decision   To mature* is used in business to mean *vencerse* (a bond, a bill, insurance, etc.). El bono **se vence** en 1998. *The bond will mature in 1998. Maduración* translates as "maturation," as well as "ripening."

maestría / mastery   *Maestría* is "mastery" as "talent, skill, knowledge." *Maestría* is also used in some countries to mean "master's degree"; in other countries the term *licenciatura* is used. Pablo Picasso pintaba con gran **maestría**. *Pablo Picasso painted with great skill (talent, mastery). Mastery* also means *autoridad* (f.), *dominio, supremacía*. El diplomático llegó a **dominar** cinco lenguas. *The diplomat gained mastery of five languages.*

maestro / maestro, master   *Maestro* means "maestro" in music and also "master" in the sense of "expert in" (art, painting, etc.). However, the everyday meaning of *maestro (maestra)* is "teacher, schoolteacher."
obra maestra = *masterpiece*
llave maestra = *master key*
abeja maestra = *queen bee*
maestro de ceremonias / *master of ceremonies   Master* also means *dueño, señor, amo, patrón* (m.). ¿Quién es el **dueño** de la casa? *Who is the master of the house?*   no depender de nadie / *to be one's own master   Maestre* (m.) is an old term for "grand master" (of a military or religious order). Lope de Vega fue **maestre** de Calatrava. *Lope de Vega was grand master of Calatrava.*

mágico / magic   *Mágico* is "magic(al)" as an adjective and "magician" *(mago)* as a noun. In a figurative sense, *mágico* means "wonderful, marvelous."   varita **mágica** / *magic wand*   La fantasía crea un mundo **mágico**. *Fantasy creates a magic (magical) world.* Sus palabras tuvieron un efecto **mágico** sobre la audiencia. *His words had a wonderful effect on the public. Magic* is also a noun for *magia*.
por arte de magia = *by magic*
magia blanca / *white magic*   Para los niños Disneylandia es un mundo de **magia**. *For children, Disneyland is a world of magic.*

magisterial / magisterial *Magisterial* does not mean "magisterial"; rather, it means "related to teaching." La carrera **magisterial** no es muy larga. *The course of study to become a teacher is not very long.* *Magisterial* means *autoritario, oficial, dominante, pomposo.* El director habló con un tono muy **dominante** (autoritario). *The principal spoke in a magisterial tone of voice.* *Magistral* is translated as "masterly, excellent." La actuación del grupo fue **magistral.** *The group's performance was masterly (masterful, excellent).*

malicia / malice *Malicia* is not "malice" but "wickedness, slyness, subtlety, suspicion." *Malice* means *malevolencia, mala voluntad, ojeriza, rencor* (m.), *maldad* (f.), and in legal terms, *intención delictuosa.* [The basic difference is that *malice* always suggests an "active ill will, a desire to harm," whereas *malicia* suggests a "passive harm or evil."] "Con **malevolencia** para nadie, con caridad para todos" (Abrahán Lincoln) *"With malice toward none, with charity for all" (Abraham Lincoln)* No le guardo **rencor** a ella. *I bear her no malice.* *Maliciar(se)* means "to fear, suspect, go bad." No **malicies** que te quieran engañar. *Don't suspect that they want to deceive you.*

malicioso / malicious *Malicioso* is not as strong as "malicious." It is more accurately translated as "suspicious, improper, sly." El comediante usó expresiones **maliciosas.** *The comedian used improper expressions.* *Malicious,* however, means *malévolo, rencoroso, malo,* and in legal terminology, *delictuoso, doloso.*
daño **doloso** = *malicious damage*
una mirada **malévola** / *a malicious look*

mandato / mandate *Mandato* and *mandate* both refer to "political term, judicial warrant or order." *Mandato,* however, has a wide range of meanings: "command, order (*una orden* of any kind), term of office," and in the legal world, "power of attorney." El **mandato** del presidente dura seis años en México. *The president's mandate lasts six years in Mexico.* El **mandato** (la orden) del dictador era difícil de cumplir. *The dictator's order was difficult to carry out.*

manejar / manage *Manejar* is "to manage" (a tool, a machine, a person), but both terms have additional meanings. *Manejar* is "to drive (a vehicle), to handle or wield" *(operar),* and in a figurative sense, "to boss, to lead by the nose." [*Manejar* is the term used in the Americas for "to drive"; *conducir* is the term used in Spain.] **manejar** el tinglado / *to pull strings* No sé **manejar** (operar) este aparato. *I don't know how to run (to manage) this machine.* Los taxistas del mundo **manejan** (conducen) como locos. *Taxi drivers of the world drive like crazed people.* *To manage* is a frequently used term in English to cover many situations: *administrar, dirigir, dominar, conseguir* (i), *arreglárselas.* [In the Spanish spoken in the United States, the term *manachear* is used conversationally for "to manage"; however, this term has not found its way into any dictionary to date.] Se las **arregló** para ver al presidente. *He managed to see the president.* ¿Puedes **venir** a las diez? *Can you manage ten o'clock?* Ella **domina** a su marido. *She manages (dominates) her husband.* *Manager* is translated as *gerente* (m.), *director* (m.), and *administrador* (m.); however, the English term is used extensively in some Latin American countries and has been included in some dictionaries. Tienes que hablar con el **administrador.** *You have to speak to the manager.*

manera / manner *Manera (modo)* is exactly *manner* ("way").
sobre manera = *exceedingly*
no hay manera = *there is no way*
de esta **manera** / *after this **manner**, in this way* Me contestó de **mala manera**.
He answered me rudely. **Manners**, the plural form, is translated as *modales* (m.),
educación (cortesía), *costumbres* (f.). La **educación** hace al hombre. *Manners
make the man.* ¡Vaya **modales**! *Where are your **manners**?* Es de mala educación
interrumpir. *It is bad **manners** to interrupt.* comedia de **costumbres** / *comedy
of manners*

mango / mango *Mango* and *mango* both stand for the tropical fruit, as well as
the tree on which it grows. But in Spanish, *mango* has an everyday meaning
of "handle" (of a tool) that has different names, according to the tool: "stick"
(of an umbrella or a broom), "stock" (of a whip), "hilt" (of a sword or dagger),
"helve, haft" (of a tool or weapon in general). Me comí dos **mangos**. *I ate two
mangoes (mangos).* El **mango** del cuchillo es de plástico. *The knife **handle** is made
of plastic.* Ella espantó el ratón con un **mango de escoba**. *She scared away the
mouse with a **broomstick**.*

manía / mania *Manía* and *mania* share the idea of "fad, craze, obsession." *Manía*
also means "oddity, eccentricity, idiosyncrasy," and in a figurative sense, "habit"
or in the worst sense of the word, "bad habit." **manía** de grandezas /
megalomania **manía** depresiva / *depressive psychosis* Tiene la **manía** de
comerse las uñas. *He has the **bad habit** of biting his fingernails.* El viejito tiene
manías raras. *The old man has strange **eccentricities**. **Maníaco*** is exactly "maniac,
maniacal," meaning "mad, crazy, fanatic, faddish." Again, the Spanish term
frequently means "eccentric, odd, cranky, fussy, finicky." Los **maníacos** necesitan
tratamiento médico. *Maniacs need medical treatment.* Henry Higgins fue un
lingüista **maniático**. *Henry Higgins was a **finicky** linguist.*

manifestación / manifestation *Manifestación* is "manifestation" as "declaration,
statement, a display or showing (of emotion, of nature, etc.)"; and in recent times,
it has come to mean "(public) demonstration, mass meeting." hacer una
manifestación / *to hold a **demonstration**; to demonstrate* La policía disolvió
la **manifestación**. *The police broke up the **demonstration**.*

manifiesto / manifesto, manifest *Manifiesto*, as a noun, means "manifesto" ("a
political statement"); as an adjective it exactly means "manifest" ("evident,
obvious, clear"). poner de **manifiesto** / *to show; to reveal* Es un error
manifiesto. *It is a **manifest** (an obvious) mistake.* Su actitud hacia la música moderna
fue **manifiesta**. *Her attitude toward modern music was **clear** (manifest).*

mansión / mansion *Mansión* does not exactly mean "mansion" but any "house,
dwelling, shelter, lodging." Nowadays, the term *mansión* is more literary than
common. Hay **mansiones** pequeñas y pobres. *There are small, poor **houses** (dwell-
ings).* *Mansion* in English suggests a grander place: *casa solariega, casa grande,
palacete* (m.), *palacio*. Mi casa no es un **palacio**. *My house is not a **mansion**.*

mantel / mantel, mantle   *Mantel* (m.) is neither "mantel" nor "mantle." *Mantel* stands for "tablecloth" or "altar cloth." El **mantel** hace juego con las servilletas. *The **tablecloth** matches the napkins.* *Mantel* means *repisa, manto* (of a fireplace). El **manto** (la repisa) de la chimenea está lleno de fotos. *The **mantel** of the fireplace is full of photos.* *Mantle* means *manto, capa* in both a real and a figurative sense. bajo el **manto** de la noche   /   *under the **mantle** of the night (under the cloak of darkness)*

mantener / maintain   *Mantener* (ie) and *to maintain* both mean "to support, affirm, keep up." *Mantener* also means "to feed, sustain, hold (celebrate)." **Mantengo** mi opinión. *I **maintain** my opinion.*   **mantener** una conversación   /   *to keep up a conversation*   **mantener** la carne fresca   /   *to keep the meat fresh*   **mantenerse** a pan y agua   /   *to feed oneself on bread and water*

mantilla / mantilla   *Mantilla* is "mantilla," which was borrowed from Spanish, and means "a woman's scarf (of lace), worn over the head and shoulders." In Spanish, the plural *mantillas* sometimes means "baby clothes" or a "shawl" or "blanket" (for a baby).
estar en mantillas = *to be in diapers* (in the beginning)
Muchas novias españolas se casan con una **mantilla** blanca. *Many Spanish brides get married in a white **mantilla**.* Ella envolvió al niño en **mantillas**. *She wrapped the baby in swaddling clothes.* Ya he salido de **mantillas**. *I wasn't born yesterday.*

manufactura / manufacture   *Manufactura* and *manufacture* share the idea of "the making of goods by hand or by machine."[Note that *fabricación* is used more frequently when a machine is used; *confección* is used in reference to the making of clothes.] *Manufacturar* is "to manufacture." *To manufacture* is translated as *manufacturar,* as well as *fabricar* (when a machine is used) and *confeccionar* (of clothing). In a figurative sense, *to manufacture* is used in the sense of *fabricar* or *forjar* (a story). En Los Angeles se **confecciona** mucha ropa. *A lot of clothing is **manufactured** in Los Angeles.* Los italianos **fabrican** buenos zapatos. *Italians **manufacture** good shoes. Manufacturer* translates as *fabricante.* ¿Quién es el **fabricante** de esas aspiradoras? *Who is the **manufacturer** of those vacuum cleaners?*

marca, marco / mark   *Marca* and *mark* share the idea of "sign *(señal,* f.*),* scar *(cicatriz,* f.*),* label." Each term has additional meanings. *Marca* also means "brand, make, trademark, score *(resultado)."*
de marca = *outstanding*
marca registrada = *registered trademark*
¿De qué **marca** es el coche de Juan? *What **make** of car does John have?* Es un imbécil de **marca mayor**. *He's a **first-class** idiot. Marco* means "frame, framework, goalpost (in football)." Ese cuadro tiene un **marco** detallado. *That picture has a detailed frame. Mark* also means *calificación* or *nota* ("grade"), *huella, mancha, objetivo* or *blanco, marco* (German currency). Pablo Picasso dejó su **huella** en pintura. *Pablo Picasso left his **mark** on painting (in the art world).*   dar en el **clavo**   /   *to hit the **mark***

marchar / march *Marchar* and *to march* both mean "to walk with steady steps" *(desfilar)*, for example, in military style. In Spanish, *marchar(se)* has a wide range of meanings, such as "to go away, leave, work, go, run (function), operate." **Se marchó** de aquí a las dos. *He left here at two o'clock.* Todo **marcha** sobre ruedas. *Everything is running like clockwork.* Este reloj no **marcha** bien. *This watch doesn't work well.* Todo **marcha** bien. *Everything is going well.*

margen / margin *Margen* (m., f.) is "margin" (of a page) in a real sense and "limit (of error), liberty of action" in a figurative sense. Both terms mean "profit" *(ganancia)* in the business world. In addition, *margen* means "edge, border *(lindero)*, bank (of a river), opportunity, pretext, cause." [The *Academia Real* and Larousse admit that *el margen* and *la margen* are the same thing, but popular usage is *la margen* for "river bank" and *el margen* for the other meanings.]
dar margen para = *to give occasion for*
Las **márgenes** del río están verdes. *The river banks are green.* vivir al **margen** de la sociedad / *to live on the fringes of society* el **margen** de ganancias / *profit margin* por un escaso **margen** / *by a narrow margin, narrowly* **Marginal** means "marginal" (on the border), usually on a "lower limit." Both *marginal* and *marginal* are used in the modern sense of "living on the fringes of society."

marino / marine *Marino (marinero)* is not "marine" but "sailor, seaman." As an adjective, *marino (marítimo)* means exactly "marine." The feminine noun, *marina*, means "navy." ¡Colón fue un **marino** portugués, no italiano! *Columbus was a Portuguese, not an Italian, sailor!* la **marina** mercante / *the merchant marine* azul **marino** / *navy blue* brisa **marina** / *sea breeze* La ballena es un mamífero **marino**. *The whale is a marine mammal.* Marine translates as *infante* (m.) *de marina* and the plural *marines* means *infantería de marina.* A *marine* (soldier) is *un infante.* ¡Cuéntaselo a tu abuela! *Tell it to the marines!* Si no regresas pronto, mandaré a los **infantes**. *If you're not back soon, I'll send for the marines.*

masa / mass *Masa* and *mass* both refer to "indefinite matter, a large quantity or bulk" and in the plural both refer to "a group or aggregate of people." The main meaning of *masa,* however, is "dough (of flour), mortar (plaster)." El lago se convirtió en una **masa** de hielo. *The lake became a mass of ice.* La rebelión triunfó en manos de las **masas**. *The rebellion triumphed in the hands of the masses.* El pan se hace con **masa** de harina. *Bread is made with flour dough. Mass* also means *misa* as a "religious ceremony."
misa mayor = *High Mass*
medios de comunicación = *mass media*
Se durmió en la **misa**. *He fell asleep during mass.*

masacre / massacre *Masacre* (f.) means "massacre" ("the killing of innocent or defenseless people"). The only distinction is that *masacre* refers only to people, whereas *massacre* refers to people and animals. *Masacre* is used primarily in Latin America; *matanza* is used in Spain. [Actually, *matanza*, applied to animals, refers to the task of killing or slaughtering a pig and all the work involved. The *matanza* is a celebration for the "peasants" and occurs only once a year per household.] El rey

Herodes decretó la **masacre** (matanza) de los niños inocentes. *King Herod decreed the* **massacre** *of innocent children.*

máscara / mascara *Máscara* is not "mascara" but "mask" in a real sense, as well as the figurative sense of "pretense."
máscara antigás = *gas mask*
baile de **máscaras** (mascarada) / **masquerade** *ball* quitar la **máscara** a alguien / *to unmask someone* La **máscara** antigás puede salvarte la vida. *A gas* **mask** *can save your life.* **Mascara** is eye makeup and is translated as *rímel* (m.). Ella tiene que usar **rímel** especial para que los ojos no se le pongan rojos e hinchados. *She has to use special* **mascara** *so that her eyes don't become red and swollen.*

masivo / massive *Masivo* means "massive" in the sense of "enormous, of the masses." un aumento **masivo** de precio / *a* **massive** *increase in price* *Massive* also means *macizo, sólido, imponente.* El anillo es de oro **macizo**. *The ring is made of* **massive** *gold.*

masón / mason *Masón* (m.) is "mason" ("freemason"). *Mason* also means *albañil* (m.), *cantero.* El **albañil** trabaja en la construcción. *A* **mason** *works in construction.* *Masonería* is translated as "masonry" ("freemasonry"). La **masonería** es una organización internacional. *Freemasonry is the name of an international organization. Masonry* also translates as *albañilería, mampostería* ("brickwork, construction"). La **albañilería** es cada día más cara. *Masonry gets more expensive every day.*

matador / matador *Matador* (m.) and *matador* both mean "bullfighter" *(torero).* *Matador* also means "killer, murderer," as a noun and "killing, murderous" as an adjective. In a figurative sense, *matador* means "backbreaking, tiring, painful." el cuchillo **matador** / *the* **murderous** *knife* Partir leña es una tarea **matadora**. *Splitting wood is a* **backbreaking** *task.*

materia / matter *Materia* and *matter* both mean "substance, subject" *(asunto).* *Materia* also refers to "subject" or "course" (in school).
materia prima = *raw material*
¿Qué pasa? = *What's the matter?*
La **materia** que más odio es la química. *The* **subject** *I hate most is chemistry.* índice de **materias** / *table of* **contents** en realidad / *as a* **matter** *of fact* **No pasa nada.** *Nothing's the matter.*

material / material *Material* (m.) means "material" ("matter, substance") as a noun. *Material,* as an adjective, means "material" ("not spiritual"). Cemento es un **material** de construcción. *Cement is* **material** *used in construction.* **material** escolar / *teaching* **materials** *Material* also means *tela, tejido,* and as an adjective, it means *esencial, fundamental,* and in a court of law, *pertinente.* *Material- mente* means "absolutely, utterly." *Materially,* on the other hand, means *considerablemente, físicamente.*

materializar / materialize *Materializar* is not exactly "to materialize" in the sense of "to become fact, to be realized." The syntactic usage of both terms is different. *Materializar* takes an object and means "to visualize, consider material something that is not." The reflexive *materializarse* is an everyday term for "to become materialistic." ¿Cómo **materializas** la idea de la muerte? *How do you* **visualize** *the concept of death?* Se **materializó** cuando ganó el gordo de la lotería. *He* **became materialistic** *when he won the lottery. To* **materialize**, on the other hand, never takes an object and is used to mean *realizarse, resultar, cristalizar.* Las supuestas ganancias del negocio nunca se **realizaron** (cristalizaron). *The alleged benefits of the business never* **materialized.**

maternal / maternal   *Maternal* and *maternal* share the meaning of "motherly, the best qualities of a mother." *Maternal (mother)* also means *materno* ("related to the mother by blood"). Note the contrast between these two columns:

abuela materna = *maternal* **amor maternal** = *motherly love*
   grandmother   **de manera maternal** = *in a motherly way*
lengua materna = *mother* **figura maternal** = *mother(ly) figure*
   tongue

Mi nodriza fue una alemana **maternal.** *My nurse was a* **motherly** *(maternal) German woman.*

maternidad / maternity   *Maternidad* (f.) has the two meanings of *maternity:* "pregnancy" and "maternity hospital." It also has a third meaning of "motherhood." La **maternidad** es el privilegio más grande de la mujer. **Motherhood** *is a woman's greatest privilege.*

matiné / matinée   *Matiné* (f.) has not been included in the latest dictionary of the *Real Academia;* nevertheless, it is an accepted term in other dictionaries and is used in Latin America to mean "matinée" ("a spectacle or performance in the early afternoon"). Me gusta ir al cine en la **matiné** del viernes para ver los estrenos. *I like to go to the movies for the Friday* **matinée** *to see the new releases.*

matriculación / matriculation   *Matriculación* means "registration" for vehicles, etc., and "enrollment, registration" in a school. La **matriculación** (matrícula) en la universidad se hace con computadoras. *Registration (matriculation) at the university is done through computers. Matriculation* (as well as the corresponding verb, *to matriculate*) is not used much in the United States and should be considered an archaic term. *Matricular(se)* means "to register, to enroll." (It is not used to mean "to register in a hotel.")

matrimonio / matrimony   *Matrimonio* and *matrimony* share the meaning of "the state of being married." In Spanish, *matrimonio* is used more frequently with the meanings of "married couple, married life, a marriage" *(casamiento, boda).*
fuera de matrimonio = *out of wedlock*
El **matrimonio** se lleva muy bien. *The* **married couple** *gets along very well.*   un joven **matrimonio** / *a young* **married couple**   partida (acta) de **matrimonio** / *certificate of* **marriage**   cama **matrimonial** / **double bed**

matriz / matrix   *Matriz* (f.) and *matrix* both mean "womb, uterus; mold for casting; row of numbers." *Matriz* is also an adjective, meaning "central, main." [The plural of *matriz* is *matrices;* likewise, the plural of *matrix* is *matrices.*]
casa matriz = *headquarters, main office*

matrona / matron   *Matrona* and *matron* share the sense of "mature, elderly woman; guardian of women or children." *Matrona* also means "midwife" *(partera)*, "searcher" (at customs). La **matrona** del orfanatorio se hace respetar por los niños. *The matron at the orphanage is well respected by the children.* La **matrona** que me ayudó a nacer fue mi tía Lucía. *The midwife who delivered me was my Aunt Lucy.*

mayor / mayor, major   *Mayor* is not "mayor" but "older, adult, bigger, major (great of age)," as an adjective. As a noun, *mayor* means "adult, ancestor." The plural form *mayores* is translated as "ancestors."
mayor de edad = *of majority, legal age*
libro mayor = *ledger*
plaza mayor = *main square*
al por mayor = *wholesale*
Mi casa es **mayor** que la tuya. *My house is bigger than yours.* Mi amigo es **mayor** que yo. *My friend is older than I.* una señora **mayor** / *an elderly lady* Tiene dos hijas **mayores**. *She has two adult daughters. Mayor*, on the other hand, is a noun and means *alcalde* (m.); *mayoress*, which is infrequently used nowadays, means *alcaldesa. Major* means *mayor, importante, considerable* as an adjective, and *especialidad* (f.) or *carrera* (in school) as a noun.

media / media   *Media* is not "media" but "stocking, mean (in statistics)" as a noun. It is "half" (when placed in front of a noun) and "average" (when placed after a noun) as an adjective. [*See also the entry for* **medio**.] [In some Latin American countries, *media* is used to mean "sock."] Note the contrast in meanings in the following examples:
media naranja = *half an orange*
profesor medio = *average professor*
Las **medias** son más largas que los calcetines. *Stockings are longer than socks.* hacer 60 kilómetros de **media** / *to do an average of 60 kilometers Media*, on the other hand, is translated as *medios (de comunicación, de publicidad, de información).* Los **medios de comunicación** nos unen, nos informan, nos compran... *Mass media unites us, informs us, buys us....*

mediano / median   *Mediano* is "median" as a "middle line, point" in geometry. However, the adjective *mediano* means "average, middling, moderate, mediocre." Compré una sandía **mediana**. *I bought an average watermelon.* tomate de tamaño **mediano** / *a medium-size tomato* cerveza **mediana** / *mediocre beer* un trabajo muy **mediano** / *a very middling piece of work Median* means *mediana* or *promedio* in statistics, and *zona intermedia* in reference to roads and freeways.

médico / medical   *Médico* is "medical" as an adjective and "doctor, physician" as a noun. [*See also the entry for* **doctor**.] Un matasanos es un **médico** falso. *A quack is a false physician.* receta **médica** / *medical prescription Medical* is a noun meaning *reconocimiento médico* ("medical exam"), in addition to its meaning as an adjective.
escuela de medicina = *medical school*

cuerpo de sanidad = *medical corps*
Medicina is "medicine" as a career and as a remedy (also called *medicamento*).

medio / medium *Medio* means "medium" as "average" and as "a means of communication." *Medio* also refers to "means" as a noun. As an adjective, however, it has two meanings: (1) "middle, half" when placed before a noun; (2) "average" when placed after a noun. [*See also the entry for* **media.**]
medio litro = *half a liter*
alumno medio = *average student*
El poeta Horacio abogaba por un **medio** feliz. *The poet Horace advocated a happy medium.* El perro estaba en **medio** de la carretera. *The dog was in the middle of the highway.* El fin no justifica los **medios**. *The end does not justify the means.* Sírveme **media** taza de café. *Give me half a cup of coffee.*

memoria / memory *Memoria* means "memory" as the "power, ability to remember." In Spanish, *memoria* also means "report, essay, memorial, legacy." The plural *memorias* is used for "memoirs." **memorias** (recuerdos) de la infancia / *childhood memories* aprender de **memoria** / *to learn by heart (to memorize)* si mal no **recuerdo** / *if memory serves me* guardar una **memoria** (un recuerdo) agradable / *to have (cherish) a pleasant memory*

memorial / memorial *Memorial* (m.) means "memorial" as a "document," usually a "petition." *Memorial* in English means *monumento (conmemorativo).*
Día de los Caídos = *Memorial Day*
monumento a los caídos = *war memorial*

menor / minor *Menor* and *minor* share the idea of "lesser in size, amount, number, or extent." *Menor* also translates as "smaller/smallest, younger/youngest, lesser/least." [In English, a distinction is made between the comparative and superlative forms of an adjective (i.e., *smaller* for comparing two nouns; *smallest* for comparing more than two). However, in Spanish, *menor* is always used, the only distinction is the article *el* or *la* before the adjective to indicate the superlative: *El carro azul es menor que el rojo.* ("The blue car is *smaller* than the red one.") *El carro azul es el menor de todos.* ("The blue car is the smallest of all of them.")]
al por menor = *retail (store, sale)*
tono menor = *minor key*
tribunal de menores = *juvenile court*
Juanito es el m**enor** de la familia. *Johnny is the youngest in the family.* No tengo la **menor** idea. *I don't have the faintest (least) idea.* Los **menores** de edad no votan. *Minors do not vote.* Es un mal **menor**. *It is a lesser evil.* película no apta para **menores** / *movie not suitable for minors (i.e., an X-rated movie)* *Minor* in English also means *secundario, sin importancia,* and *nimio* ("insignificant, trivial") as an adjective and *menor* (m.) *de edad* as a noun. Es un problema sin **importancia**. *It's a minor problem.*

menos / minus *Menos* is "minus" in subtraction as the symbol (-). It is also used every day to mean "less, not so, fewer, least" and, as a preposition, "except, but."

al menos = *at least*   ni mucho menos = *far from it*
en menos de = *by less than*   menos mal = *thankfully*
a menos que = *unless*   lo menos = *at least*
Es el alumno **menos** inteligente de la clase. *He's the **least** intelligent student in the class.* Te daré cualquier cosa **menos** eso. *I'll give you anything **but** that.* Hay tres lápices **de menos.** *Three pencils are **missing**. Minus* in English has three different translations. In reference to numbers, it means *negativo,* as in *un número negativo* ("a minus or negative number"). In reference to temperature, it refers to "below zero" or *bajo cero.* As a colloquialism, *minus* means *despreciable* as in *una cantidad despreciable* ("a minus quantity"). *Ese tipo es un **cero** a la izquierda. That guy is a **minus** quantity.*

mental / mental   *Mental* and *mental* both refer to the "mind" *(la mente). Mental* in colloquial English has downgraded its meaning as a noun to mean *chiflado, anormal, chalado* ("crazy").
prueba de inteligencia = *mental test (intelligence test)*
Ese muchacho es un caso **anormal.** *That boy is a **mental** case.* Debe estar un poco **chiflado.** *He must be a bit **mental.***

mercantil / mercantile   *Mercantil* is "mercantile" in the sense of "commercial," but the Spanish term is sometimes used in a pejorative sense to mean "mercenary, money-grubbing" *(codicioso).* [*Mercantilismo* means "mercantilism" in the best sense of the word, "the business of trading," as well as the worst sense of the word, "profit over moral values." It is interesting to note that these two denotations are reversed in the Spanish and English dictionaries. In the *Real Academia,* the negative meaning is given first, followed by the positive meaning. In *Webster's,* the order is reversed.]
marina mercante = *merchant marine*
sociedad mercantil = *trading company*
El buen espíritu **mercantil** puede convertirse en **mercantilismo.** *A good **mercantile** mentality can become **mercantilism** (money-grubbing).*

mermelada / marmalade   *Mermelada* is "marmalade," not only made of orange but also made of other fruits. For this reason, *mermelada* also translates as "jam" or "preserves." pan tostado con **mermelada** de fresa / *toast with strawberry preserves* **mermelada** de naranja amarga / *orange **marmalade***

mero / mere   *Mero* is "mere" in the sense of "pure, simple." *Mero* is used in Mexico to mean "real" *(verdadero),* as well as "right, only, self." *Mero* is also used as an adverb, meaning "exactly." el **mero** hecho / *the **mere** fact* Es el **mero** amo. *He is the **real** boss.* Llegó a la **mera** hora. *She arrived **right** on time.* Son **mero** las dos. *It's **exactly** two o'clock.* ser el **mero** malo / *to be wickedness itself* yo **mero** / *myself* *Meramente (simplemente)* translates as "merely, purely, solely" and in Mexico, "exactly, really." Estaba **simplemente** (meramente) tratando de ayudar. *I was **merely** (only) trying to help.*

mesa / mesa   *Mesa* and *mesa* are both used in geography for "high plateau" *(altiplano).* In Spanish, *mesa* also means "table, desk," and in a figurative sense, "food" (on the table), as well as "general or presiding committee."

mesa electoral = *electoral college*
mesa extensible = *extension table*
mesa de tijera (plegable) / *folding **table*** **mesa** redonda / ***round-table*** *conference* En casa de mi tía siempre hay buena **mesa**. *At my aunt's house, there's always good **food** (on the table).* La **mesa directiva** se reunió ayer. *The **presiding committee** met yesterday.*

mesura / measure *Mesura* is not "measure" but "moderation, dignity, reserve, composure." El delegado de Perú habló con **mesura**. *The delegate from Peru spoke with **moderation**. Measure means medida, regla, compás (m.; in music).*
hecho a la medida = *made to measure*
en gran **parte** / *in large **measure*** excesivamente / *beyond **measure*** Si no puedes contar los **compases**, no cantes. *If you can't count the **measures** (beats), don't sing.*

metrópoli / metropolis *Metrópoli* (f.) [note that the word is not spelled with an *s*] means "metropolis" in the sense of "main city, center of population, culture, etc." *Metrópoli* also means "mother country." España es la **metrópoli** de Hispanoamérica. *Spain is the **mother country** of Hispanic America. Metro* (short for *metropolitano*) is used to mean "subway." El **metro** es un buen sistema de transporte en Madrid y México. *The **subway** is a good transportation system in Madrid and Mexico City.*

mimar / mime *Mimar* is not "to mime" but "to spoil, pamper, cuddle, pet (people)." Los abuelos suelen **mimar** a los nietos. *Grandparents usually **spoil** their grandchildren. To mime means remedar, imitar, representar (with gestures). Mimo* means "pampering, spoiling, petting (of people)." *Mime* means *pantomima* ("theater with gestures instead of words"). [In old Spanish, *mimo* and *pantomima* were equivalent to *mime* in English. Nowadays, *pantomima* has the pejorative meaning of "foolishness."]

mímica / mimicry *Mímica* is "mimicry" as "mime, gesticulation, sign language." Los hispanos usan mucha **mímica** (gesticulación) cuando hablan. *Hispanics use a lot of **gesturing** (gesticulation) when they speak. Mimicry* in English sometimes takes the negative connotation of *remedo, monería, bufonada, pantomima* (see note above). El comediante trató diferentes **bufonadas** (monerías). *The comedian tried different **mimicries** (impressions).*

mina / mine *Mina* is "mine" in the real sense of "the extraction of minerals," and in the figurative sense of "a source of money, wisdom, knowledge, etc." *Mina* and *mine* are also explosive devices planted in the ground or placed underwater. In addition, *mina* in Spanish is used for "lead" or "tip" (of a pencil). una **mina** de información / *a **mine** of information* La **mina** del lápiz contiene plomo. *The **tip** of a pencil contains lead.*

minimizar / minimize *Minimizar* was finally included in the latest dictionary of the *Real Academia*, with the meaning of the English word *to minimize* ("to reduce to a minimum, disparage"). Possible synonyms in Spanish include *rebajar,* *aminorar*, and in the worst sense, *menospreciar, denigrar, quitar méritos.* Se trata de **minimizar** (aminorar) los riesgos del viaje. *One must try to minimize the risks of the trip.* El jefe quiere **minimizar** (quitar méritos) el trabajo del empleado. *The manager wants to minimize the merit of the clerk's work.*

minoría / minority *Minoría* is "minority" as the opposite of "majority." It should not be confused with *menoría,* which translates as "minority" ("under legal age") and also "subordination, infancy." Los hispanos son la **minoría** más grande en los Estados Unidos. *Hispanics are the largest minority in the United States.* La **menoría** de edad es hasta los 21 años en muchos países. *Minority of age (the state of being a minor) lasts until the age of 21 in many countries.* **Minoridad** (f.) is an archaic word, according to the *Real Academia.*

minuto / minute *Minuto* and *minute* are both "60 seconds" and figuratively, "a moment." The feminine form in Spanish, *minuta* means "draft, payroll, memorandum, menu." [Note that the dictionary of the *Real Academia* does not include "menu" as a meaning of *minuta;* nevertheless, other dictionaries accept that meaning and, what is more important, millions of Hispanics use the word every day in restaurants.] La **minuta** tiene muchos platos de mariscos. *The menu shows many seafood dishes.* ¡Un **momento**! *Just a minute!* En el **momento** en que... *The minute that...* ahora mismo / *this very minute Minute* is also an adjective meaning *menudo, diminuto, detallado.* (Note that the pronunciation of the adjective form in English is different.) The plural *minutes* means *acta(s)* (of a meeting). [Some countries use the singular *acta;* others, the plural *actas.*]
a última hora = *at the last minute*
Nos hizo una relación **detallada** del accidente. *He gave us a minute account of the accident.* La secretaria leyó las **actas** (el acta). *The secretary read the minutes.*

miserable / miserable *Miserable* in Spanish means "extremely poor, stingy, sordid, wretched, destitute." La familia vive en una choza **miserable** en los suburbios de la ciudad. *The family lives in a sordid shack in the city's slums. Miserable* suggests *desdichado, infeliz, angustiado.* [In Spanish, *miseria* and *miserable* are based on a cultural fact: the lack of means for survival, what would be called "extreme poverty" in the United States. In English, *misery* and *miserable* stress the psychological idea of *desgracia, dolor, tristeza* that generally is a good share of poverty.] El perro se sentía **triste** cuando su dueño lo abandonó. *The dog felt miserable when his owner abandoned him.*

miseria / misery *Miseria* and *misery* are basically "poverty," but there are fundamental differences based on cultural differences. In Spanish *miseria* suggests the idea of "extreme poverty, squalor, pittance, destitution."
¡una **miseria**! = *a mere nothing! a pittance!*
Los campesinos viven en la **miseria**. *The peasants live in extreme poverty. Misery* is better translated as *pena, tristeza, desgracia, desdicha, dolor* (m.). Hay muchas familias en la **desdicha**. *There are many families living in misery.*

mistificación / mystification *Mistificación* does not mean "mystification"; instead, it means "hoax, deceit, mockery, trick." Sus palabras amargas son una

mistificación de la Biblia. *His bitter words are a* **mockery** *of the Bible. Mystification,* however, means *desorientación, confusión, complejidad* (m.), *misterio.* El éxito de los trucos mágicos depende de la **confusión** del público. *The success of magic tricks depends on the* **mystification** *of the audience.*

mitin / meeting *Mitin* (m.) comes from the English word *meeting,* but the two terms do not share exactly the same meaning. *Mitin* refers to a "political or social rally." [The plural of *mitin* is *mítines.*] Los rebeldes tuvieron un **mitin** secreto. *The rebels had a secret* **meeting.** *Meeting* has many denotations: *reunión, junta, sesión, entrevista, encuentro, cita.*
sesión pública = *open meeting*
celebrar una junta = *to hold a meeting*
El presidente levantó la **sesión.** *The president adjourned the* **meeting.** Tuve una **cita** con el director. *I had a* **meeting** *with the director.* tomar la palabra / *to address the* **meeting**

mixtura / mixture *Mixtura* and *mixture* share the idea of "mixing ingredients," but the Spanish term is hardly used, except in a pharmacy to refer to preparing medicines. Sometimes *mixtura* is used in a pejorative sense for a "mixture" or "concoction" of drinks or food. *Mixture* is an everyday word, meaning *mezcla,* both in a real and a figurative sense. Un plato de paella es una **mezcla** de pollo, puerco, mariscos y arroz. *Paella is a* **mixture** *of chicken, pork, seafood, and rice.*

moda / mode *Moda* only means "mode" in the phrase *à la mode,* which both languages borrowed from the French. *Moda* primarily means "fashion, style."
a la moda = *fashionable*
de moda = *in style*
¿Qué te parece la **moda** de los sombreros anchos? *What do you think of the* **style** *of wide hats? Mode* means *modo, manera, método, forma.* Hay muchos **métodos** de vender zapatos. *There are many* **modes** *(ways) of selling shoes.*

modelar / model *Modelar* is "to model" ("to work as a model"). [The *Real Academia* does not recognize this meaning; however, many other dictionaries do.] *Modelar* also means "to mold, form, shape, pattern." **Modelamos** la cera para hacer un busto. *We are* **molding** *the wax to make a bust.* **Modelar** es el sueño de muchas jóvenes. *Modeling is the dream of many young women.* **modelar** el alma de una persona / *to form (to shape) a person's mind To model* also means *presentar* (a dress, new shoes, etc.), *seguir* (i.) *un modelo, posar* or *modelar* for an artist, photographer, etc. Ella **posó** (modeló) para Picasso. *She* **modeled** *(posed) for Picasso. Modelador / modeladora* is "modeler or model" ("one who works as a model"), whereas *modelista* means "dress designer."

modesto / modest *Modesto* has most of the same meanings as *modest:* "humble, simple, unassuming, shy"; however, *modesto* seems to emphasize the material aspect and is often translated as "poor, needy." Nació en una familia **modesta.** *He was born into a* **modest** *family.* Gana un sueldo **modesto** (moderado). *She earns a* **modest** *salary.* Son personas **modestas.** *They are* **poor** *(needy) people. Modest,* on the other hand, stresses the moral side: *decente, recatado, pudoroso.* Es una joven **pudorosa**. *She is a **modest** young woman.* **Modestia** shares the basic idea of *modesty*, but it sometimes stresses the idea of "simplicity, need." *Modesty*, again, seems to emphasize the moral side with the meanings of *decencia, pudor* (m.), *recato*.

mole / mole   *Mole* (f.) has kept the Latin meaning of "mass, bulk, volume." *Mole* (m.) also is the name of a Mexican dish made with chocolate-seasoned chili sauce, although there is no relation between the two words. Esta roca pelada es una **mole** enorme. *That bare rock is a huge **mass**.* *Mole* in English, which has the same Latin origin as *mole*, has a limited usage as *rompeolas* (m.) or *malecón* (m.; "breakwater, jetty"), as well as *muelle* (m.; "dock, harbor"). Of a different origin, the English word *mole* also stands for *lunar* (m.; "beauty mark") and the animal *topo*. *Mole* is also used for *espía* ("spy"). Caminamos un rato por el **malecón**. *We walked for a while along the **mole**.* Tiene un **lunar** cerca de la boca. *She has a **mole** near her mouth.* Los **topos** se comen mis rosales. *The **moles** are eating my rosebushes.*

molestar / molest   *Molestar* is not "to molest" but "to annoy, bother, disturb, inconvenience, pester." Me **molestan** una barbaridad los mosquitos. *The mosquitoes **bother** me an awful lot.* Me **molesta** un zapato. *My shoe is **hurting** me.* Perdone que lo **moleste**. *I'm sorry to **bother** you.* ¿Le **molestaría** prestarme cinco dólares? *Would you **mind** lending me five dollars?* To *molest* has downgraded its meaning to convey negative sexual connotations: *faltar al respeto, ofender, meterse con alguien.* Lo acusan de **faltar el respeto** a menudo a la secretaria. *They accuse him of frequently **molesting** (harassing) the secretary.*

moneda / money   *Moneda* and *money* share the concept of "currency, legal tender," but *moneda* is also used for "coin" or "change" (hard cash). In this respect, *moneda* contrasts with *billete* (m.; "paper money"). *Moneda* is also used to mean "mint" (of money). [Note that *dinero* also means "money" in general, but *dinero* is not used to mean "currency." Colloquially, many words are used to mean "money": *plata* is used colloquially in many countries; *lana* is used in Mexico; *parné* (m.) or *perras* or *pelas*, in Spain; *reales* (m.), in Venezuela; and *chavo*, in Puerto Rico.]
acuñar moneda = *to mint money*
moneda falsa = *counterfeit money*
Se ruega **moneda** fraccionaria. *Please tender the exact fare.* ¿Sabes cuál es la **moneda** de China? *Do you know what the **currency** is in China?* **moneda** cantante y sonante / *cold, hard cash* *Money*, on the other hand, is used in the figurative sense of "wealth, property" and is translated as *dinero*. The plural form *monies* means *fondos*. [Note that *dineros* is never used.] El **dinero** llama al **dinero**. *It takes **money** to make **money**.* tirar el **dinero** por la ventana / *to throw **money** down the drain* El tiempo es **oro**. *Time is **money**.*

montar / mount   *Montar* is "to mount" (a horse, a bike, a picture, a play, guns, jewels, guard). In addition, *montar* means "to go up, get on, get into, amount to, assemble or put together (something that comes in parts), cover (a female)." [Note the prepositions used after *montar*: *montar a caballo; montar en burro; montar en coche.*] **Montó** el diamante en el anillo. *He **mounted** the diamond in the ring.*

No me gusta **montar** en avión. *I don't like **to go up** in an airplane.* Ayúdame a **montar** la bicicleta nueva. *Help me **to assemble** (put together) my new bicycle.* La cuenta **montó** a ochenta dólares. *The bill **amounted** to eighty dollars. To mount* is used less frequently than its Spanish cognate because there are many colloquial terms that replace it, such as *to ride* (horses, bicycles), *to get on, to set* (jewels).

monte / mount *Monte* (m.) and *mount* share the idea of "a small mountain," but each term has additional meanings. *Monte* also means "forest, woodland," and in some Latin American countries, "wild country." **monte de piedad** = *pawnshop* echarse al **monte** / *to take to the **hills*** Los perros corrieron al **monte**. *The dogs ran into the **wild country**.* No todo el **monte** es orégano. *Life is not just a bowl of cherries. Mount* also means *montura, cabalgadura* (of a horse), *soporte* (m.) or *montadura* (of jewels), *borde* (m.; of a photograph), *cureña* (of a cannon). En ese establo hay **monturas** muy caras. *There are expensive **mounts** in that stable.* El joyero trabaja en la **montadura** del diamante. *The jeweler is working on the diamond **mount** (mounting).*

monumento / monument *Monumento* and *monument* both apply to "something lasting or outstanding," such as statues, buildings, churches, writings that serve as a memorial. In Spanish, *monumento* is used more loosely than its English cognate in the sense that any "sepulcher" is a *monumento* (according to the *Real Academia*) and any building of a certain interest deserves the term *monumento*. [In English, *monument* used to be "any statue, any tomb," for example, in Shakespeare's works; however, this use is now obsolete. On the other hand, *a national monument* may refer to a mountain or other geographical area such as the Grand Canyon. In Spanish, *monumento* never refers to a geographical location.] Toda la ciudad antigua de Toledo es un **monumento** nacional de España. *All of the old city of Toledo is a national monument in Spain.*

moral / moral, morale *Moral* (f.) means the same thing as the plural *morals* in English ("principles of conduct, ethics"; *ética*), as well as the word *morality*. Also as a noun, *moral* means the same thing as the word *morale (estado de ánimo)*. As an adjective, *moral* translates as "moral," with the meaning "relating to morality." In botany, *moral* (m.) is the tree that bears *moras* ("mulberry tree"). La **moral** del senador es sospechosa. *The senator's **morals** are suspect.* Nuestra **moral** es alta. *Our **morale** is high. Moral* in English also means *moraleja* or *enseñanza* (of a story). **costumbres** relajadas / *loose **morals*** Todas las fábulas tienen **moraleja**. *Every fable has a **moral**.*

moralizar / moralize *Moralizar* and *to moralize* both refer to "moral principles" in general but in different ways. The emphasis of *moralizar* is on the negative side, as a reproach, meaning "to admonish, warn, reprove mildly." El cura **moralizó** sobre los males del divorcio. *The priest **warned** about the evils of divorce. To moralize* emphasizes the positive side: *mejorar la moral, sacar lecciones morales, aprender.* El Papa trata de **mejorar la moral** de todo el mundo. *The Pope tries **to moralize** (improve the morals of) the whole world.*

moribundo / moribund   *Moribundo* is "moribund" ("dying") and applies only to people. El **moribundo** pidió un sacerdote. *The dying man asked for a priest. Moribund,* on the other hand, is used with organizations, corporations, clubs, etc.; it's never used with people. There is no direct translation in Spanish: *en decadencia, a punto de extinguirse.*   una sociedad **en decadencia** / *a moribund society*

moroso / morose   *Moroso* is not "morose" but "slow, tardy, lingering" and in the business world, "delinquent" (regarding payment, an account, a check). Perdió el avión por ser **moroso.** *He missed his flight because he was tardy.* No me gustan los pagos **morosos** porque salen caros. *I don't like delinquent payments because they end up being costly. Morose* has negative denotations such as *malhumorado, hosco, sombrío, taciturno, mohíno* ("gloomy, somber, angry, moody").   una persona **sombría** / *a morose person*

mortificar / mortify   *Mortificar* is "to mortify" ("to humiliate, punish"). In Latin America, *mortificar* is used with the meaning of "to bother" *(molestar),* "to try one's patience," and even worse, "to torment." Un alumno me **mortificó** con preguntas inoportunas. *A student was trying my patience with ill-timed questions.* No me **mortifiques** con estas tonterías tuyas. *Don't bother me with your nonsense.*

mote / mote   *Mote* (m.) does not mean "mote"; rather, it means "nickname, motto." El **mote** (apodo) de Cervantes es "El Manco de Lepanto". *Cervantes' nickname is "The One-handed Man of Lepanto". Mote* in English means *mota* ("speck," for example, of dust).

motivo / motive   *Motivo* and *motive* share the idea of "reason, cause." *Motivo* also means "motif" (in music, art, etc.).
con mayor **motivo** = *even more so*
sin **motivo** alguno / *for no reason at all; for no apparent motive*   No abandonaré mi puesto bajo ningún **motivo.** *I won't leave my post under any circumstances. Motive (motor)* is also an adjective, meaning *motor, motriz, cinético.* Se estudia la fuerza **motriz** aun en el tercer año de primaria. *Motive (motor) force is studied even in the third grade of elementary school.*

moto / motto   *Moto* (f.) is not "motto" but the shortened form of *motocicleta* ("motorcycle"). The English *motto* is *lema* (m.), *divisa, mote* (m.)
Mi **lema** es "siempre listo". *My motto is "always ready."*

mover / move   *Mover* (ue) shares with *to move* the concepts of "to change place or location, push, carry, pull, stir, wag (tail / *rabo*), incite." *To move* has the additional meanings of *mudarse* (to change from one house to another, to go to reside in another place) and *conmover* (ue) (feelings, heart). Se **mudaron** de Chicago a Miami. *They moved from Chicago to Miami.* Se **conmovió** al ver tanta pobreza. *He was moved when he saw so much poverty.*

móvil / mobile   *Móvil* (m.) means "motive" as a noun and "mobile, movable" as an adjective. ¿Cuál fue el **móvil** del crimen? *What was the motive for the crime?* París es un "festival **móvil**". (Hemingway) *Paris is "a movable feast." (Hemingway)*

Mobile is sometimes better translated as *portátil* or *transportable* (home), depending on the context.
casa transportable = *mobile home*

mula / mule *Mula* is a "mule" (female) and is the basic term used to refer to this animal. However, *mulo* refers directly to a "male mule." In both English and Spanish, the terms are used to refer to people who are stubborn *(testarudo)* or stupid *(estúpido)*.
testarudo como una mula = *as stubborn as a mule*
La **mula** es una buena bestia de carga en terreno montañoso. *The mule is a good pack animal on mountainous terrain.* *Mule,* in addition, refers to *babucha* or *chancleta* (lounge slipper) and also *mula eléctrica* ("electric engine") to tow boats along a canal. La señora tiene unas **babuchas** de muchos colores. *The lady has a very colorful pair of mules. Mulero (arriero)* translates as "muleteer, mule driver."

mundano / mundane *Mundano* is not "mundane" but "worldly, earthly, social, fashionable." In other words, *mundano* retains the original Latin meaning.
vida mundana = *social life*
placeres mundanos = *worldly pleasures*
Tienes ideas **mundanas.** *You have worldly ideas. Mundane,* however, has downgraded its denotation to mean *vulgar, trivial.* No hablemos de un tema tan **vulgar.** *Let's not talk about such a mundane topic. Mundial* is the adjective that refers to "world" as in *Primera Guerra Mundial* (the First World War). La Cruz Roja es una organización **mundial.** *The Red Cross is a worldwide organization.*

murmurar / murmur *Murmurar* and *to murmur* share the meaning of "to mutter, complain." The basic meaning of *murmurar,* though, is "to gossip," and in a poetic sense, "to ripple" (water, wind, a stream). Las aguas **murmuran** en el arroyo. *The waters ripple in the creek.* Mi suegra nunca **murmura** de mí. *My mother-in-law never gossips about me. To murmur* also means *susurrar* or *cuchichear* ("to whisper") or, in more simple speech, *hablar en voz baja.*
soplo cardíaco = *heart murmur*

musa / muse *Musa* means "muse" ("any of the nine goddesses") and, in common speech, "source of artistic inspiration." El poeta sólo escribe cuando siente la inspiración de la **musa.** *The poet only writes when he feels the inspiration of the muse. Muse,* as a noun, means *meditación, contemplación.* As a verb, *to muse* means *meditar, ponderar.* El pintor está **meditando** sobre su próxima obra de arte. *The painter is musing about his next work of art.*

muscular / muscular *Muscular* and *muscular* both refer to "muscles" as part of the anatomy. Siento un dolor **muscular** en el muslo. *I feel a muscular pain in my thigh. Muscular* is also used in English to refer to people who are *fornido, musculoso, fuerte* ("brawny"). ¡Qué hombre tan **fornido** (musculoso)! *What a muscular (strong) man!*

musical / musical *Musical* and *musical* both apply to anything "related to music." In Spanish, however, the term is used to apply only to things. *Musical* in English

165

applies both to people and to things. The word is also a noun that means *obra* or *programa* (m.) or *comedia musical.*

apreciador de música = *a musical person*

Lágrimas y sonrisas fue una **obra musical** con Julie Ándrews. The Sound of Music was *a* **musical** *with Julie Andrews.* José Lecuona era un buen **apreciador de música.** *José Lecuona was a very* **musical** *person.*

N

nacional / national *Nacional* means "national" as "having to do with the nation." In some contexts, **nacional** is better translated as "domestic": *vuelo **nacional*** ("domestic flight"), *mercado **nacional*** ("domestic market"). The plural ***nacionales*** was the "national militia" during the Spanish Civil War.
himno nacional = *national anthem*
renta nacional = *national income*
producto nacional bruto (PNB) = *gross national product (GNP)*
No se puede fumar en Estados Unidos en los vuelos **nacionales**. *In the United States, you can't smoke on **domestic** flights.* *National* in the United Kingdom stands for *súbdito, ciudadano* ("citizen"). Los escoceses son **ciudadanos** del Reino Unido. *The Scots are **nationals** of the United Kingdom.*

natural / natural *Natural* and *natural* share the idea of "arising from or relating to nature" and also the figurative sense of "simple, normal, usual." Both terms have additional meanings. In Spanish, **natural** also means "fresh (fruit), straight (whiskey), native (of a country), life-sized (for example, a portrait), illegitimate (child)." *Natural* (m.) is also a noun, meaning "nature, character, native (of a country)." Me gusta la guayaba **natural**. *I like **fresh** guava.* Un **natural** de Río de Janeiro es un carioca. *A **native** of Rio de Janeiro is a "carioca."* Es de un **natural** celoso. *He has a jealous **nature**.* Los **naturales** ya no viven desnudos. *The **natives** no longer go naked.* *Natural* is also an adjective in English that means *instintivo* (behavior), *nato* (talent of an artist). As a noun, *natural* also means *persona dotada* ("gifted person"), *éxito inmediato* ("a sure hit, success"). El deseo de sobrevivir es **instintivo**. *The desire to survive is **natural**.* Es la mujer **apropiada** para ese trabajo. *She is a **natural** for that job.* **Naturaleza** means the same thing as *nature*. However, it is also used in the expression **naturaleza muerta** ("still-life" painting).

naval / naval *Naval* is "naval" and "nautical." *Naval* is used to refer to all kinds of boats and ships—military, merchant, fishing, or recreational. Because of its wide meaning, good equivalents in English are "nautical" and "marine." combate **naval** / **naval** *(sea) battle* base **naval** / **naval** *base* agregado **naval** / **naval** *attaché* Ese restaurante tiene un motivo **naval**. *That restaurant has a **nautical** motif.* *Naval* in English refers only to the branch of the armed forces, i.e., the navy *(armada, marina)*.
oficial de la armada = *naval officer*
observatorio de la marina = *naval observatory*

nave / nave *Nave* (f.) and *nave* are "the main aisle in a church," but in Spanish, **nave** also means "ship (in the air, at sea), vessel, large building (in factories, for storage, etc.)." Queen Mary es la **nave** más grande del mundo. *The Queen Mary is the largest **ship** in the world.* El rancho tiene una **nave** para almacenar trigo. *The ranch has a large building for storing wheat.* se alquila **nave** industrial / *industrial premises for lease* quemar las **naves** / *to burn one's bridges* *Nave* in English also means *cubo* ("hub") of a wheel. *Naveta* is the "censer" (shaped like a small boat) that is used in church ceremonies.

navegar / navigate *Navegar* means "to navigate" ("to steer a ship"), as well as "to sail" and even "to fly." Los aviones **navegan** a una altura de más de 30.000 pies. *Planes fly at an altitude of more than 30,000 feet.* *Navegación,* similarly, means "navigation", as well as "sailing, flying." *Navegante* translates as "navigator," as well as "sailor" *(marinero)*. Algunos **navegantes** (marineros) vivían más tiempo en el mar que en la tierra. *Some sailors used to live at sea more than on land.*

nebuloso / nebulous *Nebuloso* and *nebulous* share the idea of "vague, obscure, indefinite (ideas)." *Nebuloso* is still used with the original meaning of "cloudy, hazy, misty." [According to Webster's dictionary, *nebulous* with the meaning of "cloudy" is an archaic term.] Muchas teorías filosóficas tienen conceptos **nebulosos.** *Many philosophical theories contain nebulous concepts.* La montaña se ve **nebulosa** por la madrugada de otoño. *The mountain looks hazy in the early morning in the fall.*

nefario / nefarious *Nefario* is an archaic term in Spanish for "nefarious" ("very wicked, villainous, criminal"). [Note, though, that the *Real Academia* does not recognize *nefario* as archaic.] *Nefarious* is most accurately translated as *malvado, impío, inhumano.* La conducta **malvada** del criminal fue condenada. *The criminal's nefarious conduct was condemned.*

negar / negate *Negar* (ie) shares with *to negate* the concept of "to deny, refuse, say no." *Negar* can be more polite than *to negate,* with the meaning " to decline (an invitation), to disclaim (a responsibility)." The reflexive form *negarse* means "to refuse, to reject" *(rehusar).* No **niegues** que estás equivocado. *Don't deny that you are wrong.* Se **negó** a la invitación de asistir a la fiesta. *He declined the invitation to attend the party.* Se **niega** a pagar. *She refuses to pay. To negate* also has the meaning of *invalidar, anular.* El permiso quedó **anulado.** *The permit was negated.*

negociador, negociante / negotiator *Negociador* (m.) means "negotiator" as a noun and "negotiating" as an adjective. *Negociante* (m., f.) is not "negotiator" but "merchant, dealer," and even "businessman, businesswoman."
negociante al por mayor = *wholesale merchant*
Mi amigo es un buen **negociante** en carros importados. *My friend is a good imported car dealer.*

negociar / negotiate *Negociar* is not exactly "to negotiate." *Negociar* suggests "to deal, to trade" in ordinary business. *To negotiate* is usually used for special or difficult business dealings and a more accurate translation would be *gestionar.* ¿Quiénes van a **gestionar** el problema entre los palestinos y los israelís? *Who is going to negotiate the problem between the Palestinians and the Israelis?*

nervio / nerve *Nervio* and *nerve* both refer to the units of the nervous system, and in a figurative sense, both share the idea of "energy, vigor, strength."

ataque de nervios = *a fit of nerves*

estar hecho un manojo de **nervios** / *to be a bundle of nerves* poner los **nervios** de punta / *to have one's nerves on edge; to be very much on edge* A pesar de sus años no le faltan **nervios** (energía). *In spite of his age, he doesn't lack energy. Nerve* in English has downgraded its figurative sense to mean *sangre fría, caradura, descaro, insolencia.* The plural, *nerves,* means *nerviosismo, nerviosidad* (f.).

¡Qué descaro! = *What nerve!*

El empleado tiene mucha **caradura.** *The employee has a lot of nerve.* No podía dominar su **nerviosismo.** *He couldn't control his nerves.*

nervioso / nervous *Nervioso* and *nervous* both are related in the technical sense of "relating to the nervous system." Nevertheless, each term has other figurative meanings. *Nervioso* suggests "excited, wiry, nervy, jittery."

depresión nerviosa = *nervous breakdown*

Estoy **nervioso** porque voy a ver a mi padre después de diez años. *I'm excited because I'm going to see my father for the first time in ten years.* ¡No te pongas **nervioso!** *Take it easy!/Calm down!* Se pone **nerviosa** antes de la fiesta. *She becomes jittery before a party. Nervous,* on the other hand, suggests *miedoso, asustadizo, tímido, atemorizado.* Está **atemorizado** porque una muchacha lo invitó a bailar. *He's nervous because a girl asked him to dance. Nerviosidad* (f.) suggests "agitation, (a state of) nerves, impatience, irritability." *Nervousness* suggests *timidez* (f.)*, miedo.*

nicho / niche *Nicho (hornacina)* is "niche" as a "recess in a wall for a statue, vase, etc." *Niche,* however, is also used with the figurative meaning of *buena colocación, buen puesto.* Encontró un **buen puesto** en la administración de la empresa. *He found his niche in the company's administration.*

níquel / nickel *Níquel* (m.) means "nickel" (also spelled *nickle*), the metal. In some Latin American countries, *níquel* is used for the coin worth *cinco centavos* (possibly influenced by the nickel of the United States) and is also used for "money" in general. (The plural of *níquel* is regular: *níqueles.*) [*Traganíqueles* ("nickel swallower") is a name for the cola and soft-drink vending machines in some countries. The *traganíqueles* is as old as the first vending machines when a bottle of cola used to cost a nickel or so. Note that actually *níqueles* have disappeared in most Hispanic countries.] Los abuelos recuerdan los días en que una Coca-Cola costaba dos **níqueles.** *Grandparents remember the days when a Coca-Cola cost two nickels.*

norte / north *Norte* (m.) means "north" as a cardinal point and, in a figurative sense, "aim, goal, guide." As an adjective, *norte* means "northern, northerly." **rumbo norte** = *northerly direction*

La prosperidad del país debe ser nuestro **norte.** *The prosperity of the country should be our aim.* **norte** de brújula / *magnetic north*

nota / note *Nota* and *note* share most meanings, with the exception of *nota* meaning "grade" or "mark" (in school). Espero buenas **notas** este semestre. / *expect good grades this semester. Note* is also used for *billete* (m.; "banknote"), *importancia,* or *renombre* (m.).

un pagaré = *a promissory note*
notabilidad = *a person of note*
escritor **de nota** (de renombre, de fama) / *a writer **of note** (famous)*

notable / notable *Notable* and *notable* both emphasize the good qualities of people or things as "worthy, remarkable, outstanding, famous." In Spanish, *notable* also refers to some quantity or amount and means "considerable." [In Spain and some other countries, *notable* is the school grade below *sobresaliente* ("outstanding") and is the equivalent of a *B*. Apparently, in other countries, *notable* is the highest grade on the scale, the equivalent of "merit" or *A*.] Pablo Picasso nos dejó muchas obras **notables**. *Pablo Picasso left us many **notable** works.* El estafador se llevó una cantidad **notable** de dinero. *The swindler stole a **considerable** amount of money.*

noticia / notice *Noticia* is not "notice" but "news item, information." *Notice* means *aviso, advertencia, letrero, anuncio, cartel* (m.; "poster"), *dimisión, plazo*. **dar un despido** = *to give notice*
en seguida = *at a moment's notice*
hasta nuevo aviso = *until further notice*
sin previo aviso = *without notice, with no notice*
una semana **de plazo** *a* / *week's **notice*** llamar la **atención** / *to attract **notice** (attention)* El **aviso** prohíbe fumar. *The **notice** (sign) says "no smoking." Noticiar* means "to notify, to give notice." *To notice* means *observar, notar, fijarse en.* No **se fijó en** mi sombrero. *He didn't **notice** my hat. Notición* (m.) means "big news, bombshell."

notorio / notorious *Notorio* is not "notorious" but "famous, noted, well-known, evident." Su generosidad es **notoria**. *His generosity is **well-known**.* Su acento alemán es **notorio**. *Her German accent is **evident**. Notorious*, although meaning "famous," usually conveys negative qualities. Possible meanings are *infame, de mala reputación, mala publicidad*. [*Notorio* and *notorious* both mean "famous," but the English term is often associated with negative words such as *crime, criminal*, etc.; whereas the Spanish term preserves the original sense of "famous" in reference to anything or anybody.] un criminal **infame** / *a **notorious** criminal* un asesinato **vil** / *a **notorious** murder*

novedad / novelty *Novedad* (f.) and *novelty* share the concept of "newness, innovation, new product." *Novedad* also means "news, change," and the plural *novedades* stands for "latest fashions, news." Esta tienda vende muchas **novedades**. *This shop sells plenty of **novelties**.* sin **novedad** / *nothing new (no change)* Aquí vendemos **novedades**. *We sell the **latest fashions** here.* ¿Sabes la última **novedad**? *Have you heard the latest **piece of news**? Novelties*, the plural form in English, translates as *productos nuevos*, referring to small, often cheap, cleverly made articles, usually for play or for adornment.

novel, novela / novel *Novel* (m.) is not "novel" (the adjective) but "new, inexperienced, beginner, novice, newcomer." Es un escritor **novel**. *He is a **beginning** (new) writer. Novel*, as an adjective in English, is not used frequently in everyday language. However, it means *raro, extraño*. Fue una experiencia **rara** para nosotros. *It was a novel experience for us.* **Novela** means "novel" (the noun) in literature and also has the figurative meaning of "story, lie." **Novelón** (m.) is one of the terms for "soap opera." In Spain, the term *culebrón* (m.; "big snake") is used and in other countries, the terms *telenovela* and *radionovela* are used.

novela rosa = *romance*

novela policiaca = *detective story*

La **telenovela** (el culebrón) *"Crystal"* de Venezuela hizo furia en España. *The Venezuelan soap opera "Crystal" was a big hit in Spain.*

núcleo / nucleus *Núcleo* and *nucleus* are both scientific terms. However, in Spanish *núcleo* is also a common term for "kernel, center (of population), area, core." El **núcleo** de esta población es muy antiguo. *The center of this town is very old.* Me gusta mi **núcleo** residencial. *I like the residential area I live in.*

nulo / null *Nulo* and *null* both mean "void *(sin valor)*, zero, nonexistent." *Nulo* also applies to people, meaning "useless." **nulo** y sin valor / **null** and void hombre **nulo** / **useless** man **Nulidad** (f.) is "nullity" ("the state of being null or void") and also refers to "incompetence, incapacity" (in people). El gerente es una **nulidad**. *The manager is a nonentity (an incompetent).* To nullify means *anular, invalidar, hacer nulo.* [Note that in Spanish there is no such word as *"nulificar."*] No se puede **anular** el contrato. *It's not possible to nullify the contract.*

numeración / numeration *Numeración* and *numeration* both mean "numbering" or "counting." *Numeración* also means "numbers, numerals," and "pagination (of a book)." la **numeración** arábiga / *Arabic* **numbers** la **numeración** del libro / *the* **pagination** *of the book* Han cambiado la **numeración** de la calle. *The house* **numbers** *have been changed.*

numeral / numeral *Numeral* and *numeral* are both adjectives for "related to numbers." *Numeral* is also a noun in English that means *número, cifra.* Los **números** romanos son letras en realidad. *Roman* **numerals** *are really letters.*

nupcial / nuptial *Nupcial* and *nuptial* are both adjectives, meaning "of marriage" or "of a wedding." In Spanish, *nupcial* is used more frequently than *nuptial* in English. marcha **nupcial** / **wedding** march banquete **nupcial** / **wedding** *banquet (feast, reception)* vestido **nupcial** (de novia) / **wedding** *dress* Nuptials, the plural form, is translated as *nupcias, casamiento, boda.* The English words *wedding* and *marriage* are the everyday terms used instead of *nuptial.* hijos de segundas **nupcias** / *children from a second* **marriage** Carlos contrajo segundas **nupcias**. *Charles remarried.*

O

obituario / obituary   *Obituario* and *obituary* both refer to "deceased people" but in different ways. In Spanish, *obituario* is the "death register" ("recording of the dead") in a church, a funeral home, or a hospital. Morones no figura en el **obituario** de la parroquia. ¿Estará vivo? *Morones doesn't appear in the parish **death** **register**. I wonder if he's alive.* *Obituary* means *necrología,* which is the newspaper section dedicated to the dead. ¿Te gusta leer las esquelas de **defunción** (nota necrológica)? *Do you like to read the **obituary** notices in the paper?*

objetar / object   *Objetar* and *to object* mean "to bring forward as a reason, to adduce." Le **objeté** que no lo podríamos hacer. *I **objected** (protested) that we would not be able to do it.* *To object* also has some negative connotations: *oponerse a, desaprobar* (ue), *rechazar,* and figuratively, *molestar.* Ella **se opone** a tocar el piano. *She **objects** to playing the piano.* ¿Le **molesta** que fume? *Do you **object** (mind) if I smoke?* *Objeción,* similarly, means "objection" as "reasoning against, protest." *Objection* in English also means *oposición, desaprobación, antipatía.* El proyecto tuvo gran **oposición**. *There was great **objection** to the project.*

objetivo / objective   *Objetivo* and *objective* share the idea of "target, aim," but the Spanish term also means "lens" (in eyeglasses, in cameras). El ladrón fue captado en el acto de robar por el **objetivo** de la cámara. *The thief was caught in the act of robbing by the camera **lens.***

obligación / obligation   *Obligación* is "obligation" in various senses, and in the business world it means "bond" *(título).* The plural *obligaciones* is used in the figurative sense of "family," especially "children." La **obligación** antes que la devoción. *Business before pleasure.* No faltes a tus **obligaciones**. *Don't neglect your **obligations**. (Don't fail in your **duty**.)* Algunas **obligaciones** son una buena inversión. *Some **bonds** are a good investment.*

obsequio(s) / obsequies   *Obsequio(s)* does not mean "obsequies" but "presents, gifts" and in a figurative sense, "honor, kindness."
obsequio del autor = *complimentary copy*
La recepción fue en **obsequio** del artista. *The reception was in **honor** of the artist.* Se deshizo en **obsequios** con ella. *He lavished **attention** on her.* *Obsequies* (which is always plural) means *exequias (funerales),* ("funeral or burial rites"). Ayer se celebraron las **exequias** del senador fallecido. *They held the **obsequies** for the deceased senator yesterday.* *Obsequiar* means "to give, offer, honor, lavish attention." Me **obsequiaron** con una copa de vino español. *They **offered** me a glass of Spanish wine.*

obsequioso / obsequious   *Obsequioso* is not "obsequious" but "attentive, complying, obliging." ¡El gerente es una persona tan **obsequiosa**! *The manager is such an **obliging** person!* *Obsequious* has downgraded its original meaning and has taken on negative shadings: *servil, adulón, zalamero.* La secretaria es muy **servil** (zalamera) con el jefe. *The secretary is very **obsequious** (servile) to her boss.*

observar / observe   *Observar* and *to observe* share the ideas of "to notice, look at, see, fulfill, remark," and "to celebrate" (a holiday, for example). *Observación* shares all the meanings of *observation*, and it also translates as "reproof, reprimand." La maestra estricta hace **observaciones** a los alumnos perezosos. *The strict teacher reprimands lazy students.*

ocasión / occasion   *Ocasión* and *occasion* both mean "favorable time, opportunity, chance, happening, motive." In Spanish, *ocasión* sometimes means "bargain." **mercancía de ocasión** (de lance) = *bargain* Tuve la **ocasión** (oportunidad) de visitar el Perú. *I had occasion (the opportunity) to visit Peru.* La **ocasión** hace al ladrón. *Opportunity makes the thief.* *Occasion* may also refer to *acontecimiento señalado, momento especial.* **de vez en cuando** = *on occasion* Brindemos en este **momento señalado**. *Let's make a toast on this occasion.* estar a la altura de las **circunstancias** / *to be equal to the occasion* *Ocasional* and *occasional* mean "for an occasion; accidental." un poema **para el caso** / *an occasional poem* *Ocasionalmente* and *occasionally* share the same distinctions as the adjectives *ocasional* and *occasional. Occasionally* is used sometimes to mean *de vez en cuando, una que otra vez.* Vamos al teatro **de vez en cuando.** *We go to the theater occasionally.*

oculto / occult   *Oculto* is not "occult" but "hidden, concealed." ciencias **ocultas** / *occult sciences* El ladrón está **oculto** en el campo. *The thief has hidden in the countryside. Occult* is not used anymore with the original meaning of "hidden"; rather, it has taken on the sophisticated sense of "hidden for a special reason." Possible translations include *secreto, esotérico, impenetrable, misterioso. Occult,* as a noun (preceded by definite article), translates as *artes ocultas.* Lo hace con un motivo **misterioso.** *He is doing it for an occult (mysterious) motive.* Tuvieron una ceremonia **secreta.** *They held an occult ceremony.*

ocupar / occupy   *Ocupar* and *to occupy* both mean "to take possession of, to engage oneself in, to employ." The reflexive *ocuparse* plus the preposition *de* translates as "to take care of, look after, deal with, see to." *Ocuparse* with the preposition *en* means "to occupy oneself with, to engage in." Irak **ocupó** Kuwait en 1990. *Iraq occupied Kuwait in 1990.* El armario **ocupa** demasiado lugar. *The wardrobe (armoire) takes up too much space.* asiento **ocupado** / *seat taken* ¡**Ocúpate** de tus cosas! *Mind (take care of) your own business!* Ella **se ocupa** mucho **de** sus gatos. *She takes good care of her cats.*

ocurrencia / occurrence   *Ocurrencia* and *occurrence* share the concept of "incident, coincidence," but the basic denotation of *ocurrencia* is "bright idea, witticism, funny thought." **tener ocurrencia** = *to be witty* Nadie se esperaba tal **ocurrencia** (suceso). *Nobody was expecting such an occurrence (incident).* ¡Tienes cada **ocurrencia**! *What funny ideas you get! Occurrence* primarily means *acontecimiento, suceso. Ocurrente* means "witty, imaginative, full of ideas." Carlota es una gerente muy **ocurrente** con los productos. *Charlotte is a very imaginative manager with the products.*

173

ofender / offend   *Ofender* and *to offend* both mean "to insult, to hurt (one's feelings), to displease." However, *ofender* also means "to hurt (physically)." The reflexive *ofenderse* translates as "to get upset, to fall out with."
sin ofender = *no offense*
Ese mal olor me **ofende** bastante. *That bad odor **offends** (displeases) me a lot.* To *offend against* ("to violate a law or rule") is *delinquir, infringir la ley.* Fue a la cárcel por **infringir** la ley. *He went to jail for **offending against** the law.*

ofensa / offense   *Ofensa* is not "offense" but "insult, affront, injury (with words)." Recibió varias **ofensas** de un cliente enfadado. *He received several **insults** from an angry customer. Offense* primarily means *delito, falta* (in sports), *infracción de la ley, escándalo.*   **crimen** de pena capital / *capital **offense*** No tenía la intención de **ofender.** *No **offense** was intended.*

ofensivo / offensive   *Ofensivo* means "offensive," in the sense of "attacking." *Offensive* also means *insultante* (with people), and *desagradable* (with smell). *Ofensivamente* and *offensively* share the same similarities and differences as their respective adjective forms.

oficial / official   *Oficial* is "official" as an adjective, meaning "holding an office, formal and ceremonious." As a noun, *oficial* (m.) means "clerk (in public service), skilled worker, officer (in the military or on a police force)."
un informe oficial = *an official report*
Trabaja de **oficial** en el juzgado. *He works as a court **clerk.** Official,* as a noun, refers to *funcionario, directivo, dignatario.* Es un **funcionario** del gobierno. *He is a government **official.***

oficio / office   *Oficio* is not "office" but "trade, occupation, profession, service (in church), official letter." El gobernador mandó un **oficio** al alcalde. *The governor sent an **official letter** to the mayor.* Esos son gajes del **oficio.** *Those are **occupational** hazards.* Juan es albañil de **oficio.** *John is a mason by **trade.** Office* means *oficina, despacho,* as well as (public) *cargo* or *posición.*
entrar en funciones = *to take office*
oficina de colocación / *employment **office** (agency)*

oficioso / officious   *Oficioso* is not "officious" but "unofficial, informal (document), willing, diligent, industrious."
una mentira oficiosa = *a little white lie*
de fuente oficiosa = *unofficially, from an unofficial source*
Es un oficial muy **oficioso.** *He is a very **diligent** clerk. Officious,* on the other hand, means *entrometido* ("meddlesome"), *molesto.* Nuestro vecino es muy **entrometido.** *Our neighbor is very **officious.** **Oficiosamente** suggests "unofficially." Officiously* means *entrometidamente.*

óleo / oil, oleo   *Óleo* is "oil" in painting and also in church services.
pintar al óleo = *to paint in oils*
Oil used for cooking is *aceite* (m.; *óleo* in this sense is rather literary). *Oil* as a natural resource is *petróleo* and *carburante* (m.; "fuel"). Engines need *oil* as a lubricant, which translates as *aceite* (m.).

pozo de petróleo = *oil well*
tanque petrolero = *oil tanker*
quemarse las pestañas = *to burn the midnight oil*
El **petróleo** es el oro negro. *Oil is black gold.* encontrar una **mina de oro** / *to strike oil* La paella se cocina con **aceite** virgen de oliva. *Paella is cooked with virgin olive oil.*

ómnibus / omnibus *Ómnibus* (m.) means "omnibus, bus" and the term is used in a few countries. Other terms include the following: *autobús* (m.; is used in most countries), *guagua* (Caribbean), and *camión* (m.; Mexico). The smaller *minibús* also has many variants; among them, *colectivo* (Peru, Argentina), *buseta* (Colombia), and *combi* (m.; Mexico). When *ómnibus* is used with trains, it becomes *tren ómnibus,* which is a slow train that makes frequent stops and is best translated as "local train." El **tren ómnibus** se demora cinco horas; el rápido llega en dos horas. *The local train takes five hours; the fast train arrives in two. Omnibus* ("edition") in English also means *antología.* As an adjective, it means *que abarca varias cosas.* Literalmente *ómnibus* quiere decir que es "para todos". *Literally,* **omnibus** *means that it is "for everybody."*

opcional / optional *Opcional* has finally been included in the latest dictionary of the *Real Academia,* after being used by millions of speakers for many years. *Opcional* is the most common term used to mean "optional." Other synonyms include *optativo, facultativo, discrecional.* Es **opcional** escribir "enseguida" o "en seguida". *It is optional in Spanish to write enseguida or en seguida.*

operación / operation *Operación* is more formal than *operation,* although both terms share the same idea. *Operación* is used for surgery, as well as for military and business operations. *Operation* is commonly translated as *manejo, trabajo, dirección, explotación, funcionamiento, obra, actividad* (f.).
telefonista = *telephone operator*
explotación de la fábrica / *operation* of the factory el **manejo** de una grúa / *the operation of a crane* estar en **vigor** (una ley) / *to be in operation (a law)* Las **obras** empiezan mañana. *Operations begin tomorrow.*

operar / operate *Operar* is used less frequently than *to operate;* however, *operar* is used for "to perform surgery" and is a rather formal term for "to manage, maneuver, work, bring about." *To operate,* on the other hand, is a useful word with a wide range of meanings: *llevar a cabo, gobernar* (ie), *trabajar, explotar, manejar, mantener* (ie) *en servicio, funcionar, dirigir.* ¿Quién **dirige** esta compañía? *Who operates this company?* La máquina **funciona** con electricidad. *The machine operates on electricity.* **obrar** con libertad / *to operate freely.*

oportunidad / opportunity *Oportunidad* (f.) translates better as "opportuneness" or "timeliness" than "opportunity." *Opportunity* in most cases means *ocasión.* La **ocasión** hace al ladrón. *Opportunity makes the thief.*

oportuno / opportune *Oportuno* is almost exactly "opportune" ("suitable, timely, advisable"), but the Spanish term is also used to describe people who are "quick and witty."

en el momento oportuno = *at the right moment*
una llegada **oportuna** / *a **timely** (opportune) arrival* Tomó las medidas **oportunas.** *He took the **appropriate** measures.* El presidente fue muy **oportuno** al contestar. *The president was very **quick and witty** in his answer.*

oposición / opposition *Oposición* means "opposition" in all its denotations; however, *oposición* (usually in the plural form, *oposiciones*) is also used to mean a "competitive examination" (for example, for a position). el líder de la **oposición** / *the leader of the **opposition*** ganar las **oposiciones** a una cátedra / *to win a chair in a **competitive examination***

optimista / optimist, optimistic *Optimista* means "optimist" and "optimistic" (the noun and adjective, respectively). *Optimista* is used only with people. El **optimista** ve el vaso medio lleno, no medio vacío. *The **optimist** sees the glass as half-full, not half-empty. Optimistic,* on the other hand, is used to refer to both people and things. Possible translations for *optimistic* to describe situations, words, things, etc. include *esperanzador, prometedor, positivo, alentador.* Es un signo **prometedor.** *It is an **optimistic** (promising) sign.* Ella nos dio un discurso **alentador.** *She gave us an **optimistic** speech.*

oración / oration *Oración* and *oration* share the idea of a "formal public speech" *(discurso). Oración* also means "prayer" and "sentence" or "clause" (in grammar). El obispo pronunció la **oración** fúnebre. *The bishop gave the funeral **oration.*** La letanía es una serie de **oraciones.** *The litany is a series of **prayers.*** estar en **oración** / *to be in **prayer*** parte de la **oración** / *part of **speech***

orbe / orb *Orbe* (m.) and *orb* mean "sphere, earth," but in Spanish, *orbe* is used in the figurative sense of "world." El Papa es un personaje conocido en todo el **orbe.** *The Pope is a well-known person throughout the **world.***

orden, ordenar / order *Orden* (m.) means "order" ("arrangement"), whereas *orden* (f.) means "order, command, religious order" and also "warrant, decree, nature."
la orden del día = *the order of the day*
cumplir las **órdenes** / *to obey **orders** Order,* for example, of merchandise, translates as *pedido* (of products).
cheque nominativo = *check to order*
La secretaria hizo dos **pedidos** de zapatos. *The secretary placed two **orders** for shoes. Ordenar* means "to order" ("to arrange, fix, command") and also "to ordain" (bishops, priests, etc.). *To order* food or goods is translated as *pedir* (i), *encargar, hacer un pedido.* ¿Ya **pediste** la comida? *Did you **order** dinner already?* Ayer **encargué** un abrigo. *Yesterday I **ordered** a coat.*

ordenanza / ordinance, ordnance *Ordenanza* and *ordinance* both mean "disposition, bylaw, order." However, *ordenanza* (m.) also means "orderly (in a hospital, in the military), mail clerk." Una **ordenanza** de mi ciudad prohíbe lavar el coche en la calle. *An **ordinance** in my city prohibits washing the car in the street.* El **ordenanza** limpia las botas del coronel. *The **orderly** shines the colonel's boots. Ordnance,* on the other hand, means *artillería, armas,* or *pertrechos militares.*

ordinario / ordinary *Ordinario* and *ordinary* share the basic idea of "common, usual, normal, mediocre." *Ordinario,* though, has downgraded its denotation to describe people (not things) who are "vulgar, rude, coarse." [Nonnative speakers of Spanish should exercise caution and refrain from using *ordinario* to refer to an individual. In some dialects, referring to a person as *ordinario* can result in an embarrassing situation.] El coche **ordinario** (usual) de Europa es pequeño. *The **ordinary** (average) car in Europe is small.* ¡Qué palabras más **ordinarias** usó el juez! *What **vulgar** language the judge used!*

organismo / organism *Organismo* shares with *organism* the technical meaning of "individual, animal, or plant with organs." The Spanish term, however, also applies to "organizations, institutions" such as the United Nations or NATO. El hombre es un **organismo** mucho más complicado que una ameba. *A human being is a much more complicated **organism** than an amoeba.* La ONU es un **organismo** que busca la paz del mundo. *The UN is an **institution** searching for world peace.*

organización / organization *Organización* exactly means "organization." Nevertheless, there are differences in meaning that stem from differences in culture, perhaps deriving from the degree to which each culture stresses organization as a quality. *Organization* is a key word in American English and has many translations in Spanish:

asociación	arreglo
unión	comunidad
orden (f.)	organismo
sociedad (f.)	corporación
agrupación	organización

Es una **asociación** para ayudar a los pobres de la ciudad. *It's an **organization** for helping the city's poor.* El sindicato es una **sociedad** (unión) de obreros para su beneficio. *The union is an **organization** for the benefit of the workers.*

órgano / organ *Órgano* and *organ* both apply to parts of the body and to the musical instrument, but the Spanish term applies also to a "body" or "organization," and in a figurative sense, "agent, means, spokesperson."
órgano de manubrio = *barrel organ*
armónica = *mouth organ, harmonica*
El **órgano** legislativo es una de las tres divisiones del gobierno. *The legislative **body** is one of the three divisions of the government.* El sindicato de los camioneros es un **órgano** muy activo. *The truck drivers' union is an active **organization**.*

orientación / orientation *Orientación* and *orientation* share both the real and figurative meanings of "a position relative to the compass; awareness, guidance, etc." In Spanish, *orientación* has a wider scope because it includes the meaning of "exposure (of a building), aspect, prospect." La casa tiene buena **orientación** al sur. *The house has a good southern **exposure**.* con **orientación** al mediodía / *facing south; with a southern **aspect** (exposure)* El decano dio **orientación** general a los alumnos nuevos. *The dean gave a general **orientation** to the new students.*

oriente, oriental / orient, oriental *Oriente* (m.) and *Orient* are regions of Asia, that include China, Japan, etc. In Spanish, however, *oriente* is an everyday word for "east," almost as commonly used as *este* (m.).

Oriente Medio = *Middle East*
Extremo Oriente = *Far East*
Cercano Oriente = *Near East*

El sol sale por el **oriente**. *The sun rises in the **east**. Oriental* means "Oriental," as well as "eastern." Valencia está en la región **oriental** de España. *Valencia is in the **eastern** region of Spain.*

oro / ore *Oro* is not "ore" but "gold." In Spanish, *oro* is the source of many idiomatic expressions.

mina de oro = *gold mine; bonanza*
pan de oro = *gold leaf*
chapado de oro = *gold-plated*

Ore means *mineral* (m.) or *mena*.

El **mineral** de hierro se extrae de las minas para procesarlo. *Iron **ore** is extracted from the mines for processing.*

orquesta / orchestra *Orquesta* is "orchestra" (note the spelling in Spanish has only one *r*), but the Spanish term is used loosely to refer to any kind of "band." *Orchestra* in English is also used to refer to the *platea* (in some countries, the *patio de butaca*) in the cinema or theater.

butaca de patio = *orchestra seat*

Las butacas de **platea** son los asientos más caros del teatro. *The **orchestra** seats are the most expensive ones in the theater. Orquestar* means "to orchestrate" ("to compose, arrange music"). *To orchestrate* is used loosely to refer to *preparar, combinar*. Los alumnos **prepararon** una recepción para los profesores. *The students **orchestrated** a reception for the professors.*

ortografía / orthography *Ortografía* is exactly "orthography, spelling." (Note that *spelling* is the everyday term used in English.) La profesora cometió una falta de **ortografía** cuando escribió "elije". *The professor made a **spelling** error when she wrote elije.*

oscuro / obscure *Oscuro* basically translates two English terms. In a real sense, it means "dark" (colors, without light). In a figurative sense, *oscuro* means "obscure" ("without light, not clear, not well-known, gloomy, black, shady").

azul oscuro = *dark blue*
un porvenir oscuro = *a gloomy future*
un asunto oscuro = *a shady affair*

llevar una vida **oscura** / *to keep in the **background*** Es un escritor **oscuro**. *He is an **obscure** writer. Oscurecer*, similarly, means "to darken" in a real sense and "to obscure" in a figurative sense. **oscurecer** la verdad / *to **obscure** the truth* Ella **oscurece** a sus hermanos. *She **leaves** her brothers **in the shade**.*

ostensible / ostensible *Ostensible* in Spanish does not mean "ostensible"; rather, it means "obvious, evident, open, conspicuous, visible." Cometió un error **ostensible**. *He made an **obvious** mistake. Ostensible* in English has lost its original meaning and now is used to mean *aparente, supuesto, presunto.* El **supuesto** problema se solucionó pronto. *The **ostensible** problem was resolved quickly.* ***Ostensiblemente*** means "clearly, openly, obviously." *Ostensibly* means *aparentemente, supuestamente.*

overol / overall *Overol* (m.) is a loan word from English for "overalls" and both the Spanish and the English refer to the same garment. In some countries, however, the plural *overoles* is used, but in others, the singular is preferred. [In Spain, workers wear the *mono,* which is another version of the *overol.*] Los niños se ponen el **overol** para jugar y no mancharse. *The children put on their **overalls** to play without getting dirty.* *Overall* is also an adjective meaning *global, total,* and is an adverb, meaning *en conjunto.*
coste total = *overall cost*

oxidar / oxidize *Oxidar* is "to oxidize" in chemistry and "to rust" in everyday speech. *Oxidarse* translates as "to get rusted, to become rusty." El tubo **se ha oxidado.** Debemos cambiarlo. *The pipe **has rusted.** We must replace it.* ***Oxidado*** means "rusty." *Óxido* means "oxide" in technical terminology, but the everyday word for the concept is *rust.*

P

paciencia / patience *Paciencia* exactly means "patience," according to all the dictionaries, but there are clear cultural differences between the two terms. [*Patience* suggests the virtue of waiting "with human hope," whereas *paciencia* seems to refer to the virtue of waiting "without human hope but with God's hope"—in other words, a "hopeless patience." For example, if a Hispanic government official says *"¡Tenga paciencia!"* actually he or she is saying that the problem probably cannot be solved or that it will take forever.] probarle a alguien la **paciencia** / *to try someone's patience* armarse de **paciencia** / *to muster one's patience* Con **paciencia** se gana el cielo. *Slow and steady wins the race.* tomar algo **con paciencia** / *to take something calmly*

paciente / patient *Paciente* and *patient* are both adjectives for people "with patience." Both terms are also nouns, with a slight difference in meaning. *Paciente* (m., f.) is only used when a person is sick or in the hospital. If the person is a "customer" of the doctor, the word *cliente* is used. El hospital está lleno de **pacientes**. *The hospital is full of patients. Patient*, on the other hand, refers to the sick person being treated by the doctor as well as to the customer of the doctor. According to context, an appropriate translation is either *paciente* or *cliente*. Hace diez años que soy **cliente** del Dr. Doll. *I have been Dr. Doll's patient for ten years.*

padre / padre *Padre* is "father" and also "priest" (or "father" as a title in the church). The plural form *padres* means "parents" or "ancestors." Colloquially, *padre* and *padrísimo* are used in modern Mexico as adjectives meaning "fantastic" *(estupendo)*. In all Hispanic countries, *padre* is used in colloquial speech as an adjective to mean "very big."
un éxito padre = *a big hit, an enormous success*
un susto padre = *quite a scare, a great scare*
A **padre** ganador, hijo gastado. *A wage-earning father produces a spendthrift son.* una paliza de **padre** y señor mío / *a hell of a beating* darse la vida **padre** / *to live it up Padre* is a loan word from Spanish that means "priest" and is usually translated as *capellán* (m.; "chaplain or priest for a school or the armed forces").

paje / page *Paje* (m.) means "page" as "a servant to a person of high rank." In Spanish the term is historical, a key word in the past. el **paje** de un rey / *a king's page Page* has changed with time to mean *botones* (m.; "bellboy"), *acomodador* (m.; "usher"). The word also means *página* (of a book or magazine) and *plana* (of a newspaper).
en primera plana = *on the front page*
el **botones** de un hotel / *the page of a hotel* Trabaja de **acomodador** en el senado. *He works as a page in the Senate.*

paleta / palette *Paletas* and *palettes* are used by painters, but the Spanish term also means "shovel, (ping-pong) paddle, shoulder blade," and in colloquial speech, "front teeth." In Spain and Mexico, *paleta* also means an "ice-cream bar." Los niños juegan con **paletas** en la arena de la playa. *The children are playing with their shovels in the sand on the beach.*

palma / palm *Palma* and *palm* share the sense of "tree, a part of the hand," and both terms stand for a symbol of "triumph" *(triunfo).* The plural form *palmas* is used to mean "applause."
llevarse la palma = *to triumph, to win*
palma datilera / *date palm, date tree* Te conozco como la **palma** de la mano. *I know you like the back (palm) of my hand.*

palpitante / palpitant *Palpitante* and *palpitant* both refer to "heartbeat." *Palpitante* is used in the figurative sense of "exciting, passionate, thrilling." La telenovela tiene momentos **palpitantes** de amor. *The soap opera has some thrilling love scenes.* *Pálpito* is used in Latin America for "hunch, feeling, presentiment."

panel / panel *Panel* (m.) and *panel* share the meaning of "section of a wall, door, or window; a board for instruments, controls." *Panel* is used in Latin America as "panel" in English, meaning "jury, group of people to present a discussion." (In Spain *panel* is not used with this meaning; instead, *jurado* or *mesa redonda* is used.) In some countries, *panel* is also used to mean "billboard" (for advertisements). El **panel** (jurado) escogió la reina del carnaval. *The panel (jury) selected the queen of the carnival.* Un **panel** (una mesa redonda) de expertos dirigió la discusión. *A panel of experts led the discussion.* Los anuncios en **paneles** son caros, pero efectivos. *Billboard advertisements are expensive but effective.* Panel in English also translates as *paño* (of a dress).

papá, papa / papa *Papá* and *papa* (or "daddy") are terms for "father." In Spanish, *papá* is the everyday word for "father," along with *padre*, which is the more formal term. **Papá** Noel / *Father Christmas* Papa in English is generally used only by children. *Papa* (m.) means "Pope" and *papa* (f.) means "potato" in Latin America. [Note that *patata* means "potato" in Spain and that in Latin America, *papa del aire* is translated as "yam."] no saber ni **papa** de / *to know "beans" about (know nothing)* **papa** dulce (batata) / *sweet potato*

papel / paper *Papel* (m.) and *paper* both stand for "thin material used for writing or printing." In the theater and in a figurative sense, *papel* also means "role, part."
papel glaseado = *glossy paper*
hacer un papel = *to play a part*
Ella tiene un buen **papel** en la obra. *She has a good part (role) in the play.* **papel** de estraza / *brown paper* Paper also means *periódico, ensayo, ponencia, comunicación;* in the plural, *papers* is the everyday term for *documentos.* To paper is *empapelar* or *pulir con lija* (to sandpaper).
semanario = *weekly paper*
en **teoría** / *on paper (in theory)* poner por escrito / *to put down on paper* libro

en rustica / **paperback** book   Escribí dos **monografías** este curso. I wrote two **papers** this school year.

paquete / packet   **Paquete** (m.; *cajetilla*) means "packet" (a small container or package, for example, for cigarettes). However, **paquete** also means "package, parcel," and in a figurative sense, "heavy task, hard job."
paquete postal = *parcel post*
de paquete = *brand-new*
un coche **de paquete** / a **brand-new** car   ¡Vaya un **paquete**! What a job! Packet is also used for *carpeta*, *sobre* (m.; of tea, etc.). Me dieron una **carpeta** con la información pedida. They gave me a **packet** of the information requested.

par / pair, par   **Par** (m.) and *pair* ("couple") both refer to "two things, a set of two." In Spanish, **par** is also an adjective meaning "equal, even (number)."
de par en par = *wide open*
sin par = *peerless, matchless, without equal*
un **par** de horas / a **couple** of hours   jugar a **pares** y nones / to play odds and **evens**   Pair in English also applies to *pareja* ("a couple") and *yunta* (of oxen).   unas tijeras, una tijera / a **pair** of scissors   una **pareja** de recién casados / a **newlywed couple**   Par in English is a noun, meaning *igualdad* (f.), and in the business world, *paridad* (f.), *valor* (m.) *nominal*. In golf, *par* translates as *par, recorrido*.
a la par = *at par, at the same time*
ser típico / to be **par** for the course   ser igual a / to be on a **par** with

parábola / parable, parabola   **Parábola** is a true cognate of both *parable* ("story") and *parabola* (in mathematics). **Parabólico** means "parabolic" in mathematics; however, the feminine form **parabólica** is the Spanish rendition of "satellite dish" (for television). México es el primer país del mundo en **parabólicas** por persona. Mexico leads the world in **satellite dishes** per capita.

parada / parade   **Parada** means "parade" only in terms of a military parade. The primary meaning of **parada** is "stop, stand" (of taxis, for example), "break, pause." En esta equina no hay **parada** de autobús. There is no bus **stop** at this corner. Parade, on the other hand, refers to *desfile* (m.), *presentación*, and figuratively, *alarde* (m.), *ostentación*, *gala*.   un **desfile** de carrozas / a **parade** of floats   **presentación** de modelos / fashion **parade**   Nos hace **alarde** (ostentación) de erudición. He **parades** his learning before us.

parcela / parcel   **Parcela** is not only "parcel" (of land) but also "particle, small piece." Las **parcelas** más caras están cerca de la playa. The most expensive **parcels** (lots) are near the beach. Parcel also means *paquete* (m.), *partida* (of goods), and figuratively, *sarta* or *montón* (m.; for example, of lies).
paquete postal = *parcel post*
El **paquete** de libros llegó averiado. The **parcel** (package) of books arrived damaged. Nos contó un **montón** de mentiras. He told us a **parcel** (pack) of lies. **Parcelar** means "to parcel out" ("divide in plots"). To parcel also means *empaquetar* or

embalar, envolver (ue). (Note that in American English *to package* is more commonly used.)

parcial / partial *Parcial* and *partial* share several meanings, such as "incomplete, biased, unjust." vista **parcial** / *a* **partial** view un juicio **parcial** (injusto) / *a* **partial** judgment *Partial* in English is used in the figurative sense of *aficionado* ("fond of"), *con predilección por. Partiality* translates as **favoritismo.** Ella es **aficionada** a los bombones. *She is partial to chocolates.* tener **favoritismos** / *to show* **partiality**

pariente / parent *Pariente* (m.) does not mean "parent" but "relative" ("someone related by blood or marriage").
pariente político = *in-law*
Tengo **parientes** por toda España. *I have* **relatives** *all over Spain. Parent* is translated as *padre* or *madre* to refer to a specific parent; *parents* is translated as *padres* (and in some countries, informally as *papás*).

parque / park *Parque* (m.) is "park" with all its meanings, as well as "parking" (according to the *Real Academia*). It also means "depot" ("warehouse"). [In Madrid and all Spanish cities, there are *parkings* (m.), the term popularly used for a commercial place where one pays to park a car.] *Parquear* is used in some countries for "to park." Other countries use *aparcar* or *estacionar.*
parque de artillería = *weapons depot*
Me gusta visitar el **parque** zoológico. *I like to go to the* **zoo** *(zoological park).* **parque** de atracciones / *fairground; theme* **park**

parroquial / parochial *Parroquial* is not "parochial" but "parish" (as an adjective). Se oyen las campanas **parroquiales.** *One can hear the* **church** *bells. Parochial,* in everyday language, has shifted from the meaning of "parish" to a figurative sense of a state of mind that is limited ("narrow-minded"): *estrecho, local, localista, pueblerino.*
escuela privada, escuela parroquial = *parochial school*
tener una mentalidad **pueblerina** (estrecha) / *to have a* **parochial** *outlook Parroquiano,* on the other hand, has lost the original meaning of "member of a parish church" and has become "a regular customer of a store," and in a negative sense, "a regular customer of a bar." El bar de la esquina siempre está lleno de **parroquianos.** *The corner bar is always full of* **regular customers.**

parsimonia / parsimony *Parsimonia* is not "parsimony" but "moderation, temperance, calmness, slowness."
con parsimonia = *calmly*
Camina con mucha **parsimonia** (cachaza). *He is walking very* **slowly.** Llevan una vida de **parsimonia** (frugalidad). *They live a life of* **moderation.** *Parsimony* translates as *tacañería, avaricia.*

parsimonioso / parsimonious *Parsimonioso* means "moderate, calm, unhurried." *Parsimonious* means *tacaño, avaro, muy frugal.* [This is a typical case of an adjective that has downgraded its original meaning. It is difficult to pinpoint how a word crosses a fine line of meaning, for example, from "moderate" to "stingy" and even from "frugality" to "stinginess."] Es **tacaño** con su dinero. *He is **parsimonious** with his money.* ¿Es **muy frugal** la gente de Monterrey? *Are the people from Monterrey parsimonious?*

parte / part *Parte* (f.) translates as "part" with several meanings, according to context. *Parte* as a masculine noun means "dispatch, message, communiqué (military), report (of news or weather)." El general mandó **un parte** urgente al presidente. *The general sent an urgent **communiqué** to the president.* Me enteré de la noticia en **el parte** de las dos de la tarde. *I found out the news on the two p.m. **report**.*

partición / partition *Partición* and *partition* share the idea of "division, distribution." La **partición** de la herencia trajo división entre los hermanos. *The **partition** of the inheritance divided the brothers. Partition*, however, is also a term used in construction to mean *tabique* (m.), which is a "thin wall." La directora mandó poner **tabiques** entre las oficinas. *The director ordered **partitions** built between the offices.*

participar / participate *Participar* and *to participate* both mean "to take part, share, have a share." The Spanish term also means "to inform, notify, announce (news)" and in the business world, "to invest" (money). Nos **participó** que se casará en mayo. *He **informed** us that he's getting married in May.* **participar** de la misma opinión / *to share the same opinion Participación* similarly means "participation" ("taking part, sharing in"), and it also means "notice" *(aviso)* and in the business world, "shares (stocks), investment." **participación** en los beneficios / *profit **sharing*** Tengo **participaciones** en esta empresa. *I have **shares** (stock) in this company.*

particular / particular *Particular* does not mean "particular" but "special, peculiar to, individual, personal, private." As a noun, *particular* (m.) means "matter, subject, point, item, private individual, civilian."
lecciones particulares = *private lessons*
profesor particular = *private tutor*
particular de una región / *peculiar (unique) to a region* No sé nada de este **particular**. *I know nothing about this **matter**.* vestido de **particular** / *dressed as a **civilian*** nada de **particular** / *nothing special Particular*, on the other hand, means *concreto, detallado, exigente, delicado*. As a noun, *particular* means *detalle* (m.), *pormenor* (m.), *dato*. Es muy **exigente** con la puntualidad. *He is very **particular** about punctuality.* entrar en **pormenores** / *to go into particulars*

partir / part *Partir* and *to part* share the idea of "to divide." However, in Spanish, *partir* means "to divide into any number or amount," rather than "to divide by two or into two" like its English cognate. *Partir* and *to part* both mean "to break, split." *Partir* in Spanish means "to share" *(compartir)*, "to cut, chop." *Partir de* means "to leave, set off."
a partir de (+ time or place) = *starting from* (+ time or place)
Se partió el cristal de la ventana. *The window **broke**.* **partir** una manzana / *to*

cut (to share) an apple   **Partió de** la estación temprano. *He left (set off from) the station early.*   **partir** la cara a uno   /   *to break someone's neck*   ¡Que te **parta** un rayo!   *To hell with you!* *(May you be **struck** by lightning!)* *To part* also translates as *separar, despedirse* (i). *To part (one's hair)* is *hacerse la raya.* [Note that *to part* always suggests "by two."] **Se separó** de ella en malos términos. *He **parted** from her on bad terms.*

pasable / passable   *Pasable* and *passable* suggest "adequate, good enough, acceptable." Sus notas son **pasables**. *His grades are **passable**. Passable* in English also refers to a road as *transitable* and to a river as *atravesable*. Es una carretera vieja pero está **transitable**. *It's an old road but still **passable**.*

pasaje / passage   *Pasaje* (m.) and *passage* both mean "a section of a book" and "passageway" *(pasadizo)*. *Pasaje* also means "fare, ticket" (for a plane, train, boat, etc.) and "passengers" (on a plane, etc.).   un **pasaje** del *Quijote*   /   *a **passage** from* Don Quijote   Todo el **pasaje** del avión murió en el accidente. *All the **passengers** on the plane died in the accident. Passage* is also *pasillo, corredor* (m.), *paso* (of time), *travesía* ("crossing"), and *aprobación* (of a law). [*Passage* used to be a term for *billete* (m.; "ticket") for traveling by boat or ship, not for any other mode of transportation. It also used to mean *facilidades* (f.; "facilities") on a ship.] Es un **corredor** amplio y largo. *It's a long, wide **passage** (hall).*   el **paso** del tiempo   /   *the **passage** of time*   la **aprobación** de un proyecto de ley   /   *the **passage** of a bill*

pasar / pass   *Pasar* is "to pass" in most of its denotations. The Spanish term also means "to happen, to suffer, to swallow (food), to turn over (a page)."
pasar el rato = *to kill time*
pasar por alto = *to omit, to ignore*
pasar(lo/la) bien = *to have a good time*
No le **pasó** nada. *Nothing **happened** to him.*   **pasarse** de la raya   /   *to go too far*   ¿Cómo lo (la) **pasas**? *How are you doing? To pass* also means *aprobar* (ue) (a test or exam). [Note that *aprobado* is the equivalent of a *D.*] No **aprobó** las matemáticas. *He did not **pass** mathematics.*

pasivo / passive   *Pasivo* and *passive* share the same meanings as adjectives. *Pasivo* is used as a noun in financial language to refer to "liabilities."
en el pasivo = *on the debit side*
activo y pasivo = *assets and liabilities*

pasta / pasta, paste   *Pasta* and *pasta* both refer to Italian food such as ravioli, as well as to the dough to make the dish. In Spanish, *pasta* also means "pastry or cookie, cover (of a book), paste (as a doughy substance; for the teeth)" and figuratively, "makings" ("aptitude") and in Spain, "dough" (slang for "money").
de buena pasta = *good-natured* (person)
pasta de dientes = *toothpaste*
pasta de madera = *wood pulp*
Me gustan las **pastas** de chocolate. *I like chocolate **pastries**.* Miguel tiene **pasta** de torero. *Michael has the **makings** of a bullfighter.* Estoy sin **pasta**. *I'm broke. (I have no **dough**.) Paste* is also used for *cola* or *goma* ("glue"), *barro* ("clay").

Usamos **cola** (engrudo) para pegar cosas. *We use* **paste** *(glue) to stick things together.*

pastar / paste   *Pastar* is not "to paste" but "to graze, pasture." El ganado **pastaba** tranquilamente. *The cattle* **was grazing** *peacefully. To paste* is translated as *pegar* or *colar* (ue) (with glue). Tengo que **pegar** estas dos tablas. *I have* **to paste** *these two boards together.*

pastel / pastel   *Pastel* (m.) and *pastel* are both terms used in art to refer to "a painting done with crayons" and "crayon." The everyday meaning of **pastel** in Spanish is "cake, pastry, cookie, pie" and, in a figurative sense, "mess, bummer, failure."
descubrir el pastel = *to spill the beans, to tell all*
pintar al pastel = *to paint in pastels*
dibujo al pastel = *pastel drawing*
pastel de almendras / *almond* **pastry**   La fiesta resultó un **pastel**. *The party was a* **bummer**. *Pastel* is also used in English to refer to "a light or pale color."
azul claro = *pastel blue*

pastilla / pastille, pastil   *Pastilla* and *pastille* or *pastil* are both derived from the French and mean "tablet, lozenge, pellet." *Pastilla* also means "bar or cake (of soap), piece or bar (of chocolate)."
pastilla de café con leche = *toffee*
pastilla para la garganta / *throat* **lozenge** *(pastille)*   Necesito una **pastilla** de jabón para bañarme. *I need a* **bar** *of soap to take a bath.*

pastor / pastor   *Pastor* (m.) is the Latin and Spanish term for "shepherd." In Spanish-speaking countries, *pastor* is used to refer to a "protestant minister." *Pastor* is also used in a figurative sense to refer to any religious leader, such as a bishop or priest (*pastor* of souls). Es el **pastor** de la iglesia metodista. *He is the* **pastor** *of the Methodist church. Pastor* is used in English for "clergyman" or "priest." Appropriate translations would be *párroco* ("head of the parish") or *sacerdote* (m.; "priest"). El **párroco** tiene a su cargo una parroquia. *The* **pastor** *is in charge of the parish.*

patente / patent   *Patente* is "patent" as an adjective, meaning "obvious, evident." *Patente* (f.) is also a noun, meaning "patent" as an "official document for an invention." The Spanish term, however, is used loosely to refer to any "license" or "authorization" to operate a business. In some countries, *patente* is used to mean "license plate" (of a car).
charol = *patent leather*
hacer patente = *to show clearly*
Mi tío tiene la **patente** de vender la marca Gucci en su tienda. *My uncle has the* **authorization** *to sell the Gucci brand in his store.*

paternal, paterno / paternal   Paternal means "paternal," in the sense of "fatherly, having the qualities of a father." amor **paternal** / *fatherly (paternal) love*   Paterno, on the other hand, means "paternal" in the sense of "related by blood." mi abuelo **paterno** / *my* **paternal** *grandfather (father's father)*

patético / pathetic   *Patético* is not "pathetic' but "moving, distressing, tragic." Fue un discurso **patético** (conmovedor). *It was a moving (touching) speech. Pathetic* means *lastimoso, de pena, malísimo.* Es una mujer **lastimosa.** *She is a pathetic creature.* Es un torero **malísimo.** *He's a pathetic bullfighter.* ¡Es una **pena**! *It's pathetic! Patetismo* translates as "pathos."

patio / patio   *Patio* does not exactly mean "patio"; rather, it has a wide range of meanings: "yard (in general), playground, schoolyard, orchestra pit (in the theater)." Hay muchos rosales y naranjos en el **patio.** *There are many rosebushes and orange trees in the yard. Patio* is a word that was borrowed from Spanish, and its meaning is generally restricted to "a paved area adjacent to a house, usually with tables, chairs, etc." This meaning of *patio* is generally called a *terraza* in Spanish and sometimes is called a *patio andaluz* ("Andalusian patio"). En verano me gusta comer en la mesa de la **terraza** (del patio). *In the summer I like to eat at the table on the patio.*

patriota / patriotic, patriot   *Patriota* means both the adjective "patriotic" and the noun "patriot." In addition, it means "fellow countryman" or "fellow countrywoman" *(compatriota).* Los dos ministros son de Andalucía. Son **patriotas** (compatriotas). *The two ministers are from Andalusia. They are fellow countrymen.*

patrocinar / patronize   *Patrocinar* and *to patronize* share the idea of "to sponsor, support." *To patronize* sometimes downgrades its connotation to express *tratar con aire protector,* which implies arrogance on the part of the subject. *To patronize* also means "to frequent a place (restaurant, store, etc.)" and is translated as *frecuentar, ser cliente fiel de.* [There is no such accepted term as *"patronizar"* in Spanish. It is considered an anglicism.] El gerente **trata** a María **con aire protector.** *The manager patronizes Mary.* Los borrachos **frecuentan** esta cantina. *Drunks patronize this bar.*

patrón, patrono / patron   *Patrón* (m.) means "patron" only in the expression *santo patrón* ("patron saint"). *Patrón* primarily refers to people, with the meaning of "boss, master, owner, skipper" and refers to things, with the meaning of "pattern, standard (model)."
patrón oro = *gold standard*
Donde hay **patrón** no manda marinero. *The boss is the boss. (Where there is a skipper, the sailor doesn't command.)* Hasta los desesperados tienen su (santo) **patrón.** *Even the desperate have their patron (saint).* **patrón** de vestido / *dress pattern Patrono* means "employer, sponsor," and it is also used in the expression for "patron saint": *santo patrono.*
patrona = *patroness, landlady*
Mi **patrono** me paga cada semana. *My employer pays me every week. Patron,* however, translates as *patrocinador* (m.), *cliente* (m.).
patrocinador de las artes = *patron of the arts*
Patronato translates as "patronage, sponsorship," as well as "board of trustees."

peculiar / peculiar   *Peculiar* is not "peculiar" but "characteristic, typical, particular." Este sombrero es **peculiar** de México. *This hat is typical in Mexico. Peculiar* in English has downgraded its original meaning of "characteristic" to become *raro, extraño, singular* ("odd, queer"). Está un poco **chalado** (raro). *He's a bit peculiar.* Don Jones era un hombre millonario, pero muy **extraño**. *Don Jones was a millionaire but a most peculiar man.*

pena / pain *Pena* is not "pain" but "sorrow, grief, trouble, pity, (legal) punishment, penalty." The plural form *penas* suggests "hardships, toils, torments (in hell)."
a duras penas, apenas = *barely*
pena capital = *capital punishment*
pena de muerte = *death penalty*
¡Qué pena! = *What a shame (pity)!*
Siento **pena** en decírtelo. *I am **sorry** to inform you about it.* Pasó por muchas **penas** de joven. *He experienced a lot of **trouble** in his youth.* ¡Allá **penas**! *That's not my **worry**!* *Pain* refers to *dolor* (m.) as physical pain, and in a figurative sense it means *pena, sufrimiento.* The plural form *pains* suggests *dolores de parto* ("labor pains"), *esfuerzos.* Se esmeró en acomodar a sus invitados. *She took great **pains** to please her guests.*

penalidad / penalty *Penalidad* (f.) means "suffering, hardship." las **penalidades** de la vida / *the **hardships** of life* *Penalty* means *castigo, sanción,* and in the business world, *recargo, multa.* [In European *fútbol* (m.; "soccer"), the word *penalty* (m.) has been borrowed from the English. In Mexico and some other countries, *penal* (m.) is used instead.] Me dieron una **multa** por pagar atrasado. *They charged me a **penalty** for the late payment.* Un **penalty** (penal) es un gol casi seguro. *A **penalty** is almost a sure goal.*

penalizar / penalize *Penalizar* has finally been included in the dictionary of the *Real Academia* with the meaning of "to penalize," but only as it applies to sports. *To penalize* in general means *castigar, penar, sancionar.* **Fue sancionado** con 25 años de cárcel. *He **was penalized** with 25 years in prison.*

pendiente / pending, pendant *Pendiente* and *pending* are adjectives to describe something "not finished." However, *pendiente* also means "hanging" or "sloping" in a real sense and "outstanding" in a figurative sense. *Pendiente* (f.) is also a noun, meaning "slope" and as a masculine noun, it means "earring" and also "pendant."
cheques pendientes = *outstanding checks*
pedidos pendientes = *pending orders*
estar pendiente de = *to be waiting for*
una **pendiente** muy suave / *a very gentle **slope*** Es una carretera muy **pendiente**. *It's a very **sloping** road.* Lleva **pendientes** de oro. *She is wearing gold **earrings.***

penitencia / penitence, penance *Penitencia* means "penitence" (the corresponding feeling is *arrepentimiento*) and "penance," as well as "punishment, detention (in school, for example)." Está haciendo **penitencia**. *He is doing **penance**.* La maestra le dio una hora de **penitencia**. *The teacher gave him an hour in (on) **detention**.*

pensión / pension   *Pensión* and *pension* both mean "retirement pay" *(jubilación).* In Spanish *pensión* also means "boardinghouse, charge for room and board." [*Jubilación* is used for "retirement" and "retirement pay." In parts of Latin America the word for both concepts is *retiro.*]
media pensión = *partial board*
pensión vitalicia = *annuity, life annuity*
Ella tiene buena **pensión** (jubilación). *She has a good pension.* Una **pensión** es más barata que un hotel. *A boardinghouse is cheaper than a hotel.* **Pensionado** means "pensioned" as an adjective and "boarding school" *(internado)* as a noun. **Pensionista** means "boarder" (in a private school). **Pensionar** means "to give a pension." *To pension (off)* translates as *jubilar, retirar.*

percibir / perceive   *Percibir* and *to perceive* both mean "to hear, see, sense." Each term has additional meanings. *Percibir* also means "to collect" or "to receive" (money). **Percibí** (divisé) un barco a lo lejos. *I could perceive a boat in the distance.* ¿**Percibes** mucho dinero en tu negocio? *Do you make (receive) much money in your business? To perceive* also means *darse cuenta de, comprender.* **Se dio cuenta de** que lo estaban vigilando. *He perceived that he was being watched.*

perdonar / pardon   *Perdonar* and *to pardon* share the idea of "to forgive, to excuse." *Perdonar* is also used for "to miss" *(perder,* ie), "to overlook" *(omitir),* "to spare (effort)." **Perdone** la molestia. *Excuse me for bothering you.* **Perdone** que se lo diga. *Pardon my saying so.* Juan no **perdona** una ocasión de contar un chiste. *John doesn't miss a chance to tell a joke.* Ella no **perdona** ni un detalle. *She doesn't overlook a detail.*

perentorio / peremptory   *Perentorio* is not "peremptory" but "imperative, urgent, pressing." Es **perentorio** que sigas adelante. *It's imperative that you keep going. Peremptory* refers to *áspero, brusco, autoritario.* Mostró una actitud muy **brusca.** *He had a very peremptory attitude.*

perfeccionar / perfect   *Perfeccionar* means "to perfect" ("to complete, make perfect"). However, the term in Spanish does not necessarily achieve "perfection"; rather, it can mean "to improve, to make better" or simply "to brush up on" (a subject). Quisiera **perfeccionar** mi francés antes de ir a París. *I would like to brush up on my French before going to Paris.*

persecución / persecution   *Persecución* is "persecution" as "torment, oppression." The term in Spanish can also have the less serious meaning of "chasing, pursuing."
manía persecutoria = *persecution complex*
La **persecución** del ladrón por la policía alcanzó velocidades de 100 millas por hora. *The police chase of the thief reached speeds of 100 miles per hour.*

perseguir / persecute, prosecute   *Perseguir* (i) similarly means "to persecute, torment, harass, oppress" *(atormentar),* but it also has the less serious meaning of "to chase, pursue" and in a figurative sense, may even have the positive connotation of "to aim for, to keep up." In legal terminology, *perseguir* translates as "to prosecute." **perseguir** el bienestar del pueblo / *to pursue the well-being* *of the people* **perseguir** (agobiar) con sus demandas / **to harass** *(pester) with one's demands*

personaje / personage *Personaje* (m.) means "personage" ("important person"), as well as "character" (in literature). El **personaje** de Don Quijote es famoso. *The* **character** *of Don Quijote is famous.*

personal / personal, personnel *Personal* and *personal* are both adjectives for "individual, private." *Personal* (m.) as a noun means "personnel" ("staff, employees") and in a broad sense, "people."
personal de la empresa = *company staff*
Había mucho **personal** (gente) en la graduación. *There were many* **people** *at the graduation.* *Personalizar* exactly means "to personalize."

persuasión / persuasion *Persuasión* and *persuasion* both suggest "causing to do something by reasoning or convincing." El predicador habló con gran **persuasión**. *The preacher spoke with great* **persuasion**. *Persuasion* also means *creencia* (religious or political), *convicción, religión, secta.* Su **creencia** religiosa no le permite tomar. *His religious* **persuasion** *doesn't allow him to drink.*

perverso / perverse *Perverso* and *perverse* share the basic idea of "wicked, corrupt," but each term has different shades of meaning. In Spanish, *perverso* takes on the strong sense of "evil, depraved, vicious." Es un hombre muy **perverso**. *He's a very* **depraved** *man. Perverse,* on the other hand, sometimes has the meaning of *obstinado* or *terco, adverso* or *contrario.* Tiene un sentido de justicia **contrario**. *He has a* **perverse** *sense of fairness. Perversidad* (f.) suggests "depravity, viciousness." *Perversity* usually means *obstinación* or *terquedad* (f.), *espíritu* (m.) *de contradicción.* No trates de luchar contra la **obstinación** famosa del director. *Don't try to fight the director's notorious* **perversity**.

peste / pest *Peste* (f.) is not "pest" but "plague, stink, stench" and in a figurative sense, "evil, corruption, pestilence." The plural form *pestes* translates as "curses." La **peste** bubónica mató muchas vacas. *The bubonic* **plague** *killed many cows.* Ese puro tiene mucha **peste**. *That cigar has a bad* **stench**. Se fue echando **pestes**. *He left, spitting* **curses**. *Pest,* on the other hand, means *insecto* and in a figurative sense, *lata* or *molestia* ("bothersome person"), *rollo* or *lata* ("a bore" or "a bothersome thing"). Esos niños son una **lata**. *Those children are* **pests**.

petulancia / petulance *Petulancia* is not "petulance" but "insolence, flippancy, arrogance" *(arrogancia).* Me molesta la **petulancia** del joven. *The young man's* **arrogance** *bothers me. Petulance* suggests *malhumor* (m.), *irritabilidad* (f.). *Petulante* means "arrogant, insolent, flippant" *(presumido).* La chica es más **petulante** cada día. *The girl grows more* **insolent** *every day. Petulant* means *malhumorado, irritable.* Es tan **irritable** que no quiere escuchar nada ni a nadie. *He is so* **petulant** *that he won't listen to anything or anybody.*

picar / pick *Picar (cavar)* is "to pick" in the sense of "to dig up (soil, rocks), to peck (birds)." *Picar* also has the following meanings: "to sting, bite (animals, insects), pierce, burn (hot pepper), spur on (a horse), punch (a ticket), itch, chop up or dice (meat, onions)," and figuratively, "to wound (an ego), nettle, pique."

The reflexive form *picarse* has the additional meanings of "to get angry, decay (teeth), go rotten, spoil." "To pique" is rendered by *picar* in the sense of *ofender* (to offend), *herir* (ie, i), *irritar*, or, less seriously, *estimular* (to excite, arouse). El cocinero está **picando** cebolla. *The cook is dicing (chopping) onions.* Me **pica** la espalda. *My back itches.* ¿Qué mosca le **ha picado**? *What's eating him?* El jefe **picó** mi amor propio. *The boss wounded my ego.* Se **picaron** las manzanas. *The apples got rotten (spoiled).* To pick means *escoger, recoger, escarbarse* (teeth), *hurgarse* (nose). *To pick on* is *criticar; to pick out* is *escoger; to pick over* is *buscar en;* and *to pick up* is *levantar, alzar.* No lo puedo **levantar**. *I can't pick it up.*

pico / pick *Pico* and *pick* share the meaning of "a heavy tool used to break up soil or rock." *Pico* also means "beak" or "bill" (of a bird), "corner" (of a hat, table, etc.), or "lip, spout, peak" (of a mountain) and in a figurative sense, "mouth, lips." The variations, *pica* and *piqueta* mean "a small pick."
treinta y pico = *thirty-something; thirty-odd*
Para escalar montañas se usa un **pico** (una piqueta). *To climb a mountain, you need a pick.* El pelícano tiene un **pico** muy largo. *The pelican has a very long bill.* tener un **pico de oro** / *to have the gift of gab* trabajar de **pico** y pala / *to work like a slave* Tiene 40 años y **pico**. *He is forty-odd years old.* Son las dos y **pico**. *It's a little after two o'clock.* Pick, on the other hand, means *selección* ("choice"), *plectro* or *púa* (for a guitar), *cosecha* or *recolección* ("harvest"), and figuratively, *lo mejor, la flor y nata* ("the pick of the crop").

pieza / piece *Pieza* and *piece* are both used in reference to games, sets, music, material, and weapons; but each term has additional uses. *Pieza* also means "part (of an engine), room, sample."
pieza de recambio (repuesto) = *spare part*
La vajilla viene con 48 piezas. *The set of china comes with 48 pieces.* Mi casa tiene cinco piezas (cuartos). *My house has five rooms.* Piece has the basic meaning of *pedazo* or *trozo*, and it also means *pasaje* (m.; of a book), *parcela* (of land). (*Piece* is the "countable" term used with nouns that literally cannot be counted (for example, *advice, news*). When used like this, *piece* has no translation: "a piece of advice" becomes *un consejo*, "two pieces of furniture" becomes *dos muebles*.) ¿Quieres un pedazo de tarta? *Do you want a piece of cake?* Compramos una parcela de terreno. *We bought a piece of land.*

pila / pile *Pila* shares with *pile* the meaning of "heap, mass of things" (*montón*, m.). *Pila* also means "sink" (in Spain), "(electric) battery or cell, font (in church), loads, trough (*bebedero*)" and "fountain" (in America).
nombre de pila = *first name*
Tengo una **pila** de cosas que hacer. *I have a pile of things to do.* Necesito **pilas** para la linterna. *I need batteries for the flashlight.* La **pila** de la iglesia tiene agua bendita. *The church font contains holy (blessed) water.* Tienen una **pila** de niños. *They have loads of children.* Pile, on the other hand, also means *pilote* (m.; support), *estaca* ("stake"), *pelo* (of carpets, materials), *mole* (f.; "big building"), *fortuna* (money). El edificio tiene **pilotes** enormes. *The building has huge piles (pilings).* Ganó una **fortuna** en acciones. *He made a pile on the stock market.*

pimiento / pimento   *Pimiento* means "bell pepper, sweet pepper." *A* "hot pepper" is called *ají* [m.] in the Caribbean and neighboring regions, and *chile* [m.] in Mexico and other countries, where peppers come in different colors, sizes, and flavors. *Pimentón* (m.), which is called *pimienta roja* in some countries, is "paprika." The feminine *pimienta* means "pepper" (black or white) and, figuratively, means "wit, fun, excitement."
sal y pimienta = charm (figuratively)
La fiesta necesita un poco de **pimienta**. *The party needs a little **excitement**.* La chica tiene **pimienta**. *The girl has **wit**. Pimento* in English is the red variety of bell pepper, called *pimiento morrón*, that is used as a relish, for example, in stuffed olives. Me gustan las olivas rellenas de **pimiento morrón**. *I like olives stuffed with **pimento**.*

pinchar / pinch   *Pinchar* does not mean "to pinch"; rather, it means "to puncture, prick, spur," and in a figurative sense, "to tease, goad, stir up, annoy." *Pinchar* is also a colloquial term for "to inject."
ni pincha ni corta = *he (she) has no say in the matter*
Las espinas **pinchan**. *Thorns **prick**.* Le **pinché** para que bailara con María. *I **teased** (goaded) him into dancing with Mary.* Me **pincharon** demasiado en el brazo. *They **injected** me a lot in the arm. (They **gave** me too many **shots** in the arm.) To pinch* means *pellizcar, pillarse* (fingers), *apretar* (ie) (shoes), and in a figurative sense, *quitar* or *robar, herir* (ie, i) (pride), *economizar* or *tacañear.* Se **pilló** el dedo con la ventana. *He **pinched** his finger in the window.* escatimar gastos / *to **pinch** pennies*

pipa / pipe   *Pipa* and *pipe* share the meanings of "a device for smoking" and "a cask (for wine or oil)." *Pipa* also stands for "seed, pip (of fruit), reed (a *lengüeta* in a musical instrument)," and "belly" (in Latin America).
pipa de la paz = *peace pipe*
El jerez se guarda en **pipas** de roble. *Sherry is kept in oak wood **pipes** (casks).* Las **pipas** de girasol contienen aceite. *Sunflower **seeds** contain oil. Pipe* also means *tubo, tubería, cañería; flauta* or *flautín* (m.; musical instrument); *cañón* (m.; of an organ). The plural *pipes* stands for *gaitas* ("bagpipes") and is a familiar term for *cuerdas vocales* ("vocal cords"). [In translating *pipe,* note that *tubería* and *cañería* are used as a "set of pipes," in other words, the plumbing system. In everyday speech, these words are used as equivalents of *tubo.*]
órgano de cañón = *pipe organ*
la **tubería** del agua / *the water **pipes*** Los gallegos tocan la **gaita**. *Galicians play the **pipes** (bagpipes).*

piquete / picket   *Piquete* (m.) means "picket" as "a band of strikers, stake, post, squad" *(m.; pelotón).* The Spanish term is also used for "sting" *(pinchazo),* "small hole," and in some countries, "yard." El culpable fue ejecutado por el **piquete** (pelotón) de ejecución. *The convicted man was executed by the firing **squad** (picket).* El **piquete** de la abeja me causa dolor. *The bee **sting** is giving me some pain. Picket* also means *manifestación* ("riot, demonstration"), *retén* (m.; of fire fighters, police officers). La policía puso un **retén** alrededor de la casa. *The police put a **picket** around the house.*

plan / plan *Plan* (m.) and *plan* both mean "project, schedule, scheme, idea, intention." The Spanish term also means "attitude" *(actitud,* f.*)*, "way, manner" *(modo)*, and in a figurative sense, "date" *(cita)*, "boyfriend, girlfriend."
a todo plan = *on a grand scale*
en plan de broma = *as a joke*
plan de estudios / *course* of study; study **plan** ¿Qué **planes** (proyectos) tienes ahora? *What are your* **plans** *now?* Si sigues con ese **plan** no te irá bien. *If you keep up that* **attitude***, things will go badly for you.* María no tiene **plan** esta noche. *Mary has no* **date** *tonight.* *Plan* in English also means *plano* ("map").

planta / plant *Planta* and *plant* share two meanings: "tree, bush, or shrub" and "factory." *Planta* also means "floor, story (of a building), sole (of the foot), staff (of a company), ground plan" *(plano)* and in a figurative sense, "appearance."
planta baja = *ground floor*
la **planta** (plantilla) de la compañía / *the* **staff** *of the company* ¿Te molesta la **planta** del pie? *Does the* **sole** *of your foot bother you?* tener buena **planta** / *to have a good (nice)* **appearance** *Plant* also means *maquinaria,* as well as *estratagema, trampa.* Use la **maquinaria** con cuidado. *Use the* **plant** *(machinery) carefully.*

plantar / plant *Plantar* means "to plant" (trees, flowers, etc.), but *plantar* is also used figuratively to mean "to throw someone out, to found, set up." The reflexive *plantarse* means "to arrive quickly, to stand firm." Plantó a la secretaria en la calle. *He* **threw** *the secretary* **out** *into the street.* Se plantó delante de la puerta. *He* **stood** *in the doorway.* *To plant* also means *cultivar* (the land), *colocar* (by hiding), *establecer* or *instalar.* **sembrar** (plantar) maíz / *to plant corn* Mi hermano **cultiva** trigo en su rancho. *My brother* **plants** *(raises) wheat on his farm.*

plataforma / platform *Plataforma (estrado)* means "platform" as "a raised stage or flooring." *Plataforma* is also used in the figurative sense of "stepping-stone." **plataforma** móvil / *moving* **sidewalk** Te va a servir de **plataforma** para la fama. *It will serve you as a* **stepping-stone** *to fame.* *Platform* also means *andén* (m.; at a bus or train station), *programa* (m.; of a political party), *andamio* ("scaffold" used by builders, etc.). La gente espera en el **andén**. *The people are waiting on the* **platform**. Apoyó el **programa** republicano. *He supported the Republican* **platform**.

plato / plate *Plato* is "plate" as "a shallow dish," but *plato* is also used for any kind of dish, as well as "course (in a meal), a plateful," and "a pan, scale, tray" (of a scale).
no romper un plato = *to be harmless*
platillo volante = *flying saucer*
Sirvieron cinco **platos** en el banquete. *They served five* **courses** *at the banquet.* Esaú vendió sus derechos por un **plato** de lentejas. *Esau sold his rights for a* **plateful** *of lentils.* *Plate* also means *placa, chapa, lámina, plancha, base* (f.; in baseball), *matrícula* ("registration" of a vehicle). **matrícula** del carro / *license* **plate** Mira la **lámina** de la página 13. *Look at the* **plate** *(illustration) on page 13.*

plausible / plausible *Plausible* and *plausible* share the basic idea of "praiseworthy, commendable, acceptable, reasonable." However, there is a subtle difference in interpretation. In Spanish, *plausible* refers to the positive aspect of the meanings. *Plausible* in English stresses the negative aspect of the meanings, as though the meaning were superficial or suspicious. The following are possible interpretations for *plausible:*
1. *aceptable*, but...(I have my doubts).
2. *recomendable*, but...(not wholeheartedly).
3. *honesto*, but...(I reserve my suspicions).
4. *digno de elogio*, but...(with reservations).
Another possible way to solve the problem of the interpretation of *plausible* is to add an adverb of doubt, such as the following: una decisión *posiblemente* **aceptable** / *a **plausible** decision* un candidato *aparentemente* **recomendable** / *a **plausible** candidate*

plaza / plaza *Plaza* was incorporated into English with the meaning of "public square, commercial or service center." In Spanish, however, *plaza* has additional meanings: "job, post, market, town, bullring, seat (in cabs, in the theater)." La **plaza** de Salamanca es muy artística. *Salamanca's **plaza** (main square) is very artistic.* Hay una **plaza** vacante en la tienda. *There is a **job** opening at the store.* El teatro es antiguo y sólo tiene 600 **plazas**. *The theater is old and only has 600 **seats** (accommodations).*

pluma / plume *Pluma* translates as the formal term *plume* (of a bird), but the common translation is *feather*. In addition, in Mexico and the Caribbean *pluma* means "pen, quill, penmanship," and figuratively, "writer, style (of writing)." In some Latin American countries, *pluma* is "faucet" or "tap"; however, in other countries *grifo, espita, llave* (f.) are used for "faucet." colchón de **plumas** / **feather** bed vestirse con **plumas** ajenas / *to strut in borrowed **plumes*** El periodista vive de su **pluma**. *A journalist lives by his **pen**.* Esta **pluma** gotea. *This **faucet** leaks.* *Plume* in English is used nowadays only to mean "a large, showy feather" and is best translated as *pluma decorativa*.

plus / plus *Plus* (m.) is a noun in Spanish, meaning "bonus" or "extra pay." Los obreros reciben un **plus** por Navidad. *The workers receive a **bonus** for Christmas.* *Plus* in English has three functions with different meanings:
1. Adjective: *positivo*, as in a *plus* number *(número positivo)*.
2. Noun: *cantidad positiva, signo más*.
3. Preposition: *más*.
[Note that the plural of *plus* is *plusses* in British English and *pluses* in American English.]
signo más = *plus sign*
Cuatro **más** dos son seis. *Four **plus** two is six.* Voy a llevar un baúl **más** una maleta. *I am going to take a trunk **plus** a suitcase.* **más** de dos libras / *two pounds **plus*** Recibió la nota de B+ (B **más**). *He received a B+ (B **plus**).*

polar / polar *Polar* is "polar" as "relating to the poles."
casquete polar = *polar ice cap*
Polar in English is also used in the figurative sense of *opuesto, contrario*, and

also with the idea of *central, guía.* La gerencia y el sindicato tienen ideas **opuestas.** *Management and the union have **polar** views.*

político / political, politic *Político* means "political" as an adjective, and as a noun, it means "political" and "in-law" (family relative), as well as "politician." In a figurative sense, *político* stands for the word *politic*, which means "polite, diplomatic, clever, astute, tactful, wary." Synonyms in Spanish for this meaning of *político* include *prudente, astuto, sagaz, ingenioso.* The feminine noun *política* means "politics" (the social science) and "policy, tactics" *(póliza).*
hermano político (cuñado) = *brother-in-law*
político hábil = *tricky politician*
La honradez es la mejor **política.** *Honesty is the best **policy.*** Juan fue **político** con todos sus parientes. *John was **polite** to all his relatives.*

póliza / policy *Póliza* means "policy" in the sense of a "contract." *Póliza* also means "voucher, certificate."
póliza de seguros = *insurance policy*
Policy in English translates as *póliza, política, programa* (m.; "platform"), *normas de conducta* (of a newspaper), *principios, sistema* (m.), *táctica, actitud* (f.).
política exterior = *foreign policy*
¿Sería buena **táctica** aceptar la invitación? *Would it be good **policy** to accept the invitation?* las **normas de conducta** de la empresa / *company **policy***

polo / polo *Polo* and *polo* both are a "sport played on horses." But in Spanish, *polo* is also "(North or South) pole, focus, zone, area" and "ice-cream bar" (in Spain).
polo acuático = *water polo*
Juan y María son **polos** opuestos. *John and Mary are like opposite **poles.*** **polo** de desarrollo / *development **area*** La discoteca es un **polo** de atracción de la juventud. *The discotheque is a **focus** of attraction for young people.* Pole in English also means *poste* (m.; telegraph), *pértiga, polaco* ("of Polish origin").

pompa / pomp *Pompa* and *pomp* both stand for "splendor, magnificence, display," but *pompa* also means "(soap) bubble, puff (on clothes)." The plural form *pompas* is translated as "funeral" in the common expression *pompas fúnebres* ("funeral ceremony"). El rey Salomón tenía mucha **pompa.** *King Solomon used to display a lot of **pomp.*** Me gusta jugar con **pompas** de jabón. *I like to play with soap **bubbles.*** *Pomposo* exactly means "pompous." *Pomposidad* (f.) is "pomposity."

ponderar / ponder *Ponderar* and *to ponder* share the idea of "to consider, think over, weigh (in one's mind)" *(sopesar).* However, *ponderar* also means "to praise highly, speak highly (of)." El jefe **ponderó** (reflexionó) mucho sobre ese asunto. *The boss **pondered** (thought over) that matter considerably.* **Ponderó** las proezas del difunto. *He **praised** the dead man's deeds **highly.*** No **ponderes** tanto esa novela. *Don't **speak** so **highly** of that novel.*

popa / pop, pope   *Popa* means neither "pop" nor "pope." *Popa* is the "stern" of a ship.
de popa a proa = *from top to bottom; from stem to stern*
Todo va viento en **popa**. *Everything is going well. Pop* means *explosión, taponazo* (of a bottle opening), *gaseosa* or *refresco, música popular*. La botella de buen champán tiene un gran **taponazo**. *A bottle of good champagne makes a big pop. Pope* means *Papa* (of the Catholic Church).

populación / population   *Populación* and *population* share the meaning of "the act of populating" *(poblar)*. La **populación** de los Estados Unidos empezó en el siglo XVII. *The **population** of the United States began in the seventeenth century. Population* also means *población* ("the number of people"). La **población** de España ha sido de 37 millones por varios años. *The **population** of Spain has been 37 million people for several years.*

popular / popular   *Popular* and *popular* share the idea of "common, prevalent, for the public, folkloric." [In Spanish, *popular* stresses the meaning of "folkloric," but in its latest dictionary, the *Real Academia* has included the meaning of "*acepto y grato al pueblo*"; in other words, it is now the equivalent of *popular* in English.]
precios populares = *popular prices*
Julio Iglesias es **popular** (bien conocido) en muchos países. *Julio Iglesias is **popular** in many countries.*   educación **popular**   /   *education **of the people*** *Popular* in English is also translated as *bien conocido, estimado, democrático, de moda.*
ropa de moda = *popular (fashionable) clothes*
elección democrática = *popular election*
Es muy **estimado** por sus amigos. *He is very **popular** among his friends.*

portátil / portable   *Portátil* means "portable," as is *ordenador* (m.) *portátil* ("portable computer"). The word *portable* does not exist in Spanish.

portento / portent   *Portento* is not "portent" but "marvel, wonder, prodigy." El muchacho es un **portento** en música. *The boy is a musical **prodigy**. Portent* means *augurio* ("omen"), *presagio, signo*. *Portentoso* means "marvelous, prodigious, strange." *Portentous,* on the other hand, means *siniestro, de mal agüero* ("ominous"). Me dieron una noticia **de mal agüero**. *They gave me **portentous** news.*

portero / porter   *Portero* and *porter* both mean "doorman, doorkeeper," according to the original word in Latin, but both terms have other meanings as well. *Portero* also means "janitor, caretaker, goalkeeper." [Note, in soccer, the word for "goalkeeper" is *guardameta* rather than *portero*.] El **portero** mantiene limpio el edificio. *The **janitor** keeps the building clean.*   **portero** de tribunal   /   *court **usher*** **portero** eléctrico   /   *intercom* *Porter* has the additional meanings of *maletero, mozo, conserje* (m.) or *bedel* (m.; in government buildings). El **mozo** llevó el equipaje al tren. *The **porter** took the luggage to the train.*

posar / pose   *Posar* means "to pose" (for a photo or as a model), but it also means "to settle upon" or "to perch"; "to lodge, put, lay, put down (on the floor)." El pájaro se **posó** en la copa del árbol. *The bird **perched** in the treetop.* **Posó** su mano sobre mi hombro. *He **laid** his hand on my shoulder. Pose* (f.) means "pose" (in modeling or as a pretense), as well as "exposure" (in photography).

poseer / possess *Poseer* is "to possess" ("to own, have"), as well as "to know perfectly" (an issue, a language) and "to have sexual relations with a woman." The reflexive form *poseerse* takes on the meaning of "to control oneself." María **posee** el francés y el español. *Mary knows French and Spanish perfectly. Poseído* refers to people who own things, "possessed, owned." However, when *poseído* is applied directly to people, it means "full of oneself, conceited, arrogant." [*Una persona poseída* refers to "a person who is possessed by the devil or evil spirits."] A nadie le gusta la gente **poseída**. *Nobody likes conceited people.*

posible / possible *Posible* and *possible* are exactly the same as adjectives. *Posibles* (m., pl.) refers to "means, property, resources."
lo mejor posible = *as well as possible; the best possible*
de ser posible = *if possible*
Ella tiene más **posibles** que yo. *She has more resources than I do.*

posición / position *Posición* and *position* share the ideas of "social or physical place, job, status, posture, rank." Ocupa una **posición** alta (un cargo alto) en la compañía. *He has a high position (post) in the company. Position* has the additional meanings of *actitud* (f.), *opinión, condiciones* (pl. only), *lugar* (m.), *sitio, situación.* Están en **condiciones** de casarse. *They are in a position to marry.* ¿Cuál es la **situación** de Europa? *What's the geographical position of Europe?* Ponte en mi **lugar**. *Put yourself in my position.* ¿Cuál es su **opinión** de las reformas democráticas de los estados bálticos? *What is your position on democratic reforms in the Baltic states?*

poste / post *Poste* (m.) and *post* both stand for "pole (for a flag, telephone wires, etc.), pillar, picket, goalpost."
poste indicador = *signpost*
Los **postes** de la luz son altísimos. *The utility posts (poles) are very tall. Post* also means *puesto* or *trabajo, correo* or *correos* (office), *factoría, meta* or *salida* (in sports).
factoría = *trading post*
Correos queda a dos cuadras de aquí. *The post office is two blocks from here.* ¿Ha venido el **correo**? *Has the post (mail) come?* (chiefly British)   estar más sordo que una **tapia** *(fence)* / *to be as deaf as a post*

postura / posture *Postura* and *posture* share the idea of "position, attitude, stand," but *postura* also means "laying (of eggs), egg *(huevo)*, bid (at an auction), bet *(apuesta)*." Una mala **postura** echa a perder la columna. *Bad posture ruins the spine.* Su **postura** no es clara. *His position is not clear.* Las **posturas** siguen subiendo en la subasta. *The bids keep going up at the auction.* Aquí tiene una **postura** fresca. *Here is a fresh egg.*

pote / pot *Pote* (m.) is not "pot" but "jug, jar, pan, flowerpot," and in some countries, "can" *(lata).* Los antiguos guardaban las monedas de oro en **potes**. *The ancients used to keep their gold coins in jars. Pot* also means *olla, puchero, orinal* (m.; "chamberpot"), and in a figurative sense, *(premio) gordo, marijuana.* The plural *pots* is used figuratively to mean *montones* (m.; *una gran cantidad*).

[*Marijuana,* one meaning of *pot,* may also be spelled *mariguana* or *marihuana.*]
lo que haya = *potluck*
montones de dinero = *pots of money*
el gordo de la lotería = *lottery jackpot*
La cocina está llena de **ollas.** *The kitchen is full of **pots.*** ¿Es legal fumar **marijuana** en México? *Is it legal to smoke **pot** in Mexico?*

potencia / potency *Potencia* and *potency* both stand for "power, strength." *Potencia* also means "power (a strong nation), virility." The plural *potencias* means "faculties" (of memory, will, etc.).
potencia de un motor = *power of an engine*
en potencia = *in the making*
Se reunieron las **potencias** europeas. *The European **powers** held a meeting.* El viejito anda bien de sus **potencias.** *The old man still has all his **faculties.***

práctica / practice *Práctica* shares almost all its meanings with *practice;* nevertheless, *práctica* is sometimes used to mean "custom, tradition." The plural *prácticas* suggests "practicum, internship, training." La siesta es una **práctica** establecida en la cultura hispana. *The siesta is an established **custom** (practice) in Hispanic culture.* Los futuros maestros tienen un año de **prácticas.** *Future teachers have one year of **internship** (on-site training).* *Practicable* is not only "practicable, feasible" but also "passable" (road, etc.). Esta carretera no está **practicable** para camiones ni autobuses. *This road is not **passable** for trucks and buses.*

práctico / practical *Práctico* and *practical* are almost equivalents in the sense of "handy, convenient, comfortable." *Práctico* also describes people as "expert." As a noun, it means "coastal pilot." Ella está muy **práctica** en computadoras. *She is very **expert** in computers.* *Practical* also means *verdadero* ("true") in some contexts: "a *practical* disaster" *(un verdadero desastre).*
broma pesada = *practical joke*
enfermera sin título = *practical nurse*
Prácticamente does not mean "practically" but "in practice, by practice." *Practically* means *realmente, efectivamente, casi.* Ocurrió hace **casi** un año. *It happened **practically** a year ago.*

precinto / precinct *Precinto* not "precinct" but "(lead) seal" and "(paper) seal" (of a bottle, for example).
violación de precinto = *breaking of seals*
Para abrir la botella hay que romper el **precinto.** *You have to break the **seal** to open the bottle. Precinct* means *recinto* ("grounds"), *zona, frontera, distrito electoral.* El **recinto** de la catedral es amplio. *The cathedral **precinct** is vast.* Cada votante tiene que ir a votar al **distrito electoral** indicado. *Each voter has to vote in his or her assigned **precinct.** Precintar* means "to seal, to place a seal (on packages, bottles, etc.), to seal off."

preciosidad / preciosity *Preciosidad* (f.) is not "preciosity" but "charm, beauty, marvel." ¡Qué **preciosidad** de niña! *What a lovely child!* Esta pulsera es una **preciosidad.** *This bracelet is a **beauty.** Preciosity* has the negative meaning of "fastidious refinement" and is translated as *preciosismo, amaneramiento* (of style). ¿Te gusta el **preciosismo** barroco de esta iglesia? *Do you like the baroque preciosity of this church?*

precioso / precious *Precioso* and *precious* share the meaning of "valuable, priceless, dear." In addition, *precioso* means "pretty" or "beautiful," and in a figurative sense, "delightful, wonderful."

metales preciosos = *precious metals*

Es una criatura **preciosa**. *She is a beautiful baby. Precious* is also used at times to mean *afectado* (manners), and it is used as a term of endearment for *querida, preciosa*. In colloquial English, *precious* is used as an adverb, meaning *muy, perfecto*.

muy poco = *precious little*

un perfecto imbécil = *a precious (perfect) fool*

Esta foto es muy **valiosa** (querida) para mí. *This photo is very precious (dear) to me.* Tiene gestos **afectados**. *She has precious (mannered) gestures.* Se pondrá furioso si estropeas su **querido** auto. *He'll be furious if you damage his precious car.*

precipicio / precipice *Precipicio* and *precipice* share the meaning of "steep cliff, abyss," but both terms are used figuratively with different meanings. *Precipicio* suggests "downfall, ruin, a psychological abyss." Desde el divorcio de su mujer, está hundido en un **precipicio** sin salida. *Since the divorce from his wife, he has sunk into an inescapable abyss. Precipice*, on the other hand, suggests the figurative meaning of *riesgo* ("risky situation").

precipitar(se) / precipitate *Precipitar(se)* and *to precipitate* both mean "to throw, hurl down" *(depeñar)*. In addition, *precipitar(se)* also means "to rush, act recklessly."

no precipitarse = *to take one's time*

No **te precipites**; todavía hay tiempo. *Don't rush; there's still time left.* To precipitate also means *causar, provocar*. El déficit nacional **provocó** el desastre. *The national deficit precipitated the disaster.*

preciso / precise *Preciso* and *precise* both suggest "exact, accurate, clear, concise." The Spanish term also means "necessary, needy."

para ser preciso = *to be precise*

Es **preciso** que llegues a tiempo. *It's necessary for you to arrive on time. Precise*, on the other hand, sometimes takes on the meaning of *meticuloso* ("finicky"), *detallado, puntual*. El jefe es **meticuloso** en ese asunto. *The boss is precise on that matter. Precisamente* means "precisely" in the sense of "exactly, just," and it also means "as a matter of fact, in fact, especially." **Precisamente** ayer comí con ella. *In fact I ate with her yesterday.* Vine **precisamente** a verte. *I came especially to see you. Precisely* suggests *meticulosamente, en punto*.

¡Eso es! = *Precisely!*

a las seis en punto = *at precisely six o'clock*

Precisión means "precision, exactness, accuracy," as well as "need."

precoz / precocious *Precoz* and *precocious* are used to describe children who, early on, show intelligence or special talent. In Spanish, *precoz* also applies to fruits or crops, meaning "early, premature." [The plural of *precoz* is *precoces*.]
una cosecha precoz = *an early crop*
Mozart fue un niño muy **precoz** en música. *Mozart was a very **precocious** boy in music.* Este año las peras vinieron **precoces**. *This year the pears ripened **early**.*

predicamento / predicament *Predicamento* does not mean "predicament"; instead, it means "esteem, prestige, influence." Ella tiene mucho **predicamento** en literatura comparada. *She has a lot of **prestige** (influence) in (the field of) comparative literature.* *Predicament* means *apuro, aprieto, trance* (m.), *situación difícil*. Pasó muchos **apuros** (trances) para llegar a triunfar. *He went through many **predicaments** before he managed to succeed.*

premio / premium *Premio* does not mean "premium" but "prize, award, reward."
premio gordo = *grand prize*
El **premio** Nobel es muy apreciado. *A Nobel **prize** is valued highly. Premium* means *prima, cuota* in the business world. As an adjective, *premium* means *excelente, de primera calidad.*
ser muy solicitado = *to be at a premium*
Las **primas** del seguro suben cada día más. *Insurance **premiums** are going up more and more.*

premisa / premise *Premisa* means "premise" only in philosophy as a "statement" or "proposition in a syllogism." *Premises* (the plural form) is used with the meaning of *local* (m.), *edificio, parte* (f.) *inicial* (of a deed).
en el local = *on the premises*
La **parte inicial** de esta escritura está clara. *The **premises** of this deed are clear.* Este **edificio** está bien cotizado. *These **premises** are highly rated.*

preocupado / preoccupied *Preocupado* and *preoccupied* share the meaning of "concerned, worried."
estar preocupado por = *to be preoccupied about*
Estoy **preocupado** por el futuro de Rusia. *I am **preoccupied** (concerned) about the future of Russia. Preoccupied* also has the meaning of *distraído, absorto, ensimismado* ("absent-minded"). Está **absorto** en la última novela de Gabriel García Márquez. *He's **preoccupied** with the latest novel by Gabriel García Márquez. Preocupar(se)* and *to preoccupy* likewise share the meaning of "to worry, to care."
¡No se preocupe! = *Don't worry!*
To preoccupy also means *distraer, absorber, ensimismar.* La música clásica le **ensimisma** (absorbe) completamente. *Classical music **preoccupies** her completely.*

preparación / preparation *Preparación* and *preparation* both mean "the act of preparing, the state of readiness, a medical prescription." La **preparación** para llegar a ser médico requiere muchos años. *The **preparation** (training) for becoming a doctor takes many years. Preparation* also means *tarea* or *deberes* (m.; "homework"). The plural *preparations* translates as *preparativos.* Hago mis **deberes**

para el colegio todas las noches. *I do my **preparation** for school every night.* Hizo todos los **preparativos** para el largo viaje. *He made all the **preparations** for the long trip.*

prescribir / prescribe *Prescribir* means "to prescribe" with the idea of "to decree, to order." El Congreso **prescribió** (ordenó) una subida de impuestos en el licor. *Congress **prescribed** (decreed) a tax increase on alcoholic beverages. To prescribe* also means *recetar* (remedies or medicine). El médico **recetó** descanso absoluto. *The doctor **prescribed** complete rest.*

prescripción / prescription *Prescripción* and *prescription* both mean "rule, norm, precept." *Prescription* also means *receta* (for medicine, etc.). una **receta** para la tranquilidad de espíritu / *a **prescription** for peace of mind*

presentación / presentation *Presentación* means "presentation" and "introduction" (of people, of witnesses). Figuratively, it means "appearance." Tiene buena **presentación** en clase. *He has a good **appearance** in class.* In addition, *presentación* is used for "performance."

presentar / present *Presentar* and *to present* both mean "to offer, give, propose, show, submit, come up." However, *presentar* also means "to introduce" (people, witnesses) and "to perform" (in the theater). The reflexive form *presentarse* translates as "to introduce oneself," and "to turn up, appear, come to, apply (for a position)." ofrecer un aspecto lúgubre / *to **present** a dismal outlook* Se **presentó** a la policía. *He **turned himself in** to the police.* Te **presento** a mi esposo. *Let me **introduce** you to my husband.* Permita que me **presente**. *Allow me to **introduce myself.*** El perro **plantea** un problema. *The dog **presents** a problem.*

presente / present *Presente* (m.) does mean "present, gift" as a noun; although the everyday word for "gift" is *regalo*. *Presente* is a more formal term. As a noun, it also means the "present (time)" and in grammar, the "present (tense)." ¿Cuántos **regalos** (presentes) recibiste para tu cumpleaños? *How many **presents** (gifts) did you receive on your birthday? Presente* as an adjective also means "present" *(actual)*. In business correspondence, *la presente* means "this letter."
tener presente = *to keep in mind*
en el presente = *at the present time*
los presentes = *those present; the audience*
mejorando lo presente = *present company excepted*

preservar / preserve *Preservar (proteger)* means "to preserve" as "to protect, safeguard." *To preserve* has additional meanings such as *poner en conserva* (food), *conservar* or *guardar* or *mantener* (ie) (peace, traditions, dignity, silence, etc.). Estados Unidos trató de **mantener** la paz en el Golfo Pérsico. *The United States tried **to preserve** the peace in the Persian Gulf. Preservativo* means "preservative" ("chemical substance to preserve food"), but in the contemporary world, *un preservativo* has become an important term, meaning "condom, contraceptive." La venta de **preservativos** ha aumentado mucho a causa del SIDA. *The sale of **condoms** has increased greatly because of AIDS.*

presidente / president   *Presidente* (m.) translates as "president," but the use of the titles is not always parallel in both languages, even within the Spanish-speaking world. A *presidente* is the head of a republic, an assembly, a club, a committee ("chairman"), of a parliament ("speaker"), of the Council of Ministers ("premier"), of a court of justice ("presiding magistrate"). [The *Real Academia* accepts *presidenta* with two meanings: (1) the woman who presides and (2) the wife of the *presidente*. Perhaps someday the meaning of *presidente* will change to "the husband of the *presidenta*."] *President* in the United States also applies to the head of a university, a bank, or a company. In the Hispanic world, a university usually has a *rector* (m.), and a bank has a *director* (m.). La **rectora** de la universidad decidió jubilarse. *The **president** (rector) of the university decided to retire.*

presumido / presumed   *Presumido* is not "presumed" but "conceited, pretentious, presumptuous." A nadie le gusta la gente **presumida**. *Nobody likes conceited people.* *Presumed*, on the other hand, means *supuesto, presunto, posible*. No sabemos quién es el **presunto** ladrón. *We don't know who the **presumed** thief is.*

presumir / presume   *Presumir* does mean "to presume" with the meaning of "to assume, suppose," but the main idea of *presumir (de)* is "to be conceited, boast, brag, put on airs." **Presume** de ser valiente. *He **brags** about being brave.* To *presume* is also used with the meaning of *atreverse a* ("to dare to"), *permitirse, aventurarse*, and it sometimes takes the negative meaning of *abusar*. **abusar** de la hospitalidad de alguien / *to **presume** on someone's hospitality*

presunción / presumption   *Presunción* and *presumption* both mean "supposition." The basic meaning of *presunción*, however, is "conceit, vanity, presumptuousness." Su **presunción** lo hace odioso. *His **conceit** makes him hateful.* **presunción** (suposición) legal / *legal **presumption*** *Presumption* also means *atrevimiento, osadía*. Su **atrevimiento** no tiene límites. *His **presumption** has no limits.* *Presunto (supuesto)* stands for "supposed, assumed, presumed, would-be." Es el **presunto** autor del crimen. *He is the **presumed** perpetrator of the crime.* el **presunto** poeta / *the **would-be** poet* **presunto** heredero / *heir apparent*

pretender / pretend   *Pretender* is not "to pretend" but "to intend, try, seek (a job)," as well as "to woo, court (a woman)." **Pretendió** convencerme. *She **tried** to convince me.* El jefe **pretende** a la secretaria. *The boss **is courting** the secretary.* To *pretend* means *fingir, aparentar, suponer, disimular*. **Fingió** estar enfadada. *She **pretended** to be angry.* *Pretendiente* means "suitor, wooer," as well as "applicant, candidate, claimant (of an inheritance)." La viuda rica tiene muchos **pretendientes**. *The rich widow has many **suitors**.* *Pretender* translates as *hipócrita* (m., f.), *fingidor* (m.). It does share one use with *pretendiente*: (m.) "pretender to the throne" is the same as *pretendiente al trono*.

pretensión / pretension   *Pretensión* and *pretension* share the meaning of "claim" (*reivindicación*). *Pretensión* also refers to "aim, aspiration, vanity." Tiene la **pretensión** de ser director. *He has the **aspiration** of being the principal.* *Pretension* also means *pretexto, excusa*. No puedes justificar esos **pretextos**. *You cannot* justify those **pretensions**. **Pretencioso** (also spelled **pretensioso**) means "pretentious" as "faking greatness, vain, conceited." un muchacho **pretencioso** / *a conceited boy* *Pretentious* has upgraded its negative meaning to also refer to things or places that are "elegant" or "deluxe." The Spanish translation of this concept is *elegante, lujoso.* Tiene una casa muy **elegante**. *She has a pretentious house.*

prevaricar / prevaricate *Prevaricar* does not mean "to prevaricate"; instead, it means "to break the law, transgress, betray a trust, corrupt (an official employee)." Se fue a la cárcel por **prevaricar**. *He went to jail for breaking the law.* *To prevaricate* means *mentir* (ie, i), *tergiversar* ("to misrepresent, twist the truth"), *evadir la verdad.* **Tergiversa** los hechos en sus comentarios. *He prevaricates with the facts in his comments.* *Prevaricador* means "dishonest." Ese funcionario es un **prevaricador**. *That official is a dishonest man.* *Prevaricator* means *mentiroso, tergiversador* (m.). *Prevaricación* means "abuse of trust, breaking of the law." *Prevarication,* on the other hand, means *mentira, tergiversación.*

prevención / prevention *Prevención* is not "prevention" but "precaution, warning," and in some countries, "police station." In certain contexts, it also means "prejudice." Las botellas de licor de México tienen una **prevención** contra el daño del alcohol. *Bottles of liquor in Mexico show a warning about the dangers of alcohol.* tener **prevención** contra uno / *to be prejudiced against someone* *Prevention,* on the other hand, translates as *impedimento, protección.* El **impedimento** del cáncer es importante. *The prevention of cancer is important.*

prevenir / prevent *Prevenir* (ie) stands for "to warn, foresee, take precautions." Más vale **prevenir** que curar. *It is better to take precautions than to cure. ("An ounce of prevention is worth a pound of cure.")* *To prevent* means *impedir* (i), *evitar.* para **evitar** accidentes / *to prevent accidents*

previo / previous *Previo* basically means "previous," but the syntactic functions of the two terms are not necessarily the same. As an adjective, *previo* also means "prior, earlier, preliminary"; as a preposition, *previo* means "after, following." Observe estas ideas **previas** sobre el tema. *Notice these preliminary ideas on the subject.* la pregunta **previa** / *the previous question* **Previa** consulta a los socios, alquilamos el edificio. *Following (after) consultation with the members, we rented the building.* **previo** pago / *after payment; on payment* **previo** aviso / *after notification; prior notice* *Previous* is also used colloquially for *prematuro, apresurado* ("hasty"). *Previous to* is a preposition, meaning *antes de.* Fue una decisión **apresurada**. *It was a previous (hasty) decision.* Revise su trabajo **antes de** mandarlo. *Check your work previous to (prior to) sending it.*

prima / prime *Prima* is not "prime" but "(female) cousin, bonus (on wages), premium (for insurance), first string (of a guitar, etc.)."
materia prima = *raw material*
Muchas empresas dan una **prima** por Navidad. *Many companies pay a bonus for Christmas.* *Prime,* on the other hand, also means *lo mejor, flor y nata* (f.) as a noun, and *principal, primordial, selecto, primo* (in mathematics), as an

adjective. In the business world, it is used in the phrase *prime cost*, which is *coste* (m.) *de producción* in Spanish.

primer ministro = *prime minister*
sumamente importante = *of prime importance*
en **perfecto** estado / *in prime condition* estar en **lo mejor** de la vida / *to be in one's prime* Números **primos** son 1, 3, 5, 7, 11, 13, 17. *Prime numbers are 1, 3, 5, 7, 11, 13, 17.*

primitivo / primitive *Primitivo* and *primitive* share the same meaning when they refer to people as "simple, uncivilized." *Primitivo* also applies to things to refer to something "original." Muchos indios de México llevan una vida **primitiva.** *Many Mexican Indians live a primitive life.* Un diamante, una vez cortado, no puede volver a su forma **primitiva.** *Once it is cut, a diamond cannot return to its original state. Primitivamente* likewise means "primitively," as well as "originally."

principal / principal *Principal* and *principal* share the idea of "main, important" as adjectives. carretera **principal** / *main* road lo **principal** / *the principal (main) point Principal* in English is also a noun, meaning *director* (m.; of a school); in the commercial world, it means *capital* (m.; of a loan); and in legal terminology, it means *autor* (m.; of a crime). El **director** del colegio lo decidió. *The school principal made the decision.* El **capital** a pagar es de un millón de dólares. *The principal to be paid is one million dollars.* The noun *principle* translates as *principio, regla, ley, esencia.*
principios morales / *moral principles* por principio / *on principle.*

privado / private *Privado* basically means "private" ("personal, confidential"). However, *privado de* (from the verb *privar de*) means "deprived of, without."
vida privada = *private life; privacy*
en público y en **privado** / *in public and in private* información **privada** (confidencial) / *private information* **privado de** alimentos / *deprived of food Private* is widely used, for example, as *particular* (lessons, home, car, secretary), *íntimo* (wedding, funeral), *raso* (soldier), *secreto* (matter), and *reservado* (in one's affairs). *Private* is not translated at all when the context is obvious: "private citizen" is translated simply as *ciudadano*; "private income," as *renta.* [*Private* and *privacy* reflect an important cultural value in the United States and therefore are key terms, more so than the equivalent terms in Spanish.]
partes pudendas = *private parts*
maestro **particular** / *private teacher* Juan tiene una fortuna **personal.** *John has private means.* Lo discutimos **a puerta cerrada.** *We discussed the matter in private.*

probar / probe, prove *Probar* (ue) does not mean "to probe" but "to prove" as "to test, demonstrate." In addition, *probar* means "to try on (clothes), taste (food), attempt, try" *(intentar).* La cocinera **prueba** todos los platos. *The cook tastes all her dishes.* Me **probé** el traje nuevo. *I tried on the new suit. To probe* means *sondear, penetrar, investigar.* Están **investigando** sobre las transacciones de la compañía. *They are probing into the company's transactions. To prove,* in addition to its shared meaning with *probar,* sometimes means *verificar, comprobar* (ue). **verificar** la denuncia / *to prove the accusation*

procedente / proceeding *Procedente de* and *proceeding from* mean the same thing ("coming from"). *Procedente* is also an adjective, meaning "proper, reasonable, sensible." avión **procedente de** Roma / *flight proceeding from Rome* / Su conducta fue **procedente**. *His conduct was proper. Proceeding* is used as a noun, with the meaning of *acción, proceder* (m.). The plural *proceedings* means *debates* (m.), *beneficios* (of a nonprofit organization or charity), *actas* (of a meeting), and *publicación* (of a conference, of Congress). los **beneficios** de la rifa / *the proceedings from the raffle* La secretaria del club leyó las **actas**. *The secretary of the club read the proceedings.*

proceder / proceed *Proceder* and *to proceed* share the sense of "to go ahead, come from, act, advance." In addition, *proceder* means "to be advisable, to behave, to be sensible, to be relevant." As a noun, *proceder* (m.) means "behavior, conduct." ¡**Proceda** (avance, siga) con cuidado! *Proceed with care!* **Procede** hacerlo despacio. *It is advisable to do it gently (slowly).* **Procedió** con mucha generosidad. *He behaved with great generosity.* Su **proceder** fue impecable. *His behavior was impeccable.*

procesión / procession *Procesión* is "procession" ("religious ceremony"). Both terms are also used in a figurative sense to mean "series, string (of events)." *Procesión* is also used colloquially to mean "trouble, problem." La **procesión** va por dentro. *Still waters run deep. Procession* also refers to *desfile* (m.; "parade"), *comitiva, cortejo.* Un **cortejo** de barcos seguía el yate del rey. *A procession of ships followed the king's yacht.* la **comitiva** del presidente / *the president's procession* la **comitiva** fúnebre / *funeral procession*

proceso / process *Proceso* and *process* share the idea of "method, system, systematic change." *Proceso* also means "trial" or "lawsuit" *(pleito)*, "course, progress."
informática = *data processing*
en curso = *in progress*
proceso mental / *mental process* El **proceso** es una novela de Kafka. *The Trial is a novel by Kafka.* en el **proceso** de una vida / *in the course of a lifetime* **procedimiento** de fabricación / *manufacturing process*

procurar / procure *Procurar* is not "to procure" but "to try, attempt, strive, secure, bring."
procurar que = *to make sure that*
Procure llegar a tiempo. *Try to arrive on time.* Este niño sólo me **procura** satisfacciones. *This child brings me nothing but satisfaction.* **Procuramos** cambiar de actitud hacia Rusia. *We are striving to improve our attitude toward Russia. To procure* means *conseguir* (i), *proporcionar, llevar a la prostitución.* No pude **conseguir** el libro. *I couldn't procure the book. Procurer* is a noun in English that means "one procures" whether legally or illegally. Primarily it means *proxeneta* (m., f.; "go-between, pimp"). La profesión de **proxeneta** es inmoral. *The profession of a procurer is immoral.*

producto / product   *Producto* and *product* share the meanings of "industrial article" and figuratively, "result." In addition, *producto* refers to "produce" (in agriculture) and "proceeds" (of a sale). In the commercial world, *producto* means "yield, benefit."
producto derivado = *by-product*
productos alimenticios = *foodstuffs*
productos de belleza = *cosmetics, beauty products*
productos de consumo = *consumer goods (products)*
Me gustan los **productos** frescos del campo. *I like fresh farm **produce**.*   **producto nacional bruto (PNB)** / *gross national **product** (GNP)*

profano / profane   *Profano* and *profane* share the idea of "worldly, not sacred, irreverent." *Profane*, however, has extended its meaning to *malhablado* ("foul-mouthed"), *soez* ("rude or dirty language"), *blasfemo.* El borracho profería palabras **soeces.** *The drunk was using **profane** language. Profanity*, along with its shared meaning with *profanidad* (f.) of "impiety," is often used in the plural to refer to bad language: *palabrota* ("vulgar word"), *taco* ("swear word"), *blasfemia.* ¡No tienes por qué decir **palabrotas!** *You don't have to use **profanity** (profanities)!*

proferir / proffer   *Proferir* (ie, i) does not mean "to proffer"; instead, it means "to utter, speak" and sometimes has the downgraded meaning of "to hurl (insults), to use bad language." El presidente **profirió** un discurso contra el terrorismo internacional. *The president **uttered** (gave) a speech against international terrorism.* Cuando lo detuvieron, **profirió** insultos. *When he was arrested, he **hurled** insults at them. To proffer* means *proponer, ofrecer, brindar.* Rehusó la mano **brindada.** *He refused the **proffered** hand.*

profesor / professor   *Profesor* (m.) is used in most Spanish-speaking countries as "teacher" of any school, as well as being a cognate of *professor,* which usually is restricted to colleges and universities and to refer to lecturers. [Some countries, such as Mexico, use *maestro* more often than *profesor.* In other countries, *catedrático (-a)* is used to refer to "high school teacher" and "university professor." In Spain, *catear* (from *catedrático*) is the colloquial term for "to flunk."]
profesor particular = *private tutor, private teacher*
profesor auxiliar = *assistant professor*
profesor titular = *full professor*
profesor visitante = *visiting professor*
Don José es **profesor** de primer grado. *Don José is a first-grade **teacher**.* Ella es **profesora** (catedrática) auxiliar en Harvard. *She is an assistant **professor** at Harvard.* El **catedrático** (profesor) me cateó en matemáticas. *The **teacher** flunked me in mathematics. Profesorado* translates as "teaching staff." El **profesorado** está bien preparado. *The **teaching staff** is well prepared.*

programa / program   *Programa* (m.) means "program" ("plan, procedure"), as well as "syllabus, curriculum." Un **programa** semestral se compone de 16 semanas. *A **syllabus** for a semester involves 16 weeks.* El **programa** de español contiene literatura y lingüística. *The Spanish **curriculum** includes literature and linguistics.*

progresivo / progressive *Progresivo* means "progressive" ("in progress") to refer to programs, taxes, actions, etc. el desarrollo **progresivo** del país / *the country's progressive development* *Progressive* also refers to *progresista* ("in favor of reform") to describe newspapers, people, government, etc. un periódico **progresista** / *a progressive newspaper*

progreso / progress *Progreso* not only means "progress" as "improvement," but also means "an increase" of any kind. El suicidio juvenil está en **progreso**. *There is an increase in juvenile suicide.* *Progresismo* means both "progressionism" ("believing in progress") and "progressivism" (a political doctrine). ¿Crees en el **progresismo**? *Do you believe in progressionism?*

prolongación / prolongation *Prolongación* is "prolongation," as well as "extension" (of a city, street, etc.) and "overtime" (in a game). La **prolongación** norte es grande. *The northward extension is big.* La **prolongación** es de sólo 10 minutos. *Overtime is only 10 minutes.*

prolongar / prolong *Prolongar* means "to prolong," as well as "to extend, last (longer), end late." La sesión se **prolongó** más de lo previsto. *The meeting lasted longer than expected.* *Prolongado* means "prolonged" and "lengthy." Este año tuvimos unas vacaciones **prolongadas**. *This year we had a lengthy vacation.*

promoción / promotion *Promoción* means "promotion" in the sense of "increase in salary and/or position." In addition, *promoción* means "graduation class or group." una **promoción** a gerente / *a promotion to manager* La **promoción** de 1950 se reunió en el colegio. *The graduates of 1950 got together at the school.* *Promotion* also is used in business and marketing (primarily in the United States) to mean *publicidad* (f.). [In some Latin American countries, *promoción* is used in the sense of *promotion* in business and marketing *(publicidad).*]
escalafón = *promotion list*
Las empresas gastan muchos millones en **publicidad**. *Companies spend millions of dollars on promotion.*

pronto / pronto, prompt *Pronto* and *pronto* (which is a loan word in English that comes from Spanish) both mean "without delay." *Pronto* and *prompt* share the idea of "quick, fast, rapid." *Pronto* also stands for "willing, ready," and as an adverb means "early" or (in America) "suddenly."
lo más pronto posible = *as soon as possible*
por de pronto; por lo pronto = *for the time being*
Está **pronta** para ayudarnos. *She is ready to help us.* Cuanto más **pronto** mejor. *The sooner the better.* Necesito una respuesta **pronta** (inmediata). *I need a prompt reply.* *Prompt* also suggests *en punto* ("sharp, on the dot") and, in business, *disponible.* a las cinco **en punto** / *at five o'clock prompt (sharp)*

propaganda / propaganda *Propaganda* is not exactly "propaganda" but "promotion" (of ideas, policies, etc.) and in the business world, "publicity, advertisement." Se gastan muchos millones en **propaganda** en los medios de comunicación. *Millions are spent on advertising in the mass media.* *Propaganda* has a pejorative meaning nowadays: *engaño, falsedad* (f.), *doctrina, ideas falsas.* [Originally *propaganda* in English had the meaning of "promotion of ideas, doctrines, etc. to further one's cause." Actually the origin of the term is religious: the *propagation* of faith. The current meaning, though, conveys the negative idea of "deception, distortion."] Ese artículo contiene muchas **ideas falsas** sobre Kuwait. *That article contains a lot of propaganda about Kuwait.*

propiedad / property, propriety *Propiedad* (f.) means "property" (estate, house, money, etc.) and in a figurative sense, "quality" (or "characteristic"). *Propiedad* also means "ownership, proprietorship."

derechos de propiedad = *copyright*
derecho de propiedad = *ownership rights*
propiedad industrial = *patent rights*
Esta granja es de **propiedad** particular. *This farm is private **property**. Propriety,* on the other hand, means *conveniencia, decoro, corrección, convenciones* (social). Se expresa con **corrección**. *He expresses himself with **propriety**.*

propio / proper *Propio* is "proper" in grammar. However, the basic meaning of *propio* is "own, very, same, typical of, particular, peculiar."

propio de su edad = *natural (typical) for his or her age*
nombre propio = *proper noun*
un defecto **propio** de los españoles / *a fault **typical** of the Spaniards* Vivo en mi casa **propia**. *I live in my **own** house.* hacer lo **propio** / *to do the **same*** Me lo contó en sus **propias** palabras. *He told me in his **own** words.* Le di el paquete en **propias** manos. *I gave him the parcel **personally** (in person). Proper* has many other meanings and uses; however, basically it means *correcto, decoroso, apropiado, adecuado.* Una camiseta no es **apropiada** para ir a la fiesta. *A T-shirt is not **proper** attire for the party.*

proporcionar / proportion *Proporcionar* is not "to proportion" but "to afford, furnish, give." Los padres **proporcionan** educación a sus hijos. *Parents **furnish** (provide) an education to their children. To proportion* means *balancear, correlacionar* and, in a medical sense, *dosificar.* El juez debe **balancear** el castigo con el crimen. *The judge must **proportion** the punishment to the crime.*

prorrogar / prorogue *Prorrogar* (ue) is "to prorogue" in the sense of "to defer." *Prorrogar* primarily means "to extend, prolong." Me gustaría **prorrogar** las vacaciones. *I would like **to extend** my vacation. To prorogue* in English also has a limited, specialized meaning of "to adjourn" a session of the legislature or of parliament. Suitable translations are *concluir, terminar.* El parlamento **concluyó** la sesión. *The parliament **prorogued** the session. Prórroga* means "extension, deferment" and in Spain it applies to "overtime" in sports. *Prorogation* means *fin* (m.), *conclusión.*

prospecto / prospectus, prospect *Prospecto* does not mean "prospect." *Prospecto* means "prospectus" as "booklet, brochure, statement that describes a project or enterprise." María escribió un **prospecto** sobre la nueva empresa. *Mary wrote a **prospectus** on the new business. Prospect* is a catchy word with many different meanings, such as *perspectiva, esperanza, expectativa, posibilidad* (f.), *porvenir* (m.), *futuro cliente.* tener **porvenir** / *to have **prospects*** tener un trabajo en

perspectiva / *to hold out a* **prospect** *for the job* Hay que buscar **futuros clientes**. *It's necessary to find new* **prospects**.

protector / protector *Protector* (m.) and *protector* both mean "defender, guardian." However, *protector* also means "patron" (of the arts) and "mouthpiece" (in boxing, football, etc.). As an adjective, *protector* means "patronizing." Mecenas fue **protector** famoso de las artes en la Italia del Renacimiento. *Mecenas was a famous* **patron** *of the arts in Italy during the Renaissance.* Sociedad **protectora** de animales / *Society for the Prevention of Cruelty to Animals* **Protección** means "protection, defense," as well as "patronage" (of the arts).

proveer / provide *Proveer* and *to provide* share the idea of "to supply, furnish." The Spanish term also stands for "to fill" (a vacancy) *(vacante, f.)* and "to rule, make a ruling, resolve." **Proveyó** el puesto (la vacante) a su sobrino. *He* **filled** *the post by hiring his nephew.* no **proveer** (dar) lo suficiente para vivir / *to not* **provide** *a decent living*

providencia / providence *Providencia* and *providence* both refer to "God as provider" or "divine care or guidance." In addition, *providencia* means "measure, step, decision." Tomó las **providencias** necesarias para emigrar a Chile. *He took the necessary* **steps** *(measures) to emigrate to Chile.*

provisión / provision *Provisión* and *provision* both mean "supply." The plural *provisiones* refers to "provisions" (food, equipment). In the business world, *provisión* means "cover" or "funds." hacer **provisión** de café / *to get in a* **supply** *of coffee* **provisión** de fondos / *reserve funds Provision* in English also means *disposición, ley* (f.). Las **disposiciones** de la ley son severas en este caso. *The* **provisions** *of the law are severe in a case like this.*

provocar / provoke *Provocar* and *to provoke* share the idea of "to cause, incite, irritate." In Colombia and other countries, *provocar* is used like *gustar* to mean "to feel like, to like." **provocar** (causar) risa / *to provoke laughter* Me **provoca** una taza de café. *I* **feel like** *(having) a cup of coffee.*

provocativo / provocative *Provocativo* and *provocative* both mean "causing, inciting, stimulating." *Provocativo* has downgraded its denotation to mean "offensive, irritating." palabras **provocativas** / *irritating words Provocative*, on the other hand, has taken on sexual shades of meaning: *sugestivo, provocador, insinuante*. La modelo lleva un vestido **insinuante**. *The model is wearing a* **provocative** *dress.*

proyección / projection *Proyección* shares with *projection* the idea of "showing films, slides." *Proyección* also means "emission" (of liquids). El volcán tiene una gran **proyección** de lava. *The volcano has a large* **emission** *of lava. Projection* also means *saliente* (m.), *saledizo*, as well as *futuro, pronóstico*. El tejado tiene un **saliente** muy agudo. *The roof has a sharp* **projection**. el **pronóstico** del presupuesto para los próximos cinco años / *the budget* **projections** *for the next five years*

proyectar / project *Proyectar* and *to project* share the ideas of "to plan, design, show pictures." In addition, *proyectar* means "to throw, hurl." ¿Quién **proyectó** esta catedral? *Who **designed** this cathedral?* **Proyectó** la moneda al mar. *She **threw** the coin into the sea.* *To project* also translates as *sobresalir, resaltar, destacar.* Esta novela **hace resaltar** los valores humanos importantes. *This novel **projects** important human values.*

proyecto / project *Proyecto* and *project* both mean "plan, scheme." They only differ in the meaning of *proyecto* as "bill, proposition" (for legislation). **proyecto de ley** = *legislative bill*

prueba / probe *Prueba* is not "probe" but "test, quiz, evidence, sampling (of food), sign, token, event (in sports), (photographic) print, fitting (of clothes), circumstantial evidence (in a trial)."
poner a prueba = *to put to the test*
a toda prueba = *with complete confidence*
piloto de prueba = *test pilot*
a prueba de bomba = *bombproof, shellproof*
a prueba de bala = *bulletproof*
Aquí está la **prueba** de su delito. *Here is the **evidence** (proof) of his crime.* María le dio un regalo como **prueba** de amor. *Mary gave him a gift as a **token** of love.* *Probe*, on the other hand, means *investigación, sondeo, encuesta, exploración* and in medical terminology, *sonda.* Es necesaria una **investigación** de la firma. *A **probe** of the firm is called for.*

publicar / publish *Publicar* means "to publish" (books, papers), but it also means "to publicize, make public, announce, proclaim." Todos los periódicos **publicaron** esa noticia insignificante. *All the newspapers **published** that unimportant news item.* *To publish* also means *editar* (books, magazines). El catedrático **editó** un libro de poemas de García Lorca. *The professor **published** a book of poems by García Lorca.*

público / public *Público* and *public* are adjectives and nouns for "audience, spectators, people (in general)." The usage of the two terms is parallel, although the Spanish term is used more frequently than the English—for example, to refer to "customers (of a store), (television) viewers, readers (of books, newspapers, etc.)."
casa pública (Spain) = *brothel*
relaciones **públicas** / *public relations* Cada escritor tiene su **público.** *Every writer has his or her **readers** (followers).* La tienda está llena de **público.** *The store is full of **customers.*** sacar al **público** / *to publicize*

pudín, budín / pudding *Pudín* (m.) and *budín* (m.) both are loan words from the English *pudding.* The *Real Academia* almost writes a complete recipe for *budín* in its dictionary; the recipe is quite different from the one found in Webster's. [Note that *budín* is, in fact, a cognate, but *pudín* is considered an anglicism.]

pueblo / pueblo, people *Pueblo* means "village, town, common people, country (nation)." todos los **pueblos** de América / *all the **countries** in the Americas* Los

pueblos de Castilla son pequeños. *Castilian **villages** are small.* **pueblo** de mala muerte / *hick **town*** hacer un llamamiento al **pueblo** / *to call on the common people* Pueblo was borrowed from the Spanish to refer to *aldea india,* and by extension, *indios* (especially Hopi and Zuñi, who live in *pueblos*). *People,* on the other hand, means *pueblo* as "nation, common people"; however, *gente* (f.) is used to refer to people in general. [Note that *people* is always plural, whereas *gente* and *pueblo* are singular.]

puesto / post *Puesto* and *post* share the meaning of "job" or "position" *(empleo),* "station" (military). In addition, *puesto* means "stall, stand, small shop, seat, place." tener un buen **puesto** / *to have a good **job** (post)* En la feria hay muchos **puestos.** *There are many **stalls** at the fair.* **puesto** de periódicos / ***newsstand*** el **puesto** del piloto / *the pilot's **seat*** *Post,* on the other hand, also means *poste* (m.; "pole"), *palo, estaca, correo* or *casa de correos, cartas* (chiefly British), *factoría* ("trading post").
correos = *post office*

pulcritud / pulchritude *Pulcritud* (f.) does not mean "pulchritude" but "neatness, tidiness, cleanliness," and figuratively, "fastidiousness." Nos admiró la **pulcritud** de su estudio. *The **neatness** of his studio surprised us.* *Pulchritude* means *belleza* (physical beauty). Nunca vio tanta **belleza** reunida en una mujer. *He never saw so much **pulchritude** together in one woman.* *Pulcro* translates as "neat, tidy, clean, immaculate." Tiene una casa muy **pulcra.** *She has a very **tidy** home.*

pulir / polish *Pulir* means "to polish" (metal, glass, marble) and, figuratively, "to refine, finish off," but each verb has additional meanings. In colloquial British speech, *polish* also means "to sell off, steal, pinch." [In some countries, *embolar* is used to mean "to polish, shine" (shoes); in some other countries, *limpiar, lustrar,* and *dar brillo* are used.] Hay que **pulir** un poco a este niño. *This child needs a little **polishing.*** To *polish* also translates as *embolar, limpiar, lustrar, dar brillo* (see note above), as well as *encerar* (floor, furniture). In colloquial speech, *to polish off* means *zampar* ("to eat quickly"), *despachar, liquidar, cepillarse* ("to kill"). La criada **enceró** los pisos de madera. *The maid **polished** the wood floors.* Se **zampó** dos pollos. *He **polished off** two chickens.* El jefe nunca **embola** sus zapatos. *The boss never **polishes** (shines) his shoes.*

pulóver / pullover *Pulóver* (m.) has not been included in the latest dictionary of the *Real Academia;* nevertheless, as a loan word from the English *pullover,* it is used daily in many Latin American countries, just as in Spain the words *jersey* and *suéter* have been borrowed from the English. [Note that the plural of *pulóver* is *pulóveres.*]

pulpa, pulpo / pulp *Pulpa* exactly means "pulp" (of wood, of fruit, tissue, dental). Este tomate tiene mucha **pulpa.** *This tomato has a lot of **pulp.*** *Pulpo* means "octopus." *Pulp* is also used colloquially to describe a *novela* (or *revista) de poca categoría.*
hacer papilla = *to reduce to pulp*
Yo no leería esa **novela** tan baja. *I wouldn't read that **pulp** novel.* Los dos coches se hicieron **papilla** cuando chocaron de frente. *Both cars were reduced to **pulp** when they collided head on.*

211

pulso / pulse   *Pulso (latido)* and *pulse (beat)* have the same meaning in anatomy. In addition, *pulso* means "steady hand" and, in a figurative sense, "care, caution." In Latin America *pulso* is used for "bracelet" *(pulsera)* because it is worn on the wrist (where the pulse is taken).
ganar algo a pulso = *to get something the hard way*
tomar el **pulso** a alguien   /   *to take someone's pulse*   obrar con **pulso**   /   *to proceed with caution*   Dibuja con buen **pulso.** *He draws with a steady hand. Pulse* is also used in music to mean *ritmo, compás* (m.), *vibración,* and is used with leguminous vegetables to refer to the edible seeds such as *guisantes* (m.; "peas"), *frijoles* (m.; "beans"), etc. La música moderna tiene **ritmo** rápido. *Modern music has a fast pulse. Pulsación* and *pulsation* are used also to mean *pulse/pulso* as "beat." *Pulsación* is used as well to mean "touch (on a piano, of a typist), strum (guitar, banjo), tap (on a typewriter keyboard)."
pulsaciones por minuto = *words per minute*

pulverizar / pulverize   *Pulverizar* means "to pulverize," as well as "to spray, atomize" and, in a figurative sense, "to smash, shatter, waste, dissipate." Pulverizó su fortuna en dos años. *He wasted his fortune in two years.* Pulverizó el vaso de cristal. *She shattered the glass.*   pulverizar una teoría   /   *to tear a theory to pieces   Pulverización* means "pulverization" (of solid matter) and "spray" (of perfumes, crops). *Pulverizador* (m.) means "pulverizer," as well as "spray gun (for painting), spray, atomizer (for perfumes)." El perfume se va pronto con el **pulverizador.** *Perfume disappears quickly with an atomizer.*

punto, punta / point   *Punto* and *point* share various meanings: "dot, idea, place, spot, point (of a pen or pencil), score (in sports)." *Punto* also means "period (the punctuation mark), stitch, moment, holes (in belts, in shoes), comma (for decimals)." [In Hispanic and European countries, decimals are written with a comma *(,)* rather than a decimal point. For example, *dos dólares y medio* is written as $2,50. However, Mexico has recently changed to the system used in the U.S. and would express the same amount as $2.50.] En ese **punto** no estamos de acuerdo. *We do not agree on that point.*   cinco **coma** siete (5,7)   /   *five point seven (5.7)*   con **puntos** y comas   /   *in full detail   Punta* is used for "point ('sharp end' of a pencil, a nose, a knife, etc.), (finger) tip, nail" *(clavo),* and "sourness" (of wine).
horas punta = *rush hour*
Point, in addition to its shared meanings with *punto* and *punta,* means *fin* (m.), *propósito, buena idea, sentido.*
al grano = *to the point*
No acabo de ver tu **propósito.** *I don't quite see your point.*   fuera de **propósito**   /   *beside the point*   en este **momento**   /   *at this point* in time

puntuación / punctuation   *Puntuación* and *punctuation* both refer to the mechanics of writing a language (for example, with "punctuation marks"). In addition, *puntuación* stands for "score, scoring," and in some countries it is used to mean "grade" *(nota)* for a school class. Tuve buena **puntuación** en el examen de historia. *I got a good grade (score) on the history test.*

puntuar / punctuate *Puntuar* stands for "to punctuate" ("to write punctuation marks"), as well as "to score (points in sports), to grade (papers, tests)." Hugo Sánchez **puntuó** en la primera mitad con dos goles. *Hugo Sánchez scored two goals in the first half.* To punctuate also means *recalcar, destacar, interrumpir.* En su discurso, ella **destacó** la idea de triunfar con el esfuerzo personal. *In her speech, she punctuated the idea of succeeding through personal effort.* El silencio **fue interrumpido** con la tos rítmica del niño inquieto. *The silence was punctuated by the rhythmical coughing of the restless boy.*

pupila, pupilo / pupil *Pupila* and *pupil* only share the meaning of "pupil of the eye." Otherwise, *pupila* and *pupilo* do not mean "pupil" but "boarder" (one who pays room and board), and in a figurative sense, "ward" (one who is under custody or guardianship) *(protegido).* [*Pupilo, pupila* used to refer to an "orphan" or "minor" (with a guardian); however, this meaning has become obsolete.]
tener pupila = *to be sharp*
estar a pupilo = *to be on room and board*
casa de pupilos = *boardinghouse*
Ella está de **pupila** en una pensión. *She is a boarder at a boardinghouse. Pupil,* on the other hand, also means *alumno, discípulo.* Todos los **alumnos** la aprecian. *All the pupils like her.*

puridad / purity *Puridad* (f.) is not "purity" but "secrecy, secret." [The original meaning of *puridad* was *pureza* ("purity"), but later the term came to mean the "secrecy" that was associated with the "purity" of the body.] *Purity* means *pureza* and is used to refer to people as well as things such as metals, water, etc.

puro / pure *Puro* and *pure,* as adjectives, share the basic meaning of "chaste, without mixture, untainted." *Puro* also means "sheer (luck, chance), plain, simple, straight (a drink)," and in America, "only, just." As a noun, *puro* means "cigar." [The original expression was *cigarro puro,* but over the years, *cigarro* was dropped.] El anillo es oro **puro**. *The ring is pure (solid) gold.* la **pura** verdad / *the plain (simple) truth* un **pura** sangre / *a thoroughbred (horse)* La vi por **pura** casualidad. *I saw her by sheer chance.* De **puro** gordo no cabe por la puerta. *He's so fat that he can't fit through the door.* Yo fumaba **puros** en Cuba. *I used to smoke cigars in Cuba.*

púrpura / purple *Púrpura* in its everyday meaning is not technically "purple" but "crimson." In a figurative sense, *púrpura* translates as "purple" to refer to *dignidad* (f.; "dignity"), because *púrpura* ("royal purple") was the color worn by such dignitaries as kings, counts, cardinals, popes, etc. [There is an illness, called *púrpura* in Spanish and *purpura* in English, that is characterized by purplish patches on the skin.] Los cardenales todavía usan ropa de color **púrpura**. *Cardinals still wear clothing the color of crimson. Purple,* in every language, means *morado* or *violeta.* Me encanta contemplar el cielo **morado** de la tarde. *I love to watch the purple sky in the evening.*

Q

querella / quarrel *Querella* is used with the figurative meaning of "quarrel" as "disagreement." The basic meaning of *querella,* though, is "complaint, lament." In old Spanish, the term used to mean "moan, groan." Hay una **querella** de años entre los dos hermanos. *There is a long-standing **disagreement** between the two brothers.* Tengo una **querella** contra él. *I have a **complaint** against him. Quarrel,* on the other hand, means *disputa, pelea, riña, camorra.* Busqué una **pelea** con mi prima. *I picked a **quarrel** with my cousin.* No tengo nada en contra tuya. *I have no **quarrel** with you.* hacer las paces después de una **riña** / *to make up after a **quarrel***

quieto / quiet *Quieto* is not "quiet"; instead, it means "still, calm, tranquil, motionless." La criatura está muy **quieta.** *The baby is very **calm.*** ¡Todo el mundo **quieto!** *Nobody move!/Everyone **keep still!*** ¡Déjame **quieto!** *Leave me **alone** (in peace)! Quiet,* on the other hand, means *silencioso, callado, descansado, sencillo* or *discreto, privado* or *íntimo.* In business, as well as other activities, *quiet* means *encalmado, inactivo.*
¡**Cállate!** = *Keep quiet! Shut up!*
Un diplomático debe saber **callarse** en cinco lenguas. *A diplomat should know how to **keep quiet** in five languages.* El teatro está **silencioso.** *The theater is **quiet.*** Hay un **silencio** sepulcral. *It is as **quiet** as the grave.* La bolsa estuvo **encalmada** hoy. *The stock market was **quiet** today.*

químico / chemical *Químico* is not only "chemical" but also, as a noun, is "chemist." The feminine form *química* is the science of *chemistry.* Un **químico** debe saber mucha **química.** *A **chemist** must know a lot of **chemistry.***

quinto, quinta / quint *Quinto* means "fifth." In Spain, *quinto* is the term for a "new soldier, recruit." *Quinta,* the feminine form, means "farm" (along with *hacienda, granja, estancia, rancho, finca, predio, campo*). In Spain, *quinta* is the term for "military draft, conscription." Subí por la escalera hasta el **quinto** piso. *I walked upstairs to the **fifth** floor.* entrar en **quintas** / *to reach **draft** age. Quint* is short for *quintuplet,* which is translated as *quintillizo* in Spanish. [In card games, *quint* means *quinta,* or "five cards of the same suit."] Mi vecina tuvo **quintillizos.** *My neighbor had **quints** (quintuplets). **Quíntuplo** means "quintuple" ("five times more"). El **quíntuplo** de cinco es veinticinco. *The **quintuple** of five is twenty-five. **Quintuplicar** means "to quintuple" ("to make five times as great or as many").

quiosco / kiosk *Quiosco* means "kiosk" ("an open pavilion or house"), as well as "bandstand, newsstand, stand, pavilion." In general, *quiosco* is used more frequently in Spanish than in American English. Si pasas por un **quiosco** me compras el periódico de hoy. *If you go by a **newsstand,** buy me today's paper.*

quitar / quit *Quitar* does not mean "to quit"; instead, it means "to take away, take off, steal, subtract, turn off (the radio or TV set)." ¿Quién me **quitó** el bolígrafo? *Who **took** my pen?* **quitar** la vida a alguien / *to **take** someone's life* Le **quitó** el bolso de las manos. *He **snatched** the bag from her hands.* To quit means *dejar de, parar, abandonar* (a job or a place), *marcharse, salir de, dimitir* (a job). [The past tense of *to quit* is *quit;* the past participle is *quitted.*] No debes **abandonar** ese trabajo. *You shouldn't **quit** that job* Salió de la fiesta temprano. *He **quit** (left) the party early.* Dejó a su mujer. *He **quit** (left) his wife.* ¡**Deja** de molestarme! ***Quit** bothering me!*

R

ración / ration *Ración* means "ration" as "a share (of something); a food allowance." In Spanish, *ración* also translates as "helping, portion," for example, in a restaurant.
a ración (adverb) = *meanly, stingily*
Los soldados comen su **ración** diaria. *The soldiers are eating their daily* **rations**. Sírvete otra **ración** de pollo. *Have another **helping** of chicken.* tener su **ración** de / *to have (get) one's **share** of* **ración** de hambre / *pittance of food* *Racionar* and *to ration* share exactly the same meanings. [Note in the example that the article *el* is required after *racionar*.]
racionar el pan = *to ration bread*

radio / radio, radius, radium *Radio* (m.) translates as "radio" (set, wireless), as well as "radius (of a circle, a bone), radium (the metal), spoke (of a wheel or tire), scope, range (of action), outskirts (of a town)." [In some countries, *la radio* is used instead of *el radio* to refer to the "radio set."] Los **(las) radios** son baratos (baratas) hoy día. *Radios (radio sets) are cheap nowadays.* La bicicleta tiene dos **radios** (rayos) rotos. *The bicycle has two broken **spokes**.* Muchos pobres viven en el **radio** de la ciudad. *Many poor people live in the **outskirts** of the city.*

ranchero / rancher *Ranchero* is normally used to mean "farmer" in Latin America, but *ranchero* also means "camp cook." Los **rancheros** hispanos no llegan a ser ricos. *Hispanic **ranchers** (farmers) do not become rich.* El **ranchero** del cuartel es todo un desastre. *The **mess cook** at the barracks is a complete disaster. Rancher,* on the other hand, also translates as *hacendado, vaquero, ganadero* [Primarily, *rancher* in English refers to someone who raises animals such as horses, cattle, etc.] Hay muchos cuentos folklóricos sobre los **ganaderos** de Texas. *There are many folk tales about Texas cattle **ranchers**.*

rancho / ranch *Rancho* is used in Latin America for "ranch," but it also means "shack, hut, mess (communal food)," and in a figurative sense, "bad food, swill." Los campesinos viven en **ranchos** pobres. *The peasants live in humble **shacks**.* Los soldados se quejan de su **rancho** diario. *The soldiers complain about their daily **mess**. Ranch* also translates as *hacienda, granja, finca.*

rango / rank, range *Rango* means "rank" as "class, position," but in Latin America, it also means "luxury, pomp." mantener su **rango** / *to maintain one's standing* Tiene el **rango** de catedrático. *He has the **rank** of full professor* persona **de alto rango** / *high-class person* *Rank* also translates as *fila, grado.* The plural *ranks* means *tropa, filas, soldados rasos.* El alcalde se unió a las **filas** demócratas. *The mayor joined the democratic **ranks**. Range* has a wealth of meanings such as *sierra, cadena,* or *cordillera* (of mountains), *campo* or *galería* (for shooting), *extensión, alcance* (m.), *esfera, escala.* Esa **cordillera** es la más bella, pero la más peligrosa. *That **mountain range** is the most beautiful,* *but the most dangerous.* El piloto tiene un **campo** limitado de visión por la neblina. *The pilot has a limited range of vision because of the fog.*

rapar / rape *Rapar* does not mean "to rape"; instead, it means "to shave" or "to give a close haircut." Le dije al barbero que me **rapara** bien. *I told the barber to give me a close haircut.* To rape means *violar* ("to force sexual intercourse"). *Rape* (m.) means "a quick shave, a rough haircut."
al rape = close (cut)
dar un **rape** a alguien / *to give someone a scolding; to tell someone off*
Rape translates as *violación*. El número de **violaciones** ha aumentado últimamente. *The number of rapes has increased lately.*

raptar / enrapture *Raptar* means "to kidnap, abduct." Los terroristas **raptaron** al niño y piden un millón por su rescate. *The terrorists kidnapped the child and are asking a million in ransom.* To enrapture translates as *extasiar, arrobar, embelesar.* Ella está **extasiada** delante del galán. *She is enraptured by the lead actor.*

rapto / rapt *Rapto* is a noun, meaning "kidnapping, abduction (of a person)" and figuratively, "rapture, ecstasy, impulse." El **rapto** es un delito execrable. *Abduction (kidnapping) is an execrable crime.* Rapt, which is a little-used adjective in English, means *extasiado, entusiasmado, absorto, ensimismado.* atención **profunda** / *rapt attention*

raqueta / racket, racquet *Raqueta* means "racket, racquet" (for tennis) and it also refers to a croupier's "rake," as well as to "snowshoe." En la nieve se camina más fácilmente con **raquetas**. *You can walk on the snow more easily in snowshoes.* *Racket* also means *timo, estafa* ("swindle"), and in colloquial speech, *bulla, jaleo, barullo.*
estafa de narcóticos = *drug racket*
La reventa de billetes es un **timo**. *Ticket scalping is a racket.* Los muchachos hacían mucha **bulla**. *The boys were making quite a racket.* Armaron **jaleo**. *They raised a racket (made a fuss).*

raro / rare *Raro* and *rare* share the meaning of "scarce, infrequent." *Raro* also means "strange, peculiar, odd, weird."
raras veces = *seldom, rarely*
¡Qué raro! = *How odd!*
Me siento **raro** hoy. *I feel odd (strange) today.* Es un tipo bastante **raro**. *He is a pretty strange guy (fellow).* Me miraba como a un bicho **raro**. *She looked at me as though I were a strange creature.* *Rare* also translates as *poco cocinado* (meat), as well as *distintivo, de suma calidad.* Prefiero el bisté **poco cocinado** (hecho). *I like my steak on the rare side.* Tiene una colección de joyas **preciosas**. *She has a collection of rare jewels.*

rata, rato / rat *Rata* and *rat* are both the animal, but in a figurative sense, *rata (ratero)* means "petty thief, sneak thief."
rata de agua = *water rat*
rata de hotel = *hotel thief*

No había ni una **rata**. *There wasn't a **living soul**.* más pobre que una **rata** / *as poor as a **church mouse*** Ese joven se gana la vida como una **rata** miserable. *That young man makes a living as a miserable **thief**.* *Rat* is also used figuratively to mean *traidor* (m.), *canalla* (m.), *desertor* (m.). Aquí hay gato encerrado. *I smell a **rat**.* Ese **canalla** traicionó a sus compañeros. *That **rat** betrayed his friends.* ***Rato,*** on the other hand, refers to "a period of time, while." Me encanta nadar en mis **ratos** de ocio. *I love to swim in my spare **time**.* ¿Me esperas un **rato**? *Will you wait for me a **while**?*

raza / race *Raza* means "race" in reference to human beings, but it also means "strain, breed" (of animals).

de raza = *thoroughbred* (horse), *pedigree* (dog, cat), *purebred*
la **raza** humana / *the human **race*** Este caballo es de buena **raza**. *This horse is of a good **breed**.* perro de **raza** (con pedigrí) / *a **pedigreed** dog* *Race* also translates as *carrera* (cycling, horses, cars), *curso* (of a star, of time).

carrera de armamentos = *arms race*
carrera de caballos / *horse **race*** problema **racial** / *a **race** (racial) problem* **carrera** contra el reloj / ***race** against the clock (against time)*

real / real *Real* and *real* share the meaning of "true, authentic." *Real* in Spanish also means "royal" and in a figurative sense, "grand, splendid, fine." As a noun *real* (m.) was an old coin, equivalent to a quarter of a peseta. [*La Real Academia de la Lengua Española* is the "Royal Academy of the Spanish Language," a body of 28 Spanish members *(los Académicos de la Lengua)* who live and work in Madrid. The Academy has parallel organizations in every Latin American country. The *Real Academia* has been publishing dictionaries and grammars of the Spanish language since the eighteenth century when it was founded and sponsored by the *reyes* (kings), hence the distinction *real*.]

tener reales = *to have lots of money*
La vida es seria, la vida es **real**. *Life is serious, life is **real**.* El baile fue un éxito **real** (verdadero). *The dance was a **real** (true) success.* Fue una celebración **real** (regia). *It was a **grand** celebration.* No vale un **real**. *It's not worth one **red cent**.* *Real* in English also refers to "permanent or immovable things" (such as buildings, land) and figuratively, it is used to mean *por completo, todo*.

bienes raíces = *real estate*
Ese tipo es **todo** un idiota. *That guy is a **real** idiot.*

realeza / realty *Realeza* is not "realty" but "royalty." *Realty* means *bienes* (m.) *raíces*.

realizar / realize *Realizar* and *to realize* share the meaning of "to carry out, accomplish" and in the business world, "to convert into money," for example, shares of stock, assets, etc. Sometimes *realizar* simply means "to make, do." The reflexive *realizarse* figuratively means "to come true."

realizar un trabajo = *to do a job*
realizar(se) los sueños = *to make one's dreams come true*
Realizó sus proyectos exitosamente. *He **carried out** his plans successfully.* Ella **realizó** sus esperanzas. *She **fulfilled** her hopes.* *To realize* principally means *darse*

cuenta de, comprender. Al fin **me di cuenta del** error. *In the end, I realized my mistake*. **Comprendo** que me hablaste en broma. *I realize that you were only joking*.

rebatir / rebate *Rebatir* is not "to rebate" but "to refute, to repel (arguments, attacks, etc.)." No voy a **rebatir** sus ataques. *I am not going to refute his attacks. To rebate* means *reembolsar, rebajar*. Me **reembolsaron** quinientos dólares. *They rebated (refunded) five hundred dollars to me.*

reciclar / recycle *Reciclar* and *to recycle* are no longer false cognates. The *Real Academia* in its latest dictionary has included *reciclar* with the same meaning as *to recycle*. [The corresponding noun is *reciclaje* (m.) and the corresponding adjective is *reciclado* to mean "recycling" and "recycled," respectively.] Escribo mis cartas en papel **reciclado**. *I write my letters on recycled paper.* El **reciclaje** no es un mal negocio. *Recycling is not a bad business.*

recipiente / recipient *Recipiente* (m.) does not mean "recipient"; instead, it means "container, receptacle." Necesito un **recipiente** grande para la basura. *I need a large container for the garbage. Recipient* means *destinatario* (of a letter, a shipment, etc.). El **destinatario** paga el porte. *The recipient pays for the freight.*

recluso / recluse *Recluso* and *recluse* share the basic idea of "seclusion," but their actual meanings are very different. *Recluso* is used to mean "prisoner, inmate." El **recluso** no puede ver televisión. *The prisoner cannot watch television. Recluse,* on the other hand, means *solitario, ermitaño*, which indicates a self-imposed seclusion. Lleva una vida de **ermitaño**. *He is living like a recluse (hermit).*

recolección / recollection *Recolección* is not "recollection" but "harvest, harvesting, harvest time," as well as "collection, gathering" of data, information, etc. La **recolección** de cereales es en verano. *The grain harvest is in the summer. Recollection* means *memoria, recuerdo*. Tengo gratos **recuerdos** de aquel verano. *I have pleasant recollections of that summer.*

recolectar / recollect *Recolectar* means "to harvest, to gather (data)." Los campesinos **recolectan** maíz. *The farmers are harvesting corn. To recollect* means *recordar* (ue), *acordarse* (ue) *de*. No **me acuerdo de** ese incidente. *I do not recollect that incident.* si mal no **recuerdo** / *as far as I recollect*

reconocer / recognize *Reconocer* and *to recognize* both mean "to identify, to be aware of something or somebody known before." In addition, *reconocer* is also "to examine (a patient), to admit or acknowledge, to survey (terrain)." ¿No la **reconoces**? *Don't you recognize her?* El médico me **reconoce** todos los años. *The doctor examines me every year.* **Reconozco** mis faltas. *I acknowledge my mistakes.* **reconocer** la evidencia / *to bow to the evidence*

reconvenir / reconvene *Reconvenir* (ie) is not "to reconvene" but "to reproach, reprimand," and in legal terms, "to counterclaim." El director me **reconvino** por llegar tarde. *The principal reprimanded me for being late. To reconvene* means *convocar de nuevo, reanudar* (a meeting). El rector **convocó de nuevo** al profesorado. *The president reconvened the faculty.*

récord / record   *Récord* (m.) is a borrowed word from English to mean "record" as "an unsurpassed statistic" or "a top performance." *Récord* is also used in Spanish as an adjective. [*Récord* does not appear in the latest dictionary of the *Real Academia;* however, it does appear in other dictionaries, such as Larousse, and is used frequently in many Spanish-speaking countries.] ¿Cuál es el **récord** de tiempo de la milla? *What is the record time for the mile?* batir el **récord** / *to beat (break) the record*   Record in English has many other meanings: *registro, expediente* (m.; at school), *disco, actas* ("minutes"), *relación* ("account"). La universidad guarda sus **expedientes.** *The university keeps your records.* Tengo **discos** de música flamenca. *I have records of flamenco music.*

recordar / record   *Recordar* (ue) is not "to record" but "to remember, recall, remind." Te **recuerdo** que mañana es lunes. *I'm reminding you that tomorrow is Monday.* To record translates as *registrar, apuntar* or *tomar nota de, consignar* (in the minutes), *grabar* (on tape, for example). **emisión diferida** = *previously recorded broadcast* Lo **apuntó** en su cuaderno. *He recorded it in his notebook.* La BBC **grabó** el discurso. *The BBC recorded the speech.*

recrear / re-create, recreate   *Recrear* and *to re-create* share the meaning of "to create again"; *recrear* and *to recreate* share the meaning of "to amuse, entertain." The reflexive *recrearse (divertirse* [ie, i]*)* means "to enjoy, relax, take pleasure." **recrearse** en el mal ajeno / *to delight in the misfortunes of others* **Me recreo** en la lectura de novelas. *I relax by reading novels.*

rector / rector   *Rector* as an adjective means "driving" or "leading" (person), "guiding" (idea). As a noun, *rector* (m.) means "president" (of a university). Hoy día necesitamos ideas **rectoras.** *Nowadays we need guiding ideas.* fuerza **rectora** / *driving* force Unamuno fue un **rector** famoso de la Universidad de Salamanca. *Unamuno. was a famous president of the University of Salamanca.* *Rector* is always a noun in English, and it means *párroco* (of a church), *superior* (m.; of a religious convent or order).

recubrir / recover   *Recubrir* is not "to recover"; rather, it means "to cover, coat (with paint, with metal)." [The past participle of *recubrir* is *recubierto.*] La moneda está **recubierta** de oro. *The coin is covered with gold.* To recover means *recobrar, recuperar, encontrar* (ue). Japón se **recuperó** de los desastres de la guerra. *Japan recovered from the disasters of war.* La policía no alcanzó a **recobrar** el dinero robado. *The police were unable to recover the stolen money.*

recurrir / recur   *Recurrir* is not "to recur" but "to go to, resort, appeal." Si necesito dinero **recurro** a mi padre. *If I need money, I go to my father.* **Recurro** a su generosidad. *I appeal to your generosity.* To recur means *repetirse* (i), *volver* (ue) *a ocurrir.* Ese tema **se repite** a lo largo de la novela. *That theme recurs throughout the novel. Recurrente* and *recurrent* mean the same thing; however, *periódico* ("periodic, periodical") is used more frequently in this sense than *recurrente.* [Note that *recurrencia* is a false cognate for *recurrence* and was not included in the most recent dictionary of the *Real Academia.* Nevertheless, *recurrencia* is listed in Larousse as a medical term meaning "recurrence." *Recurrence* is used in English with the meaning of *repetición, reaparición, vuelta.*] La **reaparición** de un ruido. *The recurrence of a noise.*

reducir / reduce   *Reducir* and *to reduce* share the meaning of "to lessen, cut down, diminish." The reflexive form *reducirse* stands for "to boil down to, come down to." Todo esto **se reduce** a nada. *All this comes down to nothing.* To reduce has additional meanings such as *adelgazar* or *perder* (ie) *peso* ("to lose weight, slim down"), *degradar* (an officer). El mejor modo de **adelgazar** es comer poco. *The best way to reduce is to eat a little bit.*   **poner** una teoría en práctica / *to reduce a theory into practice*   *Reducido* and *reduced* both mean "diminished, cut down, lowered." In addition, *reducido* is a frequent term in Spanish for "small, limited, poor, confined (space), low (price)." La cosecha nos dio un rendimiento muy **reducido.** *The harvest gave us a very poor yield.*

referencia / reference   *Referencia* is the same as *reference* with all its denotations, but *referencia* also means "report, account."
por **referencias** = *by hearsay*
libro **de consulta** / *reference book*   Nos dio una **referencia** completa de su viaje. *He gave us a complete account of his trip.*

referir / refer   *Referir* (ie, i) and *to refer* both mean "to relate, mean, be speaking about." However, *referir* also means "to tell of, recount." No me **refiero** a usted. *I am not referring to you.* Refirió su vida en cinco minutos. *He told the story of his life in five minutes.* To refer also means *remitir, dirigir, enviar, calificar, consultar.* Remitió el estudiante al director. *She referred the student to the principal.* Véase la página 10. *Refer to page 10.* Consulte los archivos para eso. *Refer to the archives for that.*

reflejar / reflect   *Reflejar* means "to reflect" in the sense of "to mirror, to bend or throw back heat, light, sound, etc." El espejo **refleja** la luz. *The mirror reflects light.* La felicidad **se refleja** en su rostro. *Happiness is reflected in his face.* To reflect on means *reflexionar, meditar,* and sometimes it takes on a negative shading such as *desacreditar, perjudicar, desprestigiar.* Sus fuertes palabras **perjudicaron** su honradez. *Her strong words reflected on her integrity.* Esa acción lo **descredita.** *Such an act reflects on him.*

reflexión / reflection   *Reflexión* means "reflection" (of light or heat, "meditation, remark"). Los vampiros no tienen **reflexión** en el espejo. *Vampires have no reflection in a mirror. Reflection* also means *reproche* (m.), *crítica.*
pensándolo bien = *on reflection*
Es una **crítica** de su trabajo. *It is a reflection on his work.*

reforma / reform   *Reforma* means "reform" as "social or political change for improvement." In addition, *reforma* means "repair, alteration, redecoration, remodeling."   cerrado por **reformas** / *closed for repairs*   Hicimos algunas **reformas** en la cocina. *We did some remodeling in the kitchen.*   **reformatorio** / *reform school*

reformar / reform *Reformar* and *to reform* mean "to cause social or political change," but *reformar* also means "to repair, alter (clothes), renovate, remodel." El sastre **reformó** mi chaqueta. *The tailor **altered** my jacket.*

refrán / refrain *Refrán* (m.) is not "refrain"; instead, it means "saying, proverb." El *Quijote* está lleno de **refranes**. *Don Quijote is full of **proverbs**.* según reza el **refrán** / *as the **saying** goes Refrain* stands for *coro* or *estribillo* ("part of a song or poem that is repeated").

refrenar / refrain *Refrenar* does not mean "to refrain" but "to restrain, curb, check." **Refrenó** el caballo. *He **checked** the horse. To refrain means abstenerse de, guardarse de.* Hay que **guardarse** de las malas lenguas. *One must **refrain** from gossiping.*

refresco / refreshment *Refresco* does not exactly mean "refreshment" because it does not include "food or snacks" as *refreshment* does. Sirvieron **refrescos y bocadillos** en la recepción. *They served **refreshments** at the reception.*

refundir / refund *Refundir* is not "to refund" but "to recast, rewrite, rehash (a paper, a story)." **Refundió** su ponencia para publicarla. *He **rewrote** his paper in order to publish it. To refund means reembolsar, reintegrar, devolver (ue).* Le **reembolsaron** los gastos. *They **refunded** (reimbursed) his expenses.*

regalar / regale *Regalar* and *to regale* share the meaning of "to treat royally" *(agasajar, tratar a cuerpo de rey).* However, the primary meaning of *regalar* is "to give" (a present or gift) and has the figurative meaning of "to flatter, caress." Mis abuelos me **regalan** (tratan a cuerpo de rey) cada vez que los visito. *My grandparents **regale** me every time I visit them.* Le **regalé** un brillante para su cumpleaños. *I **gave** her a diamond for her birthday.* **regalar** al oído / *to flatter To regale* also is used infrequently to mean *deleitar, entretener* (ie). Nos **entretenía** en el viaje con sus cuentos de misterio. *During the trip, he **regaled** us with his mystery stories.*

regalía / regalia *Regalía* is not "regalia" but "privilege, prerogative, (salary) bonus." Todavía los gobernantes tienen sus **regalías**. *Government officials still have their **privileges**. Regalia means insignias, galas, atributos* (of an office). **de punta en blanco** = *in full regalia* Los catedráticos lucían sus **galas** en la graduación. *The professors wore their **regalia** at the graduation ceremony.*

régimen / régime, regimen *Régimen* (m.) and *régime* share the meaning of "political rule," but *régimen* is used much more frequently than its cognate and is often translated as "system." *Régimen* also shares with *regimen* the idea of "a systematic plan" (for dieting, undergoing therapy, etc.). [The plural of *régimen* is *regímenes*.] **régimen de vida** = *way of life* Los **regímenes** dictatoriales no permiten los derechos del individuo. *Dictatorial systems (régimes) do not allow rights for individuals.* el **régimen** de Franco / *Franco's régime* El médico me puso a **régimen** estricto por el colesterol. *The doctor put me on a strict regimen (diet) because of cholesterol.*

registrar / register, registrar   *Registrar* means "to register" except in the sense of "to register in a school." The primary meaning of *registrar* is "to search, inspect, check," as well as "to notice, note." [Note that *registrar* is not always "to inspect officially"; it can simply be "to go through or check over."] No me **registraron** el equipaje. *They didn't inspect my luggage.* Se **registró** un aumento de criminalidad. *An increase in the crime rate was noticed.* Se **registró** todos los bolsillos, pero no encontró la llave. *He went through all his pockets, but he didn't find the key.* To register also means *matricularse* (in a school), *certificar* (a letter), *presentar* (a complaint), *expresar* (an emotion), *percibir, darse cuenta de.*
carta certificada = *registered letter*
Presentó varias quejas. *He registered several complaints.* **Me matriculé** en cinco cursos. *I registered in five courses.* No **acusó** sorpresa alguna sobre mi llegada inesperada. *She registered no surprise at my unexpected arrival. Registrar* is a noun in English to refer to "the keeper of records" at a university, for example. The equivalent term in Spanish is *registrador* (m.).

regresar / regress   *Regresar* is not "to regress" but "to return, come back" and in Latin America, "to give back" *(devolver,* ue*).* Ayer **regresamos** de vacaciones. *We came back (returned) from vacation yesterday. To regress* means *retroceder.* Después de disgustarse con tantas reformas, el profesorado está **retrocediendo.** *After becoming displeased with so many reforms, the faculty is **regressing.** Regreso* means "return journey" or simply "return." *Regress* translates as *regresión, retroceso.*

regulación / regulation   *Regulación* and *regulation* share the meaning of "rule, ordinance, law." However, *regulación* is used frequently to mean "control."
regulación de precios = *price control*
regulación de nacimientos = *birth control*
regulación de un curso de agua   / *regulation* of a waterway   *Regulation* in the plural form *regulations* translates as *reglamento* or *reglamentación.* Cada empresa tiene su **reglamento.** *Every company has its own **regulations.***

regular / regular   *Regular* as an adjective means "regular" in the sense of "normal, current, proper." However, in Spanish *regular* has downgraded its original denotation to mean "average, mediocre, not bad, so-so, nothing special." Lleva una vida **regular** (ordenada). *He leads a **regular** (ordered) life.* Es completamente **regular** (normal). *It's perfectly **regular** (normal).* ¿Cómo estás? — **Regular.** *How are you? — Oh, **so-so.*** Es un libro **regular.** *It's an **average** book. Regular,* on the other hand, may have several meanings, such as *asiduo, permanente, verdadero, estupendo.*
un cliente asiduo = *a regular customer*
el personal permanente = *the regular staff*
un verdadero idiota = *a regular idiot*
un tipo estupendo = *a regular guy*

relación / relation   *Relación* means "relation" as "relationship, connection, narration." In addition, *relación* means "list, record, report, account."

tener relaciones con = *to have dealings with*
No guarda **relación** con eso. *It bears no **relation** to that.* Aquí está la **relación** de los empleados. *Here is the **list** of employees.* Hace un año que tienen **relaciones**. *They have been **going out** (dating) for a year.* **Relation**, on the other hand, also means *pariente* (m.), *parentesco.* The plural *relations* means *parientes*, as well as **relaciones** *(públicas, comerciales, políticas, diplomáticas, sexuales, etc.).* ¿Qué **parentesco** tiene contigo? *What **relation** is he to you?*

relajar, relajación / relax, relaxation *Relajar* means "to relax" and *relajación* means "relaxation" but only in a sense of "letting up, slackening, loosening." The two terms in Spanish are used primarily to describe a "loosening" or "slacking off" of morality, power, discipline, etc. Only occasionally do the terms have the meaning of "to rest, calm down, enjoy." **Relajaron** las reglas durante nuestra visita. *They **relaxed** the rules during our visit.* To *relax* and *relaxation* are used primarily with the meaning of *descansar, descanso, recreo, desahogo.* ¡Tranquilo! ¡Cálmate! = *Relax!*
aflojar la mano / *to relax one's grip* Siéntate y **descansa** (relájate). *Sit down and relax.*

relativo / relative *Relativo* is an adjective that translates as "relative" ("related one to the other, not absolute").
en lo relativo a = *in regard to*
"Frío" es un término **relativo**. *"Cold" is a relative term.* **Relative** is also a noun in English that means *pariente, parienta.* Sus **parientes** viven en Canadá. *His **relatives** live in Canada.*

relevante / relevant *Relevante* does not mean "relevant" but "outstanding, excellent." Es un escritor **relevante**. *He is an **outstanding** writer.* **Relevant** means *pertinente, relacionado a.* Esa sugerencia es **pertinente a** nuestro problema. *That suggestion is **relevant** to our problem.*

relevar / relieve *Relevar* means "to relieve" in the sense of "to replace, exonerate, take over from." Los centinelas se **relevan** cada hora. *The sentries **relieve** each other every hour.* To *relieve* has other denotations, such as *aliviar, mitigar, liberar, destituir,* and in the most positive sense, *alegrar.*
hacer sus necesidades = *to relieve oneself*
limpiar a alguien la cartera = *to relieve someone of his wallet*
La medicina me **alivió** mucho. *The medicine **relieved** me quite a bit.* Le **liberamos** de sus preocupaciones. *We **relieved** him of his worries.* La **destituyeron** de su puesto. *They **relieved** her of her post.*

relieve / relief *Relieve* (m.) is "relief" as "embossing" and also means "prominence, social standing."
poner de relieve = *to emphasize*
alto relieve / bajo relieve = *high relief / bas-relief*
Es una familia de **relieve**. *It is a family of **social standing**. Relief* has the primary meaning of *alivio, auxilio, socorro, beneficiencia.* Sentí **alivio** con la aspirina. *I felt **relief** after taking the aspirin.*

remarcar / remark *Remarcar* does not mean "to remark" but "to mark again" (that is, "re-mark"). **Remarcaron** las líneas de la calle. *They marked the lines on the street again.* To remark stands for *observar, notar, comentar.* Ella nos **advirtió** del peligro. *She remarked to us about the danger.*

remover / remove *Remover* (ue) is not "to remove" but "to stir, move (things)." Para hacer tamales **remueves** la masa. *You stir up the dough to make tamales.* To remove means *quitar, desplazar* or *despedir* (i) (people), *tachar* or *borrar* (from a list), *quitarse* (clothing), *extirpar* (in surgery). **Quítese** el abrigo, por favor. *Remove your coat, please.* ¿Quién **quitó** los libros de la mesa? *Who removed the books from the desk?* Le **extirparon** un riñón. *They removed one of his kidneys.*

rendición / rendition *Rendición* is not "rendition"; instead, it means "surrender." *Rendition* means *traducción, versión, ejecución* (in music). Una buena **traducción** nunca es fácil. *A good rendition is never easy.*

rendir / render *Rendir* (i) means "to render" in the sense of "to give" (thanks, homage, an account), and "to hand over, to give profit." In addition, *rendir* means "to surrender, to wear out, exhaust." **Rindió** homenaje al rey. *He rendered homage to the king.* Ese negocio **rinde** buen dinero. *That business renders good money (a good profit).* **Rindió** cuentas. *She accounted for her actions.* Napoleón **se rindió** en Waterloo. *Napoleon surrendered at Waterloo.* Este paseo me **ha rendido**. *This walk has worn me out.* To render also means *traducir, interpretar (arte, música).*

renovar / renovate *Renovar* (ue) means "to renovate" ("to restore, redecorate"), as well as "to renew, replace" (things or people). Acaban de **renovar** la catedral. *They just renovated the cathedral.* Es bueno **renovar** el personal de vez en cuando. *It is good to replace personnel from time to time.* **Renovación** means "renovation" ("redecoration") and "renewal."

renta / rent *Renta* means "rent" *(alquiler, m.)* as a "monthly payment for lodging, etc." *Renta,* though, also means "income" and in a broader sense, "interest, return" *(beneficio).*
renta bruta = gross income
a renta = on lease
renta vitalicia = life annuity
vivir de sus **rentas** / to live on one's private **income** *Rentable* means "profitable." Ese negocio es muy **rentable**. *That business is very profitable.* *Rentable* in English stands for *alquilable* (a house) and *arrendable* (land). Este terreno es **arrendable**. *This parcel of land is rentable.*

rentar / rent *Rentar* means "to rent" in Latin America, whereas *alquilar* is used for "to rent" in Spain. In addition, *rentar* means "to yield benefits." Se **rentan** (se alquilan) estos apartamentos. *These apartments are for rent.* To rent land translates as *arrendar (terreno).*

reparar / repair *Reparar* and *to repair* both mean "to fix, mend, renew, repay, compensate"; but *reparar en* means "to notice, pay attention."

no reparar en gastos = *to spare no expense*
No **reparé en** su presencia. *I did not notice his presence.*

reparo / repair   *Reparo* means "repair" and also "notice, warning." Frequently, *reparo* takes on a negative shade of meaning, such as "objection, fault, reservation."
poner reparos = *to raise objections*
No pongas **reparos** a la comida. *Don't look for faults with the cooking.* **Reparable** means "reparable" ("repairable"), as well as "noteworthy" *(digno de atención)*. Los daños del alma no son **reparables**. *Damages to the soul are not reparable.* **Reparación** and *reparation* both mean "redress, restoration, compensation, making up." In everyday language, *reparación* translates as "repairs" in English to refer to "fixing, mending, renewing." La iglesia necesita **reparación**. *The church needs repairs.*   taller de **reparaciones** / *repair shop*   La casa está en **reparación**. *The house is being repaired.*

réplica / replica   *Réplica* and *replica* both mean "copy, reproduction, facsimile." *Réplica* also means "(sharp) answer, retort, rejoinder."
sin réplica = *unquestionably*
No es un original sino una **réplica**. *It is not an original but a replica.*

replicar / replicate   *Replicar* does not mean "to replicate"; instead, it means "to retort, answer." **Replicó** al insulto con otro insulto. *She answered the insult with another insult. To replicate,* on the other hand, translates as *repetir* (i), *duplicar.* No se puede **duplicar** la belleza de una puesta del sol. *The beauty of a sunset cannot be replicated.*

reportar / report   *Reportar* does not mean "to report" but "to bring, get (profit, advantage, etc.)." La tienda **reporta** buenas ganancias. *The store brings in a good profit. To report* has several denotations such as *relatar, redactar (actas), presentar (un informe), declarar, hacer un reportaje, presentarse (al trabajo).* **Se presentó** ante el capitán. *He reported to the captain.* **Informó** sobre la muerte de Picasso. *She reported on the death of Picasso. Reportar* is often used to mean "to report" by Spanish speakers in the United States, but this is generally considered to be an anglicism.

reporte / report   *Reporte* (m.; *reportaje*, m.) means "report" in the sense of "news, information." un **reporte** (reportaje) sobre China / *a report on China   Report* also means *informe* (m.), *relato (relación), boletín* (m.), *reputación (fama)* and refers to a loud or explosive noise such as *disparo, cañonazo.* [In the latest dictionary of the *Real Academia, reportero* is given with the meaning of "reporter." Other dictionaries, such as Larousse, include *repórter* and *reportero* as "reporter," sometimes classifying them as an anglicisms.] Escribí dos **informes** para la clase. *I wrote two reports for the course.*   de buena **reputación** / *of good report*   Desde lejos se oían los **disparos**. *One could hear the reports from afar.*

reprobar / reprove   *Reprobar* (ue) is not "to reprove" but "to condemn, to reject (doctrine, people), to disapprove." In some countries, *reprobar* means "to fail" (an exam, a course) as the opposite of *aprobar* (ue), which is used universally for "to pass" (an exam, a course). Todo el mundo **reprueba** el narcotráfico. *Everybody **condemns** drug trafficking.* ¿**Reprueba** Ud. toda clase de música moderna? *Do you **disapprove** of all modern music?* ¡Papá, sólo **reprobé** matemáticas y química! *Dad, I only **failed** math and chemistry!* To reprove, on the other hand, translates as *censurar, criticar, reprender.* El jefe me **reprendió** sin razón. *The boss **reproved** me for no reason.*

requerimiento / requirement *Requerimiento* is not "requirement"; instead, it means "request, demand" and in legal terms, "injunction, summons." *Requirement,* however, means *requisito, condición, necesidad* (f.). Ese curso es un **requisito** para graduarse. *That course is a **requirement** for graduation.* Sus **necesidades** son modestas. *His **requirements** (needs) are simple.*

requerir / require *Requerir* (ie, i) means "to require" ("to need, call for"), as well as "to urge, beg, request." [*Requerir (a una joven)* means "to court, to woo." The classic expression is *requerir de amores.*] Se **requiere** su presencia. *Your presence is required.* **Requiero** que me acompañes. *I **urge** you to go with me.* To require is also translated as *disponer, exigir.* La ley **dispone** (exige) que lo castiguen. *The law **requires** that he be punished.* si **es preciso** / *if (it is) **required***

requisito / requisite *Requisito* means both "requirement" and "requisite," the former being much more commonly used than the latter as a noun. [*See also the entry for* **requerimiento / requirement.**]
requisito previo = *prerequisite*
Ella tiene los **requisitos** para el cargo. *She has the **qualifications** for the post. Requisite* is also an adjective, meaning *necesario, esencial.*

resentirse / resent *Resentirse* (ie, i) means "to resent" ("to feel hurt or angry about something"), as well as "to become or get weak (for example, in health), to feel the effects."
estar resentido por = *to be resentful of*
Su salud se **resintió** mucho. *His health **was getting weak**.* La casa se **resintió** con el terremoto. *The house **was weakened** by the tremor. Resentimiento (rencor,* m.) means "resentment" ("a bitter feeling of hurt"). [Although *resentirse* and *to resent* basically share the same meaning, there is an acute difference in the way the two feelings are expressed. In Spanish, *resentirse* and *resentimiento* are feelings a person keeps to himself or herself. On the other hand, *to resent* and *resentment* usually are active feelings that are expressed openly. A more accurate translation of *to resent* and *resentment* would be *ofenderse* and *ofensa*, respectively. For example, "I *resent* your words" would be translated as *Tus palabras me ofenden.*] Le guarda **resentimiento** a Juan. *He harbors **resentment** toward John.*

reserva / reserve *Reserva* means "reserve" (of character, of stock or products, of soldiers). In Spain, *reserva* also means "reservation" ("the act of booking seats, rooms, etc."), whereas *reservación* is used with this meaning in Latin America. *Reserva* is also translated as "reservation" in the sense of "objection," and it also means "reservation" as "land set aside for American Indians."
sin reserva = *without reservations*

con la mayor reserva = *with (in) the strictest confidence*
tener reservas = *to have reservations*
provisiones de reserva = *reserve supplies*
reservas en metálico = *cash reserves*
Hay muchos alimentos en **reserva.** *There is plenty of food in* **reserve.** Tengo **reservas** (reservación) en el hotel. *I have* **reservations** *at the hotel.* una **reserva** de aves / *a bird* **sanctuary**

reservación / reservation [*See entry for* **reserva / reserve.**]

resignación / resignation *Resignación* and *resignation* share the meaning of "passive acceptance, patience." Un maestro necesita **resignación.** *A teacher needs* **resignation.** *Resignation* also has the primary meaning of *renuncia* or *dimisión (de un puesto).* La **renuncia** del senador causó sorpresa. *The senator's* **resignation** *was a surprise.*

resignarse / resign *Resignarse* means "to resign (oneself), to accept passively." **Me resigné** a guardar cama. *I* **resigned myself** *to staying in bed.* To *resign,* however, principally means *renunciar* or *dimitir (de un puesto).* **Renunció** a su cargo inesperadamente. *She* **resigned** *from her post unexpectedly.*

resistir / resist *Resistir* and *to resist* share the meaning of "to withstand, endure, show strength." The reflexive form *resistirse* has the stronger meaning of "to oppose, refuse, deny." On the other hand, *resistir* may simply mean "to last, to wear well." Tú no **resistes** nada. *You* **have no stamina.** Ella **se resiste** a ayudarnos. *She* **refuses** *to help us.* El secador **resiste** todavía. *The dryer* **is holding up** *well.* Me **resisto** a creerlo. *I* **find it hard** *to believe.*

resorte / resort *Resorte* (m.) is not "resort" but "spring" (of metal). Los **resortes** de la cama están rotos. *The* **springs** *in the bed are broken. Resort* translates as *estación* or *lugar* (m.) *de recreo,* as well as *recurso* ("a going or turning to for help").
recurrir a = *to have resort to; to resort to*
el último recurso = *the last resort*
balneario = *beach (ocean, lake) resort*
Viña del Mar es un **balneario** de Chile. *Viña del Mar is an* **ocean resort** *in Chile.* un **lugar frecuentado** por mendigos / *a* **resort** *for beggars*   sin **recurrir** a la violencia / *without* **resort** *(resorting) to violence*

respeto, respecto / respect *Repeto* and *respect* both mean "regard, honor, esteem." *Respecto,* however, is not used in Spanish as a noun; it is used in adverbial expressions with the meaning of "regard, matter" and sometimes "respect."
al respecto = *on that matter*
con respecto a = *with regard to*
respecto a = *regarding*
respeto a sí mismo = *self-respect*
presentar sus **respetos** a uno / *to pay* **respects** *to someone*   con **respeto a** esa cuestión / *with regard to (with respect to) that problem*   tener **respeto** a la ley / *to have* **respect** *for the law*   **respecto a** mí / *as for me*

restar / rest *Restar* does not mean "to rest." *Restar* means "to subtract, take (away), remain, be left (over)," and figuratively, it means "to reduce, lessen." Sólo **resta** una semana de clases. *There is only one week left of classes.* La directora les **restó** la autoridad a los maestros. *The principal reduced the authority of the teachers.* To rest, on the other hand, means *descansar, reposar, apoyar, pararse* ("to stop"), *depender de.* Apoya tu cabeza en mi hombro. *Rest your head on my shoulder.* La pelota se **paró** al borde del agujero. *The golf ball rested on the rim of the hole.* **Descansa** en paz con su familia. *He is at rest with his family.*

resto / rest *Resto* means "rest" as "remaining, left." The plural *restos* stands for "remains, corpse." Sus **restos** yacen en el ataúd. *His remains lie in the coffin. Rest* also means *descanso, reposo, tranquilidad* (f.). In English, *rest* is used in a variety of expressions.
área de descanso = *rest area*
baños, servicios = *restrooms*
reposo absoluto = *complete rest*
brazo (de sillón) = *armrest*
respaldo = *backrest*
parado = *at rest*
un **descanso** de cinco minutos *a five-minute rest*

resultar / result *Resultar* means "to result" as "to turn out, come out." *Resultar* is used frequently with a variety of meanings, such as "to happen, seem, go with, match, come to, add up to, be worth." El cáncer de los pulmones **resulta** de fumar. *Lung cancer results from smoking.* Ese collar **resulta** bien con la blusa. *That necklace goes well with the blouse.* No **resulta** comer en un restaurante. *It's not worth it to eat in a restaurant.* **Resulta** que no hay dinero. *It happens that there is no money.* Ella me **resulta** simpática. *She seems nice to me.* Viene a **resultar** lo mismo. *It amounts to the same thing. Resultado* is the noun form, meaning "result." [Note that there is no such term as *"resulto"* in Spanish.]

resumir / resume *Resumir* does not mean "to resume"; instead, it means "to sum up, summarize, abridge (shorten)." **Resumió** su ponencia en la carta al editor. *He summarized his paper in his letter to the publisher. To resume* means *continuar, reanudar, reasumir* (one's duties). **Reanude** su velocidad. *Resume your speed.* **Reasumió** el mando. *He resumed command. Resumen* (m.) means "résumé" ("curriculum vitae"), as well as "summary, abstract *(sumario).* [The plural of *resumen* is *resúmenes.*]
en resumen = *in short*
Escriba un **resumen** de cincuenta palabras. *Write a fifty-word abstract.*

retaliación / retaliation *Retaliación* is listed in some dictionaries as an anglicism for "retaliation." However, technically, there is no such word in Spanish as *retaliación* and its verb form, *retaliar. Retaliation,* however, translates as *represalia, venganza, desquite* (m.).
como represalia = *in retaliation*
To retaliate translates as *vengarse, tomar represalias, desquitarse.* **Se desquitó** con un golpe. *He retaliated with a blow.*

retener / retain *Retener* (ie) is "to retain" in the sense of "to remember, keep." It also means "to hold (by force), to deduct or withhold, to restrain."
retener la lengua = *to hold one's tongue*
Retén el perro para que no se vaya. *Hold the dog so it doesn't run away.* **Retienen** 20 dólares para el sindicato. *They **withhold** 20 dollars for union dues.* To retain also translates as *guardar, conservar, contratar.* La **contrataron** para tocar el piano en la fiesta. *They **retained** her to play the piano at the party.*

reticencia / reticence *Reticencia* is not "reticence" but "insinuation, innuendo." El discurso estaba lleno de **reticencias**. *The speech was full of **insinuations**. Reticence,* on the other hand, means *reserva* and more negatively, *taciturnidad* (f.; "silence, sullenness"). *Reticente* means "insinuating, sarcastic, misleading." Sus comentarios **reticentes** me cayeron mal. *His **insinuating** remarks rubbed me the wrong way. Reticent* stands for *reservado, callado,* and *taciturno* ("gloomy, sullen"). Es una persona muy **reservada**. *She is a very **reticent** person.*

retirado / retired *Retirado* is used in parts of Latin America to mean "retired (from work)"; however, *jubilado* is the commonly used term in Spain and other Latin American countries for "retired." *Retirado* also means "secluded, remote." Está **retirada** (jubilada) desde 1988. *She has been **retired** since 1988.* una vida **retirada** / *a **secluded** life*

retirar / retire *Retirar* and *to retire* both mean "to withdraw, remove, take away, take back, retreat (militarily)," although *retirar* is used much more frequently than *to retire.* In some parts of Latin America, the reflexive form *retirarse* means "to retire" from work or from a career; in other countries, the verb *jubilarse* is used. Voy a **jubilarme** (retirarme) a los 60 años. *I am going **to retire** at 60.* Los soviéticos **retiraron** sus tropas. *The Soviets **retired** (retreated) their troops.* **Retiró** los platos de la mesa. *He **removed** the plates from the table.* **Retiré** mi dinero del banco. *I **withdrew** my money from the bank.* **Retiro** mis palabras (lo dicho). *I **take back** what I said.* To retire also translates as *acostarse* (ue) ("to go to bed"). Generalmente ellos **se acuestan** temprano. *They generally **retire** early.*

retreta, retrete / retreat *Retreta* means "retreat" ("military call, band"), and in Latin America, it refers to an "open-air concert," usually held in the plaza. Al toque de **retreta** los soldados se retiraron a dormir. *At the sound of **retreat**, the soldiers went to sleep. Retrete* (m.) means *restroom, toilet* in Spain, although nowadays, *váter* (m.) or *aseos* is used more frequently. [Note that Spaniards use the terms *retretes, váteres, servicio,* and *aseos;* whereas Latin Americans use the terms *baños, servicios,* and *lavabos.*] *Retreat* also is used for *retirada (militar),* as well as *retiro, refugio.* un **refugio** en el campo / *a country **retreat*** El mundo de los libros es su **refugio**. *The world of books is his **retreat**.*

retribución / retribution *Retribución* is not "retribution" but "remuneration, reward, payment, fee." Le dieron una buena **retribución** por salvar al niño. *They gave him a great **reward** for saving the child. Retribution* means *castigo, venganza, represalia, pena merecida.* El **castigo** debe ser justo. *Retribution should be just.*

reunión / reunion   *Reunión* is not "reunion" but "meeting, gathering, assembly." **punto de reunión** = *meeting place* Hubo **reunión** del profesorado. *There was a faculty **meeting**. Reunion* suggests a grander "meeting" than *reunión*, perhaps of war veterans or of family members. Appropriate translations would be *reunión casual, reunión anual, tertulia.*

reunir / reunite   *Reunir* is not "to reunite" but "to collect, unite, join, gather." **Reunimos** 200 dólares para los pobres. *We **collected** 200 dollars for the poor. To reunite* means *volver* (ue) *a encontrarse, reconciliarse.* La familia **vuelve a encontrarse** todos los años para Navidad. *The family **reunites** every year at Christmas time.* Después de 35 años, los hermanos **se reconciliaron**. *After 35 years, the brothers **were reunited**.*

revelar / reveal, revel   *Revelar* and *to reveal* share the meanings of "to uncover, disclose, make known." *Revelar* also means "to develop" (film, pictures). No es difícil **revelar** una foto. *It's not difficult **to develop** a photo. To revel*, on the other hand, translates as *gozar, deleitarse, divertirse* (ie, i). María **goza** bailando. *Mary **revels** in dancing.*

reversible / reversible   *Reversible* and *reversible* both mean "able to be reversed," for example, a jacket. Un suéter **reversible** no muestra la etiqueta. *A **reversible** sweater doesn't show the label. Reversible* in English is also a legal term for *revocable* (a decision). La decisión del juez es **revocable**. *The judge's decision is **reversible**.*

reverso / reverse   *Reverso* as a noun means "reverse" ("the back" of coins, medals, etc.). Una moneda tiene anverso y **reverso**. *A coin has obverse and **reverse** sides. Reverse* as a noun means *revés* (m.), *lo contrario, derrota, marcha atrás* (of a gear), *dorso* (of a page). As an adjective, *reverse* has the meaning of *opuesto, contrario.* Todo **lo contrario**. *Quite the **reverse** (opposite).* El presidente sufrió una **derrota**. *The president suffered a **reverse** (reversal). To reverse* means *invertir* (ie, i), *volver* (ue) *al revés, dar marcha atrás*, and in the legal profession, *revocar, cancelar, anular.* [Note that there is no such word in Spanish as *"reversar".*] El espejo **invierte** la imagen. *The mirror **reverses** the image.* Puse una conferencia a **cobro revertido**. *I **reversed** the (telephone) charges.* El juez **revocó** la sentencia. *The judge **reversed** the sentence.*

revertir / revert   *Revertir* (ie, i) means "to revert" in legal terminology (i.e., "to return property to its owner or heirs"). **Revirtieron** la casa a su dueño. *They **reverted** the house to its owner. To revert* also means *volver* (ue) *a* (a previous state). **Volvió a** su declaración original. *He **reverted** to his original statement. Revertible* in English translates as *reversible. Reversión* in Spanish stands for "reversion."

revisar / revise   *Revisar* and *to revise* both mean "to read over, correct, change, amend." *Revisar* is also used for "to audit (accounts), check (oil in the car, etc.)." **Revisó** (corrigió) las pruebas. *He **corrected** (revised) the quizzes.* Favor de **revisar** el aceite del carro. *Please **check** the oil in the car. To revise* is also used for *repasar* ("to review"), *enmendar* (ie). Voy a **repasar** el vocabulario. *I am going **to review** (to revise) the vocabulary.*

revisión / revision   *Revisión* means "revision" and also "audit, auditing, checking (of machines, of oil, etc.)."   No me gusta la **revisión** de impuestos. *I don't like the tax **audit**.*   *Revision* also translates as *repaso* ("review").

revolver / revolve   *Revolver* (ue) does not mean "to revolve"; instead, it means "to mix, stir up, toss, disarrange, upset (the stomach), get rough (weather, seas), turn against."   [The past participle of *revolver* is *revuelto* ("mixed up, scrambled").] **revolver la sangre** = *to make one's blood boil* **Revuelve** la masa para los tamales. *Mix the dough for the tamales.*   Su cuarto está muy **revuelto**. *His room is in disorder (a mess).*   Esto me **revuelve** el estómago. *This **upsets** my stomach.*   To revolve, on the other hand, translates as *girar, dar vueltas, repetirse* (i).   La Tierra **gira** alrededor del Sol. *The Earth revolves around the sun.*   Toda la vida familiar **se centra** en los niños. *All of family life revolves around the children.*

revulsión / revulsion   *Revulsión* is only used in medicine for a kind of "skin treatment."   *Revulsion*, on the other hand, means *asco, náuseas, repugnancia, repulsión.*   Su conducta inmoral me causa **repulsión**. *I feel **revulsion** at his immoral conduct.*

rico / rich   *Rico* and *rich* both mean "wealthy, fertile, abundant, magnificent," but the two words have other meanings, depending on the context. With food, for example, *rico* means "tasty, delicious." In Spain, *rico* is used to mean "lovely, adorable (person), gorgeous (girl)."   hacerse **rico** / *to become **rich*** ¡Qué niño más **rico**! *What an **adorable** child!*   Este pollo está bien **rico** (sabroso). *This chicken is very **tasty** (delicious).*   *Rich*, when used with food, means *fuerte, rico en calorías, opíparo* ("sumptuous").   *Rich* may also mean *generoso* (wine), *vivo* (color), and in colloquial language, *gracioso* ("funny"). Fue un banquete **opíparo**. *The banquet was **rich** (sumptuous).*

rodeo / rodeo   *Rodeo* has passed to English as *rodeo* ("show of cowboys' skills"). However, *rodeo* also means "detour, roundabout way." The plural *rodeos* is used in a figurative sense to mean "evasiveness, evading." **andar con rodeos** = *to beat about the bush* **sin rodeos** = *frankly* Hay un **rodeo** para llegar allá. *There is a **detour** on the way there.*   No me hables con **rodeos**. *Don't talk to me in circles. (Don't be evasive.)*

romance / romance   *Romance* as an adjective translates as "romance" in reference to "languages derived from Latin." The noun *romance* (m.) means "ballad" (a literary form) and "Castilian" (i.e., "Spanish language"). Los **romances** del Cid son históricos. *The **ballads** about El Cid are historical.*   *Romance* in English has several denotations such as *novela romántica* ("love story"), *amorío* or *amor(es)* (m.), *encanto* or *ensueño.*   México, tierra de **encanto** / *Mexico, land of romance*   Tuvo **amores** con varias mujeres. *He had **romances** with several women.* Las **novelas románticas** han llegado a ser un gran negocio. *Romances (romance novels) have become big business.*

ronda / round *Ronda* translates as "round" in reference to patrol, watch, mail delivery, drinks, negotiations, etc. Invito a una **ronda** más de tragos. *I'll stand one more round of drinks. Round* also means *círculo, visita* (of a doctor), *rutina, descarga, asalto* (in boxing). Cayó al suelo en el quinto **asalto**. *He fell to the floor in the fifth round.*

rondar / round *Rondar* is not "to round" but "to patrol, go on rounds, prowl" and figuratively, "threaten, court (a woman), serenade." Colloquially, *rondar* means "to be about" (years old). La gripe le está **rondando**. *The flu is threatening him.* Ella ya **ronda** los cincuenta. *She is now about fifty years old.* El policía **ronda** el vecindario. *The police officer makes the rounds of the neighborhood. To round* means *redondear, doblar* (the corner), *dar la vuelta* (an obstacle). *To round off* stands for *pulir, acabar, completar, redondear* (a number). **Completó** la tarea en dos horas. *He rounded off the work in two hours.* El total es 118, pero vamos a **redondearlo** a 120. *The total is 118, but let's round it off to 120.*

ropa / rope *Ropa* is not "rope" but "clothes, wardrobe, clothing." La **ropa** cambia con la moda. *Clothing changes with the fashions. Rope* means *soga, cuerda, ristra* (of garlic or onions), *lazo.*
ponerse al tanto = *to learn the ropes*
Los vaqueros usan **sogas** y lazos. *Cowboys use ropes and lassos.*

rostro / rostrum *Rostro* is not "rostrum" but "face, countenance."
hacer rostro a = *to face*
Tienes el **rostro** muy pálido. *Your face is very pale. Rostrum,* which is a speaker's platform, translates as *tribuna.* El orador subió a la **tribuna**. *The speaker went up to the rostrum.*

rudo / rude *Rudo* and *rude* share the meaning of "rustic, primitive, unrefined, uncultured, ignorant, unlearned." Generally, in conversation, *rudo* is used much more frequently than *rude* to express these meanings. *Rudo,* however, also means "rough, coarse, hard, difficult." Había una mesa **ruda** en el comedor. *There was a rustic (rude) table in the dining room.* Es un campesino pobre y **rudo**. *He is a poor, ignorant peasant.* Ese trabajo es muy **rudo**. *That is very hard work. Rude,* on the other hand, is used more frequently to mean *grosero, descortés, mal educado,* and sometimes expresses the negative connotation of *indecente.* Es **mal educado** apuntar con el dedo. *It's rude to point with your finger.* No seas **descortés** (mal educado). *Don't be rude.* No digas **groserías**. *Don't make rude remarks.*

rumor / rumor *Rumor* (m.) means "rumor" as "gossip, hearsay, unfounded story," as well as "murmur, soft voice, rustle, whisper (of the wind, etc.)." según los **rumores** / *rumor has it that* el **rumor** de las aguas del arroyo / *the murmur of the water in the stream* Un simple **rumor** puede hacer bajar la bolsa de valores de Nueva York. *A simple rumor can cause the New York stock market to go down.*

S

sábado / sabbath *Sábado* is the Jewish "Sabbath" and also means "Saturday."
[Note that the Christian *Sabbath* is translated as *domingo* ("Sunday").] **Sábado** significa
un día de descanso y de adoración. *The **Sabbath** means a day of rest and worship.*
Saldremos el **sábado.** *We are leaving on **Saturday.***

sacar / sack *Sacar* is not "to sack"; instead, it means "to take out, draw, pull
out, get (grades, money, rewards), take off (clothes, hat), find (faults, solutions),
stick out (tongue, chest, etc.)."
sacar la lotería = *to win the lottery*
sacar de quicio (de sus casillas) = *to exasperate*
Sacó su dinero del banco. *She **withdrew** her money from the bank.* **Sacó** la pistola
y disparó al ladrón. *He **drew** his gun and shot the thief.* **Sacó** del olvido al poeta.
*He **rescued** the poet from oblivion.* To sack means *saquear, ensacar* ("to put into
a sack"), *atrapar* (to tackle a quarterback in football).
acostarse, dormirse = *to sack out*
Los soldados **saquearon** la ciudad. *The soldiers **sacked** the city.*

saco / sack *Saco* means "sack" ("bag," *costal,* m.) and also "jacket" in Latin
America. *Saco* is also used in many expressions.
saco de dormir = *sleeping bag*
echar en saco roto = *to forget*
saco de mentiras = *pack of lies*
saco roto (manirroto) = *spendthrift*
El trigo se vende en **sacos** grandes. *Wheat is sold in large **sacks.*** Me gusta tu **saco**
nuevo. *I like your new **jacket.*** Sack means *saqueo* ("capture and plunder") and
in colloquial English it is used to refer to *cama, despido* (from a job), and *jerez*
(m.; sherry). El **saqueo** de Roma fue en 1527. *The **sack** (sacking) of Rome was
in 1527.* Caeré muerto en la **cama** en seguida. *I am going to hit the **sack** right
away.*

sal / salt *Sal* (f.) means "salt," as well as "wit, charm" *(encanto).*
sal de gema (bola) = *rock salt*
sal de mesa = *table salt*
sal de la tierra = *salt of the earth*
El comediante tiene mucha **sal.** *The comedian has quite a **wit.*** No creas en todo
eso. *Take it with a grain of **salt.*** *Salado* means "salty, salted," as well as "witty,
spirited, cute, lovely." In Cuba, *salado* means "unlucky." Hay lagos de agua
salada. *There are lakes with **salty** water.* La abuelita sabe contar unos chistes bien
salados. *Grandmother knows how to tell some **spirited** jokes.*

salario / salary *Salario* means "salary" in colloquial speech, with no distinction
between rich and poor, professionals and laborers. In the business world, there
is an acute difference between *salario,* meaning "wages," and *sueldo,* meaning

"salary, income (of professional workers)."
salario de hambre = *starvation wages*
salario básico = *minimum wage*
Los obreros trabajan mucho para ganar su **salario** modesto. *Laborers work hard to earn their humble wages. Salary,* on the other hand, translates as *sueldo* ("money received or paid for clerical or professional work").
estar a sueldo = *to be on salary*
Los profesionales reciben un **sueldo;** no se les paga por hora. *Professionals receive a salary; they are not paid by the hour.*

salón / salon, saloon *Salón* (m.) shares with *salon* the meaning of "a stylish shop, a hall for exhibition." *Salón* also means "lounge, ballroom, assembly room." En este **salón** caben cinco mil personas. *Five thousand people can fit into this hall (salon). Saloon,* however, means *cantina, taberna, bar.* Las **cantinas** eran famosas en el Oeste. *Saloons were famous in the old West.*

saludar / salute *Saludar* means "to salute" (military style) and it also means "to greet, say hello, give regards, acknowledge (people)." **Saludamos** al director del banco. *We greeted the bank manager.* No me **saluda** nunca por la calle. *He never acknowledges me in the street.* **Salúdame** a tu esposa. *Give my best (regards) to your wife.*

saludo / salute *Saludo,* similarly, means "salute" (in military style), as well as "greeting, regards, best wishes." [When guns are discharged as a salute, the word *salva* is used in Spanish and the terms *salute, volley,* and *salvo* are used in English (for example, "a 21-gun *salute*").] Salvas son una clase de **saludo** militar. *Salvos are a type of military salute.* una **salva** de veintiún cañonazos / *a twenty-one gun salute (salvo)* Reciba un atento **saludo** de, / *Yours truly, / Sincerely yours,*

salutación / salutation *Salutación* and *salutation* both refer to the greeting in a business or friendly letter, as well as to a greeting in general. *Salutación* is a formal expression of *saludo* (in a letter, in an official capacity, in daily life). *Salutación* is also used to mean "salutation" in a religious sense. [Usually, *encabezamiento* is the term used to mean "salutation" as the beginning part of a letter.] la **salutación** angélica (Ave María) / *the angelic salutation (Hail Mary)*

salvaje / salvage *Salvaje* does not mean "salvage"; rather, as an adjective, it means "savage, wild, uncivilized, primitive, brutal." In colloquial modern Spanish, *salvaje* is used to mean "fantastic, terrific." La selva tiene animales **salvajes.** *The jungle is full of wild animals.* El boxeador le dio un golpe **salvaje.** *The boxer gave him a brutal blow.* La fiesta estuvo **salvaje.** *The party was fantastic. Salvage* is a noun, meaning *salvamento, rescate* (m.), *objetos salvados* ("salvaged things"). El **salvamento** del barco no fue fácil. *The salvage of the ship was not easy. To salvage* translates as *salvar* ("to rescue, save" from shipwreck, fire, flood, etc.).

salvo / salvo *Salvo* in Spanish is not the noun for "salvo"; it is an adjective, meaning "safe, saved," and an adverb, meaning "except (for), save."
a salvo (ileso) = *safe and sound*

dejar a salvo = *to spare (safeguard)*
salvo que (a no ser que) = *unless*
salvoconducto = *safe-conduct*
El muchachito está sano y **salvo**. *The little boy is **safe** and sound.* Todos vinieron **salvo** José. *Everyone came, **except** Joe.* **salvo** el parecer de usted / **unless** I hear *to the contrary* *Salvo* in English refers to a volley of gunfire or a military salute by discharging guns. The Spanish equivalent is *salva*. [*See also the entry for* **saludar / salute.**]

sanguina / sanguine *Sanguina* only applies to a variety of orange: *naranja sanguina,* which can be translated as "blood orange." *Sanguine* means *optimista, entusiasta, confiado* and also refers to *rojo* ("bloodred"). Admiro su ánimo **optimista**. *I am amazed by his **sanguine** spirit.* *Sanguíneo* and *sanguineous* both mean "blood, of the blood, the color of blood." *Sanguíneo* is used more frequently than its cognate, with *blood* the adjective preferred over *sanguineous*.
vaso sanguíneo = *blood vessel*
Es una infección **sanguínea**. *It is a **blood** (sanguineous) infection.*

sanidad / sanity *Sanidad* (f.) does not mean "sanity"; instead, it means "health *(salud,* f.), sanitation." La **sanidad** pública es importante. *Public **health** is important.* Tenemos problemas de **sanidad** en esta ciudad. *In this city we have **sanitation** problems.* *Sanity,* on the other hand, means *cordura, sensatez* (f.), *juicio.*
recobrar el juicio = *to regain one's sanity*

sano / sane *Sano* does not mean "sane"; rather, it means "healthy, sound, intact, wholesome."
comida sana = *wholesome food, good food*
sano y salvo = *safe and sound*
Una persona **sana** no necesita remedios. *A **healthy** person does not need medicine.* Tiene principios **sanos**. *He has **sound** principles.* No quedó un plato **sano**. *There wasn't a plate left **intact**. Sane* means *cuerdo, sensato, de juicio sano* ("of sound judgment").
estar en sus cabales = *to be sane*
Una persona **cuerda** no hace eso. *A **sane** person does not do that.*

santuario / sanctuary *Santuario* and *sanctuary* share the meaning of "shrine, temple." In Latin America, *santuario* can also mean "buried treasure." El **santuario** de Lurdes es famoso. *The **sanctuary** of Lourdes is famous. Sanctuary* also means *refugio, asilo* (for persons), *reserva* (for animals), and *sagrario* (the tabernacle or high altar where the host is kept).
buscar asilo en, acogerse a = *to seek sanctuary in*

secretar / secrete *Secretar* and *to secrete* share the scientific meaning of "to form and release a liquid or secretion." La herida **secreta** un líquido feo. *The wound is **secreting** a disgusting fluid. To secrete* has the equally important meaning of *esconder, ocultar, encubrir*. **Escondimos** el microfilm donde nadie lo podría hallar. *We **secreted** the microfilm where no one could find it.*

secular / secular *Secular* and *secular* both mean "relating to worldly things, not religious, layman *(seglar).*" However, *secular* also means "century-old, age-old, ancient." El obispo también tiene deberes **seculares.** *The bishop also has secular duties.* escuela **laica** (seglar) / *secular school* estas encinas **seculares** / *these century-old live oak trees Secular* in English can have the negative meaning of *mundano, profano.* Vive una vida muy **mundana.** *She leads a very secular life.*

seguramente / securely *Seguramente* does not mean "securely." *Seguramente* has a wide range of meanings: "probably, maybe, surely, for sure, very likely." The most common usage nowadays is with the meaning of "probably." **Seguramente** no lloverá mañana. *It probably won't rain tomorrow. Securely,* translates as *firmemente, fijamente, sin riesgo, tranquilamente.* El rehén esta atado **firmemente** a la silla. *The hostage is tied securely to the chair.*

seguridad / security *Seguridad* (f.) and *security* share the meaning of "safety." In addition, *seguridad* means "certainty."
con toda seguridad = *with complete certainty*
Seguro (Seguridad) Social = *Social Security*
Hemos tomado medidas de **seguridad.** *We have taken security measures. Security* is also translated as *garantía, fianza.* In the business world, the plural *securities* means *valores* (m.), *títulos.*
bajo fianza = *on security*
Los **valores** (títulos) tiene altibajos. *Securities have ups and downs.*

seguro / secure *Seguro* means "secure" in the sense of "safe, free from care, fear, or anxiety." However, *seguro* also means "sure, certain." Mi dinero está tan **seguro** en el colchón como en el banco. *My money is as safe (secure) in my mattress as it is in the bank.* Estoy **seguro** de que él llegó. *I am sure (certain) he arrived.*

semblanza / semblance *Semblanza* means "portrait, biographical sketch"; it does not mean "semblance." Escribió una **semblanza** del poeta. *She wrote a biographical sketch of the poet. Semblance* translates as *apariencia, aspecto, imagen* (f.); and sometimes it has the negative connotation of *fingimiento* ("pretense, falseness"). Tenía **apariencia** de un condenado. *He had the semblance of a condemned man.*

sensibilidad / sensibility *Sensibilidad* (f.) means "sensibility" ("the ability to feel"), as well as "sensitivity" ("perception through the senses"). No tiene **sensibilidad** en las encías. *He has no sensitivity (feeling) in his gums.* El artista muestra una gran **sensibilidad** en este cuadro. *The artist shows great sensibility in this painting. Sensibility* is translated as *precisión* when it applies to instruments, machines, etc. The plural *sensibilities* means *susceptibilidad* (f.) as well as *sentimientos delicados.* Jamás se dio cuenta de los **sentimientos delicados** de su hijo. *He was never aware of his son's sensibilities.*

sensible / sensible *Sensible* does not mean "sensible." *Sensible* means "sensitive, feeling, sentient, noticeable, deplorable, lamentable, tender, sore." El dedo herido está muy **sensible.** *My hurt finger is very sore.* María es una mujer **sensible.** *Mary is sensitive woman.* **sensible** al tacto / *tender to the touch Sensible,* on the other hand, means *cuerdo, sensato, razonable, consciente, cómodo* (clothes, shoes). Tiene ideas **sensatas**. *She has **sensible** ideas.* Estoy **consciente** de la honra que me hace. *I am **sensible** (conscious) of the honor you do me.*

sensitivo / sensitive *Sensitivo* and *sensitive* both mean "feeling, sentient, of the senses." El delfín es un ser **sensitivo**. *The dolphin is a **sentient** being. Sensitive* also stands for *sensible, susceptible, delicado,* and in the business world, *inestable.* Es un bebé **sensible** (delicado); llora por nada. *He is a **sensitive** baby; he cries for no reason.* Es un mercado muy **inestable**. *It is a very **sensitive** market.*

sentencia / sentence *Sentencia* and *sentence* both refer to "a decision or ruling, as in a court of law." In addition, *sentencia* is also used to mean "saying, maxim" *(máxima).*
condena perpetua = *life sentence*
El juez pronunció la **sentencia**. *The judge passed **sentence**.* La **sentencia** (pena) de muerte fue abolida en España después de Franco. *The death **sentence** was abolished in Spain after Franco's death. Sentence* is used in grammar and translates as *oración.* Esa **oración** no está muy clara. *That **sentence** is not very clear.*

sentimiento / sentiment *Sentimiento* is "sentiment" ("feeling"), as well as "regret, condolences, sorrow, sense."
sentimiento del honor = *sense of honor*
Ese poema expresa un **sentimiento** bello. *That poem expresses a beautiful **sentiment**.* Me hirió los **sentimientos**. *He hurt my **feelings**.* Le acompaño en el **sentimiento**. *I share in your **sorrow**. Sentiment* also means *opinión, parecer* (m.), and in a negative sense, *sensiblería, sentimentalismo.* Ésa es mi **opinión** (parecer). *Those are my **sentiments**.* Esas nociones son **sensiblerías** románticas. *Those notions are romantic **sentiments**.*

señalar / signal *Señalar* is not "to signal" but "to mark, point out, set or fix (dates, prices), put up signs, appoint, designate." The reflexive form *señalarse* means "to stand out." Como **señalé** previamente,... *As I **pointed out** before,...* Bolívar **se señaló** por su valentía. *Bolívar **stood out** because of his valor. To signal* means *dar la señal, indicar, avisar.* Les **dio la señal** de pararse. *He **signaled** them to stop. Señal* (f.) and *signal* both mean "sign" (for traffic, railway crossings, etc.).
señales de socorro = *distress signals*
señal de ocupado (teléfono) / *busy **signal** (telephone)*

sereno / serene *Sereno,* as an adjective, means "serene" ("calm"). As a noun, *sereno* means "cool night air, night watchman." In colloquial Spanish, *sereno* is an adjective for "sober." [Traditionally in Spain, the *sereno* was a neighborhood watchman who guarded the streets and houses at night. He had keys to all the doors and opened them for people who returned late at night. Although this tradition has virtually disappeared, some communities have restored it in response to increasing incidents of crime.]
al sereno = *in the open air*
ponerse sereno = *to sober up*
Me encanta sentir las brisas **serenas** del anochecer. *I love to feel the **calm** evening breezes.* ¡Cuidado con el **sereno** de la noche! *Be careful in the cool night **air**!* Estuvo **serena** ante las noticias graves. *She was **serene** in light of the grave news.*

serio / serious   *Serio* and *serious* share the basic meanings of "grave, sincere, earnest, important"; however, the usage is not always parallel in the two languages. *Serio* also means "reliable, dependable (person), subdued (color), formal (suit)."
en serio = *seriously, really*
Lo dijo en tono **serio**. *He said it in a **serious** tone of voice.* Ella es una alumna **seria**. *She is an **earnest** (serious) student.* Es un dependiente **serio**. *He is a reliable* employee. Llevó un traje **serio** al banquete. *He wore a **formal** suit to the banquet.* *Seriedad* (f.) means "seriousness" and "reliability, dependability, honesty." ¡Qué **poca seriedad** tienes! *How **frivolous** you are!*

servicio / service   *Servicio* and *service* share most of the same denotations. *Servicio,* however, also means "servants, employees, servant's room, service charge," and in America, "toilet."
servicio permanente = *24-hour service*
en acto de servicio = *(to die) in action*
servicio a domicilio = *home-delivery service*
servicio de información = *intelligence service*
incluido el servicio = *service charge included*
El **servicio** no fuma en público. *The **employees** don't smoke in public. Service* also means *saque* (m.) in tennis, *revisión* (of a car, machine, etc.), *utilidad* (f.) or *uso* (person, machine).
vía de acceso = *service road*

servir / serve   *Servir* (i) and *to serve* have many denotations in common, such as "to help, aid, wait on, be used by," and so on. Nevertheless, there are discrepancies. *Servir* also means "to work (as a servant), to be used for, to work or function (a machine), to be useful for."
para servir a usted = *at your service*
servirse de = *to use*
¿En qué puedo **servir**le? *How may I **serve** you?/May I **help** you?* El cuchillo **sirve** para cortar carne. *The knife **is used** to cut meat.* Esta máquina no **sirve**. *This machine doesn't **work**.* ¿Para qué **sirve** llorar? *What **is the use** of crying? To serve* also means *cumplir (una condena), despachar* (in a store or shop), *ejercer* or *desempeñar* (a job).
trabajar de = *to serve as*
Está **cumpliendo** 20 años de cárcel. *He is **serving** 20 years in prison.* si la memoria **no me falla** / *if memory **serves** me right*

signatura / signature   *Signatura* means "signature" in music, typography, and printing. However, in everyday language, *signatura* means "mark, stamp, catalog number." La **signatura** del libro es PC-8000. *The **catalog number** of the book is PC-8000. Signature* is also a noun meaning *firma.* La **firma** se pone al final de la carta. *The **signature** goes at the end of the letter.*

significación / signification, significance   *Significación* means "signification" and "significance" in the figurative sense of "importance," but the ordinary meaning of *significación* is "meaning." La **significación** de *table* es "mesa". *The* *meaning* of "*table*" *is* mesa. Es un hecho de gran **significación**. *It is a fact of great* **signification** *(significance)*. *Signification* primarily means *notificación, aviso*. *Significance* primarily means *importancia, secuencia*. Its adjective form, *significant,* translates as *mucho, significativo, importante*. Nunca aprecié la **importancia** de la reunión. *I never appreciated the* **significance** *of the meeting.* dar **mucho** énfasis a / *to place* **significant** *emphasis on*

signo / sign *Signo* and *sign* both mean "indication, token, symbol." *Signo* also means "mark" in reference to punctuation.
signo de interrogación = *question mark*
El humo es un **signo** de fuego. *Smoke is a* **sign** *of fire. Sign* has many other meanings, such as *gesto* or *ademán, huella* or *rastro, letrero* or *rótulo, aviso,* (m.) *señal* (f.), *cartel* (m.), and *prueba* or *muestra*. No da **señales** de vida. *He doesn't show any* **signs** *of life.* No dejaron **rastros** de su paso. *They left no* **sign** *of their passage.* El **letrero** dice "No fumar". *The* **sign** *says "No smoking."* Da **muestras** de debilidad. *She is showing* **signs** *of weakness.* Como **prueba** de buena fe, te pago por adelantado. *As a* **sign** *of good faith, I'll pay you in advance.*

silencioso / silent *Silencioso* and *silent* both mean "noiseless, making no sound, still, quiet." Los carros nuevos son **silenciosos**. *New cars are* **silent** *(quiet). Silent* also means *callado, mudo* (not in reference to people but to describe movies, letters).
socio comanditario = *silent partner*
Ella es una persona seria y **callada**. *She is a serious,* **silent** *person.* Me gustan las películas **mudas**. *I like* **silent** *movies. Silencio* and *silence* are the same in all contexts. *Silencio* in music means "rest."
El silencio es oro. = *Silence is golden.*
silencio sepulcral = *deadly silence*
Impuso **silencio** al público. *He called for* **silence** *from the audience. Silenciar* is "to silence" ("to be silent, quiet, still") and "to hush up."
¡Cállate! = *Be silent! Hush up!*

simpatía / sympathy *Simpatía* does not mean "sympathy." *Simpatía* means "charm, liking, attraction, friendliness, fondness." Le tengo una gran **simpatía**. *I have a great* **liking** *(fondness) for him. Sympathy* means *pésame* (m.) or *condolencia, comprensión, afinidad* (f.), *lástima, compasión*.
por solidaridad = *in sympathy* (with a strike)
Ella mostró **comprensión** ese día. *She showed* **sympathy** *that day.* Subieron los precios **a la par**. *Prices rose* **in sympathy.** Le ofrecí mi **pésame** sincero. *I gave him my sincere* **sympathy.** No tengo **compasión** por un borracho. *I have no* **sympathy** *for a drunk.*

simpático / sympathetic *Simpático* means "likeable, nice, friendly, pleasant." Fue muy **simpático** conmigo. *He was very* **nice** *to me. Sympathetic,* however, means *compasivo, comprensivo* ("understanding"), *favorable, dispuesto*. Está **dispuesto** a ayudarnos. *He is* **sympathetic** *toward helping us.*

simpatizar / sympathize *Simpatizar (con)* means "to like, be friendly, hit it off." **Simpatizaron** en seguida. *They* **hit it off** *at once. To sympathize* means *comprender,* *compartir, compadecerse, condolerse.* **Compartimos** las penas con la familia. *We* **sympathize** *with the family.*

simple / simple *Simple* and *simple* both mean "uncomplicated, easy, simple-minded." When *simple* is placed before a noun, it means "just, mere, sheer, single (one)." Perdió mi libro por **simple** descuido. *He lost my book out of* **sheer** *carelessness.* Es un **simple** soldado. *He is* **just** *a soldier.* una **simple** capa de pintura / *a* **single** *coat of paint* *Simple* in English can also mean *sencillo, natural, inocente, ingenuo.*
belleza natural = *simple beauty*
Es una profesora **sencilla.** *She is a* **simple** *professor.*

simplicidad / simplicity *Simplicidad* (f.) means "candor, simpleness, frankness." Habló con toda **simplicidad.** *He spoke with total* **frankness.** *Simplicity* means *sencillez* (f.), *llaneza, simpleza, ingenuidad* (f.), *tontería.* Recuerdo sus **simplezas** (tonterías). *I recall his* **simplicity** *(foolishness).*

sindicato / syndicate *Sindicato* means "(labor) union." El **sindicato** ayuda al empleado. *The* **union** *helps the employee.* *Syndicate* applies to a "chain of newspapers" and "news agency," which are translated as *consorcio periodístico, agencia de prensa. Syndicate* has downgraded its meaning to refer to "an association of racketeers in charge of organized crime." Possible translations might include *chantaje sistematizado, crimen organizado.* Los periodistas pertenecen a un **consorcio.** *The news reporters belong to a* **syndicate.**

situación / situation *Situación* means "situation" ("place, location, state, condition"). Está en una **situación** embarazosa. *He is in an embarrassing* **situation.** Tiene una **situación** acomodada. *He is in a sound financial* **position.** Ella siempre es dueña de la **situación.** *She is always in control of the* **situation.** *Situation* also means *colocación* (a paid occupation), *oferta* (of work). **solicitudes** de trabajo / **situations** *wanted*

sobrenombre / surname *Sobrenombre* (m.) and *surname* share the meaning of "by-name, a secondary name." However, *sobrenombre* also means "nickname." Miguel de Cervantes tiene el **sobrenombre** (apodo) de *"El manco de Lepanto". Miguel de Cervantes has the* **nickname** *of "the One-Handed Man of Lepanto." Surname,* however, basically means *apellido* ("last name"). Los hispanos tienen dos **apellidos:** el del padre y el de la madre. *Hispanic people have two* **surnames:** *that of the father and that of the mother.*

socializar / socialize *Socializar* and *to socialize* share the meaning of "to nationalize." El gobierno **socializó** los bancos. *The government* **nationalized** *the banks. To socialize* nowadays has the meaning of "to take part in social activity," which in Spanish is *llevar una vida social, alternar* ("to mix, associate with people"). Juan **lleva una vida social** activa. *John* **is** *always* **socializing.**

sofisticación / sophistication *Sofisticación* has been accepted by most dictionaries with the meaning of "sophistication"; however, its original meaning (and only meaning, according to the *Real Academia*) is "falsification, adulteration."

Sophistication has the traditional meaning of *refinamiento, exoticismo, perfección,* and in a pejorative sense, *afectación.* La gente del campo no tiene el **refinamiento** de la ciudad. *Country folk lack the **sophistication** of the city.*

sofisticado / sophisticated *Sofisticado* means "sophisticated" in everyday language and means "falsified, adulterated" in its original meaning. Sus ideas **sofisticadas** fracasaron. *His **adulterated** ideas failed to work. Sophisticated* generally means *refinado, exótico, artificial* and applies to persons, as well as to ways of life, dressing, and speaking. Me parece una moda muy **exótica.** *I think it's a very **sophisticated** fashion.*

sofocar / suffocate *Sofocar,* along with its synonyms *ahogarse* and *asfixiarse,* means "to suffocate" (for lack of air). However, *sofocar* also means "to extinguish (a fire), to put down (a riot, a revolution), to stop (an epidemic)." The reflexive *sofocarse* is used in the figurative sense of "to get upset." El criminal **sofocó** (asfixió) a la víctima. *The criminal **suffocated** the victim.* Los bomberos **sofocaron** el incendio. *The fire fighters **extinguished** the fire.* ¡No **te sofoques** por tan poca cosa! *Don't **get upset** over such a little thing! Sofocado* means "suffocated, out of breath, extinguished, stopped, upset." Está **sofocada** de tanto correr. *She is **out of breath** from running so much.*

solar / solar *Solar* means "solar" ("of the sun") as an adjective. As a noun, *solar* (m.) means "lot, plot of land." *Solar (linaje,* m.*)* used to mean "lineage, family line"; from this meaning, came the expression *casa solariega,* which is still part of everyday speech. La energía **solar** es importante. *Solar energy is important.* se venden **solares** espaciosos / *large **lots** for sale* Acaban de comprar un **solar** cerca de la playa. *They just bought a **plot of land** near the beach.* Mi padre heredó la **casa solariega.** *My father inherited the **ancestral home.***

solicitar / solicit *Solicitar* means "to solicit" ("to ask for, request formally") and "to apply" (for a job)." El gobierno **solicitó** la ayuda de la Cruz Roja. *The government **solicited** help from the Red Cross.* Se **solicita** la honra de su presencia. *The honor of your presence is **requested.** To solicit,* however, has downgraded its meaning to *abordar, importunar* (as a prostitute). *Solicitud* (f.) means "solicitude" in the sense of "care, concern, attention" *(cuidado, afán,* m.*).* However, *solicitud* is a common word for "application, request (for jobs, checks, donations)." Mandé una **solicitud** para ese trabajo. *I sent in an **application** for that job. Solicitor* (especially in Great Britain) translates as *agente* (m.), *abogado, procurador* (m.; in court).

solícito / solicitous *Solícito* means "solicitous" in the sense of "obliging, worried, showing care or concern" *(diligente).* Es una enfermera muy **solícita.** *She is a very **solicitous** nurse. Solicitous* in some contexts has changed its meaning to *inquieto, molesto* ("anxious, eager"). Está **molesto** por ganarse amigas. *He is **solicitous** about making girlfriends.*

solitario / solitary, solitaire *Solitario* means "solitary" ("lonely, deserted, remote") as an adjective. As a noun, *solitario* means "hermit" and "solitaire" (a single setting of a gem, such as a diamond; a card game). The feminine form,

solitaria, is an illness called "tapeworm," as well as a female "recluse" or "hermit." Synonyms for *solitario* include *apartado, desierto, desamparado.*
estar incomunicado = *to be in solitary (confinement)*
El anillo tiene un diamante **solitario.** *The ring has a **solitaire** diamond.*

solo, sola / sole, solo   *Solo* and *solo* both refer to a musical selection or performance for or by a single artist. [The performer is *solista* and soloist, respectively.] un **solo** de tambor   /   *a drum **solo*** Plácido Domingo es buen **solista** de ópera. *Plácido Domingo is a good opera **soloist.** Solo* is also used in English to refer to a flight with one pilot: *"solo* flight." Hoy será la primera vez que vuelo **solo.** *Today is my first **solo** flight (the first time I fly **solo**). Sola* and *solo* are both adjectives that mean "sole," as well as "alone, lonely, single, unique." Ella **sola** sobrevivía. *She was the **sole** survivor.* Juan tiene una **sola** preocupación. *John has a **single** worry.*

soluble / soluble   *Soluble* means both "soluble" ("dissolvable") and "solvable" ("able to be solved"). El azúcar es **soluble** en agua. *Sugar is **soluble** in water.* Ese problema es **soluble.** *That problem is **solvable.***

someter / submit   *Someter* does not mean "to submit"; instead, it means "to subdue, conquer, master (passions)." The reflexive *someterse* stands for "to surrender, yield, undergo."
someterse a tratamiento = *to undergo treatment*
César nunca **sometió** a los vascos. *Caesar never **conquered** the Basques.* Se **sometió** a la opinión de la mayoría. *She **yielded** (bowed) to the opinion of the majority.* Se **sometió** a una operación. *He **underwent** an operation. To submit,* on the other hand, means *presentar* (reports, papers, projects, budgets, propositions, etc.), *proponer, expresar opinión.* Ella **propuso** un cambio de horario. *She **submitted** a change in schedule.*

soportar / support   *Soportar* is not "to support" but "to bear, endure, put up with, stand." No pudo **soportar** la soledad. *He couldn't **endure** the solitude.* **Soporté** su estupidez durante años. *I **put up with** his stupidity for years. To support* means *apoyar* or *respaldar* (ideas, people), *mantener* (ie), *sostener* (ie), *sustentar, corroborar* (suspicions). El sindicato **respalda** al candidato republicano. *The union **supports** the Republican candidate.* La secretaria **mantiene** a su familia. *The secretary **supports** her family. Soporte* (m.; synonyms: *apoyo, sostén* [m.], *pilar* [m.], *sustento*) shares most of the denotations of *support* (synonyms: *pillar, bracket, rest, help*).

sortear / sort   *Sortear* is not "to sort"; instead, it means "to draw or cast lots for, to raffle." Figuratively, it means "to avoid, evade, get around." [*See also the entry for* **suerte / sort.**] La parroquia **sortea** un carro en la fiesta. *The parish is **raffling** off a car at the party.* **Sortea** el problema sin resolverlo. *He **gets around** the problem without solving it. To sort* means *ordenar, clasificar, entresacar, seleccionar.* Ella **clasifica** las solicitudes antes de leerlas. *She **sorts** the applications before reading them.*

suave / suave *Suave* does not mean "suave"; rather, *suave* means "gentle, soft (to touch), smooth, even, mild"; in modern Mexico, *suave* stands for "fantastic, terrific." El terciopelo es muy **suave**. *Velvet is very soft.* más **suave** que un guante / *as meek as a lamb; as soft (smooth) as a kidskin glove* ¡Qué **suave** estuvo la fiesta! *The party was fantastic! Suave,* on the other hand, means *afable, amable, fino, diplomático,* and in the worst sense of the word *zalamero* ("cajoling"). Tienes modales **finos**. *You have suave manners.*

suburbio / suburb *Suburbio* and *suburb* share the idea of "on the outskirts"; however *suburbio* has the connotation of "slums, poor neighborhood *(barrio muy pobre).*" [In most big cities of Spain and Latin America, the poor from the rural areas have come to the city with the hope of finding a job. Very often they build shacks on the outskirts of the city and live in very poor conditions, many times without running water or electricity. This phenomenon has given the word *suburbio* its negative connotation.] Muchos pobres viven en los **suburbios**. *Many of the poor live in the slums. Suburb(s)* and *suburbia* in English have a positive connotation in the United States because they refer to an area free from the problems of a large city (for example, better school systems, accessible services, etc.). Although *suburbios* is an adequate translation, other terms may be used such as *las afueras, barrios exteriores.* Los **suburbios** de San Diego son ricos. *The suburbs of San Diego are wealthy.*

suceder / succeed *Suceder* only shares the meaning of "to follow" with the verb *to succeed.* The basic denotation of *suceder* is "to happen, occur, give place to." Juan **sucedió** a su padre en el negocio. *John succeeded his father in the business.* El accidente **sucedió** en la Calle Ocho. *The accident happened on Eighth Street.* ¿Qué **sucede**? *What is the matter? To succeed* has the basic meaning of *tener* (ie) *éxito, triunfar, salir bien.* Afortunadamente **logré** comprar la casa. *Fortunately, I succeeded in buying the house. Sucesión* and *succession* share all their meanings.

suceso / success *Suceso* is not "success" but "event, happening, occurrence, incident." Fue un **suceso** notable en el país. *It was an important event in the country. Success* translates as *éxito, triunfo, logro. Successful* is translated as *exitoso* in many dictionaries, but the *Real Academia* only recognizes *de éxito, afortunado, próspero, logrado.* Tiene un negocio **exitoso (próspero)**. *He has a successful business.*

suerte / sort *Suerte* (f.) means "sort" as "kind, class, type." However, the principal meanings of *suerte* are "luck, fate, destiny, lot."
echar suertes = *to draw lots*
de suerte que = *so that*
La florista vende toda **suerte** (clase) de flores. *The florist sells all sorts of flowers.*

suficiente / sufficient *Suficiente* means "sufficient" ("enough") and sometimes is used to mean "self-important, complacent, smug *(engreído).*" Tengo lo **suficiente** para vivir. *I have enough to live on.* Se siente muy **suficiente**. *He feels very complacent. Suficiencia* and *sufficiency* both mean "an adequate amount, capability, competence." In a figurative sense, *suficiencia* also means "conceit, self-importance, being full of oneself, complacency." Hay **suficiencia** de comida en este país. *There is a sufficiency of food in this country.* Ella tiene aire de **suficiencia**. *She looks conceited (smug).*

sufragio / suffrage *Sufragio* and *suffrage* both mean "vote, the right to vote," but *sufragio* also means "help, aid."
sufragio universal = *universal suffrage*
recuento de **sufragios** *counting of the votes* **Sufragar** is the verb form, meaning "to pay, defray, finance." **Sufragó** los gastos de sus estudios. *He paid the cost of his schooling.*

sugestión / suggestion *Sugestión* is rarely used nowadays to mean "suggestion"; rather, it means "autosuggestion, hypnotic power." *Suggestion,* on the other hand, means *sugerencia, indicación, insinuación* ("hint"). Me hizo **sugerencias** útiles para el libro. *He gave me some useful suggestions for the book.*

sugestionar / suggest *Sugestionar* is not "to suggest"; instead, it means "to influence (people), to have a hypnotic power (over people), to convince oneself." El poeta **se sugestionó** de que tenía que morir un jueves en París, y así sucedió. *The poet convinced himself that he had to die in Paris on a Thursday, and so he did.* To suggest means *sugerir* (ie, i), *proponer, indicar.* Me gusta lo que me **sugieres**. *I like what you are suggesting to me.*

sugestivo / suggestive *Sugestivo* does not exactly mean "suggestive," instead, it means "stimulating, attractive, evocative." Es un paisaje **sugestivo**. *It is an evocative landscape.* Suggestive has downgraded it connotation to mean *impropio, indecente, vulgar* ("risqué"). Esa joven lleva ropa **indecente**. *That young woman is wearing suggestive clothing.*

suizo / Swiss *Suizo* is an adjective for "Swiss" and *Suiza* is "Switzerland." However, as a common noun, *suiza* is used in some Latin American countries for "jump rope" *(comba, soga)* and in some other countries for a "beating, thrashing." Las montañas **suizas** son lindas. *The Swiss mountains are beautiful.* Vamos a saltar la **suiza**. *Let's play jump rope.*

sujetar / subject *Sujetar* does not mean "to subject." *Sujetar* means "to secure, fasten, hold, seize, tie, restrain." **Sujeta** la puerta, por favor. *Please hold the door.* To subject, on the other hand, means *dominar, someter, subyugar, supeditar.* Roma no pudo **someter** a los bárbaros. *Rome could not subject (subjugate) the barbarians.*

sujeto / subject *Sujeto* as a noun does not mean "subject" in everyday language. *Sujeto* generally means "fellow, individual, guy." *Sujeto* as an adjective means "subject" ("liable"), and also "secured, fastened, attached, tied down." [The *Real Academia* accepts *sujeto* as "subject (matter)," a denotation that was used in classical Spanish. Nowadays, that usage is obsolete.]
sujeto a la aprobación = *subject to approval*
Hay un **sujeto** a la puerta vendiendo patatas. *There's a guy at the door, selling*

potatoes. Subject means *tema* (m.), *asunto* ("matter"), *asignatura* or *materia* (in school), and *súbdito* when it applies to people. Los canadienses ya no son **súbditos** británicos. *Canadians are no longer British subjects.* No toquemos el **tema** de la política. *Let's not touch the subject of politics.* La historia es una **materia** obligatoria. *History is a required subject.*

sumario / summary *Sumario* and *summary* as adjectives both mean "brief, concise," and as nouns, "compendium" *(resumen* [m.]). In legal terminology, *sumario* means "indictment, charges."
proceso sumario = *summary proceedings*
Redactó un **sumario** muy claro. *He wrote a very clear summary.* El juez leyó el **sumario** en público. *The judge read the charges (issued the indictment) in public.*

suplantar / supplant *Suplantar* does not exactly mean "to supplant," because *suplantar* suggests "fraudulently taking the place of, impersonating," rather than "taking the place of by force or superiority."

suplir / supply *Suplir* does not mean "to supply" but "to replace, to substitute, to make up for, to cover up." Puedes **suplir** el examen con un ensayo. *You can replace the exam with an essay.* Tenemos que **suplir** la falta de ese jugador. *We have to make up for the absence of that player.* Supliremos su error. *We will cover up his error. To supply* means *suministrar, abastecer, proveer, facilitar.* Este camión **abastece** pan. *This truck supplies bread. Suplente* as an adjective means "substitute, deputy, reserve" and as a noun means "substitute, replacement." Es un maestro **suplente**. *He is a substitute teacher. Supplier* translates as *abastecedor, proveedor, suministrador.*

suponer / suppose *Suponer* means "to suppose" as "to assume" *(presuponer).* It also means "to entail, involve, mean, count for."
como es de suponer = *as is expected*
El jefe **supone** que somos honrados. *The boss supposes (assumes) we are honest.* ¿Qué se **supone** que yo diga? *What am I supposed to say?* **Supongo** que sí. *I suppose so.* El viaje **supuso** cinco mil dólares. *The trip entailed five thousand dollars. Suposición* means "supposition" ("assumption"), but it sometimes takes a downturn to mean "slander" *(calumnia).*

supresión / suppression *Supresión* is more accurately expressed as "elimination, deletion, lifting (a restriction)." *Suppression* means *represión, dominio.* la **represión** de la revuelta / *the suppression of the revolt*

suprimir / suppress *Suprimir* and *to suppress* are both used with respect to uprisings, freedom, etc. However, *suprimir* usually takes on milder shadings: "to withdraw, omit, delete, skip (details)." El gobierno **suprimió** la libertad de expresión. *The government suppressed freedom of speech.* Suprima los detalles. *Skip the details. To suppress* usually has stronger connotations, which are translated as *reprimir* or *dominar.* **Reprimió** (dominó) la supuesta rebelión. *He suppressed the alleged rebellion.*

surgir / surge   *Surgir* is not "to surge" but "to come out, arise, appear, emerge, loom, spurt (water)." La torre **surge** entre las casas del pueblo. *The tower **looms** above the village houses.* El agua **surge** entre las rocas. *The water **spurts** between the rocks.* Ayer **surgió** un problema con la computadora. *Yesterday a problem **arose** with the computer.* **To surge,** when applied to waves or the sea, means *agitarse, encresparse, picarse.* In a figurative sense, it means *abalanzarse, apoderarse.* El mar **se agitó** en la tempestad. *The sea **surged** during the storm.* Los chicos **se abalanzaron** al cuarto. *The boys **surged** into the room.* **Surge** as a noun translates as *oleaje* (m.), *oleada.*

susceptible / susceptible   *Susceptible* is used to mean "susceptible" ("touchy, sensitive," *sensible*) in reference to people. It is also used with things and circumstances to mean "liable, subject to, likely." Es un joven **susceptible** (sensible). *He is a **susceptible** young man.* La bolsa es **susceptible** de fluctuaciones diarias. *The stock market is **liable** to fluctuate daily.*

suspender / suspend   *Suspender* and *to suspend* share the meanings of "to discontinue, to postpone, to hang." In addition, *suspender* means "to delay, to adjourn" and when applied to students, it means "to fail, flunk (a test)." **Suspendimos** la reunión al mediodía. *We **adjourned** the meeting at noon.* Mi amigo fue **suspendido** en matemáticas. *My friend **failed** (flunked) mathematics.*

suspenso / suspense   *Suspenso* means "suspense" when it is used to describe novels or movies. (This meaning was accepted by the *Real Academia* in 1984.) In general, *suspenso* means "amazed, astonished, failed (student)." As a noun, *suspenso* means "failure." Es una telenovela con mucho **suspenso**. *It's a soap opera with a lot of **suspense**.* tener el corazón en **suspenso** / *to be in suspense* **Suspense** as a noun means *ansiedad* (f.), *incertidumbre* (f.), *duda, tensión.* María prefiere mantenernos en la **incertidumbre**. *Mary prefers to keep us in **suspense**.* **Suspensión** and *suspension* both mean "hanging, interruption, postponement" and *suspensión* also means "adjournment." **suspensión** de pruebas nucleares / *suspension of nuclear testing*

sustancial / substantial   *Sustancial* means "substantial, vital, essential." Nevertheless, it is used far less frequently than its cognate. *Substantial* translates as *considerable* (amount), *fuerte* or *sólido, sustancioso* or *nutritivo* (regarding food), *adinerado* ("wealthy"). Se robó una cantidad **considerable** de dinero. *A **substantial** amount of money was stolen.* El candidato tiene ideas **sólidas**. *The candidate has **substantial** ideas.*

sustituir / substitute   *Sustituir* and *to substitute* have the same meaning: "to replace." They differ in syntax in that *sustituir* is followed by a direct object, which is followed by *por* and an object. On the other hand, *to substitute* reverses the order of the objects. Acabo de **sustituir** el carro viejo por uno nuevo. *I just **substituted** a new car for the old one.* **Sustituyó** a la maestra enferma. *He **substituted** for the sick teacher.* *Substitute* translates as *sustituto* (for a person) and *sustitutivo* (for things). María trabaja de maestra **sustituta**. *Mary works as a **substitute** teacher.* Prefiero usar un **sustitutivo** del azúcar. *I prefer to use a sugar **substitute**.*

T

tabaco / tobacco   *Tabaco* and *tobacco* both refer to the plant and the product. In some Latin American countries, *tabaco* is used to mean "cigar." (In Spain and other countries, *puro* is used.) A tobacco field is a *tabacal* (m.), and the adjective form is *tabacalero* (for example, *la industria tabacalera*).
tabaco rubio = *Virginia tobacco*
tabaco en polvo = *snuff*
El **tabaco** es original de America. *Tobacco is originally from America.* El guajiro fumaba un **tabaco** enorme. *The peasant was smoking a huge cigar.*

tabla / table   *Tabla* and *table* only share the meaning of "list, chart." The basic meaning of *tabla* is "board, plank, index (of a book), scale (of salaries)." The plural form *tablas* means "stage" in the theater.
hacer tablas = *to draw, to tie (in a game)*
tabla de planchar = *ironing board*
a rajatabla = *strictly, to the letter*
Hice una cerca de **tablas**. *I made a fence out of boards.* **tabla** de salvación / *last hope (of salvation)* **tablas** reales / *backgammon (game)* *Table* means *mesa, meseta* (in geography), and in statistics, it also translates as *cuadro, lista, tarifa* ("price table").
poner la mesa = *to set the table*
Prefiero una **mesa** redonda. *I prefer a round table.*

tableta / tablet   *Tableta* and *tablet* share the meaning of "pill" *(pastilla)* for medicine and "pad" (of paper) for writing. In addition, *tableta* means "bar" (of chocolate), and as the diminutive of *tabla*, it means "small plank, small board, block (of wood)." una **tableta** para dolor de cabeza / *a headache tablet* Necesito una **tableta** (un bloque) para escribir. *I need a tablet to write on.* Una **tableta** de chocolate tiene muchas calorías. *A chocolate bar has many calories.* Encendí la chimenea con **tabletas** de madera. *I started a fire in the fireplace with blocks of wood.*

tacto / tact   *Tacto* means "tact" in the figurative sense of "delicate sensitivity, know-how, diplomacy" *(tino, discreción, diplomacia). Tacto* also means "(the sense of) touch" and "touching" (the act of touching).
tener tacto = *to be tactful*
mecanografía al tacto = *touch-typing*
El diplomático necesita buen **tacto**. *A diplomat needs tact.* El **tacto** es un sentido crucial para los ciegos. *Touch is a crucial sense for the blind.*

talón / talon   *Talón* (m.) is not "talon" but "heel" (of a foot, of a shoe), as well as "stub, voucher, coupon." In Spain, *talón* is used for "check" (of a bank). Arranque el recibo y guarde el **talón**. *Tear off the receipt and keep the stub. Talon,* on the other hand, means *uña, garra, zarpa* (of a bird of prey). El águila arrebató el conejo en sus **garras**. *The eagle grasped the rabbit in its talons.*

tapa / tape, tap *Tapa* is not "tape" but "lid, top (of a bottle), cover (of a book), round (of beef)." [In Spain, *tapas* are appetizers or tidbits—such as olives, peanuts, cheese, sausage, omelettes—that are served in a bar to accompany a drink. The expression *ir de tapas* means to go from bar to bar, drinking and sampling the different *tapas*.] La **tapa** del baúl está abierta. *The trunk **lid** is open.* Este libro tiene **tapa** (pasta) dura. *This book has a hard **cover**.* El viernes nos **fuimos de tapas**. *Last'Friday we went **bar-hopping**.* *Tape* means *cinta* (strip), *cinta adhesiva, cinta (magnetofónica)* for recording. Tengo muchas **cintas** de Julio Iglesias. *I have many Julio Iglesias **tapes**.* *Tap* ("blow") translates as *palmadita, golpecito*. When it means "faucet," it translates as *llave* (f.), *grifo, espita*, depending on the country. "Tap dance" is *zapateado*. "Beer on tap" is *cerveza de barril*.

tarifa / tariff *Tarifa* means "tariff" as a list or table of rates to be paid for certain merchandise or services, for example, in customs. Strictly speaking, *tarifa* does not stand for the fees to be paid, which are generally expressed as *arancel* (m.) or *derechos de aduana;* however, in common usage, *tarifa* and *tariff* are used to mean both the fees and the table. In addition, *tarifa* is used for "rates" (for example, subscription rates) and "fares" (for taxicabs, buses, etc.) [In modern Spanish, *tarifa* and *arancel* are used as synonyms, especially since international commerce has increased so considerably in the last few decades. The tariff tables were established after World War II by GATT (General Agreement of Tariffs and Trade). A new agreement in 1990 failed to achieve changes.] Los productos importados están sujetos a **tarifas** (aranceles) internacionales. *Imported goods are subject to international **tariffs** (fees).*

tarta / tart *Tarta* means "tart" but is used to mean "cake" in most Spanish-speaking countries.
tarta (pastel) de manzana = *apple tart*
La **tarta** de boda era enorme. *The wedding **cake** was huge.* *Tart*, on the other hand, is usually translated as *pastel* (m.). As an adjective, *tart* means *agrio, ácido* (taste), and in a figurative sense, *áspero, cáustico* (attitude). In modern English, *tart* as a slang term for *fulana, puta* is not commonly used, having been replaced by "hooker." La maestra le dio una respuesta **cáustica**. *The teacher gave him a **tart** (caustic) reply.*

temperamento / temperament *Temperamento* means "temperament" in the best sense of the word—"natural disposition." Tiene un **temperamento** tranquilo. *He has a quiet **temperament**.* *Temperament*, however, has downgraded its meaning to stand for *carácter caprichoso, violento, inconstante*. Tiene el **temperamento** caprichoso de una diva. *She has the **temperament** of a prima donna.* *Temperamental* has only the negative meaning of *caprichoso, inestable, inesperado, violento;* and it applies to machines, as well as to people. Fue una reacción **inesperada**. *It was a **temperamental** reaction.* Este ascensor es **caprichoso**. *This elevator is **temperamental**.*

templo / temple *Templo* means "temple" as a building for religious worship, and it appears in prayers and songs of all religious denominations. Nevertheless, *iglesia* is used in Hispanic countries for a Catholic church, whereas *templo* is

used to mean the place of worship of any other denomination, including Protestant, Jewish, Mormon, etc. Figuratively, especially in South America, *como un templo* is used to mean "huge, first-rate, excellent." [Generally, *iglesia* is used to apply to all churches in the sense of "religious denomination."]
una mujer como un templo = *a real woman*
Los protestantes cantan en el **templo**. *Protestants sing in* **church**. La misa se celebra en la **iglesia** parroquial. *Mass is celebrated at the parish* **church**. *Temple* is used as the place of worship for those of the Jewish faith *(sinagoga)*. In anatomy, *temple* is *sien* (f.).

temporal / temporal   *Temporal* and *temporal* share the meanings of "not spiritual, of this world, eternal, secular" *(secular, profano, pasajero)*. In Spanish, *temporal* also means "temporary, tentative." As a noun, *temporal* (m.) translates as "storm, tempest."
los bienes temporales = *temporal (worldly) goods*
El Papa tiene poder **temporal** y espiritual. *The Pope has* **temporal** *and spiritual power*. Mi trabajo es **temporal** (provisional). *My job is* **temporary** *(seasonal)*. El **temporal** vino con lluvias fuertes. *The* **storm** *brought heavy showers*. *To temporize* translates as *contemporizar*.

tendencia / tendency   *Tendencia* and *tendency* share the meaning of "inclination, constant disposition." *Tendencia* also means "trend" (as a current style or vogue). El niño tiene la **tendencia** a enfermarse. *The baby has the* **tendency** *to get sick*. nuevas **tendencias** musicales / *new* **trends** *in music*

teniente / tenant   *Teniente* (m.) does not mean "tenant" but "lieutenant." As an adjective, *teniente* means "holding, owning" (from *tener*) and is a colloquial term for "stingy, tightfisted." **Teniente** es un grado militar. *Lieutenant is a military rank*. *Tenant* translates as *inquilino, arrendatario*. Los **inquilinos** tienen algunos derechos. *Tenants have some rights*.

tenis / tennis   *Tenis* (m.) comes from the English word *tennis*, and it applies to the game, as well as to the "(tennis) court" and the "(tennis) shoes."
colgar los tenis = *to die*

tentar / tempt   *Tentar* (ie) means "to tempt" in the sense of "to induce, entice." *Tentar* also means "to touch, to grope for, to feel." Formerly, it was used to mean "to try, attempt," and some dialects, for example in Mexico, still use it with this meaning. El demonio **tentó** a Jesús tres veces. *The devil* **tempted** *Jesus three times*. El ciego iba **tentando** las mesas. *The blind man was* **groping** *for the tables*.

tentativo / tentative   *Tentativo* was finally recognized by the *Real Academia* in its latest dictionary with the meaning of "tentative." The feminine form *tentativa* is a frequently used noun, meaning "attempt, try." Este programa es **tentativo** (provisional). *This is a* **tentative** *program*. Tuvieron éxito en la tercera **tentativa**. *They were successful on the third* **attempt**.

teórico / theoretic(al) *Teórico* and *theoretic(al)* share the same meaning. Although *"teorético"* sometimes appears in writing, it technically does not exist in Spanish.

término / term *Término* means "term" in the sense of "word, an indefinite period of time." *Término* also means "end, limit, boundary." In addition, *término* means "terminal," the final station for a train or bus. [Although *término* is used for any period of time, it does not apply to a specific "term," such as a semester or quarter. For these applications, the words *semestre* (m.) and *trimestre* (m.) are used.]
poner término a = *to put an end to*
por término medio = *on the average*
buscar un término medio = *to look for a compromise (middle ground)*
No entiendo los **términos** legales. *I do not understand legal* **terms.** Pongamos **término** a la discusión. *Let's put an* **end** *to the dispute.* *Term* translates as *período, plazo* (of time), *trimestre* (at a university, school). The plural *terms* translates as *condiciones* (of a contract, of payment).
a la larga = *in the long term*
en el futuro próximo = *in the short term*
llegar a un acuerdo = *to come to terms*
en un **plazo** de ocho días / *in a* **term** *(period) of eight days (one week)* El **trimestre** empieza en febrero. *The school* **term** *starts in February.* La empresa ofrece **facilidades** de pago. *The company offers easy payment* **terms.**

testimonial / testimonial *Testimonial* is a legal term, as is the English adjective *testimonial,* meaning "documentary evidence." declaración **testimonial** / *testimonial declaration* *Testimonial* as a noun goes beyond the courtroom to mean *testimonio, recomendación, homenaje* (m.), *certificado.* Se hizo un **homenaje** al pintor. *They gave a* **testimonial** *to the painter.* Para hacerte ciudadano necesitas un **certificado** de buena conducta. *To become a citizen, you need a* **testimonial** *of good conduct.*

timbre / timbre *Timbre* (m.) and *timbre* (also spelled *timber*) are "quality of sound." In addition, *timbre* means "doorbell, small bell, postage (for mailing), seal (fiscal)." [In English, *timbre* and its alternative spelling should not be confused with *timber,* meaning *bosque* (m.), *madera, árboles* (m.).]
tocar el timbre = *to ring the doorbell*
El **timbre** de su voz es agudo. *The* **timbre** *of his voice is sharp.* La carta necesita **timbre.** *The letter needs* **postage** *(a stamp).*

tímido / timid *Tímido* means "timid" as "easily frightened" *(asustadizo),* and it also means "shy, bashful." una respuesta **tímida** / *a timid reply* ¡Venga, no seas **tímido**! *Come on, don't be* **shy**!

tinte, tinto / tint *Tinte* (m.) means "tint" as "hair coloring" *(tinte de pelo).* Primarily, *tinte* means "dye, the process of dyeing (giving a permanent color)." *Tinto,* on the other hand, means "tinted, dyed, stained" *(teñido)* and also "dark red." In Spain, *tinto* is red wine and in some Latin American countries, "black coffee." No es el color natural del cabello. Tiene un **tinte.** *It isn't her natural hair color. She uses a* **tint.** En España se bebe mucho **tinto.** *They drink a lot of* **red**

wine** in Spain.* En Colombia la gente bebe mucho **tinto**. *In Colombia, the people drink a lot of **black coffee**. Tint,* on the other hand, more commonly means *tono, matiz* (m.) (of color). In printing, *tint* means *fondo claro* ("light background"). Su suéter tiene un **tono** rojizo. *Her sweater has a reddish **tint.

tipo / type   *Tipo* and *type* share the meanings of "kind, class, model, character (in print), individual (person)." However, *tipo* has a variety of meanings, according to its context. For example, it means "rate" when it is applied to money; "figure, shape" when it is applied to a person's physique; and both *tipo* and *tipa* are commonly used to mean "fellow, chap, guy, character." ¿Qué **tipo** de coche tiene Ud.? *What **type** (kind) of car do you have?* Los **tipos** son demasiado pequeños para leerse. *The **type** (character) is too small to read.* El **tipo** de cambio subió un poco. *The **rate** of exchange went up a little.* Esa chica tiene buen **tipo**. *That girl has a pretty **figure**.* ¿Quién será ese **tipo** raro? *I wonder who that strange **guy** is.* ¡Qué **tipo** más extraordinario! *What an extraordinary **fellow**!* **Tipificar** and *to typify* both mean "to exemplify, to symbolize."

tiquete / ticket   *Tiquete* (m.), which is used in several Spanish-speaking countries, has been included in the latest dictionary of the *Real Academia* as a loan word from English, meaning "ticket" *(boleto, billete* [m.]*)*. In some countries, *tiquete* has been shortened to *tique*. Both *tiquete* and *ticket* mean "receipt, voucher, bonus, pass, admission." Los **tiquetes** (las entradas) de cine son cada día más caros. *Movie **tickets** are getting more expensive every day.*

tirar / tire   *Tirar* is not "to tire" but "to throw, toss, drop, spill, pull, shoot, knock down, give away (price), take (pictures), print." **Tira** una foto del niño. *Take a picture of the child.* ¿Cómo estás? — **Tirando**. *How are you doing?* — *So-so.* To *tire* translates as *cansar(se)*.
agotar = *to tire out, to wear out*
Estoy **agotado**. *I'm all **tired** out.* Me **canso** de la computadora. *I'm **tired** of the computer.*

titular / titular   *Titular* and *titular* are both adjectives that mean "holding a title, in title only." *Titular* (m.) is also a noun, meaning "title holder, holder (of a passport, etc.)." The plural form *titulares* means "headlines" (in a newspaper).
profesor titular = *titular professor*
Es catedrático **titular** de historia. *He is a **titular** professor of history.* No puedo creer estos **titulares**. *I cannot believe those **headlines**. Titular* is also a verb, meaning "to title, to call (a book, novel, etc.)."

título / title   *Título* not only means "title" (of a book, etc.) but also means "degree, diploma, bond." The plural form *títulos (valores,* m.*)* means "securities" in the stock market.
título de propiedad = *title, deed*
título de licenciado / *bachelor's **degree*** Algunos bancos venden **títulos** sin fondos. *Some banks sell junk **bonds**.*

tobogán / toboggan   *Tobogán* (m.) has been added to the latest dictionary of the *Real Academia* with the same meaning as *toboggan* in English. In addition, *tobogán* applies to the "slide" or "chute" at a pool and to the device itself, "sled." [*Tobogán* should not be confused with *trineo*, which translates as "sleigh."] Los niños se divierten con el tobogán. *The children are enjoying their toboggan.* El tobogán está muy empinado. *The chute is very steep.*

topar / tope *Topar con* is not "to tope" but "to run into, bump into, come across." The reflexive *toparse con* is "to meet, encounter." El borracho topó con la columna. *The drunk bumped into the pillar.* To *tope* is used primarily in British English to mean *beber demasiado* (liquor).

tope / top *Tope* (m.) is not "top" but "end, butt, bumper (for a vehicle, for example), bang *(golpe, m.)*, masthead."
hasta el tope = *to the brim*
a (al) tope = *crammed full*
fecha tope = *deadline*
Choqué con el **tope** del otro coche. *I ran into the bumper of the other car.* Top is used to mean many things: *trompa, trompo* (a toy), *sostén* (m.; of a bikini), *blusa, copa* (of a tree), *tapa* (of a pan), *tejado, techo, cima, cumbre* (f.), *coronilla* (of the head), *parte* (f.) *superior* (of anything).
de pies a cabeza = *from top to bottom; from head to toe*
en lo alto de la escalera / *at the top of the stairs*

tópico / topic *Tópico* may or may not be a false cognate, depending on the source. The *Real Academia* considers it a false cognate and gives the following meanings: as a noun, "external medicine"; as an adjective, "trivial, commonplace, trite." Other sources, such as Larousse and Moríñigo, agree that in America, *tópico* means "topic" *(asunto, tema* [m.], *materia).* Los intelectuales no hablan de temas **tópicos.** *Intellectuals do not talk about trivial subjects.* La profesora nos dio una lista de **tópicos** (temas) para los informes. *The teacher gave us a list of topics for the reports. Topical* translates as *moderno, de actualidad.* En este curso, leemos sobre asuntos **de actualidad.** *In this class, we read about topical matters.*

tormento, tormenta / torment *Tormento* and *torment* are exactly the same. *Tormenta,* however, means "storm, tempest, blizzard" and figuratively, "argument, fight, misfortune." Todos sufrimos **tormentos** en la vida. *We all suffer torments in life.* La **tormenta** me despertó anoche. *Last night the storm woke me up.* una **tormenta** en un vaso de agua / *a tempest in a teapot*

tornar / turn *Tornar* and *to turn* share the idea of "to change, become, transform." *Tornar* also means "to return, give back." *Tornarse* means "to go back" (return).
tornar en sí = *to regain consciousness*
En las Bodas de Caná el agua se **tornó** en vino. *The water turned into wine at the Wedding of Cana.* To turn has many meanings: *girar, dar vueltas, volver* (ue), *doblar* or *voltear (a corner), desviar, trastornar, pasar de (age), sobrepasar.*
encender; prender = *to turn on (light, appliance)*
apagar = *to turn off*
excitar; gustar = *to turn on (a person)*
tocarle a uno = *to be one's turn*

Dale una vuelta a la derecha al televisor. *Turn the television set to the right.* La tierra **gira** en el eje. *The earth **turns** on its axis.*

total / total *Total* means "total" ("complete") as an adjective and also as a masculine noun. However, *total* in Spanish is also an adverb, meaning "so, finally, after all." *Eso supone una ignorancia* **total.** *That presupposes **total** ignorance.* **Total** *que no dijo nada en serio. So he didn't say anything serious.* **Total** *que no se decidió a hacerlo. She didn't decide to do it **after all.***

totalizar / total *Totalizar* appears in the latest dictionary of the *Real Academia* with the meaning of "to total" *(sumar, ascender* [ie], *montar).* *Los gastos* **totalizaron** *como 3.000 dólares. The expenses **totaled** about 3,000 dollars. To total* has come to mean "to destroy completely," in reference to automobile accidents. An accurate translation in Spanish is *destruir por completo.* *Mi auto se* **destruyó por completo** *en el accidente. My car was **totaled** in the accident.*

traducir / traduce *Traducir* is not "to traduce" but "to translate, render" and, in a figurative sense, "to result in, bring about." *Una persona bilingüe sabe* **traducir** *los gestos y las palabras. A bilingual person knows how **to translate** gestures and words. To traduce* means *calumniar, difamar* ("to defame"). *Traductor* (m.) means "translator." *Traducer* means *calumniador* (m.), *difamador* (m.). *El* **calumniador** *tendrá su merecido. The **traducer** will receive his punishment.*

tráfico / traffic *Tráfico* means "traffic" (after final acceptance by the *Real Academia*) and is synonymous with *tránsito, circulación.* Originally *tráfico* meant "trade" as a business and is still used in reference to the business of "drug trafficking" *(narcotráfico).*
semáforo; señal de tráfico = *traffic light*
tráfico de mujeres = *white slavery*
tráfico rodado / *road* **traffic** *policía de* **tráfico** (tránsito) / **traffic** *police (cop) Traficante* (m.) suggests a shady "dealer, trafficker." *Traficar* and *to traffic* share the meaning of "to trade, to deal" *(comerciar, negociar)* and can refer to legal or illegal trade. However, both are increasingly being used to refer to illegal trade.

trampa / tramp *Trampa* is not "tramp"; instead, it means "trap, cheating, trick, pitfall, ambush, hoax."
hacer trampa = *to cheat*
Tiene trampa (pega). = *There's a catch.*
Cayó en la **trampa** *como un ratón. He walked into the **trap** like a mouse. (He was caught in the **trap** like a rat.) ¿Qué alumno nunca ha hecho una* **trampa**? *What student has never tried to **cheat?** Hecha la ley, hecha la* **trampa.** *Laws are made to be **broken.** Tramp* refers to *caminata, vagabundo, vapor* (m.; "freighter") and is a slang word for a woman of loose morals, *prostituta, fulana.* *Ella es la* **prostituta** *de la ciudad. She is the town **tramp.** Tramposo* is the adjective for "cheating, swindling, lying" *(mentiroso).*

trance / trance *Trance* (m.) does not mean "trance." *Trance* means "critical moment, awkward situation *(mal paso),* tight corner."
a todo trance = *at any cost*

Pude sacarlo de un **trance** difícil. *I managed to get him out of a **tight corner**.* en **trance** de muerte / *at the **point** of death Trance, on the other hand, means éxtasis (m.), rapto.*

transacción / transaction *Transacción* and *transaction* share the meaning of "deal, settlement" *(trámite* [m.], *negociación)* in the world of business. La **transacción** se hizo en dos horas. *The **transaction** was completed in two hours. Transaction in the plural form, transactions, refers to the end result of nego-* tiations: *actas, memorias, actuaciones.* **Actas** de la Junta Directiva / **Transactions** of the Board of Directors

trascendente / transcendent *Trascendente* is not "transcendent" but "important, significant." *Transcendent* means *extraordinario, sobresaliente, excelente. Trascendencia* means "significance, importance." Esta entrevista tiene una gran **trascendencia** para mí. *This interview has great **significance** for me. Transcendence* (or *transcendency*) means *superioridad* (f.), *excelencia.* Nadie discute la **superioridad** de esta teoría. *No one will argue about the **transcendence** of this theory.*

trascender / transcend *Trascender* is not "to transcend" but "to spread to, to reach, to leak (news)." El olor **trascendía** hasta el patio. *The smell **spread** to the patio.* **Ha trascendido** la noticia. *The news **has leaked** out. To transcend* means *superar, exceder, rebasar.* El acontecimiento **supera** (excede) nuestra capacidad para comprenderlo. *The event **transcends** our ability to understand it.*

traslación / translation *Traslación* is not "translation" but "transfer, moving" *(traslado).* Los gastos de **traslación** (traslado) son deducibles si la distancia es más de 35 millas. *Moving expenses are deductible if the distance is more than 35 miles. Translation* means *traducción.*

traspasar / trespass *Traspasar* is not "to trespass"; instead, it means "to pierce, go through (as a bullet), transfer, make over (a store, a player), break, violate (a law), cross over." Lo **traspasó** con la espada. *He **pierced** him (ran him through) with the sword.* **Traspasé** la tienda a mi sobrino. *I **transferred** the store to my nephew.* **Traspasaron** el arroyo. *They **crossed over** the creek. To trespass,* on the other hand, means *entrar ilegalmente, abusar, invadir* (privacy), *usurpar* (rights).
¡Prohibido el paso! = *No trespassing!*
Traspaso means "transfer, sale, transferred property, transgression." *Trespass* means *entrada ilegal, violación* (of property), *ofensa* (in religion). Perdona nuestras **ofensas.** *Forgive our **trespasses.***

tratado / treaty, treatment *Tratado* means "treaty" ("an agreement between two countries about trade, peace, etc.") and "treatise" (of a book). *Tratado* is also an adjective from *tratar* and means "dealt with, discussed, treated." Hay que respetar el **tratado** de paz. *The peace **treaty** must be respected.* Me gustó su **tratado** sobre los pájaros. *I enjoyed her **treatise** on birds. Treatment,* on the other hand, translates as *tratamiento. Trata* translates as "trade," especially in reference to slaves and slavery: *trata de esclavos* ("slave trade").

tratar / treat *Tratar* and *to treat* both mean "to deal with, discuss, assist, cure."
tratar con = *to associate with*
tratar de = *to try to, to attempt*
Traté de dejar de fumar tres veces. *I tried to stop smoking three times. To treat,*
in addition, means *invitar, convidar, agasajar.* Mi suegra nos convidó a almorzar.
My mother-in-law treated us to lunch.

traza / trace *Traza* is not "trace"; instead, it means "appearance, look, plan,
scheme."
tener traza de = *to look like*
Juan tiene traza de maestro. *John has the appearance of (looks like) a teacher.*
Trace translates as *rastro, huella, senda, pista, línea, trazo.* El criminal no dejó
huella ninguna. *The criminal left no trace at all.*

trazar / trace *Trazar* and *to trace* both mean "to draw, sketch, outline." Trazó
una semblanza del ladrón. *He drew (traced) a picture of the thief. To trace* also
means *calcar* or *copiar, seguir* (i), *rastrear.* Los niños calcaron el dibujo de sus
cuadernos. *The children traced the picture in their books.* La policía siguió la pista
del ladrón. *The police traced the route of the thief.*

tren / train *Tren* (m.) and *train* both refer to a "vehicle on rails." However, *tren*
also means "style of life, way of living, pace, speed."
tren de cercanías = *suburban train*
vivir a todo tren = *to live in style*
Lleva un tren de vida de millonario. *He has the lifestyle of a millionaire. Train,*
in addition, means *cola* (of a long dress), *procesión, comitiva, serie* (f.; of
events). El vestido de boda tiene una cola de dos metros. *The wedding dress has
a train that is two meters long. To train* means *entrenar* (persons), *amaestrar*
(animals), *guiar* (plants). Amaestré a mi perro a ponerse de pie y caminar. *I trained
my dog to stand up and walk.*

tronco / trunk *Tronco* is "trunk" (of a tree, of a body), and in a figurative sense,
it means "lineage" (of a family). *Tronco* is also a familiar word for "blockhead"
("a stupid person"); however, in some dialects, *tronco* and the augmentative
form *troncazo* mean "strong, healthy." La secuoya tiene el tronco muy grueso.
The sequoia has a very thick trunk. María siempre duerme como un tronco. *Mary
always sleeps like a log.* A pesar de sus 60 años es un tronco. *He is very healthy
in spite of being 60 years old.* Es un tronco; no aprende nada. *He is a blockhead;
he never learns anything. Trunk,* on the other hand, also means *trompa* (of an
elephant), *baúl* (m.; the luggage, storage compartment of a car), *línea interurbana*
(a telephone party line). The plural form *trunks* means *bañador* (m.), *trusa*
("swimming suit"). Los baúles antiguos eran artísticos. *The antique trunks were
artfully made.* Las trusas modernas son multicolores. *Modern swimming trunks are
very colorful.*

truculento / truculent *Truculento* does not mean "truculent"; it means "atro-
cious, horrifying, ghastly." Fue una escena truculenta. *It was a ghastly (horrifying)
scene. Truculent* means *belicoso, agresivo, feroz, salvaje.* Los padres castigaron

a su hijo por ser **agresivo.** *The parents punished their son for being* ***truculent.*** Los terroristas son **salvajes.** *Terrorists are* ***truculent*** *(cruel, savage).*

tubo / tube *Tubo* and *tube* both mean "a hollow cylinder" (for liquids). In Spanish, *tubo* also means "pipe" for carrying water, petroleum, natural gas, etc.
tubo de ensayo = *test tube*
Hay muchos **tubos** debajo de la casa. *There are many* ***pipes*** *under the house. Tube* is a current slang word for "television" and in England is the word for "subway" *(metro).*

tuna / tuna *Tuna* is not "tuna" but "cactus pear, prickly pear, (a kind of) cactus" and also "a group of student minstrels." [The students of the *tuna* dress in medieval clothing; play guitars, lutes, and mandolins; and sing folkloric songs, as well as love songs with which they serenade young ladies. An individual member of the *tuna* is called a *tuno.*] El nopal da la fruta llamada **tuna.** *The nopal cactus bears the fruit called* ***prickly pear.*** *Tuna* in English is short for *tuna fish* and translates as *atún* (m.). Me fascina la ensalada de **atún.** *I love* ***tuna*** *salad.*

turbulencia / turbulence *Turbulencia* means "turbulence" ("disorder, riot, commotion, violent weather"). The Spanish word, however, suggests "unruliness, boisterousness"—in other words, a "noisier" turbulence. No hubo **turbulencias** en el vuelo. *We had no* ***turbulence*** *during the flight.* ***Turbulento*** means "turbulent," although in Spanish the word suggests "boisterous, unruly, rowdy." [These differences in shades of meaning are evidence of the strong influence that culture has on the language used by its speakers.] El quinto grado es demasiado **turbulento.** *The fifth grade is too* ***rowdy.***

tutor / tutor *Tutor* and *tutora* mean "guardian, protector" and usually refer to legal matters. La tía es **tutora** de su sobrino. *The aunt is her nephew's* ***guardian.*** *Tutor,* on the other hand, means *maestro* or *profesor* (m.) *particular.* Necesito un **maestro privado** de álgebra. *I need a* ***tutor*** *in algebra.*

U

ulterior / ulterior *Ulterior* and *ulterior* share the sense of "later, subsequent, further." Nadie sabe los resultados **ulteriores** que tiene la revolución. *No one knows the subsequent results of the revolution. Ulterior* has downgraded its connotation in English to mean *oculto* ("hidden, undisclosed"), *interesado.*
segunda intención = *ulterior motive*
Parece tener motivos **ocultos.** *She seems to have* **ulterior** *motives.*

último / ultimate *Último* is "ultimate" in the sense of "last in order." In addition, *último* seems to stress the idea of time and space, lending itself to translations such as "last, latter (of two), latest, farthest back *(de atrás)*, top *(de arriba)*, bottom *(de abajo)*, lowest (price)."
a la última = *up-to-date*
a últimos de mes = *at the end of the month*
estar en las últimas = *to be on one's deathbed*
Subí la escalera hasta el **último** piso. *I walked upstairs to the* **top** *floor.* Estos son los **últimos** precios. *These are the* **lowest** *prices. Ultimate,* on the other hand, has changed to emphasize the reason for being "last" and translates as *definitivo, esencial, fundamental.* ¿Cuál es la verdad **fundamental**? *What is the* **ultimate** *truth?* Su meta **definitiva** es la perfección. *His* **ultimate** *goal is perfection.* **Últimamente** means "finally" *(por último)*, as well as "lately, recently." La gasolina subió de precio **últimamente.** *Gas prices went up* **recently** *(lately). Ultimately* translates as *en el fondo, básicamente* ("basically"). **En el fondo** creo que tienes razón. *I think you are right* **ultimately.**

ultramarino / ultramarine *Ultramarino* and *ultramarine* both mean "from overseas, from beyond the sea" *(de ultramar)* as adjectives. As a noun, the plural form *ultramarinos* means "groceries, grocery store." Es dueño de una tienda de **ultramarinos.** *He is the owner of a* **grocery store.** *Ultramarine* is a noun, meaning *azul marino (de ultramar).* La camisa es de color **azul marino.** *The color of the shirt is* **ultramarine.**

único / unique *Único* in front of a noun means "only, sole, one and only." After a noun, *único* means "unique" as "having no equal, extraordinary, unparalleled." Es un suceso **único** (sin igual) en la historia. *It is a* **unique** *(an unparalleled) event in history.* Es la **única** librería que conozco en el pueblo. *It is the* **only** *bookstore I know of in town.* Esa misma librería es **única** (especial). *That same bookstore is* **unique.** *Unique* sometimes takes a downturn to mean *extraño, raro* ("strange, unusual"). Su conducta es **extraña.** *His behavior is* **unique.** *Únicamente* means "only, solely, just." **Únicamente** quiere llegar a Boston. *He* **only** *(just) wants to get to Boston. Uniquely* translates as *extraordinariamente, extrañamente.* Ella actúa **extrañamente.** *She is acting* **uniquely** *(strangely).*

unidad / unity, unit *Unidad* (f.) usually translates as "unit" and sometimes "unity" ("cohesion, oneness, continuity"). *Unidad* and *unit* share the sense of "a unit of measure, a monetary unit, etc." Figuratively, **unidad** is used to mean "unity, harmony, union."

coste por unidad = *unit cost*

Las **unidades** de combate están listas. *The combat **units** are ready.* No hay **unidad** en sus proyectos. *There is no **unity** in his plans.* **Unit** is a very common word, perhaps as a reflection of the English-speaking culture. In addition to its shared meanings with *unidad*, it means *centro* (research unit), *servicio* (department), *fábrica, elemento, aparato, máquina, equipo.* La familia es el **elemento** básico de la sociedad. *The family is the basic **unit** of society.*

uniforme / uniform *Uniforme* means "uniform" ("plain, steady") and also "even, level (surface)" as an adjective. As a noun, *uniforme* (m.) means "uniform." [In most Latin American countries, grammar and high school students still wear uniforms, in both public and private schools. This has been a long-standing tradition in Hispanic culture.] Los colores del cuadro se ven **uniformes**. *The colors in the picture seem **uniform** (plain).* Es un terreno muy **uniforme**. *It is a very **even** terrain.*

unión / union *Unión* and *union* have the shared meanings of "uniting, fusion, junction, harmony, marriage." La **unión** hace la fuerza. *In **union** is strength.* La pareja vive en perfecta **armonía** (unión). *The couple lives in perfect **harmony** (union).* **unión** aduanera / *customs **union*** *Union*, on the other hand, is also a labor term, meaning *sindicato (de trabajo).* The *Union* is also used to apply to the United States *(los Estados Unidos).* [Note that *unionism* translates as *sindicalismo*, and *unionist* and *union* (as an adjective) translate as *sindicalista*.] El **sindicato** intenta ayudar a los trabajadores. *The **union** tries to help the workers.*

universidad / university *Universidad* (f.) is both "university" and "college." [*See the entry for* **colegio / college**.] *Universitario* is the adjective for "university, college."

ciudad universitaria = *university town; college town*

Para llenar este puesto se necesita una persona con educación **universitaria**. *To fill this post, a person with a **university** (college) education is needed.*

urbano / urban, urbane *Urbano* and *urban* both mean "of a city or town, not of the country." La sociedad moderna es más **urbana** que rural. *Modern society is more **urban** than rural.* *Urbane* translates as *cortés* ("polite"), *atento, refinado.* The usage of *urbano* as "polite, courteous" is obsolete. Su comportamiento es **cortés**. *Her behavior is **urbane** (notably polite).* *Urbanidad* (f.) and *urbanity*, however, share the meaning of "politeness, courtesy." En mi escuela rural estudiábamos las reglas de **urbanidad** a partir del tercer grado. *In my rural school we studied the rules of **courtesy** beginning in the third grade.*

urgir / urge *Urgir* has the basic idea of the English *to urge*, but their syntactic combinations are so different that they should be considered "dangerous" if not "false" cognates. *Urgir* translates as "to be urgent, to be pressing," with the person involved as the indirect object of the verb. A Juan le **urge** terminar la carta. *It **is urgent** for John to finish the letter.* Nos **urge** resolver el problema del SIDA. *It is **urgent** that we resolve the problem of AIDS.* El asunto **urge** mucho. *The matter is very **urgent**. To urge*, on the other hand, means *incitar, estimular,* *encarecer, pedir* (i). *To urge* takes a person as the direct object. Juan me **incitó** a que lo visitara. *John urged me to visit him.* El senador **pidió** una reforma contra la inflación. *The senator urged for a reform against inflation.*

urna / urn *Urna* means "urn" as "a large vase," but *urna* also means "ballot box, glass case." The plural form *urnas* refers to "elections."
ir a las urnas = *to go to the polls*
Guarda las cenizas de su tía en la **urna** encima del tocador. *He keeps his aunt's ashes in the urn on the dresser.* Las **urnas** son el símbolo de libertad. *Ballot boxes are the symbol of liberty.*

usar / use *Usar* (synonyms: *emplear, utilizar*) means "to use" ("to make use, to put into service, to practice") and it also means "to wear," as well as "to wear out." A algunas muchachas les gusta **usar** minifaldas. *Some girls like to wear miniskirts.* To use sometimes means *consumir, gastar, tratar, aprovechar,* and as an auxiliary verb it means *acostumbrar, soler* (ue). **Solía** ir a la playa más a menudo. *I used to go to the beach more often.* Esta locomotora todavía **consume** carbón. *This engine still uses coal.* **Aprovecha** todo su tiempo libre para leer. *He uses all his free time for reading.* Las cosas ya no son lo que eran. *Things aren't what they used to be.* *Usado* (synonym: *de segunda mano*) means "used" ("put to work, employed for"), and it also means "worn" (clothes), and "worn-out" *(deteriorado, gastado).* Se venden coches **usados.** *Used cars sold here.* Esas llantas ya están muy **usadas.** *Those tires are already very worn out.* *Usuario* means "user" ("consumer").

utilidad / utility *Utilidad* (f.) means "utility" ("use") and also "usefulness, profit." No le veo ninguna **utilidad** a ese aparato. *I don't see any usefulness in that machine.* Ese negocio deja muchas **utilidades.** *That business yields good profits. Utility,* on the other hand, is also used for "public service" such as power, water, gas, telephone. The plural form *utilities* applies to *acciones* ("shares") in the public service companies. No me gusta pagar los **servicios.** *I don't like to pay for utilities.* En mi cartera tengo acciones de las compañías aéreas y en la **compañía del gas.** *In my portfolio, I have stocks in the airlines and in the gas utilities.*

V

vacación / vacation *Vacación* is "vacation," although the plural form *vacaciones* is used more frequently than the singular. *Vacaciones* ,is also translated as "recess" and in British English, "holiday(s)." *Tuve mis vacaciones retribuidas. I had my paid vacation (holiday).* *To vacation* is translated as *tomar* or *pasar las vacaciones.* There is no such word in Spanish as "*vacacionar.*" *Pasamos las vacaciones en Puerto Vallarta. We vacationed in Puerto Vallarta.*

vacante / vacant *Vacante* means "vacant" ("empty, free, available") as an adjective, but *vacante* (f.) is also a noun for "vacancy" ("a vacant position, a job opening," *not* "an available room in a hotel"). [A hotel sign indicating "No vacancies" would read *¡Completo!*] *Hay dos puestos vacantes en la tienda. There are two vacancies (job openings) at the store.* Vacant has other denotations, such as *vacío* (house, room), *libre, disponible* (seat, room), *vago, perdido* (stare). *Hay un cuarto disponible en el hotel. There is one vacancy (one room vacant) at the hotel. El chico tiene una expresión vaga. The boy has a vacant expression.*

vago / vague *Vago* means "vague" ("not clear, blurry, hazy") when it applies to ideas, concepts, theories, etc. When it applies to people, *vago* means "lazy, idle" and as a noun is translated as "loafer" and even "tramp, vagabond." *No me gustan las promesas vagas. I don't like vague promises. No aprueba los cursos por vago. He's failing his courses because he's lazy. No tengo la más mínima idea. I don't have the vaguest idea. Vaguedad* (f.) translates exactly as "vagueness." *Vagancia* is a colloquial term for "laziness." *La vagancia es mala consejera. Laziness is a poor counselor.*

vagón / wagon *Vagón* (m.) is only a "railway car, railway wagon."
vagón de primera clase = *first-class car* (on a train)
Este tren lleva ocho vagones de viajeros. This train has eight passenger cars (coaches). Wagon, on the other hand, applies to *carro* or *carruaje* (m.; "a horse-drawn wagon"), *furgón* (m.; for freight). A *station wagon* translates as *furgoneta* or *camioneta. Los carros de bueyes eran lentos. Ox wagons (oxcarts) were slow.*

válido / valid *Válido* means "valid" as "having legal force, sound" *(vigente),* referring to laws, objections, etc. Referring to the body, *válido* means "robust, fit, strong." [The opposite of *válido* is *inválido* (or *minusválido*), which is used to mean "handicapped, disabled."] *Las últimas elecciones son válidas. The latest elections are valid. Se necesitan hombres válidos para trabajo de construcción. Fit (able) men are need for construction work. Los accidentes de coche han dejado a centenares de jóvenes inválidos en sillas de ruedas. Car accidents have left hundreds of young people disabled and in wheelchairs.*

valiente / valiant *Valiente* and *valiant* both mean "courageous, brave." In addition, *valiente* means "boastful, braggart" and sometimes refers to a person's body, meaning "healthy, strong." In colloquial language, *valiente* is used ironically to convey its opposite meaning, and is translated as "fine, some."

dárselas de valiente = *to boast; to be a bully*
¿Los soldados son siempre **valientes**? *Are soldiers always valiant?* A pesar de sus años está **valiente**. *He is healthy in spite of his age.* ¡**Valiente** amiga tienes! *A fine friend you have!* ¡**Valiente** tonto eres! *Some (what a) fool you are!*

valor / valor, value *Valor* (m.) means "valor" ("courage, bravery") when it applies to people; nevertheless, when it applies to things, it means "value, good quality, merit, worth, credit, importance." In a figurative sense, *valor* means "important figure, valuable person." The plural form *valores* means "securities, bonds (in the stock market)."
valor nominal = *face value*
El general es un hombre de gran **valor** (valentía). *The general is a man of great valor.* El oro tiene más **valor** que la plata. *Gold has more value than silver.* Cervantes es uno de nuestros grandes **valores**. *Cervantes is one of our most important figures.* Los **valores** tienen muchos altibajos. *Securities have many ups and downs. Valuable* translates as *valioso* as an adjective and as *objeto de valor, joya* as a noun. (There is no such word as *"valuable"* in Spanish.) Las **joyas** están en la caja de caudales. *The valuables are in the safe. Valorar* and *valorizar* are synonyms for *to value*, meaning "to estimate, to raise the value, to esteem (people)." **Valoramos** mucho al director. *We greatly value our principal.*

vapor / vapor *Vapor* (m.) means "vapor" as "steam, mist, fumes, fog" and it also means "steamer, steamship."
a todo vapor = *at full speed; full steam ahead*
Me gustan las papas al **vapor**. *I like steamed potatoes.* El vino fermentado deja escapar **vapores**. *Fermented wine gives off fumes.* ¿Quién inventó el **(barco de) vapor**? *Who invented the steamship?* Nos divertimos en el **vapor** de ruedas. *We enjoyed ourselves on the paddle steamer. Vaporizador* (m.; synonym, *pulverizador*, m.) translates as "vaporizer" ("atomizer, spray").

variante / variant *Variante* (f.) means "variant" ("different version, a changing word or thing") as a noun. *Variante* as an adjective means "variable." Hay dos **variantes** de esa canción. *There are two versions of that song.* "Periodo" es una **variante** de "período". *Periodo is a variant of período.*

varios / various *Varios* means "various" *(distintos)* and "several" (of the same kind). As a pronoun, *varios* means "some." The singular form *vario, varia* means "varied" ("diverse, different"). Compré **varias** frutas maduras. *I bought various ripe fruits.* **Varios** salieron muy temprano del concierto. *Some left the concert very early.*

vaso / vase *Vaso* does not mean "vase"; instead, it means "drinking glass, glassful, tumbler." *Vaso* also means "(blood) vessel" to refer to arteries and veins and it is used to mean "cups" employed in religious ceremonies. [The *Real Academia* mentions *vaso* as a synonym of *jarrón* (m.; "vase"), but this use seems to be archaic. Certainly, the term was used by authors in the last century, but it is not employed by modern authors.] Sírveme un **vaso** de agua. *Serve me a glass of water.* Los **vasos** sanguíneos acarrean la sangre. *Blood vessels carry the blood.* **vasos** sagrados de la iglesia / *sacred* **vessels** *of the church* Vase is translated as *jarrón, florero.* "El **jarrón** tiene trece rosas, una por cada mes". *"The* **vase** *has thirteen roses, one for each month."*

vegetal / vegetable *Vegetal* (m.) means "vegetable" in the general sense of "plant," but in the specific sense of "edible vegetables," the Spanish terms are *legumbres* (f.), *verduras, hortalizas.* Respetamos el reino **vegetal.** *Let's care for the* **vegetable** *kingdom.* Las ensaladas llevan toda clase de **verduras.** *Salads usually contain all kinds of* **vegetables.** *Vegetariano,* on the other hand, translates as *vegetarian.*

vejación / vexation *Vejación* does not mean "vexation"; rather, it means "humiliation, mortification." Le hicieron pasar una **vejación** cruel. *They made him endure cruel* **humiliation.** *Vexation* means *molestia, fastidio, disgusto.* Sentí un gran **disgusto** a causa de su conducto. *I felt great* **vexation** *at his conduct.*

vejar / vex *Vejar* is not "to vex"; rather, it is "to humiliate, to hurt." No se debe **vejar** a nadie en público. *One should not* **humiliate** *another person in public. To vex* means *molestar, fastidiar, disgustar.* Sus palabras me **molestaron** mucho. *His words were very* **vexing** *to me.*

vena / vein *Vena* and *vein* share the meanings of "blood vessel, streak *(veta),* seam, layer *(filón,* m.*)."* Figuratively, *vena* also means "right mood, gift." **vena de pintor** = *a gift for painting* Sabemos la edad de un árbol por las **venas** (vetas) del tronco. *We know the age of a tree by the* **veins** *(streaks) in the trunk.* ¿Sabes dónde está la **vena cava?** *Do you know where the* **vena cava** *is (in the body)?* Cogimos a Pablo en **vena.** *We caught Paul in* **the right mood.** Hoy está de **vena** para bailar. *Today, he's in the* **mood** *for dancing. Venal* and *venal* are both adjectives that refer to an "easily bribed or corrupted person" *(sobornable, corrupto).* Desgraciadamente, es un juez **venal.** *Unfortunately, he is a* **venal** *judge.*

ventear / vent *Ventear* is not "to vent" but "to air *(airear),* to ventilate, to dry in the wind." Abrí la ventana para **ventear** el cuarto. *I opened the window* **to air out** *the room. To vent* means *emitir, dar salida a,* and in a figurative sense, *desahogar(se), descargar* (one's feelings). **Desahogó** su ira contra la directora. *He* **vented** *his anger on the principal.*

ventilador / ventilator *Ventilador* (m.) means "ventilator" or "fan"; however, in some parts of Latin America *abanico eléctrico* is used more frequently than *ventilador.* [The *Real Academia* does not recognize *abanico* as meaning "fan, ventilator," but other dictionaries that deal with American Spanish, include this meaning.] Los españoles usan **ventiladores** eléctricos cuando hace un calor espantoso. *The Spanish use electric* **fans** *when it is frightfully hot.*

veraz / veracious *Veraz* means "veracious" ("truthful, reliable"), and it applies only to persons, according to the *Real Academia.* Confiamos en una persona **veraz.** *We trust in a* **veracious** *(reliable) person. Veracious,* on the other hand, also refers to facts, with the meaning of *verídico, verdadero.* Nadie discute sus palabras **verídicas.** *No one disputes his* **veracious** *words.*

verbo / verb *Verbo* means "verb" in grammar, but it also means "speech, style of speaking." *Verba (labia)* is a slang word for "garrulity, verbiage." Me encanta el **verbo** de los campesinos. *I love the style of speaking of the farmers.* Mi suegro tiene mucha **verba**. *My father-in-law is very talkative.*

verga / verge *Verga* is not "verge" but "penis." *Vergajo* translates as "whip" (which is made from the penis of a bull). *Verge* means *borde* (m.), *margen* (m., f.), *fuste* (m.; of a column). El chico está **al borde** de la locura. *The boy is on the verge of madness.* La niña está **a punto** de echarse a llorar. *The girl is on the verge of bursting into tears.*

verificar / verify *Verificar* and *to verify* both mean "to check or prove if something is true." In addition, *verificar* also means "to inspect, to test, to carry out, to take place, to be held, to come true (a prediction)." La aviación **verificó** un espectáculo. *The air force performed in a spectacular show.* La boda **se verificó** en la iglesia parroquial. *The wedding took place (was held) in the parish church.*

vernáculo / vernacular *Vernáculo* means "vernacular" and it is only used in Spanish as an adjective to refer to "native language, habits, arts, etc." *Vernacular* is also used as a noun with two principal meanings: "native language" *(lengua vernácula)* and "everyday language of ordinary people" *(dialecto vernáculo.)* La lengua **vernácula** de Paraguay es el guaraní. *The vernacular of Paraguay is Guaraní.* Son costumbres **vernáculas**. *They are vernacular customs.*

versátil / versatile *Versátil* is not "versatile" but "fickle, changeable, flaky, inconsistent." No me gustan los empleados **versátiles**. *I don't like fickle (inconsistent) employees. Versatile*, on the other hand, has upgraded its meaning to *talentoso, polifacético, ágil (de mente), flexible.*
mesa con varios usos = *versatile table*
Es una subdirectora **polifacética**. *She is a versatile assistant director.*

versatilidad / versatility *Versatilidad* (f.) means "fickleness, moodiness." Nuestro gerente muestra frecuente **versatilidad**. *Our manager expresses frequent moodiness. Versatility* means *talento, flexibilidad* (f.), *carácter polifacético, habilidad* (f.). Admiro los **talentos** del jefe. *I admire the boss's versatility.*

verso / verse *Verso* means "verse" (as "poetry" in general) and also "line" (of a poem). The plural *versos* means "poems." Los **versos** de Alexandre ganaron un premio Nobel. *Alexandre's poems won a Nobel prize. Verse*, on the other hand, also means *estrofa* ("stanza") and *versículo* (of the Bible). una **estrofa** de ocho versos / *an eight-line verse*

vértigo / vertigo *Vértigo* and *vertigo* are both medical terms for "dizziness, giddiness." In everyday language, though, *vértigo* is used to mean "light-headedness *(mareo)*, frenzy, whirl."
tener vértigo = *to feel dizzy*
Me dejé envolver en el **vértigo** de las fiestas. *I got caught up in the whirl of parties.* La altura me da **vértigo**. *Heights make me dizzy.*

vía / via *Vía* does not mean "via"; instead, it means "road, way, lane, railway, track, tract, passage."
por vía de = *by way of*
por vía oficial = *through official channels*
Vía Láctea = *Milky Way*
Maneje por la **vía** derecha. *Drive in the right lane.* Via is not a noun but a preposition, meaning *por, por la vía de*. Este tren va para Madrid **por** (vía de) Segovia. *This train goes to Madrid via Segovia.*

vicio / vice *Vicio* means "vice" in the general sense of "an evil habit or conduct." In Spanish, *vicio* often upgrades that meaning to refer to "fault, defect, bad habit" (such as smoking, gossiping, talking too much, etc.). *Vicio* is also a slang word for "spoiling" people *(mimo)*. La envidia es un **vicio** viejo. *Envy is an old vice.* A nadie le gusta el **vicio** de fumar. *Nobody likes the bad habit of smoking.* Le estás dando **vicio** al muchacho. *You are spoiling the boy.* Vice has downgraded its original denotation to refer to perhaps the worst vices, such as *prostitución* and *narcóticos*. Fue atrapado por la escuadra de **narcóticos**. *He was trapped by the vice squad.*

vicioso / vicious *Vicioso* is not "vicious"; rather, it is "licentious, dissolute," and less seriously, "faulty, defective, habit-forming." In some dialects, it is a slang word for "spoiled" *(mimado)*.
círculo vicioso = *vicious circle*
El rey Salomón fue muy **vicioso**. *King Solomon was very dissolute.* Fumar es una costumbre **viciosa**. *Smoking is an addictive habit.* Vicious, on the other hand, means *feroz, depravado, malvado, atroz*. The term can be used to describe persons, animals, and feelings.   crímenes **atroces** contra la humanidad / *vicious crimes against humanity*   Ese perro es un animal **feroz**. *That dog is a vicious animal.*

vigilante / vigilante, vigilant *Vigilante* (m.) means "guard, watchman, sentinel." El **vigilante** no debe dormirse. *The watchman should not fall asleep. Vigilante,* which was borrowed from Spanish, has come to mean "a member of a group organized to punish crime" *(justiciero, miembro de una asociación de guardia).* Los *Guardian Angels* son **vigilantes**. *The Guardian Angels are vigilantes. Vigilante* and *vigilant* are adjectives that mean "watchful, alert."

vil / vile *Vil* and *vile* only share the meaning "worthless" *(inútil)* when referring to things. Their meanings differ when they refer to people. *Vil* means "base, despicable." Esos productos son **viles** (sin valor). *Those are truly vile (worthless) products.* La conducta del marido ha sido **vil**. *The husband's conduct has been despicable. Vile,* when referring to people, means *malvado, depravado, repugnante, infame*. Sus acciones **depravadas** dan asco. *His vile actions are disgusting.*

villa / villa *Villa* and *villa* both mean "country house" *(quinta, chalé* [m.]*). Villa,* however, also means "town." [*Villa* is thought of as en elegant house in the countryside, usually with a garden.] Las **villas** romanas eran famosas. *Roman villas were* *famous.* Yo estudié en la **villa** de Carrión de los Condes. *I studied in the **town** of Carrión de los Condes.*

villano / villain   *Villano* does not mean "villain" nor does it mean "a person of a *villa*" in modern usage. *Villano* means "not noble, peasant" as a noun, and as an adjective, it means "impolite, coarse, rustic." *Villain* means *malvado, canalla* (m.), *maleante* (m.), and in colloquial language, *bribón* (m.). In the theater and in movies, *villain* is *el malo*. Fue un **malvado** con su familia. *He was a **villain** to his family.* ¿Quién es el **malo** de la película? *Who is the **villain** in the movie?*

vino / wino   *Vino* is not "wino" but "wine."
tener mal vino = *to have a bad temper*
El **vino** es tan viejo como Noé según la Biblia. *Wine is as old as Noah, according to the Bible. Wino, on the other hand, translates as borracho habitual, borracho empedernido.* Los **borrachos** siempre piden dinero. *Winos are always asking for money.*

violar / violate   *Violar* and *to violate* share the meaning of "to break a law, a rule, a promise." In addition, *violar* means "to rape" and "to trespass." La muchacha fue **violada** en el parque. *The girl was **raped** in the park.* Alguien **violó** mi propiedad. *Someone **trespassed** on my property. Violación,* likewise, means "violation" (of the law), as well as "rape, trespassing." Robar es una **violación** de la ley. *Stealing is a **violation** of the law. Violador* (m.) means "violator" (of the law), and also "rapist, trespasser." Los **violadores** merecen la pena de muerte. *Rapists deserve the death penalty.*

violento / violent   *Violento* and *violent* both mean "acting with force to damage or destroy." However, *violento* also means "awkward, embarrassed, difficult." Tomó el poder por medios **violentos**. *He took power by **violent** means.* Fue una tempestad muy **violenta**. *It was a very **violent** storm.* Me sentí muy **violento** en su presencia. *I felt very **awkward** in his presence. Violentar* means "to force, break into (a place), distort, twist (a text)." No es justo **violentar** un texto. *It is not fair **to distort** a text.*

virtual / virtual   *Virtual* does not mean "virtual" in everyday speech; it means "possible, potential." Only in physics does *virtual* mean "virtual": *imagen virtual* ("virtual image"). Hay mucho dinero **virtual** en este negocio. *There is **potential** profit in this business. Virtual* means *verdadero, real.* Juan es el **verdadero** jefe de la compañía. *John is the **virtual** head of the company. Virtualmente* means "possibly, potentially." *Virtually* means *prácticamente, casi.* Es **casi** imposible. *It's **virtually** impossible.* Estoy **prácticamente** seguro de eso. *I am **virtually** certain of it.*

virtuoso / virtuoso, virtuous   *Virtuoso* means "virtuoso" ("interested in the arts, skilled in music") and "virtuous" ("having moral virtue"). [The plural of *virtuoso* in English is *virtuosi* or *virtuosos*.] ¿Conoces a algún **virtuoso** del violín? *Do you know a violin **virtuoso**?* El paciente Job fue un hombre **virtuoso**. *Patient Job was a **virtuous** man.*

visa / visa   *Visa* in Spanish and *visa* in English used to be false cognates; however, the *Real Academia* has finally recognized *visa* with the meaning of "visa." Formerly, the only accepted term was *visado*. Los argentinos no necesitan **visa** para ir a España. *Argentinians do not need a **visa** to go to Spain.*

visible / visible   *Visible* and *visible* both mean "perceptible, obvious, manifest, clear." In addition, *visible* applies to people who are "famous, in the public eye, well known." *Visible* is also a colloquial word to describe a person who is "decent, presentable." La torre es **visible** desde muy lejos. *The tower is **visible** from far away.* María no tiene modo **visible** (obvio) de hacerlo. *Mary has no **visible** (evident) means of doing it.* Las estrellas de cine son muy **visibles**. *Movie stars are very much in the **public eye**.* ¿Puedo entrar? ¿Estás **visible**? *May I come in? Are you **decent**?*

visita / visit   *Visita* and *visit* both mean "the act of visiting, staying as a guest, call (by a doctor)." However, *visita* also is used to refer to "visitor" or "visitors" (*invitados*).
visita de pésame = *condolence call (visit)*
visita de médico = *a very short visit, a visit on the fly*
visita de cumplido = *courtesy call*
El domingo tenemos **visita**. *We are having **visitors** on Sunday.* Mi hermano está **de visita** en Madrid. *My brother is **on a visit** to Madrid.*

visor / visor   *Visor* (m.) is not "visor"; *visor* in Spanish is a technical word for "viewfinder, sight" in photography.
retrovisor = *rearview mirror* (of a car)
El uso del (espejo) **retrovisor** evita accidentes. *Using the **rearview mirror** helps avoid accidents.* Visor in English is a common term for *visera* (of a helmet, of a cap, on a windshield). La **visera** protege los ojos contra el sol. *A **visor** protects the eyes from the sun.*

vista / vista   *Vista* and *vista* share the meaning of "view, look, perspective." *Vista* also means "vision, eyes, sight, aspect, appearance (of something)." The plural *vistas* means "openings (such as windows and doors)" and "picture postcards."
con vista(s) al mar = *with a sea view*
uno de la vista baja = *pig* (animal)
a ojos vistas = *visibly*
pagadero a la vista = *payable on sight*
Desde esta colina hay una **vista** bonita. *There is a pretty **vista** from this hill.* Es importante examinarse la **vista**. *It's important to have your **vision** (eyes) examined.* Esa carne tiene buena **vista**. *That is a nice-**looking** piece of meat.* Me gustan las **vistas** de Cancún. *I like the **postcards** of Cancún.*

visualizar / visualize   *Visualizar* and *to visualize* are no longer false cognates. The *Real Academia* included *visualizar* in its latest dictionary with the meaning of "to visualize" ("to form a mental image, to envision"). [Formerly, *to visualize* was only acceptably translated as *imaginarse, vislumbrar*.] Describa las cosas de modo que su lector pueda **visualizarlas** (imaginarlas). *Describe the things in such a way* *that your reader can* **visualize** *them.* **Visualización,** likewise, has been accepted to mean "visualization."

vivaz / vivacious *Vivaz* and *vivacious* mean "lively, full of life." In addition, *vivaz* means "long-lived, perennial (plants), quick-witted, sharp (mind)." *Esa muchacha es muy* **vivaz.** *That girl is extremely* **vivacious.** *La encina es una planta* **vivaz** *(perenne).* *The live oak is a* **perennial** *plant.* *El jefe tiene una mente* **vivaz.** *The boss has a* **sharp** *mind.* *Vivacidad* (f.) means "vivacity" ("liveliness"), as well as "sharpness" (of mind). *A pesar de tener ochenta años, ella tiene una* **vivacidad** *mental admirable.* *Despite being eighty years old, she has an admirable* **sharpness** *of mind.*

vocacional / vocational *Vocacional* and *vocational* are no longer the same thing. In Spanish, *vocacional* has kept the original meaning of "professional" ("related to any career or profession"). *conferencias* **vocacionales** / *career (professional) lectures* Vocational in English has come to be associated with training for the "manual arts and crafts," which translates as *de artes y oficios.* *una escuela de artes y oficios* / *a* **vocational** *school*

vocal / vocal *Vocal* as an adjective means "vocal" ("related to the voice"). As a noun, *vocal* has two meanings: (1) *una vocal* (f.) means "vowel" (sound), and (2) *un vocal* (m.) means "member" (of a council, organization). *Las cuerdas* **vocales** *producen sonidos.* *Vocal cords produce sounds.* *En español hay cinco* **vocales.** *There are five* **vowels** *in Spanish.* *Juan es un* **vocal** *en la directiva escolar.* *John is a* **member** *of the school board.* Vocal in English also is used to refer to people as *ruidoso, gritón.* *Ella es muy* **gritona** *en las reuniones.* *She is very* **vocal** *during the meetings.*

volátil / volatile *Volátil* means "volatile" in the technical sense of "evaporating quickly." *El alcohol es* **volátil.** *Alcohol is* **volatile.** *Volatile* in English also applies to situations—*explosivo, inestable*—and to people—*voluble, inconstante* ("fickle"). *La situación del golfo Pérsico fue* **explosiva** *por varios meses.* *The situation in the Persian Gulf was* **volatile** *for several months.* *Su carácter* **voluble** *no le ayudará nada.* *His* **volatile** *disposition will not help him.* *Volatilidad* (f.) means "volatility" in the technical sense. *Volatility,* likewise, means *volubilidad* (f.), *inconstancia.*

voltaje / voltage *Voltaje* (m.) is the technical term for *voltage;* however, the common term for the same concept is *tensión,* for example in *alta tensión* ("high voltage"). *Un cable de* **alta tensión** *puede causar la muerte instantánea.* *A* **high-voltage** *cable can cause instant death.*

voluble / voluble *Voluble* does not mean "voluble"; rather, it means "fickle, inconstant, moody, changeable." *Perdió su puesto serio por ser* **voluble.** *He lost a serious job for being* **fickle.** *Voluble* means *locuaz, hablador, charlatán, suelto* (in speech). *¡Qué* **charlatán** *es José!* *How* **voluble** *Joe is!* *Volubilidad* (f.) means "fickleness, instability, inconstancy." *Su* **volubilidad** *es un impedimento grave.* *His* **inconstancy** *is a serious hindrance.* *Volubility* means *locuacidad* (f.), *verbosidad* (f.), *soltura* (of speech). *Su* **locuacidad** *puede ser positiva.* *Her* **volubility** *can be positive.*

voluntario / voluntary, volunteer   *Voluntario* means "voluntary" ("willful, intentional") as an adjective, and "volunteer" as a noun. Se piden donaciones **voluntarias.** *Voluntary contributions are requested.*   un ejército de **voluntarios** / *an army of volunteers*   *Voluntary,* in some cases, translates as *espontáneo* ("arising from the mind without constraint").

voraz / voracious   *Voraz* means "voracious" ("greedy in eating, devouring") and, in a figurative sense, "raging, destroying (as floods, fires, etc.)." Las pirañas son animales **voraces.** *Piranhas are voracious animals.* Un fuego **voraz** destruyó la casa. *A raging fire destroyed the house. Voracious* is also used in a figurative sense to mean *insaciable, ávido* (reader, collector, etc.). María es una lectora **insaciable.** *Mary is a voracious reader.*

voz / voice   *Voz* (f.) and *voice* both mean "sound, tone, singer." In addition, *voz* means "shout, cry, word, rumor, vote."
voz cantante = *main voice*
voz pública = *public opinion*
de viva voz = *in person*
a voz en cuello = *shouting*
un secreto a voces = *an open secret*
a media voz = *in a low voice*
Sin **voz** no habría lenguajes. *There is no language without voice.* No necesitas dar **voces** aquí. *You don't have to shout around here.* Todos los días aprendo **voces** nuevas. *I learn new words every day.* Tengo **voz** y voto en esta comisión. *I have a vote on this committee.*

vulgar / vulgar   *Vulgar* in Spanish and *vulgar* in English do not necessarily have the same meaning, even though they are listed as cognates in many dictionaries. Common usage, as well as the *Real Academia,* distinguishes *vulgar* as a less negative concept, meaning "common, general, ordinary," and sometimes "banal, trivial, trite." [The corresponding noun is *vulgaridad* (f.)] Esa expresión es **vulgar** (común). *That expression is common.* Ese tipo tiene modales **vulgares.** *That fellow has ordinary manners. Vulgar,* on the other hand, has the more negative meaning of *indecente, grosero, descortés, de mal gusto.* [The corresponding noun is *vulgarity.*] ¡No seas **grosero**! *Don't be vulgar!* Es **de mal gusto** hablar muy alto. *It's vulgar to talk very loud. Vulgarización* means "popularization" ("to make known to the common people"). Uno de los hechos importantes de Martin Luther fue la **vulgarización** de la Biblia. *One of Martin Luther's accomplishments was the popularization of the Bible. Vulgarization* translates as *grosería, indecencia.*

Y

yaguar / jaguar *Yaguar* (m.) is used in Spain to mean "jaguar" (the animal). However, in Latin America, the term used is *jaguar* (m.), which is of Guaraní origin.

yanqui / Yankee *Yanqui* (m., f.) means "Yankee" as "a citizen of the United States." Usually *yanqui* has no negative connotation in and of itself; however, depending on the context, it can be used negatively. *Muchos* **yanquis** *viven en la colonia al este de la ciudad. Many* **Yankees** *live in the suburb to the east of the city.* Yankee, in English, has two other meanings: (1) "a native or resident of New England" and (2) "a native or resident of the northern states." The first meaning could be translated as *ciudadano de Nueva Inglaterra*, and the second could be translated as *norteño, ciudadano de los estados norteños*.

yarda / yard *Yarda* means "yard" as a unit of measurement. *Yard*, on the other hand, can be translated as *patio* or *jardín* (m.). (Some bilingual speakers in the United States do use *yarda* instead of *patio*.)

yaz / jazz *Yaz* (m.) means "jazz," according to the *Real Academia;* however, many other dictionaries list *jazz* (m.) to mean "jazz."

yérsey, yersi / jersey *Yérsey* (m.) and *yersi* (m.) are both terms used in Spain to mean "jersey" ("sweater"). In Latin America, the spelling used is *jersey* (m.), pronounced with the typical sound of *j* in Spanish.

yóquey, yoqui / yoke, jockey *Yóquey* (m.), or *yoqui* (m.), means "jockey," according to the *Real Academia*. In Latin America, however, the English spelling is used. *Yoke* is translated as *yugo* (for animals).

yuca / yucca *Yuca* and *yucca* are terms for two different plants. In Spanish, *yuca* refers to a bushy plant whose root is very white and is edible after it has been boiled or fried. *Yucca*, on the other hand, refers to a cactus plant used for decoration in the United States.

Z

zenit, cenit / zenith   *Zenit* (m.), or *cenit* (m.), means "zenith" as "a point in the sky directly overhead." *Zenith*, however, is used in a figurative sense to mean *apogeo* ("peak, highest point"). El artista está en el **apogeo** de su gloria. *The artist is at the **zenith** of his fame.*

zona / zone   *Zona* means "zone" ("area, region").
   zonas verdes = *park and garden areas*
   zona de ensanche = *development area*
   Zone is used in the expression *postal zone*, which translates as *distrito postal*. *Zone* is also an adjective used in sports to describe a kind of defense. An appropriate translation would be *zonal*. Las primas de los seguros se basan en los **distritos postales.** *The insurance premiums are based on **postal zones** (zip codes).* Este equipo se destaca por su defensa **zonal.** *This team is outstanding for **zone** defense.*